HUDSON PUBLIC LIBRARY

P9-BZO-927

1500 Words in 15 Minutes a Day

428.1 CLE
Cleveland, Ceil.

1500 words in 15 minutes a
day : a year-long plan to
learn 28 words a week

PLEASE
DO NOT REMOVE
CARD
FROM POCKET
HUDSON PUBLIC LIBRARY
3 WASHINGTON ST
@WOOD SQUARE
HUDSON, MA 01749

1500 WORDS IN 15 MINUTES A DAY

A Year-Long Plan
to Learn 28 Words
a Week

CEIL CLEVELAND

McGraw-Hill

New York | Chicago | San Francisco
Lisbon | London | Madrid | Mexico City
Milan | New Delhi | San Juan | Seoul
Singapore | Sydney | Toronto

HUDSON PUBLIC LIBRARY
WOOD SQUARE
HUDSON, MA 01749

The *McGraw·Hill* Companies

Copyright © 2005 by Ceil Cleveland. All rights reserved. Printed in the United States of America. Except as permitted under the United States Copyright Act of 1976, no part of this publication may be reproduced or distributed in any form or by any means, or stored in a data base or retrieval system, without prior written permission of the publisher.

1 2 3 4 5 6 7 8 9 0   CUS/CUS   0 9 8 7 6 5

ISBN 0-07-144325-8

McGraw-Hill books are available at special discounts to use as premiums and sales promotions, or for use in corporate training programs. For more information, please write to the Director of Special Sales, Professional Publishing, McGraw-Hill, Two Penn Plaza, New York, NY 10121-2298. Or contact your local bookstore.

 This book is printed on recycled, acid-free paper containing a minimum of 50% recycled de-inked paper.

For Jerry, whose words kept me going . . .

"Words are too awful an instrument

for good and evil to be trifled with;

they hold above all other external powers

a dominion over thoughts."

—WILLIAM WORDSWORTH

Contents

Introduction

Reaching for a word? Find it here. Get smart with 28 new words a week.

Do you often suffer from *lethologica* **(1)**? Do you have that desired word right on the tip of your tongue, and yet it escapes you? Do not *fulminate* **(2)**, develop *alopecia* **(3)**, or *defenestrate* **(4)** your desk and chair! This book can deliver *anabiosis* **(5)** without emergency room treatment. An hour and three-quarters a week of brain exercises will get you in shape.

Through the introduction of new words—using *heuristic* **(6)** methods, *paranomesia* **(7)**, and *mnemonic* **(8)** devices, we'll make you a *lexical* **(9)** genius in no time. You will be able to talk to anyone about any subject without embarrassment.

Equivocate **(10)** no more! Use precise language to sound smarter, work smarter, get smarter.

This book offers 28 new words (at least) in each of 52 chapters. Here you will see words defined and used in context, and will learn a bit about their backgrounds.

Early chapters (Part I, Weeks 1–10) are arranged thematically in areas of the liberal arts and related subjects, which will give you the verbal tools and concepts in a historical context to read, view, listen to, write about, and discuss works in these areas with confidence.

In the early chapters of Part II (Weeks 11–22—in chapters like Cool Words, Hot Words, or Not Words, for example) you will learn when and when not to use certain words. In the same part, in Trick Words and Slick Words, you will find how to use words that often confuse and trip up readers, writers, and speakers.

And in the later chapters of Part II (Weeks 23–52), you will find some words whose definitions will surprise you and make you smile. English words are often wacky and fun: *Wedbedrip*, anyone? *Quakebuttock*?

These useful words will stretch you and increase your vocabulary. You will refine your knowledge of language and become confident in your use of words in a clear, precise, sophisticated manner. Learn and enjoy. Take it from an expert: English is a precise language—and sometimes goofy!

At the end of most chapters, you will find further information about words, clichés, and idioms, and some derivations and startling details about our language.

Do the exercises included here and enjoy the *paronomasia*. Here are the meanings of the ten words we offered you as a starter at the beginning of this introduction.

1. The inability to recall the right word

2. Explode with sudden violence

3. Lose hair and become bald

4. Toss out through a window

5. Bring to life again after a state of suspended animation

6. Learning through discovery

7. Word play, puns, and games

8. Aids to memory

9. One who knows vocabulary and language

10. To hedge or be deliberately ambiguous

Ceil Cleveland, New York, 2004

1500 Words in 15 Minutes a Day

Essential Words
for the Literate Person

Words for Discussing Art

Learning the words in this section and some of the concepts behind them will give you the ability to read, view, listen to, write about, and discuss works in the liberal arts and humanities. These include art, architecture, music, philosophy, psychology, literature, and more. Study the words in each week's assignment and do the exercises.

DAY 1

| perspective | chiaroscuro | etching | mezzotint |

DAY 2

| palimpsest | pentimento | fresco | tempera |

DAY 3

| pointillism | mosaic | genre painting | collage |

DAY 4

| cave paintings | Byzantine | Gothic | Romanesque |

DAY 5

| classicism | Renaissance | baroque | rococo |

DAY 6

| realism | romanticism | impressionism | symbolism |

DAY 7

| cubism | surrealism | abstract expressionism | minimalism |

perspective	Let's put things in **perspective**—a point of view that shows the relationship between one thing and another. The word is used for objects and scenes depicted so that they appear to the eye to have the appropriate relationship and proportion to everything else in the painting. If a barn is depicted in the painting, the cows and sheep grazing near it will be proportionally smaller than the barn. As they paint, artists imagine converging lines invisible to the viewer of the painting.
	WORDS IN CONTEXT: *In the fifteenth century, Filippo Brunelleschi led a group of artists to creating* **perspective** *through manipulating vanishing points in a painting; thus, art for the first time became three-dimensional.*
chiaroscuro	The use of light and shade in a painting and the skill displayed by the painter in the management of shadows.
	WORDS IN CONTEXT: *Rembrandt was a master of* **chiaroscuro** *in his paintings, which show figures in sunlight and shadow.*
etching	The art of engraving with acid on metal. The print taken from the metal plate is also called an **etching**. A needle is used to scratch a design on the metal plate; this design is filled with ink. The plate and paper are then put into a press, which transfers the pattern to the paper. There are many variants of this process, but it appears to have been developed in Germany about 1515.
	WORDS IN CONTEXT: *The artist Albrecht Dürer made* **etchings** *on iron between 1515 and 1518, probably the earliest examples of this art. Other artists who used the process include Rembrandt, Goya, and Whistler.*
mezzotint	A method of engraving that leaves the impression of light and shadow or **chiaroscuro** on the final print after the artist scratches the surface of a copper or steel plate with a saw-toothed tool. The soft effect in the print can show every degree of light and shade from black to white without leaving a sharp line as in an **etching**.
	WORDS IN CONTEXT: **Mezzotint**, *an engraving showing light and shadow, was invented by a Dutchman, Ludwig von Siegen, in 1640, but the process came into wide use in England in the early eighteenth century.*

After studying the definitions above, use these new words in the sentences below.

1. The most popular work of Albrecht Dürer was a(n)_____of a pair of hands, palms held together in prayer.
2. Art lovers visit the Rijksmuseum in Amsterdam to see Rembrandt Van Rijn's *The Night Watch,* in which the artist uses_____to light the figures that appear to emerge out of shadows with a dramatic effect.
3. A method of engraving that gives the effect of light and shade is called_____.
4. Artists use a technique called_____to create the illusion of three-dimensional space on a flat surface.

Test Yourself: Write the letter next to the number to match word and meaning.

1. chiaroscuro   a. creating appropriate relationships in art
2. perspective   b. blending light and shade in paintings
3. etching   c. an engraving showing light and shadow
4. mezzotint   d. created by plate, paper, and press

On a separate sheet of paper, write a sentence using each of these new words.

DID YOU KNOW? Illuminated manuscripts are those produced by European monks during the Middle Ages using bright colored paints and very small ornamental decorations. The Bible and other precious books were made more visually beautiful in this manner.

palimpsest	Manuscripts inscribed on parchment in ancient Egypt were written on both sides (*recto*—front, and *verso*—back). These pages, often erased and reused, were called **palimpsests**.
	WORDS IN CONTEXT: *Some artists in contemporary times still create* **palimpsests** *by using both sides of their papers and then erasing the image so that the papers may be be used again. The residue of the first image sometimes leaves an interesting pattern when the paper is reused.*
pentimento	This is a painter's word for the evidence that an original work of art has been altered. Often the paint with which the artist has covered a mistake or a change of mind will become transparent. The original work will then become visible through the final composition. This creeping through of an image is sometimes compared to a **palimpsest.**
	WORDS IN CONTEXT: *A famous example of* **pentimento** *is El Greco's* Laocoon *in the National Gallery in Washington, D.C. There, a bodyless head that had been painted out was at some time repainted as a full-length figure. This was uncovered when the work was cleaned.*
fresco	In Renaissance Italy **frescoes**—the word means *fresh* in Italian—were created by painting on damp lime plaster. The dampness and the lime created an element that, as the wall dried, held the paint and color magnificently. All colors are not lime-proof, so the colors an artist could use were limited, but those that the wall held are clear and luminous. Da Vinci's *Last Supper* is a **fresco.**
	WORDS IN CONTEXT: *Minoans in Knossos, Greece, and Romans in Pompeii created* **frescoes** *in the fifteenth century. Because the art is successful only in dry climates,* **frescoes** *are rare in Northern Europe. Diego Rivera revived the art form in Mexico in the twentieth century.*
tempera	A painting method used in mural painting, usually applied to dry walls. **Tempera's** advantage is that it produces clear, pure colors. It is also used in combination with oil paint.
	WORDS IN CONTEXT: *In modern times, Ben Shahn and Andrew Wyeth revived an interest in* **tempera.** *In industrial art, a simplified* **tempera** *(pigment mixed with egg yolk, called* distemper*) is often used for posters.*

After studying the definitions above, use these new words in the sentences below.

1. The restoration of the painting revealed_____, indicating that the artist had at one time painted over the original work.
2. The _____was painted on a damp, lime plaster wall.
3. The monk erased the original manuscript and reused the parchment, thereby creating a_____.
4. The bright, clear mural on the dry wall was painted with_____combined with oil paint.

Test Yourself: Write the letter next to the number to match word and meaning.

1. tempera
2. fresco
3. pentimento
4. palimpsest

a. the erased first image left a pattern on the paper
b. alteration of the original painting
c. in dry climates this technique is successful
d. this element mixed with egg yolk creates distemper

On a separate sheet of paper, write a sentence using each of these new words.

DID YOU KNOW?
Most viewers believed that Michelangelo used muted and somber colors when he painted the Sistine Chapel in the Vatican, but when the mural was cleaned, people were startled to discover that the artist had used bright, clear colors. Grime and candle smoke had dimmed the murals.

pointillism	The technique of painting with dots of color to create an image. The French painter Georges Seurat (1859–1891) used dots of primary colors to execute an enormous painting, *Sunday Afternoon on the Island of Grande Jatte.* **WORDS IN CONTEXT:** *The Broadway musical* Sunday in the Park with George *took as its subject the work of Georges Seurat, whose huge painting done entirely in* **pointillism** *hangs in the Art Institute of Chicago.*
mosaic	Art made by setting small colored pieces of glass, stone, or marble in mortar to create a picture. **WORDS IN CONTEXT:** *Roman artists created* **mosaics** *using marble; later Byzantine artists in the sixth century composed pictures using small cubes of colored glass, which, in reflected light, produced a dazzling effect.*
genre painting	A realistic style of painting in which everyday life forms the subject matter, as distinguished from religious or historical painting. **WORDS IN CONTEXT:** *Dutch painter Jan Vermeer (1632–1675), who painted peasants, women in their kitchens, and other ordinary life scenes, might be called a* **genre painter** *because of his choice of subjects. However, his use of light and original interlocking shapes raises his genre work to another level.*
collage	A composition made with cut and pasted pieces of material, sometimes scraps combined with objects painted into a picture. **WORDS IN CONTEXT:** *For his beach house, the artist composed a* **collage** *of seashells, driftwood, and white pebbles.*

After studying the definitions above, use these new words in the sentences below.

1. The gold pictorial wall in the ancient palace was a _____ composed of glittering glass cubes.
2. The painting of farmers along with cows grazing in the fields beyond was an example of
   _____.
3. The _____ on her wall was constructed of bits of boot leather, pieces of an old barn door, and several horseshoe nails.
4. The _____ was executed by the artist using small colorful dots to create the image of a house.

Test Yourself: Write the letter next to the number to match word and meaning.

1. mosaic	a. artwork created with scraps and bits of materials
2. pointillism	b. an image created entirely with dots
3. collage	c. a picture composed of colored glass bits
4. genre painting	d. a painting depicting realistic life forms

On a separate sheet of paper, write a sentence using each of these new words.

DID YOU KNOW? The painting by American artist James McNeill Whistler (1834–1903), popularly known as *Whistler's Mother*, was actually given the less personal title by the artist of *Arrangement in Black and Grey, No. 1.* It hangs in the Musée D'Orsay in Paris.

cave paintings	The earliest European painters depicted animals, such as wild boar and buffalo, on the walls of caves more than 20,000 years ago. Two examples of **cave paintings** are found in Lascaux, France, and Altamira, Spain. **WORDS IN CONTEXT:** *The **cave paintings** in Lascaux, in the Dordogne region of southern France, are such a popular attraction that a replica of the cave has been made to preserve the original cave.*
Byzantine	An art style developed after Byzantium became the capital of the Roman Empire (c. 330). With monumental, stylized, rigid images set on gold backgrounds, this art appears in religious mosaics, panel paintings, and manuscript illuminations. **WORDS IN CONTEXT:** ***Byzantine** art was also created in Italy, Syria, Greece, Russia, and other Eastern countries under Byzantine influence.*
Gothic	A movement begun in France with sculpture (c. 1200) followed by **Gothic** painting (c. 1300). These art forms had been preceded by **Gothic architecture**; the first landmark structure is part of the abbey of Saint-Denis. This is a graceful, linear, elegant style more naturalistic than earlier European forms and far less rigid than Byzantine art. **WORDS IN CONTEXT:** *Tapestry, sculpture, and stained glass assumed importance in the soaring ribbed vaults of **Gothic** churches. The Pietà of the Avignon school was noted for its delicacy of expression.*
Romanesque	A style that emerged in France (c. mid-eleventh century). Ornamental, stylized, and complex in both sculpture and painting. Often used in huge **Romanesque** churches with massive barrel vaults and few wall openings, which encouraged monumental frescoes—of animal, vegetable, and religious motifs. **WORDS IN CONTEXT:** *Roman architecture was the main inspiration for **Romanesque** design, but Byzantine and Eastern influences were incorporated. The large walls of churches encouraged fresco painting.*

After studying the definitions above, use these new words in the sentences below.

1. The first known European paintings depicted animals. Called_____ this art was discovered in France and Spain.
2. _____churches with massive walls are often decorated with monumental frescoes.
3. _____art created in a graceful, linear style, followed architecture and sculpture of the same style in thirteenth-century France.
4. _____art has a gold background and is sometimes composed of mosaics.

Test Yourself: Write the letter next to the number to match word and meaning.

1. Gothic
2. Romanesque
3. Byzantine
4. Cave paintings

a. characterized by stylized figures on a luminous gold background
b. French movement characterized by grace and elegance
c. monumental, complex, and ornamental art and sculpture
d. earliest known art, composed of animal figures

On a separate sheet of paper, write a sentence using each of these new words.

DID YOU KNOW?
Hieronymus Bosch (c.1450–1516) was a Dutch painter of fantasy in the late Middle Ages. He filled a colorful canvas with weird, misshapen figures conducting themselves sinfully in *Hell;* in *Ship of Fools* he painted an allegory of humanity's immorality.

classicism	Ancient Greek and Roman art, which emphasized harmony, proportion, balance, and simplicity. Generally, **classicism** refers to art, architecture, and sculpture based on accepted standards of beauty. The elegance, symmetry, and repose of **classical** art are usually seen as the opposite of art of the romantic school (see below). **WORDS IN CONTEXT:** *Classicism in art denotes the absence of emotionalism, subjectivity, and excess enthusiasm. Artists of this school looked back in admiration to Greek and Roman models.*
Renaissance	European art, c. 1400–1600. **Renaissance** art began in Italy and stressed the forms of classical antiquity, which emphasized a realistic use of space, scientific perspective, and secular subjects. Early **Renaissance** artists were Leonardo da Vinci and Donatello; artists of the later or High **Renaissance** were Michelangelo, Raphael, and Titian. **WORDS IN CONTEXT:** *Renaissance means rebirth in French and describes the rich development of Western civilization that marked the transition from the Middle Ages to the modern age. It was a period of brilliant accomplishment in all the arts, literature, science, and scholarship. The humanist emphasis on the individual was typified in the Renaissance man—a man of universal genius—represented by Leonardo da Vinci.*
baroque	A style developed in Europe and Latin America during the seventeenth and eighteenth centuries. Works in all the arts were produced on a grand scale with a high sense of drama. In painting, deep *perspective* was developed, *chiaroscuro* was intensified, color was superbly exploited, and artists often showed a fascination with intense emotional states. **WORDS IN CONTEXT:** *Some of the artists working in the early (1590–1625), high (1625–1660), and late baroque (1660–1725) periods were Caravaggio, La Tour, Rembrandt, Vermeer, Rubens, and Claude Lorraine. The buildings in Versailles are examples of baroque architecture. In the late baroque, Italy lost its dominant position to France, with painters using lighter colors and softer forms, and baroque gave way to the rococo.*
rococo	In reaction to the grandeur and massiveness of the baroque, artists working in the **rococo** style used highly decorative, refined, and elegant forms. This style spread through eighteenth-century Europe. Parisian tapestries, furniture, and bronze art became delicate. Shells, scrolls, branches, and flowers appeared on furnishings. **WORDS IN CONTEXT:** *The major French painters of the rococo period were Watteau, Boucher, and Fragonard. In England, the furniture of Chippendale was rococo.*

After studying the definitions above, use these new words in the sentences below:

1. _____ is executed on a grand scale and exhibits high drama and emotion using perspective and chiaroscuro.
2. Art that emphasizes the harmony and balance of the art of ancient Greece and Rome is called_____art, a word that means "rebirth."
3. _____is the term given to the art of antiquity that set the standards for beauty and good taste.
4. Highly decorative art featuring refined forms and often incorporating flowers and branches is art of the_____style.

Test Yourself: Write the letter next to the number to match word and meaning.

1. rococo
2. baroque
3. Renaissance
4. classicism

a. art on a grand scale, with emotional intensity and drama
b. art that looked back to ancient Greece and Rome
c. refined and decorative—delicate flowers and branches
d. marked the transition between the Middle Ages and now

On a separate sheet of paper, write a sentence using each of these new words.

DID YOU KNOW? Some of the earliest Roman fresco figure paintings (c. 30 B.C.) are found on the walls of the Villa of Mysteries, a house located in the ancient city of Pompeii, which was covered by volcanic ash when Mount Vesuvius erupted in 79 A.D. The ash protected the site until it was discovered and excavated in the eighteenth century.

realism	The nineteenth-century art movement developed in reaction to the idealistic subject matter of the French art academy in favor of commonplace, everyday, even ugly subjects. **WORDS IN CONTEXT:** *Realism, broadly, is the representative, unembellished rendering of natural forms. Major realists include Courbet, J. F. Millet, and Daumier.*
romanticism	A European movement (late eighteenth to mid nineteenth centuries) that rejected a return to the classical ideals of *neoclassicism*. **Romanticism** emphasized emotion and spontaneous expression over reason. The subject matter was dramatic and usually painted in energetic, brilliant colors. **WORDS IN CONTEXT:** *Romantic artists were Delacroix, Gericault, Goya, Turner, and Blake.*
impressionism	A late nineteenth-century French school that emphasized transitory visual impressions often painted directly from nature. **Impressionists** focused on the changing effects of light and color on natural objects. **WORDS IN CONTEXT:** *Monet, Renoir, and Pissarro were important impressionists.*
symbolism	A painting movement that emerged in Paris in the 1880s. Subject matter was suggested, rather than presented directly, in stylized, evocative images. **WORDS IN CONTEXT:** *Symbolism grew out of literature in France in reaction to realism. Baudelaire was leader of the movement in poetry. Other symbolists included Mallarmé, Rimbaud, and Verlaine; Maeterlinck in drama; and Debussy in music. (Debussy was also considered to be a musical impressionist. Such terms may have slightly different connotations when describing different forms of artistic expression.)*

After studying the definitions above, use these new words in the sentences below.

1. A decorative painting movement in France opposed to realism was called
_____.

2. The work of artists who often worked outdoors, painting natural forms and emphasizing light and color was called_____.

3. _____artists such as Goya and Turner valued emotion more than reason and worked spontaneously.

4. _____is a nineteenth-century French art movement that rejected idealized subject matter and took ordinary, everyday objects, people, and scenes as its subject.

Test Yourself: Place the letter next to the number to match word and meaning.

1. romanticism
2. symbolism
3. impressionism
4. realism

a. poets led the way to this evocative art
b. a French school of artists who loved light and color
c. art painted from ordinary, natural forms
d. spontaneous, emotional art, dramatic and bright

On a separate sheet of paper, write a sentence using each of these new words.

DID YOU KNOW?
Vincent van Gogh (1853–1890), the great Dutch artist who experimented with color and loaded his canvases with layers of pigment using a palette knife, sold only one of his paintings during his lifetime. His paintings that now sell for millions of dollars include *The Potato Eaters, Starry Night, Sunflowers* (several versions), *The Small House of Vincent in Arles, Self Portrait, Man with Ear Cut Off*, and others.

cubism	A revolutionary movement begun by Picasso and Braque in Paris (c. 1907). In revolt against sensual, emotional art, **cubism** fragments the subject and shows it from multiple points of view simultaneously. Early works of the movement, sometimes called *conceptual realism*, show subjects as the mind, not the eye, perceives them. **WORDS IN CONTEXT:** *Cubism appeals to the intellect, creating a three-dimensional image as a puzzle. Other artists who worked in this style were Marcel Duchamp and Ferdinand Leger. Picasso's Damoiselles d'Avignon (1907) is a fine example of* **cubism.**
surrealism	A movement originating in France in the 1920s that explored the unconscious by using dreamlike images, spontaneous techniques, and surprising juxtapositions of objects. Whether humorous, eerie, or disorienting, these paintings pushed the boundaries of art. **WORDS IN CONTEXT:** *Influenced by psychoanalyst Sigmund Freud,* **surrealism** *expressed the imagination as revealed in dreams without the conscious control of reason. Joan Miró used images from the subconscious, while René Magritte and Max Ernst juxtaposed incongruous elements painted in a realistic manner. Salvador Dali used images inspired by dreams, notably in his famous painting of melting clocks.*
abstract expressionism	Emphasizing spontaneous personal expression and the act of painting itself, this movement, begun in New York City in the 1940s, ignored accepted artistic values and called attention to the surface of the painting—brush strokes and texture. **Abstract expressionism** was the first important American school of painting to influence art abroad. Major artists: Jackson Pollock, Willem de Kooning, Robert Motherwell, Hans Hoffman, Franz Kline, and Robert Rothko. **WORDS IN CONTEXT:** *Abstract expressionism greatly influenced the art that followed it, especially in the way material and color were used. Pollock (1912–1956), who dripped house paint on huge canvases, achieved lyrical and dramatic artwork using this technique.*
minimalism	Painting and sculpture reduced to pure forms and strict, systematic compositions. The movement originated in the United States in the early 1960s. **WORDS IN CONTEXT:** *In reaction to the subjectivity of* **abstract expressionism,** *artists such as sculptors Donald Judd and Carl Andre created impersonal, precise, primary structures in their work. The* **minimalism** *of Ellsworth Kelly, Kenneth Noland, and Frank Stella employed monumental, geometric forms and pure colors that had no references beyond the works themselves.*

After studying the definitions above, use these new words in the sentences below.

1. Freud influenced the movement in art called_____.
2. Works of_____appeal to the intellect and often present an image from several points of view.
3. Jackson Pollock's vigorous drip paintings are important in the_____movement.
4. The artistic technique of_____ strips art down to its basic shapes and forms.

Test Yourself: Write the letter next to the number to match word and meaning.

1. surrealism   a. art stripped to the basics
2. minimalism   b. art that presents the mind with a puzzle
3. cubism   c. emphasizes texture and brush strokes
4. abstract expressionism   d. dreamlike images from the subconscious

On a separate sheet of paper, write a sentence using each of these new words.

DID YOU KNOW?
The Armory Show was an art exhibition in 1913 in New York City at the 69th regiment armory. It included works of the European avant-garde seen for the first time by most Americans who were startled by such work as Duchamp's *Nude Descending a Staircase.* The Armory Show created a sensation and introduced modern art to the United States, an important event that changed the direction of American art.

Words for Discussing Architecture

The words in this chapter will help you understand the vocabulary of architecture over the centuries. The movements in architecture developed roughly in tandem with the movements in art. Here you may see words introduced in the earlier chapter that are relevant to a discussion of architecture as well as to art. Creating buildings and spaces that are both beautiful and useful blends imagination and technical skill.

DAY 1

| iconography | vault | mullions | buttresses |

DAY 2

| Byzantine | Romanesque | Norman | Tudor |

DAY 3

| Gothic | Renaissance | Baroque | Georgian |

DAY 4

| rococo | classical revival | Bauhaus | International Style |

DAY 5

| Andrea Palladio | Giovanni Bernini | Sir Christopher Wren | Frank Lloyd Wright |

DAY 6

| Stanford White | Ludwig Mies van der Rohe | Le Corbusier | I. M. Pei |

DAY 7

| Eero Saarinen | Frank Gehry | Robert Venturi | Robert A. M. Stern |

iconography	The study and interpretation of the symbolic meanings of images or representational figures. For example, in Christian **iconography**, the figure of the dove signifies the Holy Spirit, and the figure of a fish symbolizes Jesus. Each epoch develops its own **iconography** as, for instance, images of Buddha in Buddhism or Shiva in Hindu **iconography.** **WORDS IN CONTEXT:** *The study of **iconography** attempts to uncover the origins of symbols and the conventions from which the images arose so as to interpret them. It is essentially the study of icons—recognizable symbols.*
vault	This is basically a curved ceiling over a room made of brick, tile, blocks, or concrete. A **vault** can take several forms: *Roman vaults* were perfectly rigid and could be placed over vast spaces. Medieval systems favored the *barrel vault,* which spanned two walls in a continuous arch. The *groined vault,* at the intersection of two barrel vaults, forms four arched openings **WORDS IN CONTEXT:** *Curved "ribs" to strengthen the groins and sides of a **vault** appeared in the eleventh century and became the supporting skeleton of Gothic architecture.*
mullions	Slender vertical bars that divide panes in windows. **WORDS IN CONTEXT:** *Tudor buildings (see below) of the fifteenth and sixteenth centuries in England often used **mullioned** windows to give manor or country houses a warm, domestic look.*
buttresses	Projecting supports built into or against the external wall of a building to strengthen it, particularly when a vault or arch places a heavy load on one section. A *flying buttress* is a masonry arch that transfers the weight or thrust of a vault to a lower support. Buttresses were often ornamented with gables and sculpture. **WORDS IN CONTEXT:** *In cathedrals such as Notre-Dame de Paris, **buttresses** give the appearance of a "flying structure" and express the elasticity and equilibrium of Gothic architecture.*

After studying the terms above, use these new words in the sentences below:

1. _____ are an architectural element that include barrel, ribbed, and groined.
2. _____support and strengthen massive arches or vaults so as to transfer the weight to a lower support.
3. The study of the history and symbolic meanings of images and figures is called_____.
4. A_____is one with many panes divided by strips of wood.

Test Yourself: Write the letter next to the number to match word and meaning.

1. buttress   a. strips of wood or other material that divide window panes
2. vault   b. arch or vault supports designed to transfer weight
3. mullions   c. study of symbolic images or figures
4. iconography   d. curved ceiling over a space; there are several forms

On a separate sheet of paper, write a sentence using each of these new words.

DID YOU KNOW?
Notre-Dame de Paris (1200–1250 in the making) is a cathedral constructed of nine squares (three-times-three to represent the Holy Trinity) that create a geometric pattern and blend architecture and sculpture. Its two towers with a band of sculpted figures or gargoyles bind the immense Rose Window to the rest of the facade. In addition: Many contemporary homes built in a "traditional" style have paned windows influenced by the mullioned windows of the Tudor epoch.

Byzantine	Dating from the fifth century, a style of the Byzantine Empire after it became the capital of Rome (330 A.D.) This style was constructed with masonry around a central plan. The style made use of domes, ornamental forms, gold, stylized figures, and icons. **WORDS IN CONTEXT:** *Byzantine architecture consisted of a blend of Greek and Oriental traditions. Interiors were often decorated with mosaics and frescoes.*
Romanesque	The style of European architecture of the eleventh and twelfth centuries that was based on Roman style with round arches; massive, thick walls; and austere interiors. Huge west facades were crowned by a tower, or sometimes by twin towers. **WORDS IN CONTEXT:** *Romanesque churches were massive enough to sustain large barrel vaults, which created a somberly impressive atmosphere.*
Norman	This style was developed from 1066 to 1154 in areas conquered by the Normans: France, England, Italy, and Sicily. In France and England, Norman buildings were based on Romanesque architecture. These churches, castles, and abbeys were huge and sparsely decorated. English and French churches were cruciform (shaped like a cross) and had square towers. Often carved moldings were used along with grotesque animal sculptures. **WORDS IN CONTEXT:** *In England, the only remaining Norman architecture is the small St. John's Chapel (c. 1087) at the tower of London; in France, Norman architecture includes the earliest constructed parts of Mont-Saint Michel and two abbeys at Caen.*
Tudor	Architectural style in England prevalent during the 1485–1556 reign of the Tudors, Henry VII, Henry VIII, and Mary I. Used predominantly in manor or country houses, this style combined brickwork with half-timbers, gables, and many chimneys and emphasized a domestic look inside. **WORDS IN CONTEXT:** *Fine examples of the Tudor style are Hampton Court Palace and some colleges at Oxford and Cambridge. For private houses, think of sketches of Shakespeare and Anne Hathaway's home in Stratford-on-Avon.*

After studying the definitions above, use these new words in the sentences below:

1. Patterned after the Roman style, these _____ buildings were massive in size, had thick walls? and round arches, and the interiors were spare.
2. Based on *Romanesque* architecture, these churches and castles in the _____ style were huge, sparsely decorated, and sometimes contained sculptures of grotesque animals and carved panels.
3. Brickwork, half-timbers, square mullioned windows, and many chimneys characterize the _____ style of architecture.
4. A central plan, domes, gold, ornament, and stylized figures characterize the _____ style.

Test Yourself: Write the letter next to the number to match word and meaning.

1. Tudor
2. Romanesque
3. Byzantine
4. Norman

a. do as the Romans do: spare interiors, massive size
b. do as Will and Anne do: brick below, timber above
c. do as Romanesque does, animal carvings
d. do as the Greek and Oriental architects do

On a separate sheet of paper, write a sentence using each of these new words.

DID YOU KNOW? One of Italy's best-known groups of structures has a marble exterior and sits on a grassy piazza. Its cathedral, baptistry, and tower are fine examples of Romanesque architecture, but its major claim to fame among tourists is its campanile, whose angle continues to amaze viewers. What could this awesome piece of architecture be? **ANSWER:** The Cathedral at Pisa (begun in 1063) with its startling leaning bell tower (campanile).

Gothic	A style employed in Europe in the thirteenth, fourteenth, and fifteenth centuries characterized by pointed arches, ribbed vaults, and buttresses to support its heavy stone construction.
	WORDS IN CONTEXT: *In addition to the cathedral of Notre-Dame, the magnificent cathedral at Chartres, also in France, is a High **Gothic** masterpiece (begun after 1194).*
Renaissance	This European style of the fifteenth and sixteenth centuries began in Italy. Symmetry, simplicity, and precise mathematical relationships of the ancient Romans (and especially the concepts of the architect Vitruvius) were adapted for contemporary use.
	WORDS IN CONTEXT: *The rebirth (**renaissance**) of classical architecture began in Italy and spread through Europe, virtually ending the dominance of the **Gothic** style. Brunelleschi was the first great architect of the Renaissance, bringing back the domes, vaults, and arches used in Roman antiquity.*
Baroque	During the seventeenth and eighteenth centuries in Europe and Latin America, architecture as well as art was produced on a grand scale, emphasizing drama, energy, and mobility of form. **Baroque** buildings (Versailles, for example, and the churches of Christopher Wren) imposed order on many different forms such as complex ground plans, fountains, waterfalls, and facades that appeared to change in the light.
	WORDS IN CONTEXT: *Baroque architecture took on the plastic aspects of sculpture and was enhanced by the chiaroscuro effects of painting to emphasize unity and balance of diverse artistic parts.*
Georgian	The prevailing style of architecture in England during the reigns of George I, II, and III (1714–1830). Architects looked back to the principles of Andrea Palladio, the Italian Renaissance architect, whose formally classic buildings were primarily palaces and villas near Venice. His country houses employed a classic temple front; inside was a central hall surrounded by rooms laid out symmetrically.
	WORDS IN CONTEXT: *The **Georgian** architect, Palladio, was influenced by the Italian Vitruvius; Palladio later influenced the English architect Inigo Jones.*

After studying the definitions above, use these new words in the sentences below:

1. Architecture on a grand scale employing dramatic forms and diverse components is called_____.
2. _____architecture was the result of a rebirth of interest in classical Roman forms, and it revived domes, vaults, and other features of antiquity.
3. A classical style characterized by a symmetrical floor plan with a central hall was_____ architecture.
4. _____architecture incorporated ribbed vaults, pointed arches, and buttresses—some of them flying.

Test Yourself: Write the letter next to the number to match word and meaning.

1. Gothic
2. Georgian
3. Baroque
4. Renaissance

a. placed order on fountains, waterfalls, and diverse forms
b. looked back on the classical forms of antiquity with favor
c. influenced the architects of Versailles
d. palaces and villas with temple fronts and formal floor plans

On a separate sheet of paper, write a sentence using each of these new words.

DID YOU KNOW?
Monticello, Thomas Jefferson's home in Virginia, and other manor houses of Southern plantations were influenced by Georgian architecture of eighteenth- and nineteenth-century England. In addition: The "five and ten cent store" building on Broadway in Lower Manhattan, completed in 1913, and until 1920 the tallest building in the world, was inspired by the Gothic Houses of Parliaments in London. The architect was Cass Gilbert (1859–1934). Can you guess what building this is? ANSWER: The Woolworth Building, still standing and still beautiful.

rococo	A style that originated in France (c. 1720) and developed from the more grandiose baroque style. **Rococo** was characterized by refined use of various materials including stucco, metal, and wood, and it employed brilliant and delicate ornamentation.
	WORDS IN CONTEXT: *In contrast to the grand drama of the baroque style, rococo was linear and exquisitely refined. The major French architect was Gabriel. Italian rococo was associated with Tiepolo, who used bright, delicate decorations.*
classical revival	The architectural movement in England and the United States in the late eighteenth and early nineteenth centuries that "revived" the traditions of Greek and Roman antiquity. This movement is sometimes called *neoclassical*. The buildings constructed in this style partly resulted from architects' enthusiasm for archeological knowledge stimulated by the excavation of Pompeii and by investigations of features of ancient Greece.
	WORDS IN CONTEXT: *Ancient Roman influence predominated in the **classical revival** of this era in the United States, as seen in the design of the Virginia capital building created by Thomas Jefferson in 1785.*
Bauhaus	The style of the **Bauhaus School**, founded in Germany by Walter Gropius in 1919. A radical departure from earlier design styles, the teaching in this school emphasized functional skills and craft as these applied to industrial problems of mass production.
	WORDS IN CONTEXT: ***Bauhaus** concepts, which focused on severe economic, geometric design, were greatly controversial. Seen as too radical, they were banned by the Nazis in 1933. However, the style found international acclaim and had enormous influence on architecture, furnishings, and typography. It flourished in the United States, especially at the Chicago Institute of Design.*
International Style	A movement in the 1920s in the United States and abroad led by Mies van der Rohe, Le Corbusier, and Walter Gropius, and later practiced by Philip Johnson, the **International Style** became the dominant style of the mid-twentieth century. Architects used glass, steel, and other modern materials and focused on structure and function.
	WORDS IN CONTEXT: *The **International Style** opposed decorative details and incorporated sleek, simple lines and respect for modern materials. An extreme example of **International Style** is Philip Johnson's Glass House in New Canaan, Connecticut (1949), which consists of a glass box, a steel frame, and a brick floor.*

After studying the definitions above, use these new words in the sentences below:

1. Emphasizing function, lightening the mass of buildings, and employing glass, _____ architects grew out of the Bauhaus movement, which furiously disdained decoration and ornamentation.
2. Literally translated as "house for building," the_____movement in Germany after World War I stripped architecture of frills and brought the concept of mass production to the world of design and building.
3. _____departed from the baroque style by streamlining designs and adding delicate ornamentation.
4. _____looked back with favor on the traditions of Greek and Roman antiquity following the uncovering of the buried city of Pompeii.

Test Yourself: Write the letter next to the number to match word and meaning.

1. rococo
2. Bauhaus
3. classical revival
4. International Style

a. revived the traditions of Greek and Roman antiquity
b. school that influenced twentieth-century architecture
c. refined, delicate, and ornamental style
d. steel and glass, focus on structure and function

DID YOU KNOW?
The faculty at the Bauhaus, which began in Weimar, Germany, included artists and architects who would become world renowned figures: Paul Klee, Lyonel Feininger, Wassily Kandinsky, László Moholy-Nagy, and Marcel Breuer, along with Walter Gropius. In addition: Moholy-Nagy founded the Chicago Institute of Design after the Bauhaus was closed by the Nazis.

Andrea Palladio	(1508–1580): Influential Italian Renaissance architect whose drawings of Roman architecture and his own plans were published in *The Four Books of Architecture* (1570). He designed formally classic buildings, palaces, and villas, and his symmetrical country houses incorporated classic temple fronts.
	WORDS IN CONTEXT: *Palladio used the classical temple motifs in three famous churches in Venice: San Francisco della Vigna, San Giorgio Maggiore, and Il Redentore. He had a great influence on British and U.S. architecture.*
Giovanni Bernini	(1598–1680): The dominant figure of Italian baroque architecture, he produced dramatic works of architecture enhanced with sculpture. In 1629, he became architect of St. Peter's Cathedral in Rome and designed interior details and the great piazza in front of St. Peter's.
	WORDS IN CONTEXT: *Bernini produced David for Cardinal Borghese (c. 1620), Rape of Proserpine (1622), and Apollo and Daphne (1625)—all in the Borghese Gallery in Rome. Bernini (called Gianlorenzo) designed chapels, churches, fountains, monuments, tombs, and statues for popes.*
Sir Christopher Wren	(1632–1723): British architect, mathematician, and astronomer, Wren designed St. Paul's Cathedral in London (1675–1710) and 52 other churches in London. He also designed Trinity College Library at Cambridge University (1679–1684) and the Sheldonian Theatre at Oxford (1664–1669).
	WORDS IN CONTEXT: *After the great fire in London in 1666, Sir Christopher Wren designed a plan for rebuilding London. It was never carried out, though he did design many London structures. Wren's designs, in which he incorporated elegant spires, were greatly influential.*
Frank Lloyd Wright	(1867–1959): This great American architect respected nature and organic forms. He felt that structures should fit into their environment, take advantage of their natural settings, and be constructed of the same materials they sit on: if the setting was natural limestone, the structure should be of natural limestone. He also viewed houses not as a series of spaces but wished to "destroy the box," making the spaces flow openly from room to room.
	WORDS IN CONTEXT: *Frank Lloyd Wright designed The Robie House in "the Prairie Style," in Chicago (1909); his own home, Taliesin, in Spring Green, Wisconsin (1911, twice rebuilt), Taliesin West, home and school, Scottsdale, Arizona (1937), the famous Fallingwater, cantilevered over a water fall, taking advantage of the natural environment of its surroundings in Bear Run, Pennsylvania (1935), the Solomon R. Guggenheim Museum in New York City (1956), with its innovative spiraling ramp, and Marin County Civic Center, Marin, California (1957).*

After studying the names above, use them in the sentences below.

1. The major Renaissance architect who revived classical symmetrical forms and the Roman temple pillars on the fronts of structures was_____.
2. As great a sculptor as he was architect, _____ worked in and around St. Peter's, and other works of his can be seen in the Borghese Gallery in Rome.
3. _____designed St. Paul's Cathedral in London.
4. _____integrated materials and environment into architectural expression and was innovative in open planning, eliminating traditional room divisions in favor of fluid inner space.

Test Yourself: Write the letter next to the number to match man and work.

1. Sir Christopher Wren   a. David, Rape of Proserpine—and churches, too
2. Giovanni Bernini   b. formal, classic palaces and villas, he liked symmetry
3. Andrea Palladio   c. is known for *Fallingwater*
4. Frank Lloyd Wright   d. noted British architect of London structures

DID YOU KNOW? The 210-foot tower of Duke Chapel, a majestic structure whose stained glass windows contain more than one million pieces of glass, and which dominates the neo-Gothic West Campus of Duke University, was designed by African-American architect Julian Abele (1881–1950) in the mid-1920s.

Stanford White	(1853–1906) An American architect whose work with C. F. McKim and William R. Meade influenced New York City architecture at the turn of the twentieth century. Still standing are his Washington Memorial Arch in Washington Square Park and the elegant Century Club. His special interests were in interior design and decorative arts. **WORDS IN CONTEXT:** *The first Madison Square Garden in New York City was designed by* **Stanford White** *and his partners. White's building was more graceful than his life: He was shot and killed in Madison Square Garden by a jealous husband, Harry K. Thaw, over an affair* **White** *was having with Evelyn Nesbitt, Thaw's wife—an incident depicted in the film* The Girl in the Red Velvet Swing.
Ludwig Mies van der Rohe	(1886–1969) Commonly referred to as Mies, this German-American architect was a founder of modern architecture. He took over as director of the Bauhaus from Walter Gropius; later he moved to Chicago to teach in what is now the Illinois Institute of Technology. He pioneered internal structures that could support buildings made entirely of glass, the structural skeletons of buildings being one of his major interests. **WORDS IN CONTEXT:** *Known for his maxims, as well as for creating the vocabulary of modern architecture,* **Mies van der Rohe** *coined the phrases, "Less is more," "God is in the details," and "Form follows function."*
Le Corbusier	(1887–1965) Born Charles-Edouard Jeanneret-Gris, this Swiss architect worked in France; his book *Towards a New Architecture* (1923) had a revolutionary effect on international development of modern architecture. Drawing inspiration from industrial forms, he produced radical schemes for houses and apartments. **WORDS IN CONTEXT:** **Le Corbu,** *as he was often known, built a villa near Paris in 1923 and another,* Villa Savoie, Poissy, *in 1929. His plan for a "vertical city" was partially realized in the* Unité d'Habitation, Marseilles (1942–1952). **Le Corbusier** *also designed the Visual Arts Center at Harvard University (1961–1962).*
I. M. Pei	(1917–) A Chinese-American architect, Pei integrates structure and environment, favoring glass, stone, concrete, and steel. A champion of light, view, and public space, Pei is known for designing giant atriums—and for the design of the huge, glass Pyramids at the Louvre in Paris (1983). **WORDS IN CONTEXT:** *Among the structures designed by* **I. M. Pei** *are the East Wing of the National Gallery of Art, Washington, D.C. (1978), the West Wing of the Museum of Fine Arts in Boston (1981), and the Rock and Roll Hall of Fame in Cleveland (1996).*

After studying the architects above, use their names in the sentences below.

1. Despite his tabloid personal life,_____will be remembered by those who admire the Washington Square Arch in New York's Greenwich Village.
2. His goal being bringing nature, people, and architecture together in a "higher unity,"_____declared that "less is more."
3. Following his principles in *Towards a New Architecture,* _____designed a villa at Vaucresson, near Paris, in 1923.
4. _____favors glass, steel, stone, and concrete—and public space.

Test Yourself: Write the letter next to the number to match man and work.

1. Mies van der Rohe   a. designed the Pyramids at the Louvre
2. Le Corbusier   b. lived and died by the first Madison Square Garden
3. Stanford White   c. designed the Visual Center at Harvard
4. I. M. Pei   d. took over the Bauhaus from Gropius

On a separate sheet of paper, write a sentence using each of these names.

DID YOU KNOW?

Who designed the U.S. Capitol in Washington, D.C., setting the model for capitols throughout the United States?

ANSWER:

Charles Bullfinch (1763–1884) of Massachusetts.

Eero Saarinen	(1910–1961) A Finnish-American architect who also was noted for his furniture design, particularly chairs. His concrete-domed structures were innovative and influential. His projects included The Massachusetts Institute of Technology (1953–1956), Dulles International Airport (1958–1962), and the Gateway Arch in St. Louis (1959–1964), the last two were finished posthumously. **WORDS IN CONTEXT:** *Eero Saarinen studied and worked with his father, architect Eliel (Gottlieb) Saarinen. Together, the two designed the Berkshire Music Center in Tanglewood, Massachusetts. The younger Saarinen also designed the swooping Trans World Airlines Terminal in New York City.*
Frank Gehry	(1929–) A Canadian architect, who has vaulted to the top of every list of major architects since the turn of the twenty-first century with his design of the Guggenheim Museum in Bilbao, Spain. A titanium structure composed of sleek, curving, sensuous, and fanciful shapes, the Bilbao captures and reflects the light from every angle. Using unconventional materials, he breaks the mold of architecture as we have known it. **WORDS IN CONTEXT:** *Frank Gehry has been called more a sculptor than an architect, though his astonishing structures are considered technically masterful. In addition to the Bilbao, his work includes the Gehry House in Santa Monica, California (1978), and the Disney Concert Hall in Los Angeles (1997).*
Robert Venturi	(1925–) An architectural theorist, **Venturi** is a *postmodernist* (a leader in a style that emerged in the 1970s, characterized by references to and evocative of past styles, especially of the classical tradition). **Venturi's** work is often colorful and witty. In his books, *Complexities and Contradictions in Modern Architecture* (1966) and *Learning from Las Vegas* (1972), he advocates an unorthodox, eclectic, and humorous new vocabulary of architecture, illustrating the validity and high spirits of advertising, roadside signs, and strip malls. **WORDS IN CONTEXT:** *A&P parking lots have vitality and are a part of American culture, says **Robert Venturi,** whose colorful high-rises in Florida attest to his appreciation of "the kitsch of high capitalism."*
Robert A. M. Stern	(1939–) Another *postmodernist* whose work favors architecture preceding the Bauhaus and International Style. His large, private homes with porches and many windows in East Hampton, New York, and other locations incorporate traditional styles along with light and open spaces. **WORDS IN CONTEXT:** *Celebration, Florida, shows the handiwork of **Robert A. M. Stern.** This small community, created by the Walt Disney Company and coplanned by Stern, looks back to Main Street America—a tranquil, homey, pristine world that is an experiment in planned living.*

After studying the architects above, use their names in the sentences below:

1. _____ designed the Gateway Arch in St. Louis and the Trans World Airlines terminal in New York City.
2. The work of _____ harkens back to small-town America and planned communities. (His work could have been the model for the film, *The Truman Show.*)
3. _____ wrote the book advocating that Americans look at their current architectural environment and find vital, vibrant, and amusing patterns in the kitsch around them.
4. The architect who is breaking the mold of architecture in the twenty-first century with his unconventional materials and sculptural forms is _____.

Test Yourself: Write the letter next to the number to match man and work.

1. Eero Saarinen	a.	look to him for a pristine, gated community
2. Robert Venturi	b.	architect of the astonishing Bilbao
3. Robert A. M. Stern	c.	his work reflects popular culture, wit, and color
4. Frank Gehry	d.	swooping arches and concrete domes

DID YOU KNOW? Leonardo da Vinci (1452–1519) was not only a masterly painter and sculptor, but he was also a scientist, engineer, and architect. He worked on the Milan Cathedral and at least two others. He served as architect and engineer in Milan for Louis XII beginning in 1506. Leonardo also worked on several projects for the Vatican between 1513 and 1515.

Words for Discussing Music

Because music is composed of many different tones, to speak of music, one needs many different and special words. The vocabulary of music derives from several languages, particularly German, Italian, and French. Study the words in boldface below and practice using them in the exercises.

DAY 1

staff	bar line	measure	time signature

DAY 2

key signature	tempo	allegro	opus

DAY 3

libretto	aria	recitative	opera

DAY 4

leitmotif	impresario	adagio	andante

DAY 5

bel canto	castrati	oratorio	cantata

DAY 6

opera buffa	sonata	bagatelle	rhapsody

DAY 7

blues	jazz	swing	bebop

staff	The five horizontal lines on a sheet of music on and between which notes are written. **WORDS IN CONTEXT:** *In the treble clef, notes (played by the right hand on the piano) written in the spaces between the lines on the **staff** are these: F, A, C, E. Notes written on the lines are these: E, G, B, D, F. Notes written in the spaces of a **staff** in the bass clef (played by the left hand on the piano) are these: A, C, E, G. And notes on the lines are G, B, D, F, A.*
bar line	Vertical lines drawn along the **staff** to indicate **measures** between the lines. **WORDS IN CONTEXT:** *To divide the **staff** into **measures**, which enclose notes, **bar lines** are used.*
measure	A unit of rhythm or musical time indicated by **bar lines.** **WORDS IN CONTEXT:** *The composition contained three notes in each **measure**.*
time signature	The meter (rhythm) of a composition as shown by two numbers stacked one above the other on the **staff** at the beginning of a musical piece; the number below (4, for example) tells the kind of note (a quarter note) that represents one beat. The number above (3, for example) tells the number of those notes that make up a **measure.** **WORDS IN CONTEXT:** *The **time signature** indicates that the piece is in 3/4 time, which is the meter called for in a waltz.*

After studying the definitions above, use these new words in the sentences below:

1. There are five lines on a _____.
2. She saw three quarter notes in each_____ in the composition.
3. The _____ indicates that the piece is to be played in waltz time.
4. _____separated the measures on the staff.

Test Yourself: Write the letter next to the number to match word and meaning.

1. bar lines   a. contain(s) five horizontal lines
2. measure   b. indicate(s) the meter of the composition
3. time signature   c. vertical lines that divide measures
4. staff   d. space between bars that contain notes

On a separate sheet of paper, write a sentence using each of these new words.

DID YOU KNOW?
The waltz, a romantic dance in triple time, evolved from a German dance called the *Ländler*. The two Johann Strausses, father and son, made the Viennese waltz famous in the eighteenth century. The waltz was not introduced in the United States until the nineteenth century.

key signature	Indicates the key in which a piece should be played. Symbols called *sharps* (♯) and *flats* (♭) placed on the staff at the beginning of a composition indicate the composition's key. If there are no sharps or flats, the key is C. **WORDS IN CONTEXT:** *In the **key signature,** sharps raise the pitch of the indicated notes by a semitone (or half step); flats lower the pitch of indicated notes by a semitone.*
tempo	The speed at which a composition is played. **WORDS IN CONTEXT:** *The **tempo** in which the piece is to be played is **allegro**, as indicated by the use of that word above the staff.*
allegro	Instruction that a piece should be played quickly and briskly. **WORDS IN CONTEXT:** *The concert pianist played the piece brightly and quickly, as indicated on the score of the composition by the word **allegro**.*
opus	In music, this word simply means a work of music that is numbered. **WORDS IN CONTEXT:** *The composer numbered his work Opus 3 to distinguish it chronologically from his earlier works: Opus 1 and Opus 2.*

After studying the definitions above, use these new words in the sentences below:

1. His _____12 was numbered to follow his previous works.
2. The_____ of the composition was slow.
3. The word_____ on the sheet of music directed the musician to play quickly and briskly.
4. The_____indicated with its three flats that the work was in the key of E-flat.

Test Yourself: Write the letter next to the number to match word and meaning.

1. allegro   a. a work of a composer numbered in order of composition
2. tempo   b. indicates the key in which the piece is to be played
3. opus   c. the speed at which a composition is to be played
4. key signature   d. to be played with alacrity

On a separate sheet of paper, write a sentence using each of these new words.

DID YOU KNOW? Perfect pitch (or absolute pitch) is the ability to hear a note or even a sound and identify its precise pitch. A person with absolute pitch (whether inborn or acquired) can identify the name of the note that is being played or sounded without any external reference, such as a note on another instrument or a tuning device. If a note—C-sharp, for example—is sounded, most people just hear a note. The person with absolute or perfect pitch can say, "That is C-sharp." A person's ability to identify such notes immediately can be improved by training, practice, and drills, but it's clear that some people also have an innate capacity to do this.

libretto	The words (text) of an opera or an oratorio. The word *libretto* in Italian means "little book," or "booklet." **WORDS IN CONTEXT:** *Usually sung in Italian, the music in Donizetti's* Lucia di Lammermoor *is wonderful, but it helps to have the* **libretto** *in English.*
aria	**Arias** are solo pieces with orchestral or instrumental accompaniment in which opera singers express their thoughts and feelings. An aria is more complex and vocally difficult than a "song." **WORDS IN CONTEXT:** *Operas usually consist of* **arias** *that alternate with recitatives and ensemble pieces, such as duets, trios, quartets, and choruses.*
recitative	In opera and oratorio, a solo written in a style of singing that resembles dramatic speech. While **arias** convey emotion and the inner thoughts of a character, **recitatives** generally advance the plot. **WORDS IN CONTEXT:** *A* **recitative** *(derived from the Italian word for "reciting") has sometimes been called "a declamation in musical tones" or "sing speech." It can be accompanied by instruments playing a few chords or by a full orchestra. The* **recitative** *in Puccini's opera* Tosca *has a different sound from one, say, in Monteverdi's* Orfeo.
opera	Dramatic works dating back to the sixteenth century Italy in which almost all of the libretto is sung to orchestral accompaniment. During the Italian Renaissance, Vincenzo Galilei (c. 1520–1591)—father of Galileo—and other musicians wanted to revive Greek drama with music. This group was called *Camerata.* **WORDS IN CONTEXT:** *Peri, a member of Camerata, wrote the* **opera** *Dafne, and three years later he wrote* Euridice, *which was performed at the wedding of Henri IV of France and Maria de Medici. These are examples of the earliest operas, and both were tragic or serious operas (opera seria).*

After studying the definitions above, use these new words in the sentences below:

1. _____ are solos sung, often on a fixed note, in which the rhythm and lilt are taken from speech patterns.
2. An _____ is a solo in an opera that expresses the inner feelings of a character.
3. _____ were musical works intended to revive Greek declamatory style of drama.
4. The written text of an opera and operetta is called the_____.

Test Yourself: Write the letter next to the number to match word and meaning.

1. libretto   a. Peri wrote one of the first in 1597
2. opera   b. characters express emotions and thoughts in a solo
3. recitative   c. musical solo that advances the plot
4. aria   d. the book that provides the lyrics of an opera

On a separate sheet of paper, write a sentence using each of these new words.

DID YOU KNOW? Richard Wagner's (1813–1883) epic cycle of operas, *Der Ring des Nibelungen,* called "the Ring cycle," took 25 years to complete; in the meantime he wrote *Lohengrin* (1850) and *Tristan und Isolde* (1859). In the Ring cycle, each character has a signature melody (called a *leitmotif*) which unifies the work, informs the audience of the action, and gives the thoughts of the characters. Wagner is known for synthesizing music, poetry, story, movement, and visual art.

leitmotif	A German word meaning "a leading theme," which is a recurring theme. Each **leitmotif** is associated with a character or an idea in an opera. The **leitmotif** allows the composer to tell the story in music as it synthesizes with the action on stage. **WORDS IN CONTEXT:** *Leitmotif is associated with Wagner. In the last act of Götterdämmerung, a part of the Ring cycle, for example, every **leitmotif** associated with the character, Siegfried, is woven into a death march to enhance the plot. Mozart and Berlioz, along with other composers, also used the technique.*
impresario	From the Italian "imperiously," meaning the conductor or manager of an opera or a concert company. **WORDS IN CONTEXT:** *Impresario Sarah Caldwell (1924–) founded the Boston Opera in 1957 and became its director. She was also the first woman conductor at the New York Metropolitan Opera. The first opera this **impresario** staged was Ralph Vaughan Williams's Riders to the Sea at Tanglewood in Massachusetts. (The word **impresario** is not often used anymore; most director/managers are called musical directors.)*
adagio	From the Italian, "at ease," in music meaning a slow tempo or a slow movement. **WORDS IN CONTEXT:** *The composer had written **adagio** on the music to direct the musicians to play the movement at a slow tempo.*
andante	Also from the Italian, meaning literally "going" or "moving" to indicate a moderate tempo, or a walking pace. *Piu andante* means moving slightly faster. **WORDS IN CONTEXT:** *Andante on the score indicates that the musicians should play at a moderate tempo.*

After studying the definitions above, use these new words in the sentences below:

1. From 1958 to 1969, Leonard Bernstein was the musical director or_____ of the New York Philharmonic.
2. The music was to be played at a slow tempo as indicated by the word_____ on the sheet of music.
3. Each time the character appeared in the opera, her_____was woven into the music.
4. The orchestra played the movement_____to pick up the tempo to a moderate pace.

Test Yourself: Write the letter next to the number to match word and meaning.

1. leitmotif   a. play at a slow tempo
2. impresario   b. play at a moderate tempo
3. adagio   c. musical theme associated with a character
4. andante   d. musical director

On a separate sheet of paper, write a sentence using each of these new words.

DID YOU KNOW?

Which composers wrote the following operas?

(a) *The Magic Flute*
(b) *Falstaff*
(c) *Carmen*
(d) *Hansel and Gretel*
(e) *Porgy and Bess*
(f) *William Tell*

ANSWERS:

(a) **Mozart**
(b) **Verdi**
(c) **Bizet**
(d) **Humperdinck**
(e) **Gershwin**
(f) **Rossini**

bel canto	(Italian): Literally means "beautiful singing," a style of singing characterized by elaborate technique emphasizing the beauty of sound and the brilliance of performance rather than dramatic expression or emotion; associated with eighteenth-century Italian opera. Range, power, purity of sound, and seeming effortlessness are qualities of **bel canto.** **WORDS IN CONTEXT:** *Bel canto is a virtuoso singing style. Rossini (1792–1868), Donizetti (1797–1848), and Bellini (1801–1835) are well-known composers of bel canto opera. The term was first used to describe the florid vocal technique of castrati in the seventeenth and eighteenth centuries.*
castrati	Male singers who were castrated as boys to maintain a pure soprano or high alto voice range. These were singing eunuchs, boys castrated before puberty so their voices would remain high-pitched. In Italy and to some extent in Germany, where the Catholic Church banned women from singing during services and religious music became more complex, **castrati** sang high vocal parts (falsetto) with power and stamina. **WORDS IN CONTEXT:** *Castrati performed in Peri's Euridice (1600) and in Monteverdi's Orfeo (1607)— generally considered the first great Italian opera. Up until c. 1750, castrati were the stars of serious Italian opera. Carlo Broschi (1705–1782), known as Farinelli, and Francesco Bernardi (1680–1750) became enormously rich and famous. The last castrato, Alessandro Moreschi, who sang in the Sistine Chapel as part of the Vatican choir, lived until 1922.*
oratorio	A musical setting of a religious or epic libretto for soloists, chorus, and orchestra. **Oratorios** are performed without costumes, scenery, or theatrical effects. **Oratorios** began in the Middle Ages and took the name from St. Philip of Neri of Rome (1515–1595), who tried to attract young people to religious services in his **oratory** (a small chapel, or a religious society) by having the best musicians in the world perform sacred music. **WORDS IN CONTEXT:** *Handel's* Messiah, *Haydn's* Creation *and* The Seasons, *and Mendelssohn's* Elijah *are oratorios.*
cantata	Originally of the *Baroque* period, this term describes a vocal or choral piece with an instrumental accompaniment. German **cantatas** were usually religious works. As opposed to a *sonata,* a **cantata** is sung, rather than played. **WORDS IN CONTEXT:** *Italian cantatas of the seventeenth century were generally secular; their dramatic or pastoral subjects consisted of several arias and recitatives. Cantatas were much like early operas, though they were not staged. Allesandro Scarlatti (1660–1725) wrote 600 solo cantatas as well as hundreds of operas and oratorios. Johann Sabastian Bach (1685–1750) was a master of this form.*

After studying the definitions above, use these new words in the sentences below:

1. Handel's *Messiah* is an_____, composed of sacred music and performed without a theatrical setting or costumes.
2. Young boys who underwent mutilation to be able to sing in high, pure voices were called_____.
3. _____are vocal or choral pieces, originally secular, that are not staged theatrically as operas are.
4. Beautiful singing performed with brilliant technical form is _____.

Test Yourself: Write the letter next to the number to match word and meaning.

1. bel canto   a. seventeenth-century work much like opera, but not staged
2. oratorio   b. Mendelssohn's *Elijah* is one
3. cantata   c. Moreschi, who sang in the Vatican choir, was one
4. castrati   d. singing identified by its technical brilliance

On a separate sheet of paper, write a sentence using each of these new words.

DID YOU KNOW?
Benjamin Britten (1913–1976) was a great twentieth-century composer of opera. Critics and musicologists favor *Peter Grimes* (1945). But Britten wrote many other operas of various kinds, among them: *The Rape of Lucretia* (1946), *Albert Herring* (1947), *Billy Budd* (1951), and *The Turn of the Screw* (1954). *The Little Sweep* (1949) and *Noye's Fludd* (1958) are children's operas. *Owen Wingrave* (1971) was written for television.

opera buffa	"Comic opera" (Italian) of the eighteenth century. The subjects of **opera buffa** were humorous, light, and satirical, as was the music. The characters were not high born or mythological figures as in serious (tragic) or *seria opera;* they were ordinary people. **WORDS IN CONTEXT:** *Opera buffa often used bass voices, rarely heard in* opera seria. *In another departure from* opera seria, *which was built around solo voices and an occasional duet,* **opera buffa** *also added ensemble finales, in which three or more characters sing at the same time toward the end of the performance.*
sonata	From an Italian word that means "to play an instrument," a **sonata** is an instrumental piece that is usually written for the solo piano, or for the piano with one other instrument. Generally, the piano is presumed, and the name of the **sonata** takes the name of the additional instrument. For example, "violin sonata," and "flute sonata," indicate those instruments plus the piano. If the piano is the only instrument, the **sonata** is called a *piano sonata.* **WORDS IN CONTEXT:** *The* **sonata** *is composed of movements, with each movement differing in character and tempo. The first movement is allegro, the second is slower—adagio or andante—and the third is quick and lively. Haydn wrote more than 50* **sonatas** *for harpsichord and piano; Mozart wrote more than 20 piano* **sonatas** *and about 40 violin* **sonatas**.
bagatelle	The word is French for "a trifle." **Bagatelles** are also called *character pieces*. This describes a variety of nineteenth-century pieces for the solo piano, and they were written almost in reaction to the **sonata,** which the Romantic composers of this period considered old fashioned. In experimenting with new musical forms, they wrote shorter pieces that were not divided into movements. **WORDS IN CONTEXT:** *Beethoven, a master of classical forms and also a Romantic pioneer, was the first to use the title* **bagatelle**—*meaning a "throwaway piece," a fleeting mood piece.*
rhapsody	The title given in the nineteenth and twentieth centuries to an instrumental composition that is not divided into movements. **Rhapsodies** often incorporate folk tunes or have heroic themes. **WORDS IN CONTEXT:** *American composer George Gershwin's (1898–1937)* Rhapsody in Blue, *first performed in 1924, is a work for piano and orchestra and is one of the first serious orchestral works to include jazz idioms.*

After studying the words above, use these new words in the sentences below:

1. A_____is a work written for solo piano, or for piano and one other instrument, in three movements.
2. As opposed to *opera seria,*_____is a comic opera.
3. Written for solo piano, _____are nineteenth-century character pieces.
4. _____are orchestral compositions in one movement that are often based on folk music.

Test Yourself: Write the letter next to the number to match word and meaning.

1. sonata	a. merely a trifle, but Beethoven enjoyed it
2. bagatelle	b. a comic opera, short and light
3. rhapsody	c. a work for piano and one other instrument in three movements
4. opera buffa	d. Gershwin took this form seriously

On a separate sheet of paper, write a sentence using each of these new words.

DID YOU KNOW? Aaron Copland (1900–1990), an American composer, wrote three great orchestral works for ballet: *Appalachian Spring, Billy the Kid,* and *Rodeo*—all based on American folk melodies. He is also known for *Lincoln Portrait,* a work for narrator and orchestra, based on the writings of Abraham Lincoln.

blues	A blending of African and American music. Vocal **blues** suggest melancholia and despair. The tempo varies, but the **blues** are mostly slow and weary, while the mood ranges from depression to cynicism to satire. Lyrics generally are a narration of a story of suffering and privation in a 12-bar line.
	WORDS IN CONTEXT: *Washington Irving is credited with coining the term the blues in 1807. African-American history of the blues is traced through oral tradition to the 1860s. Slaves responded to their oppressive environment with "field holler," which gave rise to the Negro spiritual and the blues. Major early blues artists were Blind Lemon Jefferson, Ma Rainey, and Bessie Smith. African-American composer W. C. Handy popularized the blues form in about 1911.*
jazz	American musical form developed c. 1890 from African-American work songs, spirituals, and other forms employing African harmony, melody, and rhythm. New Orleans or Dixieland **jazz** developed from military music, **blues,** and the French tradition in New Orleans. Pioneer musicians were Buddy Bolden and Jelly Roll Morton.
	WORDS IN CONTEXT: *During World War I, musicians went north up the Mississippi looking for work. In Chicago, King Oliver, Louis Armstrong, and others introduced jazz to a wider audience, and young whites including cornetist Bix Beiderbecke were drawn to it. Jazz is considered by many to be the quintessential American music; it combines the discipline of classical music with the natural musician's improvisation (or spontaneous composition).*
swing	At the end of the 1920s, **swing** emerged. **Swing** bands were composed of groups from 14 to 18 musicians and featured soloists singing to background arrangements. Glenn Miller and his ensemble were influential in the development of **swing,** which made lively music for dancing.
	WORDS IN CONTEXT: *Swing had an insistent rhythm and was most often played by big bands. Notable swing leaders were Count Basie, Duke Ellington, and Benny Goodman.*
bebop	A form that grew out of jazz in the 1940s, which involved complex rhythms and harmonic sequences carried out against rapidly played melodic improvisation. A revolt against the formulas of **swing.** Notables were Charlie "The Bird" Parker and Dizzy Gillespie.
	WORDS IN CONTEXT: *Progressive jazz grew out of bebop and was inspired by swing band saxophonist Lester Young. Stan Getz and Dave Brubeck were leaders of bebop.*

After studying the definitions above, use these new words in the sentences below:

1. _____is American music that developed from African-American work songs. The Dixieland form of this music began in New Orleans.
2. Also developing from Negro "field holler" and spirituals, _____music expresses sad, melancholic, weary moods.
3. Lively music with an insistent beat,_____brought dancers to their feet in the late 1920s.
4. Jazz saxophonist Charlie Parker is especially associated with _____, which grew out of jazz and continues to evolve.

Test Yourself: Write the letter next to the number to match word and meaning.

1. blues   a. big band music to dance to; Lester liked it
2. jazz   b. slow, weary music; Ma and Bessie like it
3 bebop   c. energetic music of many varieties; the Bird liked it
4. swing   d. revolt against swing; Dizzy took it forward

On a separate sheet of paper, write a sentence using each of these new words.

DID YOU KNOW?
Jazz continues to evolve through *progressive jazz, bebop, hard bop* (notables, Sonny Rollins and John Coltrane). In the 1960s, Miles Davis and others brought *rock music* into jazz with *cool jazz,* and Ornette Coleman with *free jazz.* In the 1970s jazz reached into the past to create a music with elements of all jazz styles, epitomized in the work of the Art Ensemble of Chicago. Almost all jazz styles remain current today.

Words for Discussing Philosophy

Philosophy is one of the oldest fields of learning and one of the first to be systemized—by many philosophers and into many different systems. The following includes some of these systems (viewpoints or positions), some of the terms used by philosophers, and some of the historical movements in philosophy.

DAY 1

| metaphysics | ontology | cosmology | virtue |

DAY 2

| logic | rhetoric | ethics | aesthetics |

DAY 3

| Manichaeanism | cause | teleology | epistemology |

DAY 4

| first cause | cogito ergo sum | empiricism | social contract |

DAY 5

| skepticism | categorical imperative | zeitgeist | utilitarianism |

DAY 6

| materialism | leap of faith | pragmatism | übermensch |

DAY 7

| intuitionism | universals | analytical philosophy | existentialism |

metaphysics	The branch of philosophy concerned with the ultimate nature of reality and existence as a whole. Aristotle created the first system of **metaphysics**, which in Greek means "after physics"—the first philosophy after physics.
	WORDS IN CONTEXT: *Two branches of* **metaphysics** *are usually considered to be* **ontology** *and* **cosmology.**
ontology	The study of the nature of existence or reality.
	WORDS IN CONTEXT: *The study of the nature of being in general,* **ontology** *asks, What is real?*
cosmology	Originally a branch of **metaphysics**, **cosmology** is the systematic study of the origin and structure of the universe as a whole.
	WORDS IN CONTEXT: *To Plato (428–348 B.C.), Aristotle, and much later Kant (1724–1804),* **cosmology** *was based on metaphysical speculation; that is, thinking beyond the physical world. In later years,* **cosmology** *became a branch of the physical sciences itself.*
virtue	According to Plato, **virtue** consists of the harmony of the human soul with the universe of Ideas, which give order, intelligence, and pattern to a world in constant flux. To Plato, these Ideas (or Forms) existed independently and were the models of everything that existed in the physical world. His theory of Forms stated that it is as if we live in a cave seeing moving shadows on the wall and believe these shadows to be reality, when reality actually exists outside the cave.
	WORDS IN CONTEXT: *The Idea of Good was supreme and stood outside the physical world as the Sun is outside the Earth but constantly affects it.* **Virtue** *is the quality a person possesses who understands the Idea of Good; this understanding is necessary to enable a person to rule the state in a just manner. Persons with* **virtue** *were to Plato philosopher kings—the highest form of person.*

After studying the definitions above, use these new words in the sentences below.

1. Plato and Aristotle thought_____to be based on thinking beyond the physical world.
2. Plato thought that people with_____were of a higher nature than others, which would enable them to rule the state in a just manner.
3. _____is the general study of reality or existence.
4. The branch of metaphysics that consists of the study of the origin and structure of the universe is called_____.

Test Yourself: Write the letter next to the number to match word and meaning.

1. virtue   a. the systematic study of the universe as a whole
2. ontology   b. the quality necessary in a person to rule a state justly
3. cosmology   c. a branch of philosophy, the first after physics
4. metaphysics   d. the study of existence or being in general

On a separate sheet of paper, write a sentence using each of these new words.

DID YOU KNOW?
Plato studied with Socrates (470–399 B.C.), who taught through dialogues with his students. These dialectics—questions and answers—helped the students learn to think and argue clearly. Socrates's teachings were basically oral. Plato wrote down these conversations to illustrate his teacher's major ideas; among the early dialogues were those discussing the unity of virtue and knowledge and virtue and happiness. Plato also wrote a moving account of Socrates's last days and his death: In 399 B.C., Socrates was brought to trial on charges of corrupting young men through his teachings. (He said "the unexamined life is not worth living," and some of the questions he asked students were seen as religious heresy.) Sentenced to death, Socrates drank hemlock, a poison, and died.

logic	The study of the rules and principles that distinguish sound reasoning from poor reasoning.
	WORDS IN CONTEXT: *Aristotle (384–322 B.C.), Greek philosopher, scientist, and* **logician,** *who opened the Lyceum—a philosophical and scientific school in Athens—classified many of the rules of reasoning that make up valid or sound* **logic.**
rhetoric	The study of the techniques used to persuade and convince a reader or listener.
	WORDS IN CONTEXT: *The art or science of using words correctly in speaking or writing is called* **rhetoric.** *A* **rhetorical question** *is a question asked only for effect and to which the speaker expects no answer. Aristotle wrote a treatise on* **rhetoric.**
ethics	The study of standards of moral judgment and conduct; also the code of morals of a particular person, group, religion, or profession.
	WORDS IN CONTEXT: *In* **ethics,** *Aristotle emphasized that virtue is a mean between extremes and that people's highest goal should be the use of their intellect. Aristotle's golden mean was the* **ethical doctrine** *associated with moderation—behavior that falls exactly between too much and too little of a quality, that is, too much bravery is foolhardiness, and too little is cowardliness.*
aesthetics	Sometimes written **esthetics,** this is the philosophical study of beauty.
	WORDS IN CONTEXT: **Aesthetics** *asks such questions as What is beauty? How do we ascertain it? Are* **aesthetic** *judgments subjective or objective? How does art embody truth?*

After studying the definitions above, use these new words in the sentences below.

1. The speaker's persuasive_____ convinced the audience to vote for him.
2 The_____of the woman were reflected in the moral decisions and judgments she made each day.
3. The_____of the writer's argument was appreciated by the readers who elected to join him in his cause.
4 The beauty of the desert is an _____judgment by those who chose to live there.

Test Yourself: Write the letter next to the number to match word and meaning.

1. rhetoric   a. principles that distinguish good from bad reasoning
2. ethics   b. principles of right and wrong
3. aesthetics   c. techniques used to persuade or convince
4. logic   d. the study of beauty

On a separate sheet of paper, write a sentence using each of these new words.

DID YOU KNOW? Aristotle categorized all the areas of human knowledge of his time: physics, biology, political science, botany, and anatomy. He was a student of Plato and a teacher of Alexander the Great. He opened the Lyceum in Athens in 335 B.C., a major school of philosophy and science. He wrote of metaphysics, politics, and rhetoric, but most of his writings were lost between the fifth and twelfth centuries.

Manichaeanism	The philosophical and religious doctrine that holds that the universe, including all human life, is a struggle between the opposing forces of good and evil.
	WORDS IN CONTEXT: *The doctrine called* **Manichaeanism** *originated in Persia in the third century and was held by many throughout the following 1300 years. Good was seen as light, and evil was seen as darkness.*
cause	The agent (whatever or whoever) responsible for action, motion, or change.
	WORDS IN CONTEXT: *Aristotle thought* **cause** *falls into four types:* **material cause** *(the substance that the thing is made of),* **formal cause** *(the design of the thing),* **efficient cause** *(the maker of the thing), and* **final cause** *(its purpose or function).*
teleology	Describes a system of thought that explains a series of actions or events in terms of ends, goals, or purposes. **Teleological ethics** hold that whether an action is right or wrong depends on the consequences one expects from that action.
	WORDS IN CONTEXT: *Throughout history,* **teleologists** *have often identified purpose in the universe as "God's will." Their proof of God's existence argues that since there is a design in the world, there must be a designer, God. More recently, the evolutionary view finds purpose in the higher levels of organic life, but does not necessarily attribute that purpose to God or any transcendent being.*
epistemology	The branch of philosophy that deals with the origin and nature of knowledge.
	WORDS IN CONTEXT: *Questions of* **epistemolgy** *include: How do we gain knowledge? How much can we know? How can we justify our claims to knowing?*

After studying the definitions above, use these new words in the sentences below:

1. Some philosophers believe in innate knowledge, some claim that human experience is necessary before we can know anything, and some try to combine the two views; the branch of philosophy that deals with these questions is _____.
2. Ends, goals, and purposes are the concern of those who study _____.
3. The person, thing, or event that brings an action into being is called its _____.
4. The doctrine that holds that all life is a struggle between good and evil is called _____.

Test Yourself: Write the letter next to the number to match word and meaning.

1. teleology
2. Manichaeanism
3. epistemology
4. cause

a. the agent responsible for action or movement
b. end goals and purposes are important
c. the universe is a struggle between good and evil
d. asks What is knowledge? How can we know?

On a separate sheet of paper, write a sentence using each of these new words.

DID YOU KNOW?
St. Augustine (354–430) grew up as a Christian, then converted to Manichaeanism and taught *rhetoric* in Rome and Milan. He then embraced the teachings of Plato. He was a wayward soul who stole, visited brothels, kept mistresses, and then returned to Christianity at age 32. His influence on Christianity was immense, and both Catholics and Protestants view him as the founder of Christian theology. He renounced Manichaeansim, wrote his *Confessions* and *The City of God*, famous for its Christian view of history.

first cause	The world is an effect that requires a cause. Nothing can be a cause but God, who is the **first cause**.
	WORDS IN CONTEXT: *St. Thomas Aquinas (1225–1274) is at the apex of medieval thought. All events, he believed, have causes or explanations. All effects require causes. The fact that the world and humans exist requires a cause. That cause is God, who is the* **first cause.**
cogito ergo sum	René Descartes (1596–1650), French philosopher and scientist, wanted to discard medieval philosophy and religion and begin with what he was certain of. Beginning with "universal doubt," he found that the only thing that could not be doubted was the fact that he could think. His words were "**Cogito ergo sum**" ("I think, therefore I am").
	WORDS IN CONTEXT: *Often called the father of modern philosophy, Descartes was primarily a mathematician, and he contributed many concepts to mathematics. Rejecting authoritarian philosophers, he discarded all thought but doubt itself. The doubter must first exist, he said, and his famous* **cogito ergo sum** *became his guiding principle. From this small certainty, Descartes expanded knowledge little by little to admit the existence of God (as the* **first cause***) and the reality of the physical world.*
empiricism	John Locke (1632–1704) believed that all human knowledge ultimately derives from the five senses. Ideas were abstract—only the objects of thinking. He looked for **empirical** evidence; to Locke, the only reality was what one could see, hear, smell, touch, and taste.
	WORDS IN CONTEXT: *Locke believed only in that which he could verify by physical experience, or by what he could verify* **empirically.**
social contract	Posits that governments are expressions of the general will of the people; they express rational people's choice for the common good.
	WORDS IN CONTEXT: *Jean-Jacques Rousseau (1712–1778) was a Swiss-French philosopher whose ideas greatly influenced political thought, educational theory, and the Romantic movement in philosophy. He admired primitive peoples, whom he called noble savages, and he wrote* **The Social Contract**, *in which he stated that all humanity should enter into a contract with government to foster the goodwill of all people.*

After studying the definitions above, use these new words in the sentences below.

1. The philosopher looked to_____evidence for knowledge, believing that knowledge is derived from what one can see, hear, smell, touch, and taste.
2. Another philosopher looked for certainty by beginning with universal doubt. He eventually found something he could not doubt, and said_____, meaning "I know I exist because I am thinking."
3. Still another philosopher posited that since the world exists, it is an effect that demands a cause; he claimed that God was the_____.
4 A philosopher who admired primitive peoples wrote that all humanity should enter into _____with a government for the common good.

Test Yourself: Write the letter next to the number to match word and meaning.

1. empiricism   a. "I think, therefore I am."
2. first cause   b. a contract of goodwill with government
3. cogito ergo sum   c. the claim that the world is the effect of God
4. social contract   d. all knowledge derives from our five senses

On a separate sheet of paper, write a sentence using each of these new words.

DID YOU KNOW?
St. Thomas Aquinas, who drew on some of the ideas of Plato and Aristotle, developed the idea of the free will of each individual. Ultimately, he separated questions that were answerable through reason and experience from questions that were answerable only through faith. In doing so, he separated nationalism (philosophy) from faith (religion). Aquinas ranks with Plato and Aristotle as philosophers of influence.

skepticism	The theory that thinkers cannot attain any certain knowledge. All knowledge should be questioned and tested by, for example, *the scientific method.* **WORDS IN CONTEXT:** *Skeptics, such as David Hume (1711–1776), thought that we could not have knowledge of anything that had not been thoroughly researched. The research could be done by forming a hypothesis after objective data were systematically collected, and then testing the hypothesis empirically, in short, by the* scientific method.
categorical imperative	The philosophical theory that we should behave in such a way that, if all people behaved in this way, our social and governmental systems would be stable. **WORDS IN CONTEXT:** *The **categorical imperative** is a theory devised by Immanuel Kant (1724–1804) in* A Critique of Pure Reason. *He believed that we can know only certain aspects of physical life and that duty is the principle of volition of the will. Duty is born of respect for law, and goodwill is motivated by duty. His **categorical imperative** can be illustrated by this concept: If I tell a lie, the whole idea of truth-telling will collapse; if I break a promise, the whole idea of promise-making will collapse. Therefore, we should behave in a way that reinforces and stabilizes our social system of trust and promises.*
zeitgeist	Literally, in German, this means "time-spirit"—the spirit of the age; the trend of thought and feeling predominating in a certain era. **WORDS IN CONTEXT:** *Georg Wilhelm Friedrich Hegel (1770–1831) was a German philosopher who thought that time and history were inextricably woven together and would continue to be so. He believed that humanity would finally reach supreme self-consciousness, which he called the "Absolute Spirit." In each time/historical era, a particular time-spirit drove people. This time-spirit he called the **zeitgeist**.*
utilitarianism	This philosophy of morality holds that all actions should be judged for their rightness or wrongness by their consequences. Hence, the highest ethical good provides the greatest happiness for the greatest number of people. **WORDS IN CONTEXT:** *Jeremy Bentham (1748–1832), British philosopher and lawyer, and his student, John Stuart Mill (1806–1873), British empiricist, logician, economist, and social reformer, were the chief proponents of **utilitarianism**—the greatest good was the good that gives satisfaction to the greatest number of people.*

After studying the definitions above, use these new words in the sentences below.

1. The spirit of our age in the twenty-first century, or the_____, is vastly different from that in the century in which the word was introduced by a philosopher.
2. The_____can be illustrated by this: If I steal, or take something that does not belong to me, my action violates the system by which we live in this country.
3. If my morals and ethics simply focused on keeping me and my family happy and satisfied, I would be violating the chief principle of _____.
4. If I said that God does not exist because I cannot see, hear, touch, taste, or smell him, I would be considered a _____by certain philosophical standards.

Test Yourself: Write the letter next to the number to match word and meaning.

1. categorical imperative   a. denotes the greatest good for the greatest number
2. zeitgeist   b. if I break a promise, the whole system of promises breaks down
3. skepticism   c. the time-spirit that continues to develop into Absolute Spirit
4. utilitarianism   d. God does not exist because I cannot prove it with my senses.

On a separate sheet of paper write a sentence using each of these new words.

DID YOU KNOW?
The idealistic system of metaphysics of Georg Hegel greatly influenced philosophy. His ideas were based on a concept of the world as a single organism that developed by its own inner logic through three stages he called *thesis, antithesis, and synthesis.* Through these modes of inquiry, reason gradually emerged. He wrote *Logic* and *The Phenomenology of Mind.*

materialism	A widely held system of thought that seeks to explain the nature of the world as dependent on matter, which is the final reality. Some early Greek philosophers conceived of reality as material in nature, and the theory was renewed in the seventeenth and eighteenth centuries with the thinking of Thomas Hobbes (1588–1679) and John Locke. **WORDS IN CONTEXT:** *Thomas Hobbes, an English empiricist and **materialist** and one of the founders of modern political philosophy, argued that because men are naturally selfish, an absolute ruler is necessary. John Locke further advanced a **materialist** world view in his* An Essay Concerning Human Understanding, *though he also argued that those who governed should be held accountable to their subjects. Later, Karl Marx (1818–1883) argued that matter is the primary reality and that it obeys the dynamic laws of change: Progress occurs through conflict between opposing forces, such as that between different social classes. This is called dialectical **materialism.***
leap of faith	A philosophy advanced by the Danish philosopher and religious writer Søren Kierkegaard (1813–1855), whose ideas influenced the later philosophy of *existentialism* and who was also a major influence on modern Protestant thought. Reason, he believed, cannot help us move from a temporal existence to eternal truth; what is needed is a **leap of faith** to reach final religious truth. **WORDS IN CONTEXT:** *Kierkegaard described the various stages of existence as aesthetic, ethical, and religious. Advancing through these stages, we become increasingly aware of our relationship with God. When this leads to despair, because we cannot reason our way to a relationship with God, a **leap of faith** is required.*
pragmatism	A philosophy in which the truth of an idea is measured by experimental results and by their practical outcome. Thinking is primarily a guide to action, and the truth of any idea lies in its practical consequence. **WORDS IN CONTEXT:** ***Pragmatists** hold that truth is modified as discoveries are made. Originators of the **pragmatic** system of thinking were C. S. Pierce (1839–1914) and William James (1842–1910). A later **pragmatist** thinker was John Dewey (1859–1952), American psychologist, philosopher, and educational theorist, who emphasized that gaining knowledge required active participation and inquiry.*
übermensch	Superman. Friedrich Nietzsche (1844–1900), in reaction to Christianity's focus on the afterlife, posited the **übermensch**—the super person who exercised his will to achieve a more powerful state of being beyond mere mortals. **WORDS IN CONTEXT:** *Nietzsche was not a systematic philosopher but an individualistic moralist who sought to move beyond what he saw in Christianity as "a slave morality" to a more heroic morality. He envisioned a new society led by the **Übermensch**, or super person.*

After studying the definitions above, use these new words in the sentences below.

1. C. S. Pierce and John Dewey measured truth by its practical consequences in their philosophy of _____.
2. When people got to the end of their rope in trying to reason their way to a relationship with God, Kierkegaard posited that a _____was required.
3. That matter is the final reality and can undergo change is the philosophy of_____.
4. Nietszche thought that by using strength of will one could become an _____.

Test Yourself: Write the letter next to the word to match word and meaning.

1. leap of faith   a. matter is the final reality
2. übermensch   b. truth is measured by its consequences
3. pragmatism   c. after failing to reason one's way to God, one can take this
4 materialism   d. a man can use his will to power to become one of these.

On a separate sheet of paper, write a sentence using each of these new words.

DID YOU KNOW?
Karl Marx (1818–1883), a German social philosopher and revolutionary, originated, along with Friedrich Engels, a political philosophy introduced by *The Communist Manifesto* (1848). In his monumental work, *Das Kapital* (1863 –1894), Marx reverses Hegel's dialectical idealism (which held the monarchy to be the highest development of the state) and introduced dialectical materialism (known as Marxism), in which he viewed the history of society as the history of class struggle in which the capitalist class will be supplanted by the working class. Marxism influenced the development of socialism, which later influenced communism.

intuitionism	A British school of thought that maintained that all ethical knowledge arises from moral intuition. **WORDS IN CONTEXT:** *Henri Bergson (1859–1941), a French philosopher who held that the world contains two opposing tendencies—the life force and the resistance of matter to that force—advocated* **intuitionism**. *People know matter through the intellect, but they know the life force and time through their* **intuition**; *time to Bergson was not a unit of measurement but unrolled like a coil; consciousness to him assumed memory. Bergson wrote* Time and Free Will *and* The Creative Mind. *Bergson was awarded the Nobel Prize in Literature in 1927.*
universals	Properties of general or abstract things that apply to particulars or specific things; for example, love and empathy are **universals**, which people apply to individuals. **WORDS IN CONTEXT:** *Bertrand Russell (1872–1970), British Earl, philosopher, mathematician, and social reformer, believed that we live in a world of powerful forces of an indifferent nature; still, we, by accepting* **universals** *such as love and empathy, can live and care for others in a world of peace. In 1950, he was awarded the Nobel Prize in Literature.*
analytical philosophy	An influential school of thought of the twentieth century that emphasizes restating philosophical problems in highly structured terms, or ordinary language, based on modern logic. **WORDS IN CONTEXT:** *Ludwig Wittgenstein (1889–1951), an Austrian philosopher who studied with Bertrand Russell at Cambridge, wrote* Tractatus Logico-Philosophica *a work committed to the logic of language, which he found could not express concepts like "truth." His* **analytical philosophy** *arose from his study of linguistics; he came to the conclusion that language is a response to and a reproduction of "the real."*
existentialism	An important nineteenth- and twentieth-century philosophy that holds that there are no universal values; a person's essence is not predetermined but is based on free choice. Each person exists and then goes on a quest to find out what his or her essence is. **WORDS IN CONTEXT:** *Jean Paul Sartre (1905–1980) was a French philosopher who explored the question, "Que sais-je?" What am I? This led him to the theory that people exist to discover what they are. He is famous for proclaiming that "hell is other people," and that an individual is a lonely creature adrift in a meaningless universe with the terrifying choice to choose. Sartre declined the Nobel Prize in Literature in 1964. In the late 1960s, Sartre worked with Bertrand Russell to organize European opposition to the Vietnam War.*

After studying the definitions above, use these new words in the sentences below.

1. _____ are general and abstract properties such as love and empathy that can be applied to specific individuals or things.
2. _____ holds that individuals can gain knowledge through their intellect, but they know the life force and time through their intuition.
3. _____ is the philosophy positing that we exist and then go on a life journey to find what we are.
4. _____ holds that all philosophical problems arise from our use of language.

Test Yourself: Write the letter next to the number to match word and meaning.

1. intuitionism
2. universals
3. existentialism
4. analytic philosophy

a. emphasizes philosophy restated in ordinary language
b. love and empathy are two of these applied to individuals
c. the logic of language cannot express concepts such as truth
d. life is a quest to discover what we are

On a separate sheet of paper, write a sentence using each of these new words.

DID YOU KNOW? C. S. Lewis (1898–1963), the English author noted for his literary scholarship and his Christian beliefs, made logical arguments for and against a belief in God and other propositions for which there is no evidence. He argued that scientific truth, which demands empirical evidence, is different from religious belief, the sole evidence of which is faith.

Words for Discussing Psychology

Psychology is the scientific study of human behavior and mental processes. In this chapter you will find many of the words and concepts you need to know to discuss and write about this subject.

DAY 1

| consciousness | determinism | stream of consciousness | the unconscious |

DAY 2

| habit | self | emotion | will |

DAY 3

| id | ego | superego | displacement |

DAY 4

| collective unconscious | archetype | persona | anima/animus |

DAY 5

| mature personality | cognitive behavior | gestalt | belongingness |

DAY 6

| life cycle | identity | identity crisis | conditioned reflex |

DAY 7

| hierarchy of needs | self-actualization | congruence | self-regard |

consciousness	The state of being aware of one's own mental activity, knowing the totality of one's thoughts, feelings, and impressions.
	WORDS IN CONTEXT: *Psychologists are concerned with the **consciousness** of individuals; they study the way people think and how this affects their behavior. Though there are many different branches of psychology, all take into consideration, in one way or another, human **consciousness**.*
determinism	The first branch of psychology out of which many other branches or subdisciplines of psychology grew. **Determinism,** no longer in popular use, dealt with cause and effect. **Determinists** believe that events have causes that can be studied systematically through observation.
	WORDS IN CONTEXT: *Wilhelm Wundt (1832–1920) in Leipzig, Germany, in 1879 created a laboratory to study human behavior. It was there that he trained many people who became the founders of psychology—so many that he is often called the father of psychology. A **determinist**, Wundt studied, through trained observation of mental processes, the causes that produced certain effects.*
stream of consciousness	The theory that consciousness is not composed of disconnected mental elements; instead, mental processes flow continuously as a stream does. The **stream of consciousness** produces a kind of medium that holds every thought, feeling, and image of each individual and flows out of the past and into the future.
	WORDS IN CONTEXT: *William James (1842–1910) was a contemporary of Wundt, though he lived and worked in America and is considered by many to be America's greatest psychologist. James theorized that consciousness does not operate in distinctive parts, thus giving us the concept of **stream of consciousness**. (James gave us other concepts such as habit, self, emotion, and will that we discuss later.)*
the unconscious	In psychology, the unconscious is all psychological (mental and emotional) material that has been repressed or of which an individual is unaware or has never allowed to become a part of the conscious mind.
	WORDS IN CONTEXT: *Sigmund Freud (1856–1939), a Viennese psychiatrist, gave us the concept of **the unconscious**, an abstract repository for all material that one does not permit oneself to bring to consciousness. Freud theorized that we use defense mechanisms such as the repression of such emotions as hatred, anger, hurtful memories, and inappropriate sexual feelings, forcing them to remain in **the unconscious**, where we are not required to examine them, deal with them, or act on them as we might if they were brought to our conscious mind. (Freud, hugely influential in psychoanalysis, also gave us many terms and concepts such as id, ego, and superego that we discuss later.)*

After studying the definitions above, use these new words in the sentences below.

1. _____ suggests that events have causes that can be studied through observation.
2. The material that does not reside in our conscious mind is buried in _____, according to Freud's theory.
3. The theory that our mental processes flow like a river is called_____.
4. _____ is the state of being aware of our thoughts and feelings.

Test Yourself: Write the letter next to the number to match word and meaning.

1. the unconscious	a. the first branch of psychology
2. consciousness	b. mental processes not separated into parts
3. determinism	c. where repressed feelings and thoughts reside
4. stream of consciousness	d. being aware of our thoughts and feelings

On a separate sheet of paper, write a sentence using each of these new words.

DID YOU KNOW? William James's concept of *stream of consciousness* affected the writing of literature. One of his students was Gertrude Stein; her literary use of the fluid mental process that captures all that goes through the mind spontaneously and simultaneously was carried forward by James Joyce, William Faulkner, and others in writing and still continues today.

habit	An act performed so frequently and in the same way that it becomes automatic. **Habit** is the mechanism that produces and sustains conformity, convention, and custom.
	WORDS IN CONTEXT: *William James said that **habit** is a fixed pathway in the brain connected to a sense organ that has been stimulated by a set of muscles whose movements constitute an act. **Habit** virtually eliminates control of the conscious mind because the fixed pathways grow more pronounced with use, and a **habit** becomes an automatic act.*
self	William James said that we all have two selves: the **self-as-known** (what he called *the empirical Me*) and the **self-as-knower** (the *I*).
	WORDS IN CONTEXT: *According to James, the **self-as-knower** is simply the stream of consciousness: I do not think this stream of thoughts; I am this stream of thoughts. The **self-as-known** has three parts—the material Me (my body, my house, my possessions), the social Me (my recognition from others); and the spiritual Me (my attitudes, my mental processes, my moods).*
emotion	James turned the conventional idea of emotion on its head. He believed that when we experience an **emotion,** that **emotion** is caused by bodily changes that result from stimulation. **Emotion** is *not* caused by the way we perceive the situation.
	WORDS IN CONTEXT: *James thought that when one receives good news, this news has to stimulate our bodies before we smile or feel joyful; therefore, we do not laugh because we are happy. We are happy because we laugh. We are sad because we weep. In a sense, to James, the reaction of our bodies creates the **emotion**.*
will	Our **will** comes from our concentration on the act we are tempted to perform and its consequences. For example, we **will** ourselves not to eat a whole quart of ice cream because we know (1) it's not good for us; (2) we may get sick; (3) we will gain weight; (4) we will leave no ice cream for the next person. Increased strength of **will** comes from our experience in using our **will.**
	WORDS IN CONTEXT: *James believed that we do some things because they have become habits. Other acts, however, we do only after we think through our options deliberately. The ability to think through the options and consider the consequences of each of them before making a decision to act comes from our exercising our **will** over and over. As we exercise our **will**, we gain wisdom.*

After studying the definitions above, use these new words in the sentences below.

1. William James believed that we had two of these: the_____ and the _____. The first he called the empirical Me, and the other he called the I.
2. If you perform a _____long enough, it becomes automatic.
3. Concentrate on a proposed act and think of its consequences before deciding to do it, and you will be strengthening your _____.
4. James believed that body stimulus creates _____.

Test Yourself: Write the letter next to the number to match word and meaning.

1. habit   a. there are two of these: one as knower and one as known.
2. will   b. this diminishes the control of the conscious mind
3. emotion   c. as we exercise this, we gain wisdom
4. self   d. we are sad because we weep

On a separate sheet of paper, write a sentence using each of these new words.

DID YOU KNOW?
William James's brother was Henry James, the renowned novelist (*Portrait of a Lady, The Golden Bowl,* and others). William James, who had a profound influence on later psychologists, devoted most of his attention to philosophy and was so interested in religion that he wrote *Varieties of Religious Experience* (1902), a classic in the field. He never formulated a psychological system, but his ideas helped form current psychological thought.

id	A personality structure that consists of raw, primitive instincts, everything of a psychological nature that one is born with. In addition, the **id** includes repressed feelings and thoughts. The contents and the processes of the **id** are entirely unconscious, but the **id** (meaning "it" in Latin) supplies psychic energy that powers psychological functioning.

WORDS IN CONTEXT: *Sigmund Freud (1856–1939) gave us the concept of the id, as well as the other words and concepts of this day's assignment. The id, he said, was governed by the pleasure principle and the primary process. The pleasure principle seeks the reduction of tension or undischarged energy. To diminish painful tension and to gain pleasure, the id kicks in with the primary process that helps discharge tension by forming an image. For example, if one is angry enough with another person to want to harm that person, the primary process gives the angry person a picture in which he or she is harming the hated person. Before the angry person does harm, however, another personality structure steps in; that structure is called the ego.* |
| **ego** | When the **ego** functions properly, it governs the **id**. It controls the **id**'s actions, decides which needs must be satisfied, and prioritizes the impulsive actions of the **id**. For example, when a person's anger urges him or her to harm another, the **ego** acts as a monitor or filter to keep the angry person from doing something irrevocable or for which he or she will be punished.

WORDS IN CONTEXT: *The ego holds the id in check in three ways: It counters the pleasure principle with its reality principle by preventing the discharge of tension until an appropriate object (for anger, for example) is identified. Then the ego counters the primary process with the secondary process, which employs the higher intellectual functions. Finally, the ego creates a plan of action to see whether it will work to relieve the tension; this is called reality testing.* |
| **superego** | this personality structure has internalized the traditional values, morals, and ideals of the individual's parents and society, which have been reinforced in the individual's childhood by rewards and punishment.

WORDS IN CONTEXT: *The superego employs the conscience, which uses guilt to punish us when we violate our internalized moral values. The superego also employs the ego-ideal that rewards us by making us feel good and proud of ourselves when we follow our internalized ideals.* |
| **displacement** | This concept is important in Freud's development of the *psyche* (the mind, soul, entire functional person). When an instinct or impulse from the **id** is blocked, its energy is diverted (or **displaced**) to a substitute.

WORDS IN CONTEXT: *In displacement, for example, when the ego and the superego have blocked an angry man from harming someone with whom he is angry, the angry person finds a substitute. So when the man is prevented from beating up his overbearing boss, he comes home and shouts at his wife and sends the kids to their rooms (and kicks the cat!).* |

After studying the definitions above, use these new words in the sentences below.

1. The reservoir of inherited traits and instincts that is completely unconscious is the_____.
2. Social values and morals as interpreted by parents and internalized by children is called the_____ and controls the psyche through rewards and punishment.
3. _____is the gatekeeper to instinctive or impulsive action, which attempts to integrate the psyche, not only with itself but with the external world.
4 When untamed actions from the id are blocked, the individual may find another focus for anger, rage, or another emotion through_____.

Test Yourself: Write the letter next to the number to match word and meaning.

1. ego   a. taking out your anger in a rigorous game of handball or by drinking too much
2. id   b. governs primitive instincts using the voice of reality and testing it
3. superego   c. reminds you of your parents' or society's values and morality
4. displacement   d. the unconscious residence of instincts and primitive impulses

On a separate sheet of paper, write a sentence using each of these new words.

DID YOU KNOW?
Freud gave us many, many more psychological terms such as *life instincts, death instincts, libido,* and *cathexis.* Sexual neurosis (fear that the instincts in the id will break loose and cause problems) underlies many of Freud's theories. He believed that a person passes through several sexual stages on the way to becoming an adult; some of these are *oral stage, anal stage, phallic stage, Oedipus complex, castration complex, latency,* and *genital stage.*

collective unconscious	A mental medium the contents of which are inherited and are identical for everyone. It is the psychic residue of our evolutionary development, and it accumulates material from the experiences of human beings over generations. This term and the other terms in today's assignment were introduced by Freud's student, the Swiss psychologist Carl Jung (1875–1961). **WORDS IN CONTEXT:** *The **collective unconscious** acquires its contents from repeated experiences of many generations of human beings throughout the centuries, whereas our personal consciousness acquires its contents from our personal experiences.*
archetype	This is a universal image or concept that has held emotional significance for people over generations. Many symbols—the circle, for example—carried in the collective unconscious, mean much the same thing to people all over the world and had the same meaning (perhaps wholeness, completion, closure) from the beginning of human consciousness. **WORDS IN CONTEXT:** *The sun, for example, may be called an **archetype** of the **collective unconscious,** for its repetitive movement across the horizons throughout all the centuries of people's existence came to represent a steady, reliable god to people, whether they were Egyptian, Native American, or European. The sun god thus became a mythic **archetype.***
persona	This is a mask that one adopts to conceal one's true thoughts and feelings so as to conform better to social conventions and to protect one's privacy. **WORDS IN CONTEXT:** *A person who, for example, prefers to be alone with his or her thoughts (an introvert) often adopts the mask or **persona** of a gregarious person (an extrovert) to perform social functions in a manner viewed as appropriate by society.*
anima/animus	The **anima**, according to Jung, is the feminine side of a man's nature; the **animus** is the masculine side of a woman's nature. **WORDS IN CONTEXT:** *The woman showed **animus** toward the man who was annoying her, while the big, burly man revealed his **anima** to the child to get the child to trust him.*

After studying the definitions above, use these new words in the sentences below.

1. The image of the mother as nurturer has been an_____in the collective unconscious throughout many generations.
2. People sometimes take on a _____to mask their true feelings.
3. Being bullied by a jeering gang of classmates brought out the_____in the young girl. The male teacher revealed his_____ as he attempted to calm the abused girl.
4. The universal emotions and images of both war and peace are archetypes in the_____ of generations of people.

Test Yourself: Write the letter next to the number to match word and meaning.

1. persona
2. archetype
3. collective unconscious
4. animus/anima

a. the male side of a woman; the female side of a man
b. we adopt this to mask our genuine feelings in public
c. images carried throughout centuries of people
d. the accumulated psychic residue of our evolutionary development

On a separate sheet of paper, write a sentence using each of these new words.

DID YOU KNOW?
Carl Jung's ideal goal for each individual was to gain a selfhood. By this he meant that we must be able to differentiate each of the components of the psyche in a method he called *individuation* and then integrate all the opposing impulses of the psyche into a perfect whole— or a self.

mature personality	People who have developed a **mature personality** are those, according to American psychologist Gordon W. Allport (1897–1967), who are emotionally secure and accepting of themselves, who can relate warmly to others, who have humor and insight and an integrated philosophy of life. **WORDS IN CONTEXT:** *To Allport, the goal of people with a **mature personality** is to develop all the characteristics named above as well as something Allport called an extension of self. This involves participating in and enjoying a wide variety of activities and being able to project themselves into the future by hoping and planning.*
cognitive behavior	A term used to indicate how an individual's mind or intellect works. Swiss psychologist Jean Piaget (1896–1980) was interested in the **cognitive behavior** of children and adolescents and studied the relationships formed between the individual knower and the world that individual seeks to know. **WORDS IN CONTEXT:** *Piaget, whom many call the foremost child and educational psychologist, studied the **cognitive behavior** in the intellectual development of children to understand how children learn. He called himself a genetic epistemologist, using* genetic *to mean development;* epistemology *is the philosophical term used by Piaget to suggest the investigation of the nature and origin of knowledge.*
Gestalt	This German word refers to any concrete entity that has a definite form or shape. In **Gestalt psychology,** called *a field theory,* psychologists study the environmental field in which behavior takes place. Initially, **Gestaltists** studied perceptual wholes such as visual figures and shapes, though later they included concepts such as thinking, personality, memory, and learning as well. **WORDS IN CONTEXT:** *The earliest **Gestalt** psychologists were German: Max Wertheimer (1880–1943), Wolfgang Köhler (1887–1967), and Kurt Koffka (1886–1941). They studied behavior as it takes place in a specific environment, meaning everything that is in an individual's awareness or experience. **Gestaltists** broke that environment down into what they called figure-ground—the ground being a framework for the figure, for example, a black dot in a white square or field. The figure stands out from the ground, but the **gestalt** psychologists found that various other factors affect the way we see the figure and ground.*
belongingness	Taking a cue from the **Gestaltists,** American educational psychologist, E. L. Thorndike (1874–1949), formulated the concept of **belongingness.** By this, he meant that we see things in association with other things; that is, a table **belongs** to a chair, and a fish **belongs** to water **WORDS IN CONTEXT:** *Thorndike is known for his work in stimulus-response, in which he showed the extent to which animals will go to reach food—how, for example, a cat will pull a rope to open a door to reach food outside its cage. As a result of his experiments, he employed the field theory concepts of **Gestalt** psychology and came up with the idea of **belongingness** in the way we see our environment as a whole.*

After studying the definitions above, use these new words in the sentences below.

1. To Gordon Allport, the goal of a person was to develop a _____.
2. The way the mind works, especially in children as they learn, is called_____.
3. _____psychologists study the environment in which we behave.
4. Perceiving our environment as one thing in association with another is a concept called_____formulated by Thorndike.

Test Yourself: Write the letter next to the number to match word and meaning.

1. cognitive behavior
2. gestalt
3. belongingness
4. mature personality

a. the goal of an integrated person
b. the environment as a whole
c. the way a child's mind works
d. the association of one environmental thing with another

On a separate sheet of paper, write a sentence using each new word.

DID YOU KNOW?
German psychoanalyst Karen Horney (1885–1952) was interested in personality development. Working mostly in the United States, Horney introduced the concepts of basic anxiety and neurotic needs. Basic anxiety arises from a child's insecurities; neurotic needs are strategies that one develops to deal with anxiety and uses them so often that they become needs. Some of the needs include need for affection and approval, need for a partner, need for power, need for prestige, need for admiration, need for independence, need for perfection, need to exploit others.

life cycle	In the work of Erik Erikson (1903–1994), a children's psychoanalyst born in Germany of Danish parents, **life cycle** refers to the sequence of the five developmental stages that one must pass through before he or she gains an *identity*.
	WORDS IN CONTEXT: *Erikson's five stages of the **life cycle** include trust, autonomy, initiative, industry, and identity. A baby experiences trust through its relationship with its mother; after learning to trust their environment children develop independence and autonomy. Before children enter school, they learn to do some things for themselves, developing initiative. And during school they learn to work, developing industry. Following these four stages, children are ready at adolescence to develop an identity.*
identity	According to Erikson's theory, children, during adolescence, gain a sense of themselves as unique individuals, or an *ego identity,* from which they can develop a fully integrated **identity** as a person apart from others.
	WORDS IN CONTEXT: *In establishing their own **identity,** children recognize their own skills, talents, needs and desires, along with their own characteristics and preferences. They learn that they have some control over their own environment and that they have choices in the role they play in the world. After they have pulled all these characteristics together, they are said to have an integrated **identity.***
identity crisis	At each of the five stages, there is the danger that the appropriate development will not take place. When it does not, children become vulnerable to an **identity crisis** that might stunt their development, and they may encounter one problem after another in their adult life.
	WORDS IN CONTEXT: *An **identity crisis** can take place during any stage of the life cycle, not just in adolescence, which can delay or prevent the child from developing a strong **identity.***
conditioned reflex	Russian physiologist, I. P. Pavlov (1849–1936), gave us this word and concept, which involve *stimulus-response*. For example, food (*stimulus*) placed before a hungry person makes the person salivate (*response*). Say, a bell rings just before the food is presented. Imagine that this combination of food, salivation, and bell occurs repeatedly. Then the bell is rung in the presence of the hungry person, but the food is not presented. Nevertheless, the person salivates. This salivation in response to the ringing of the bell, but without the food, is a **conditioned reflex.**
	WORDS IN CONTEXT: *The lab experiments from which the **conditioned reflex** (sometimes called conditioned response) resulted were designed to study the brain, not human behavior. (Pavlov was a physiologist.) Yet, Pavlov, along with Freud, is considered one of the chief architects of twentieth-century psychology.*

After studying the definitions above, use these new words in the sentences below.

1. Erikson's _____ encompasses five stages of development in a child.
2. Pavlov's experiments in stimulus-response led to the concept of _____.
3. The fifth and most important phase of the life cycle is the last, the one in which an adolescent gains an _____.
4. If some condition prevents a child from developing sequentially through each of the five stages, the child may suffer an _____.

Test Yourself: Write the letter next to the word to match word and meaning.

1. identity   a. Pavlov's famous concept of stimulus-response
2. conditioned reflex b. the final stage in the life cycle
3. identity crisis   c. the state in which children finds themself if something prevents them from developing appropriately in one of Erikson's five stages.
4. life cycle   d. consists of five stages of development

On a separate sheet of paper, write a sentence using each of the new words.

DID YOU KNOW?
American psychologist B. F. Skinner (1904–1990), an objective behaviorist in the tradition of Pavlov and Thorndike, was interested in how behavior can be regulated by reward and punishment, which he called *positive* and *negative reinforcement.* He wrote a novel, *Walden Two* (1948) about a utopia based on his ideas of reward and punishment. He also wrote *Beyond Freedom and Dignity* (1971), in which he designed a society wherein the behavior of citizens was controlled by these reinforcements.

hierarchy of needs	American psychologist Abraham Maslow (1908–1970) designed a pyramid that consisted of a **hierarchy of needs**. At the bottom of this pyramid reside our **basic needs**—food, air, water, sex, and sleep. **WORDS IN CONTEXT:** *In this **hierarchy of needs**, our basic needs must be satisfied before we can go on to concern ourselves with other needs, such as safety, freedom from fear, love, belongingness, esteem, recognition, competence, dignity, and other growth needs.*
self-actualization	Maslow defined **self-actualization** as "the desire to become more and more what one is, to become everything one is capable of." This need is at the top of the pyramid, and **self-actualized** describes a fully integrated person. **WORDS IN CONTEXT:** *Describing **self-actualization** (or a **self-actualizing person**, as Maslow put it, because he believed that this is a process of becoming, not an end state), Maslow often included transcendence, needs that include knowledge, peace, aesthetics, and oneness with God. "What humans can be, they must be," Maslow, who was a humanistic psychologist, said. Humanistic psychology emphasizes the fullest realization of humanity's finest and more creative potential.*
congruence	This term in psychology comes from Carl Rogers (1902–1987), another American humanist. Rogers saw a person as an *organism* seeking a *self*. When these two are in total conjunction—the self fully reflecting the experiences of the organism—they are in **congruence,** and the person is functioning to his or her fullest. **WORDS IN CONTEXT:** *When **congruence** occurs, people are capable of seeing the world and themselves in it realistically: they do not feel anxiety or defensiveness; they do enjoy pleasurable relationships with others and are open to new experiences.*
self-regard	According to Rogers, this is to be humbly pleased with oneself; one feels worthy. **WORDS IN CONTEXT:** *Having **self-regard**, individuals feel good about themselves and are aware of their behavior; the way they are in the world and the way they would ideally like to be are not too far apart. **Self-regard** depends also on receiving positive regard from other people.*

After studying the definitions above, use these new words in the sentences below.

1. The pyramid that outlines our basic needs to our transcendent needs is called the
   _____.
2. When the organism and the self are in conjunction,_____occurs.
3. In Maslow's theory,_____occurs when we become everything a human can become.
4. When we have reached the state of_____, we feel worthwhile, according to Rogers.

Test Yourself: Write the letter next to the number to match word and meaning.

1. self-actualization
2. self-regard
3. congruence
4 hierarchy of needs

a. Maslow's pyramid of needs, outlined
b. seeing oneself and the world realistically
c. the organism and the self are in full alliance
d. becoming everything one is capable of

On a separate sheet of paper, write a sentence using each of these new words.

DID YOU KNOW?
Harry Stack Sullivan (1892–1949) was an American psychoanalyst who was interested in neuropsychiatry. He conducted investigations into schizophrenia and became the president of the William Alanson White Foundation in New York City. Deeply influenced by sociologists and anthropologists, he founded the Washington School of Psychiatry and formulated his theory of interpersonal relationships, which viewed the study of psychology as not that of one person, but rather as an interpersonal situation.

Words for Discussing Drama

Learning the words in this section will allow you to view, discuss, and write about theatrical productions and will give you an outline of the development of dramatic forms over time.

DAY 1

| Thespis | Aeschylus | Sophocles | Euripedes |

DAY 2

| Aristophanes | satyr play | protagonist | antagonist |

DAY 3

| liturgical drama | tropes | allegory | mystery, miracle, morality plays |

DAY 4

| Tudor plays | farce | Elizabethan drama | chronicle plays |

DAY 5

| Jacobean drama | Restoration drama | eighteenth-century drama | Eduardian drama |

DAY 6

| romantic rebellion | post-Edwardian drama | early twentieth-century drama | modern drama |

DAY 7

| symbolist drama | expressionist drama | theater of the absurd | contemporary drama |

Thespis	A sixth-century B.C. Greek poet who was said to have invented tragedy (c. 534 B.C.) as a dramatic form. *Tragedy* is the term used for a serious play usually concerning a troubled central character whose problems lead to a disastrous ending brought on by fate or a tragic flaw in his or her character—moral weakness, psychological maladjustment, or sometimes social pressures.
	WORDS IN CONTEXT: *Unfortunately, no work of* **Thespis** *has survived, but from his name we derive the term* **thespians**—*actors who perform dramatic roles in theatrical productions.* **Thespis** *created a musical form in which he impersonated a single character who engaged a chorus of actors in dialogue. Thus, he is known as the first dramatist and first actor.*
Aeschylus	A Greek tragedian (one who writes tragedy) who lived in 525–456 B.C. He introduced conflict into drama by creating a second character to oppose the first. He was one of the most talented Greek playwrights and one of only three great Greek tragedians whose works have survived.
	WORDS IN CONTEXT: *It is thought that* **Aeschylus** *wrote ninety plays, but only seven survive today. The earliest surviving play by* **Aeschylus** *is* The Suppliants *produced about 492 B.C. It has a chorus of fifty members and one distinct player. Other plays of his are* The Persians, Seven Against Thebes, The Orestia, Agamemnon, The Libation Bearers, The Eumenides, *and* Prometheus Bound.
Sophocles	The second great Greek tragedian (496—406 B.C.) whose works survive.
	WORDS IN CONTEXT: *The first of* **Sophocles'** *plays was* Ajax *(written between 450 and 440 B.C.), and the last was* Oedipus at Colonus, *written in 406 B.C. In between,* **Sophocles** *wrote* Antigone, Oedipus Rex, Electra, Trachiniae, *and* Philoctetes.
Euripedes	The third Greek tragedian (c. 480—407 B.C.) whose work survives.
	WORDS IN CONTEXT: *A number of* **Euripedes'** *tragedies survive, including the first,* Alcestis *(438 B.C.), and the last,* Iphigenia at Aulis *(c. 405 B.C.). Of his others, those most often mounted are* Medea, Andromache, The Trojan Women, Orestes, *and* The Bacchae.

After studying the names above, use them in the sentences below.

1. The plays of three great Greek playwrights survive, the first being_____, who wrote the earliest surviving tragedy, *The Suppliants*.
2. The father of tragedy, the poet who originated that dramatic form was_____.
3. About 17 of this great tragedian's plays survive, the first being *Alcestis*; his name was _____.
4. _____'s first play was *Ajax*; he also wrote *Oedipus Rex* and *Antigone*.

Test Yourself: Write the letter next to the number to match author and work.

1. Euripedes
2. Sophocles
3. Aeschylus
4. Thespis

a. poet after whom thespians are named
b. about 17 of his tragedies survive
c. he wrote Oedipus Rex
d. wrote the first tragedy that survives

On a separate sheet of paper, write a sentence using each of these names.

DID YOU KNOW?
In Athens during the fifth and fourth centuries B.C., annual contests were held outdoors, during which dramatists presented three serious plays and one lighter, satrical play. All of the three great Greek playwrights mentioned above (the exception is Thespis) were acclaimed for their work by their contemporaries and won many prizes in the dramatic competitions.

Aristophanes	A contemporary of the three great Greek tragedians, though a little younger (c. 448–380 B.C.), he was cheekier. He wrote many of the satirical plays that ended the cycle of three serious plays in the dramatists' competition in Athens. **WORDS IN CONTEXT:** *Aristophanes's* The Acharnians *(425 B.C.) satirizes the war policy of the Athenians, and especially of Cleon, the war party leader. In his play* The Clouds, *Aristophanes ridiculed Socrates and his followers, the Sophists, who were spreading their ideas throughout Greece. Aristophanes also wrote* Lysistrata, *in which the title character convinces the women of Greece to discontinue sleeping with their husbands until the men stopped making war. Some other works by Aristophanes are* The Wasps, The Birds, *and* The Frogs.
satyr play	In the Greek drama festivals, the name for the play that followed the tragic dramas was the **satyr play,** which usually made comic ridicule of some current event or popular myth. **WORDS IN CONTEXT:** *The **satyr play**, from which we derive the word* satire, *humorously distorted something in the culture that the audience recognized. Actors were usually dressed as **satyrs**—drunken and in goat skins—and made fun of the gloominess of tragedy. **Aristophanes** was a favorite writer of **satyr plays;** thus he is called a* satirist.
protagonist	Meaning "first actor" in Greek, a protagonist is the main character in a drama, novel, or story, around whom all the action revolves. The word began with Greek drama and is still used to indicate the major character in theater and literature today. **WORDS IN CONTEXT:** *Oedipus is the **protagonist** in Sophocles' Oedipus Rex, as Medea, who slays her children to take revenge on Jason, the children's father, is the **protagonist** in Euripides' play of that name. A **protagonist** can be either male or female.*
antagonist	The **antagonist** in a drama is the opponent—the person (or force) who opposes the **protagonist**—or the adversary of the **protagonist**. **WORDS IN CONTEXT:** *In* Medea, *mentioned above, Jason, who has put Medea aside to marry another woman after Medea has given up her own family and her native land for him, is the **antagonist**.*

After studying the definitions above, use these new words in the sentences below.

1. The character in a drama around whom all the action revolves is the_____.
2. The comic, satirical play that followed three tragedies in Athens' festivals is the

   _____.
3. The opponent of the major character in a drama is the _____.
4. The Greek playwright with a wicked sense of humor who wrote plays making fun of cultural or mythic elements was_____.

Test Yourself: Write the letter next to the number to match word and meaning.

1. satyr play	a. adversary of the main character
2. Aristophanes	b. the troubled main character
3. antagonist	c. involved comedy and goat skins
4. protagonist	d. satirical Greek writer

On a separate sheet of paper, write a sentence using each of these new words.

DID YOU KNOW? According to Plato in *The Apology,* when Socrates was on trial for his life in 399 B.C., he was more worried about the image of himself that the Athenians took from Aristophanes's *The Clouds* than he was about the specific charges against him.

liturgical drama	In the fifteenth and sixteenth centuries a kind of drama arose that had nothing to do with the earlier forms. This was devotional drama, connected with church services. These musical dramas were performed by clerics on special days. For example, a dramatization of the Nativity was performed on Christmas; the Resurrection, on Easter. WORDS IN CONTEXT: *Liturgical dramas*, were sometimes based on Old Testament narratives, for example the stories of Daniel, Jacob and Esau, or of Joseph and his brothers. Sometimes these **liturgical** plays were in Latin, as illustrated in Christ's Burial and Resurrection, a two-part play performed on Good Friday and the following Easter Sunday. At other times, **liturgical drama** was performed in the language of the day—the vernacular.
tropes	In Easter services, and later in Christmas services, words or small passages of chanted dialogue were inserted into the liturgy, and priests, taking the roles of biblical figures, acted out these bits, which were called **tropes.** WORDS IN CONTEXT: *Tropes*, small dramatizations, eventually grew into more elaborate presentations, and priests took them to the steps of the church and finally into the marketplace itself. Today, the word **trope** means a figure of speech.
allegory	A story in which people, things, and happenings have a symbolic meaning and are used for teaching morals or religious principles. WORDS IN CONTEXT: *Allegories* generally use simple one-to-one representatives—for example, "Vice" is the bad or misbehaving person, and "Virtue" is the good or moral person—to tell a story. These **allegorical** stories were intended to influence the audience's conduct.
mystery, miracle, and morality plays	These three kinds of medieval drama are distinctly different from one another but can be cast into the same category. **Mystery plays** were scriptural dramas, were spoken in the language of the day and dealt with prophets and the life of Jesus, having Old and New Testament sources. **Miracle plays,** also called *saint's drama*, dealt with a miracle, or a saint's life. **Morality plays** dealt with proper and improper conduct and pointed out a moral lesson, often with *allegorical* characters that represented particular people or social classes. WORDS IN CONTEXT: *Mystery, miracle,* and **morality plays** were presented not only in major British cities during the Middle Ages but were also taken into regional areas in what were called pageant wagons as traveling shows.

After studying the definitions above, use these new words in the sentences below.

1. Musical, devotional dramas connected with the church were called_____.
2. _____were small bits of dialogue inserted into the liturgy by priests.
3. A simple, symbolic story in which one thing represents another and teaches a moral lesson is an _____.
4. _____were three kinds of drama that dealt with religious or moral instruction in different ways.

Test Yourself: Write the letter next to the number to match word and meaning.

1. allegory
2. trope
3. liturgical drama
4. mystery, miracle, and morality plays

a. musical playlets sponsored by the church
b. in which X is the bad person and Y is the good person
c. bits of dramatic dialogue inserted into liturgy
d. taught religious and moral lessons

On a separate sheet of paper, write a sentence using each of these new words.

DID YOU KNOW?
Everyman, a morality play of only 900 lines, deals with the moment of death. Its theme is salvation or damnation, and its allegorical characters are Good Deeds and Confession on the one hand, and Good Fellowship and Goods on the other. These two pairs are in conflict, and the play's symbolic action is worked out through a law court, a pilgrimage, and a final descent into the grave. The play's author is unknown; it is perhaps a translation of a Dutch play, *Elckerlijc.*

Tudor plays	In England in the early sixteenth century (the period of the Tudor kings), these plays were written by scholars and teachers as academic exercises and therefore called *school plays.* Tragedy in this period had largely to do with characters' power struggles and political ambitions in historical settings. WORDS IN CONTEXT: *Two* **Tudor comedies** *that rose above the scholars' exercises were Ralph Roister Doister (1550–1553) and Gammer Gurton's Needle (written between 1552 and 1563). These are folksy plays in rhymed verse based on classic character types. Tragedy was imitative of earlier dramatic forms as well. Gorboduc, a* **Tudor tragedy** *of an ancient king (1561) by Thomas Sackville and Thomas Norton, carried echoes of medieval morality plays.*
farce	An exaggerated comedy of broad humor based on ridiculous or highly unlikely situations. Both *Ralph Roister Doister* and *Gammer Gurton's Needle* are **farces.** WORDS IN CONTEXT: *Initially, lively, antic* **farces** *filled interludes between acts of other plays. The word* **farce** *comes from the French—"a stuffing"—as in the stuffing and seasoning of a fowl for a feast.*
Elizabethan drama	Drama during the reign of Queen Elizabeth I (1558–1603). **Elizabethan drama** is a synthesis of classical and medieval traditions. From classical drama, it took features such as stock characters (the braggart soldier) and other characters (ghost, hero with a soliloquy). From medieval drama—miracle and morality plays—**Elizabethan drama** borrowed the use of allegory and the idea of a universal principle that ordered life. WORDS IN CONTEXT: *William Shakespeare is, of course, the most renowned* **Elizabethan dramatist,** *but many fine playwrights preceded him— Ariosto and Boccaccio, in Italy, for example, and Christopher Marlowe, Ben Jonson, and Thomas Kyd in* **Elizabethan** *England. Shakespeare often used their works to build on. In fact, the subplot for Shakespeare's Taming of the Shrew was based on a play by Ariosto, while the theme of the taming of a shrewish wife derived from popular English folk humor.*
chronicle plays	The late 1580s in England provided people with a sense of national identity after they were emancipated following their defeat of the Spanish Armada in 1588. Christopher Marlowe in *Edward II* and William Shakespeare in many such plays drew on historical writings of Raphael Holinshed and others to tell stories about characters from English history. WORDS IN CONTEXT: *Shakespeare's* **chronicle plays** *include his Henry plays and his Richard plays. In Richard III, England's fate is of more concern to the audience than is Richard's. In a* **chronicle play** *there is at least one passionate nationalistic speech to arouse patriotic zeal; in Richard III, it is John of Gaunt's description of England.*

After studying the definitions above, use these new words in the sentences below.

1. Plays imitative of earlier classic forms, which include *Gammer Gurton's Needle* and *Gorboduc* are _____ plays.
2. _____ is broad, ridiculous, antic comedy.
3. English drama that took features from both the classic and medieval traditions during the Renaissance was _____.
4. _____ were those based on English history and inspired nationalism.

Test Yourself: Write the letter next to the number to match word and meaning.

1. Elizabethan drama   a. silly plays once used between acts like stuffing
2. chronicle plays   b. took themes from classical and medieval drama
3. farce   c. featured kings, queens, and English history
4. Tudor drama   d. brought Shakespeare on the scene in London

On a separate sheet of paper, write a sentence using each of these new words.

DID YOU KNOW?
By 1592, Shakespeare was a favorite London playwright. Robert Greene, then a popular scholar-playwright among a group that had gained a monopoly of London theaters, became jealous. In his screed against actors in his play A *Groats-worth of Wit,* Greene parodies a line from Shakespeare's *Henry VI,* speaking of an "upstart crow," who "beautified with our feathers" takes himself to be "the only Shakes-scene in the country."

Jacobean drama	The drama of England during the reign of James I (1603–1625). As Queen Elizabeth declined and died, the mood of the country changed and doubt about the ordered Elizabethan universe was sown. The clash of world views created the renewal of a classic genre: satire.
	WORDS IN CONTEXT: *When James I followed Elizabeth to the throne (the Jacobean period), his lack of charm and intelligence left a gap between the court and the people. This vacuum was filled by skepticism. Critical young playwrights arose to skewer the times with satire. Among them were **Jacobean dramatists** Joseph Hall, John Marston, and John Donne, whose books were finally burned in the "bishops bonfire."*
Restoration drama	Charles I came to the throne in 1625 and was executed by Oliver Cromwell and his Puritans in 1649. Seven years earlier, Parliament had decreed that "public stage plays shall cease," and for eighteen years, theaters were dark. The story of English drama picks up again in 1660, when the throne was restored with the crowning of Charles II. **Restoration drama** lasted until the end of the seventeenth century.
	WORDS IN CONTEXT: *Charles II, who enjoyed theater, soon granted patents to Sir William Davenant and Thomas Killigrew to form acting companies. They did, and thus **Restoration drama** began with its two most distinctive forms: heroic plays and comedies of manners. In the first, actors declaimed in big speeches. Actresses appeared, Nell Gwyn, for one. **Restoration comedies of manners** are known for their witty dialogue and satirical humor, and the characters' personalities were marked by their names, for example, Sir Fopling Flutter or Sir Tunbelly Clumsey. William Congreve (The Way of the World) was one of the best comic dramatists.*
eighteenth-century drama	The theater of the eighteenth century, geared to the middle class, was alternately sentimental and good-natured comedy on the one hand, and tragic drama on the other. Notable playwrights: Nicholas Rowe (*The Ambitious Stepmother*, 1700); Horace Walpole (*The Mysterious Mother*, 1768). John Gay's *The Beggar's Opera* (1728) was a great success. But the British government did not appreciate sharp wit and imposed strict censorship laws; for the next 150 years most serious writers shunned the theater as an outlet for their work.
	WORDS IN CONTEXT: *Joseph Addison and Richard Steele wrote for The Tatler and The Spectator, two periodicals that helped form the tone of **eighteenth-century drama**. Steele later wrote comedies for the stage (The Lying Lover, 1703). The most lasting plays and playwrights of this era were Oliver Goldsmith (She Stoops to Conquer, 1771) and Richard Sheridan (School for Scandal, 1777).*
Edwardian drama	This genre followed the death of Queen Victoria in 1901 and continued through the nine-year reign of Edward VII. The two extremes of **Edwardian drama** were verse plays and serious problem plays. In between were farce, comedies of manners, domestic melodramas, and plays of sentiment and morality.
	WORDS IN CONTEXT: *The most typical **Edwardian** playwrights—those who dealt with caste, wealth, and gender in conventional ways—were Harley Granville-Barker (The Madras House, 1910) and St. John Hankin (The Return of the Prodigal, 1905). In this era, Romantic poets—Wordsworth, Coleridge, and others—also tried their hands as playwrights with varying success. The later masters were William S. Gilbert, Oscar Wilde, and George Bernard Shaw.*

After studying the definitions above, use the new terms in the sentences below.

1. _____ drama, during a time of questioning and cynicism in the reign of James I of England, consisted of much satire.
2. After Queen Victoria died, an era of _____ followed during which theaters presented everything from verse plays to problems plays and many dramatic genres in between.
3. Notable dramatists of _____ were Oliver Goldsmith and Richard Sheridan.
4. Because of the rise of the Puritans in England, theaters were dark for eighteen years; when Charles I came to the throne, theaters opened with_____.

Test Yourself: Write the letter next to the number to match word and meaning.

1. Edwardian drama   a. Joseph Addison and Richard Steele helped set the tone.
2. Jacobean drama   b. Romantic poets tried playwriting during this period.
3. eighteenth-century drama   c. Bishops' bonfire burned books of Donne, Marston, and Hall.
4. Restoration drama   d. Theaters reopened; Congreve's work was admired.

On a separate sheet of paper, write a sentence using each of the new terms.

DID YOU KNOW? George Bernard Shaw (1856–1950), an Irish playwright who worked in England, was a great admirer of Norwegian playwright Henrik Ibsen (1828–1906), who wrote "problem plays"—those dealing with contemporary social problems.

romantic rebellion	In a rebellion against Edwardian and other prevalent drama, Romantic playwrights created characters that were swept up in emotion. **Romanticism** began in Germany and by the 1820s it dominated theater in Europe. The best-known **romantic drama** is perhaps Goethe's *Faust* (in two parts, 1808 and 1832) based on the classic legend of the man who sold his soul to the devil. **WORDS IN CONTEXT:** *Romantic drama,* created by the rebellion of playwrights against the traditional stage, had a number of variants, but by many playwrights "natural man" was glorified, the artist being seen as something of a mad genius for whom the rules of the world did not apply. Victor Hugo's Hernani was the first important French **romantic** drama.
post-Edwardian drama	Featured plays of social realism, justice, and gender issues, and increasingly took on the problems of class conflict and war. After 1910, leading figures in the theater were George Bernard Shaw (1856–1950), Arthur Wing Pinero (1855–1934), and J. M. Barrie (1860–1937). All but Barrie continued to experiment with realistic problem plays; Barrie escaped reality by writing dramatic fantasies. (He had already written *Peter Pan* in 1903.) **WORDS IN CONTEXT:** *In the* **post-Edwardian** *era, younger playwrights continued to examine social issues, such as justice between the rich and poor, and antiwar drama (John Galsworthy* The Conquering Hero, *1923, in which a young man goes to war hesitantly, undergoes horrifying experiences, and denigrates his hero status). In* **post-Edwardian drama,** *women characters show spirit and spunk, especially in the works of George Bernard Shaw.*
early twentieth-century drama	Many movements lumped together as the avant-garde in this era—precursors to the modern theater. Some thought truth was to be found in the unconscious or spiritual life, and others turned to symbol, abstraction, and ritual, paralleling modern art movements. In the second decade, drama ranged from depicting the high life (Noël Coward's "boulevard comedies" *Hay Fever* and *Private Lives*) to D. H. Lawrence's dramas of emotional traumas of families (*A Collier's Friday Night*). **WORDS IN CONTEXT:** *In the* **early twentieth century,** *J. B. Priestley worked the problem play in his wartime and social dramas (*They Came to a City *and* Desert Highway, *1943), and poets W. B. Yeats and T. S. Eliot weighed in with lyrical prose and verse drama, Yeats in* The Cat and the Moon, The Resurrection *(1926–1939), and others, and Eliot in* Murder in the Cathedral *(1935).*
modern drama	German opera composer Richard Wagner believed that the playwright/composer's job was to create myths—to give "soul" to drama—and he saw a lack of unity among the different arts that comprise theatrical presentation. Wagner's vision of **modern drama** placed all the elements of a theatrical presentation under one artistic creator. To this end, he redesigned the architecture of the theater, along with dramatic presentation itself, with his Festival Theatre at Bayreuth. **WORDS IN CONTEXT:** *In his* **Modern Theatre for Modern Drama,** *Wagner replaced balconies and boxes with a fan-shaped auditorium on a sloped floor. He also redesigned theatrical lighting: each performance began in total darkness.*

After studying the definitions above, use these new words in the sentences below.

1. _____ added plays of brittle high society, but the era also included various theatrical forms: emotional domestic plays and those that made use of symbolism, the unconscious, and spiritual questing.
2. This movement, illustrated by *Faust* and *Hernani* and focusing on emotion rather than rationality, is called_____.
3. In_____, Richard Wagner attempted to create mythic theater and unify all the elements of dramatic production, including the theater itself, preferably under one creative director.
4. Some of the foremost playwrights of the _____era were Shaw, Pinero, Galsworthy, and Barrie.

Test Yourself: Write the letter next to the number to match word and meaning.

1. modern theater
2. post-Edwardian drama
3. romantic rebellion
4. twentieth-century drama

a. associated with the idea of "natural man" and mad artist
b. associated with emotional domestic plays, symbolic plays, boulevard comedy. and many genres
c. associated with dramatic myth-making and artistic unity; structure of the stage itself began to change
d. associated with spirited women, realistic problem plays, and fantasy

On a separate sheet of paper, write a sentence using each of these new terms.

DID YOU KNOW?
You may think of Richard Wagner (1813–1883) as simply a German composer, but he was also a poet, dramatist, director, conductor, essayist, author, and political activist. He wrote a play at age 14, wrote orchestral music and performed professionally at 15, entered a university at 16, and—though he had early operatic successes (*Rienzi*, 1830, and *The Flying Dutchman,*1843)—This extravagant tastes landed him in debtor's prison in Paris (1840). He also wrote *Art and Revolution,* 1849, *The Art-Work of the Future,* 1850, and *Opera and Drama,* 1851, in which he outlined his vision of modern theater.

symbolist drama	This movement in France in the 1880s took Richard Wagner's ideas about the modern theater to heart. Writers, at first French poets, stripped away conventional elements and replaced them with symbolic imagery, appealing to the unconscious rather than the rational mind. Playwrights thought themselves "impressionists" of the stage, as French artists were impressionists in art. **WORDS IN CONTEXT:** *Symbolist dramatists sought an imaginative, mystical drama of inner life. Symbolist poets Stephane Mallarmé and Paul Claudel were followed by symbolist playwrights Maurice Maeterlinck and Rainer Maria Rilke. Chekhov, Ibsen, and Strindberg adopted elements of the symbolists, as did later the American, Eugene O'Neill and Tennessee Williams.*
expressionist drama	The term **expressionism** is used in art, architecture, music, literature, and drama and is, generally speaking, a reaction to *impressionism.* **Expressionism,** antirealistic, focuses on a perceiving ego that imposes its concept of the universe on the outside world. **WORDS IN CONTEXT:** *Expressionist drama is concerned with social reform, and it values language above plot and character. Reinhard Johannes Sorge wrote the first expressionist drama (The Beggar,1911). Later came Strindberg's A Dream Play and Eugene O'Neill's The Emperor Jones and The Hairy Ape.*
theater of the absurd	1950s, individual playwrights anguished at the absurdity of the human condition. Eugene Ionesco said that the **theater of the absurd** expressed "man as lost in the world; all his actions become senseless, absurd, useless." After the devastation of World War II, playwrights wrote of situation rather than plot, and they eliminated cause and effect. Characters were reduced to archetypes in an incomprehensible universe. **WORDS IN CONTEXT:** *Ionesco's Bald Soprano (produced 1950) was the first absurdist drama. In it four characters demonstrate the pointlessness of existence. Samuel Beckett's Waiting for Godot (produced 1953) features two lost tramps, no plot, and empty banter. The waiting is more significant than Godot, a nonsense name that can stand for anything one waits for. American playwrights Edward Albee (The Zoo Story, 1959) and Arnold Weinstein (Red Eye of Love, 1961) work in the absurdist mode, as does English playwright Harold Pinter (The Room, The Homecoming).*
contemporary drama	The theater changed radically after 1956, when John Osborne's *Look Back in Anger* opened in London. Irish playwrights George Bernard Shaw and Shawn O'Casey continued to write, but American realist Arthur Miller said that the English theater was "hermetically sealed off from life." The breakthrough came when Osborne's play became a rallying point for the postwar "angry young men." **WORDS IN CONTEXT:** *In the United States, contemporary drama was psychological realism. Arthur Miller and Tennessee Williams used memory flashbacks, dream sequences, and symbolic characters. Brecht wrote documentary dramas in Germany, and American playwright David Rabe wrote a Vietnam trilogy expressing his frustration with war.*

After studying the definitions above, use these new words in the sentences below.

1. _____presented the world as pointless and incomprehensible through eliminating relationship between cause and effect and reducing language to meaningless dialogue.
2. _____is antirealistic drama in which the playwright puts himself or herself at the center to express rebellion and protest.
3. French poets led the way to_____ by using suggestive imagery and creating impressions of reality rather than the thing itself.
4. Realism, naturalism, symbolism, and poetic dialogue have all been incorporated in_____.

Test Yourself: Write the letter next to the number to match word and meaning.

1. theater of the absurd   a. slow, suggestive, dreamlike drama
2. symbolist   b. two tramps engaged in meaningless banter
3. expressionist   c. incorporates many dramatic forms
4. contemporary drama   d. subjective drama of protest

On a separate sheet of paper, write a sentence using each of these new words.

DID YOU KNOW?
In the late 1970s and beyond, dramatists incorporated bits of previous dramatic elements in their work. David Mamet in *American Buffalo* (1976), which dealt with mundane characters speaking in conversational language, Michael Frayn, Alan Ayckbourn, Dennis Potter, and others emphasized social realism.

Words for Discussing Literature

Learning the words in this section will give you the ability to read, discuss, and write about literature.

DAY 1

novel	melodrama	bildungsroman	roman à clef

DAY 2

point of view	limited narrator	unreliable narrator	persona

DAY 3

style	tone	voice	interior monologue

DAY 4

figurative language	metaphor	simile	oxymoron

DAY 5

verbal irony	Socratic irony	dramatic irony	paradox

DAY 6

plot	complication	crisis	denouement

DAY 7

epiphany	catharsis	tragic flaw	hubris

novel	An extended narrative in prose fiction. The **novel** grew out of the **novelle**, a collection of short tales in prose popular in fourteenth-century Italy, such as Boccaccio's *The Decameron* (1350). But the most important influence on the **novel** was Cervantes' *Don Quixote* (1605). Daniel Defoe is usually credited with writing the first **novel of incident** in *Robinson Crusoe* (1719), because its stories, held together by the struggle of Crusoe and mates to survive, are of more interest to readers than the characters. **WORDS IN CONTEXT:** *Samuel Richardson wrote the first English **novel of character** in* Pamela *(1740), in which the reader's interest is in Pamela, the protagonist, her motivations and development. The character is more important than the story.*
melodrama	In which good faces down bad, the pure of heart is confronted by the evil villain. Characters are one-dimensional and embody one particular emotion for the reader. Both character and plot are sacrificed for violent action and some sort of emotional showdown. No nuance of language or complication of motivation impede the action of a **melodrama.** **WORDS IN CONTEXT:** *In pulp novels and movies of the Old West, the good guys and the bad guys tangle, the good finally overpowering the bad; this genre is **melodramatic**. An early **melodrama** was* Sweeney Todd, The Demon Barber of Fleet Street *(1842).*
bildungsroman	A novel of the formation of a life follows a protagonist's development from childhood through adolescence into maturity. The main characters usually go through a spiritual crisis, a catalyst that helps them identify their role in life. *Roman* is the term for **novel** in most European romance languages. **WORDS IN CONTEXT:** *An early **bildungsroman** was Goethe's* Wilhelm Meister's Apprenticeship *(1796); later ones include Thomas Mann's* Magic Mountain *and Somerset Maugham's* Of Human Bondage. *Related is the **kunstlerroman**, or artist novel, which follows the development of an artist. Proust's* Remembrance of Things Past *and Joyce's* Portrait of the Artist as a Young Man *are examples.*
roman à clef	Pronounced "roman a clay," this French term refers to a novel with a key. The author expects the reader to find the "key" to identifying the actual people and events that comprise the characters and plot of the story. Though the novel is fiction, the characters are humorously exaggerated descriptions of real people and events, usually presented as caricatures. **WORDS IN CONTEXT:** *Aldous Huxley's* Point Counter Point *(1928) is a **roman à clef** that casts actual twentieth-century people in fictional roles with fictional names. D. H. Lawrence is matched with the critic, John Middleton Murry—people that readers of the 1920s would recognize. **Romans à clef** often have a short shelf life, since their success depends on the readers of the time finding the key, or recognizing the characters.*

After studying the definitions above, use these new words in the sentences below.

1. A novel with a simplistic plot and one-dimensional characters who confront one another is some way is a_____.
2. Finding the key to the real people caricatured and the real events exaggerated is the challenge to the reader in a_____.
3. This novel, the_____, takes the reader on a journey through the development of a character's life from childhood to maturity.
4. The first two_____were *Robinson Crusoe* and *Pamela*.

Test Yourself: Write the letter next to the number to match word and meaning.

1. bildungsroman   a. an extended narrative in fiction
2. melodrama   b. watch the protagonist as she grows up
3. novel   c. good guys and bad guys
4. roman à clef   d. spot the real people behind the fictional characters

On a separate sheet of paper, write a sentence using each of these new words.

DID YOU KNOW?
The mistress of the composer Franz Liszt, Marie d'Agoult, who bore him two children, wrote, under the pen name Daniel Stern, a roman à clef, *Nelida*, about their life together before and after she left him because of his numerous infidelities. (It has been translated from the French by Lynn Hoggard.) The name "Nelida" is an anagram of "Daniel." Bernadette Peters played Marie in the film, *Impromptu*.

point of view	Indicates the perspective in fiction from which a story is told. There are two basic story-telling perspectives—**third person point of view** and **first person point of view**. In the **third person point of view**, the speaker stands outside the story and refers to the characters as "he," "she," and "they." In the **first-person point of view**, the speaker is a character in the story and speaks as "I." **WORDS IN CONTEXT:** *Third* and *first person points of view* have subclasses. *Third person omniscient point of view*, for example, assumes that the speaker knows everything that needs to be known about characters and events in the story as well as all characters' thoughts and histories.
limited narrator	In this **point of view**, the narrator tells the story in the third person but has access to the thoughts and experiences of only one character or a very limited number of characters. **WORDS IN CONTEXT:** *Sometimes an author will tell a story by staying within the consciousness of a single character who narrates the story. The reader learns everything about one character, but will know the other characters only as presented by one* **limited narrator** *who has limited knowledge of the other characters.*
unreliable narrator	This narrator speaks in the first person "I" voice, but does not necessarily share the author's values or the author's judgment about what the author has the narrator tell us. The author manipulates the **narrator's** observations to make the reader find him or her **unreliable** or not trustworthy. At some point, the reader asks: Are we getting the straight story here? **WORDS IN CONTEXT:** *Henry James was a master of the* **unreliable narrator.** *In his stories "The Aspern Papers," and "The Liar," the reader must determine the true facts of the story being told not from the* **untrustworthy narrator,** *but from the way the author's manipulation of language and tone override or undercut the story the* **narrator** *is telling.*
persona	The Latin word for "mask" such as those actors carried to speak through in early Greek drama. **Persona** in literature is applied to the the the "I" who speaks in a novel or poem. Gulliver, for example, who tells us about his adventures in *Gulliver's Travels,* is the **persona** of the work. **WORDS IN CONTEXT:** *Calling the narrators* **personae** *emphasizes that they are as much a part of the fiction as is the story that they tell. They are not the author; the author speaks through the mask of the* **persona**—*unless through some obvious manipulation of the fictional elements the author invites the reader to identify the* **persona/narrator** *with the author.*

After studying the definitions above, use these new words in the sentences below.

1. When the author tells a story through an_____, the reader eventually comes to understand that the speaker does not share the author's values, beliefs, or vision.
2. _____ means "mask," and its use in literature indicates that the author speaks not for herself or himself.
3. A_____can get into the central consciousness of only one character or, at most, only a few characters.
4. _____is the perspective from which a speaker tells a story. The omniscient perspective is one in which the speaker is "all knowing."

Test Yourself: Write the letter next to the number to match word and meaning.

1. persona
2. limited narrator
3. unreliable narrator
4. point of view

a. you have reason to doubt the storyteller here
b. the perspective from which a story is told
c. the "mask" through which the narrator speaks
d. the storyteller does not have full knowledge and understanding of every character

On a separate sheet of paper, write a sentence using each of these new words.

DID YOU KNOW? Another narrative method in modern fiction is "stream of consciousness"—from a phrase used by psychologist William James in his *Principles of Psychology* (1890). This narrative mode captures the flow of a character's mental processes, memories, feelings, and random associations, some of them unconscious. James Joyce, William Faulkner, and Virginia Woolf employed stream of consciousness masterfully.

style	Refers to *how* writers say what they say—the diction, word choices, and word clusters, sentence structure and syntax, patterns of literal or figurative language. In traditional classifications of style, there are three levels: high, middle, and low. High style is rather grand; middle style is fairly common, and low style is plain or base.
	WORDS IN CONTEXT: *Many things make up **style** in a work of fiction. Often the concepts are more important than the terms that define them. For example, **demotic style** is everyday speech; **hieratic style** is formal, literary language. **Style** can be sober, somber, flowery, depressed, florid, exuberant, colorful, dull, elaborate, simple, and so on. The **style** of the writing helps create the **tone**.*
tone	This is the speaker's attitude toward the reader. The attitude can be formal or informal, intimidating or reticent, subtle or aggressive, arrogant or humble. **Tone** can seduce readers or put them off, create intimacy or distance.
	WORDS IN CONTEXT: *The **tone** of the speaker in fiction can be serious, ironic, comic, belligerent, mildly humorous. The **tone** is created by word choices, sentence construction, and language—high, middle, or low. The narrator can talk as if speaking to a child or in complicated academic jargon.*
voice	In fiction, the reader can often "hear" a voice beyond the persona or fictitious voices in a work. This is sometimes called *the implied author* or *the authorial presence*. The **voice** stands outside the story, but it is the sensibility that selects, orders, and presents this story in a particular way.
	WORDS IN CONTEXT: *The reader can hear the authorial **voice** in Hemingway's "The Killers." This is a very different **voice** from the one the reader hears in Virginia Woolf's Mrs. Dalloway. And then again, this implied author—the **voice** one hears as one reads—is different in Faulkner's The Sound and the Fury. The **voice** is the audio-puppeteer manipulating the speaker-puppets in fiction.*
interior monologue	A character thinking with no intervention by a narrator. Interior monologue presents a character's thoughts as they occur to him or her.
	WORDS IN CONTEXT: *An **interior monologue** is the verbal equivalent of thoughts, feeling, and sense perceptions of a character who is the central consciousness conveying a story. This can occur in fiction that is wholly stream of consciousness or in fiction in which this is simply one character's unmonitored point of view. For example, in a passage from James Joyce's Ulysses, the protagonist, Leopold Bloom, muses about a man before him: "Like him was I, these sloping shoulders, this gracelessness. My childhood bends beside me. Too far for me to lay a hand there once or lightly …"*

After studying the definitions above, use these new words in the sentences below.

1. _____ is the way in which writers say what they say—through diction, level of speaking, word clusters, sentence structure.
2. _____ is the sensibility, intelligence, or moral authority that selects and presents the story behind the story that fictitious speakers tell.
3. When a character gives an _____, he or she is letting the mind go, taking in and speaking of everything that comes into the senses, perceptions, or consciousness.
4. The speaker's attitude toward the audience or reader, which can create distance or intimacy is_____.

Test Yourself: Write the letter next to the number to match word and meaning.

1. interior monologue   a. how a writer says what he or she says
2. voice   b. the narrator's attitude toward the audience
3. tone   c. the choices of words, syntax, rhythms an author makes
4. style   d. a speaker's unconscious observations, reflections, sense perceptions

On a separate sheet of paper, write a sentence using each of these new words.

DID YOU KNOW?
In English writer Dorothy Richardson's novel *Pilgrimage*, she sustains a narrative describing her heroine Miriam Henderson's feelings, thoughts, sense impressions, and memories throughout 12 volumes of her story (1915–1930), prefiguring James Joyce and Virginia Woolf. She called this style "interior monologue."

figurative language	Is distinguished from *literal language* (standard language that we use every day) in that the way the words are used changes or extends their everyday meaning, sometimes giving emphasis, sometimes making the words appeal more to our senses, and sometimes obscuring their standard meanings.
	WORDS IN CONTEXT: *In speaking of war, leaders sometimes say, "We have 135,000 boots on the ground," meaning troops ready for action. This* **figurative language** *makes the image more visual—and even more aural. (This is called a synecdoche.) Journalists often announce, "The White House said today…" This* **figurative language** *obscures exactly who the speaker is. (This is called a metonymy.) The first example uses "boots," something that soldiers wear, for the soldiers themselves. The second uses "White House" interchangeably with the President or another official.*
metaphor	"The fog comes on little cat feet." **Figurative language** makes a statement or creates an image more vivid than the norm. For example, "The road was a ribbon of moonlight" is more vivid than. "At night the road was lighted by the moon." A metaphor equates one thing here—a road—with another thing—a ribbon. Because this road is narrow and has bends and turns, it resembles a ribbon. Because it is dark and the road is lighted by the moon, the road resembles a ribbon of moonlight.
	WORDS IN CONTEXT: *A* **metaphor** *describes one thing in terms of another to evoke a resemblance or comparison. But a* **metaphor** *must work on both the comparative and imagistic levels in which it is used. It would not work to say, "The road is a tree of moonlight," or "A bottle of moonlight," or "A kitten of moonlight."(A road has no resemblance or visual relationship to a tree, a bottle, or a kitten.) These are* **mixed metaphors** *that do not extend the meaning of the word, road, or make the image more vivid. They simply confuse the reader.* **Metaphors** *are used in both prose and poetry.*
simile	When the word *like* or *as* is used to draw comparisons or resemblances between two different things, the figure of speech is called a **simile.** For example, in the illustration above, if the writer had written: "The road is *like* a ribbon of moonlight" or, "The road lay *as* a ribbon of moonlight," the metaphor would become a **simile.**
	WORDS IN CONTEXT: *Poet Robert Burns wrote this line using a* **simile**: *"O my love's like a red, red rose." He might have made the line* **metaphoric** *by writing, "O my love's a red, red rose."*
oxymoron	An apparent contradiction. For example, to deliberately create a word with the exact meaning they want, writers may combine two words with opposite or contradictory meanings: bitter sweet; living death, open secret, dry ice, old news, civil war.
	WORDS IN CONTEXT: *The word* **oxymoron** *itself is an* **oxymoron**: *oxy means sharp or keen, and* moron *means foolish. Another word that is itself an* **oxymoron** *is* sophomore. *Soph means wise, and* more *means fool—the same root that gives us the word moron. To create an* **oxymoron,** *a writer may yoke together two words that are contradictory: original copy, pretty ugly.*

After studying the words above, use these new words in the sentences below.

1. When a writer uses words in a way that deviates from the standard use to extend the word's meaning, emphasize a point, make the image more visual, or make one word stand for another word, the writer said is to be using_____.
2. _____is a comparison between two things by using *like* or *as.*
3. Two contradictory words yoked together to create an image with an exact meaning is an_____,
4. A_____describes one thing in terms of another to create a resemblance or similarity.

Test Yourself: Write the letter next to the number to match word and meaning.

1. simile   a. sight unseen, random order, loose tights
2. oxymoron   b. she was as bright as a new penny, and her hair shone like copper
3. metaphor   c. Buckingham Palace announced today…
4. figurative language d. The sun is but a morning star.

On a separate sheet of paper, write a sentence using each of these new words.

DID YOU KNOW? Because all the examples of words in the Test Yourself exercise above are illustrations of figurative language, you would not have gone wrong by marking them as such. However, each is a different type of figurative language use; check to see if you matched each one with its most precise meaning.

verbal irony	Occurs when a speaker makes a statement in which the real meaning differs from what he or she says. A speaker might say, "It's been the best day of my life," when everything had gone wrong that day. The surface statement gives incorrect clues to what is actually going on. **WORDS IN CONTEXT:** *A character in ancient Greek comedy called the* eiron *was careless with the truth. He pretended to be less intelligent than he actually was. From this, we derive the word* **irony***, which alerts us to the difference between what is said and what is actually the case.*
Socratic irony	Socrates, to get his students to think, often acted as if he knew less than he did. This way, he encouraged students to make comments that he was aware were ill-founded, but he knew the exercise would tax their intellect. Today, we might call this "playing dumb to get a reaction." **WORDS IN CONTEXT:** *In literature,* **Socratic irony** *has produced the naive hero—a speaker who plays dumb to provoke the reader to understand that he does not mean what he says. Jonathan Swift in "A Modest Proposal," does this when he takes on the persona of a superrational economist to persuade authorities in poverty-stricken, but over-populated Ireland that eating new babies would be the answer to the country's hunger problems.*
dramatic irony	In drama or literature, a situation in which the reader and the author share information that the character does not have. In a play, for example, you can see a man with a raised knife behind the door the protagonist enters, so you anticipate something that the protagonist is not aware of. **WORDS IN CONTEXT:** *Shakespeare's* Twelfth Night *includes a scene in which Malvolio announces a good fortune coming to him that he has read about in a letter. This scene is one of* **dramatic irony***, because the audience knows this information comes from a letter with false information.*
paradox	A statement that is seemingly contradictory but on second thought, or if thought about in another way, is valid. For example, sometimes a cruel remark is kind. In war, one hears that a village must be bombed to be saved. In Christianity, one must die to gain eternal life. **WORDS IN CONTEXT:** *Sometimes* **a paradox** *is implied, as in "waging the peace." Or if one says, "I lie," then the statement must be true. Sometimes a* **paradox** *is explicit: In nature, plants must die in winter to be born again in spring. Death is in life; life is in death. In almost all poetry there is an element of* **paradox.**

After studying the definitions above, use these new words in the sentences below.

1. In an O Henry short story, the reader learns that a woman is cutting off her long, beautiful hair at the same time that her husband is buying her a comb to hold her long, beautiful hair; this is an example of_____.
2. The opening line of Jane Austen's *Pride and Prejudice* is: "It is a truth universally acknowledged that a single man in possession of a good fortune must be in want of a wife." What the narrator is really implying is that every single woman wants a rich husband. This is an example of_____.
3. In literature, one character may "play dumb" about a matter to entice another character to talk about it. This is called_____.
4. In a poem by John Donne, we find the lines: "One short sleep past, we wake eternally/ And death shall be no more; *Death, thou shalt die.*" This is an example of_____.

Test Yourself: Write the letter next to the number to match word and meaning.

1. verbal irony
2. Socratic irony
3. paradox
4. dramatic irony

a. a statement that seems contradictory but turns out to be valid
b. the reader or playgoer knows something the character doesn't
c. a character pretends to know less than he or she does about a matter to get another character's reaction
d. the intended meaning of a speaker's statement is different from what she or he actually says

On a separate sheet of paper, write a sentence using each of these new words.

DID YOU KNOW? Irony is tricky. If you use it orally, as in saying, "Well, that's a great idea," when everyone present knows the idea is patently stupid, then you are being sarcastic rather than subtly ironic. But, say, you look down to fasten your seatbelt in your car to keep yourself safe, and in looking down you fail to see an oncoming car that hits you and injures you. In this case, you have suffered cosmic irony. (The fates are against you.) An act you have committed to make yourself safe has put you in the hospital.

plot	The structure of the action in a novel or a play, its goal being to achieve a particular emotional and artistic effect. The **plot** of a work and its major characters are interdependent because the action is performed by the characters and reveals the personal qualities of the characters. **WORDS IN CONTEXT:** *In works of fiction a variety of **plot** forms may be developed to tell a story. However, basic to most fiction are these **plot** features: protagonist, antagonist, conflict, suspense, surprise, **complication**, climax, **crisis**, denouement.*
complication	After the protagonist and antagonist come into conflict with each other, the reader is often led on by suspense (what will happen next?), surprise (expectations are violated), and **complication** (the rising action of the narrative where the characters' conflict escalates along with reader suspense). **WORDS IN CONTEXT:** ***Complication** need not be based on the conflict of two characters. **Complication** may arise when a character comes in conflict with fate, with nature, with circumstances that stand between the character and a goal, or a conflict within his or her own mind. In these cases, the protagonist comes up against an antagonist that is not an individual but a force that pushes back at him or her.*
crisis	The **complication** or rising action escalates to a *climax*, which reaches a **crisis,** sometimes called the *arc of the story.* The fortune of the protagonist takes a turn—she or he overcomes the antagonist or is overcome by that person or force. **WORDS IN CONTEXT:** *At the **crisis** point in the story, the hero may die or may emerge victorious over whatever the opposing force has been. The **crisis** then leads to the falling action and **denouement**.*
denouement	This French word (pronounced "de'-noo-ma(n)" means "an unknotting" or "an unraveling." After the **crisis**, the action, which has been steadily rising, plunges; suspense is relieved, and the **denouement** begins. **WORDS IN CONTEXT:** *In the **denouement** of a story, the unraveling of mysteries and misunderstandings, questions of motivation, and **complication** occur. In some narratives, the **denouement** is followed by a reversal, in which the hero's fortune undergoes yet another change, often because the hero has discovered something new about himself or herself or the situation.*

After studying the definitions above, use these new words in the sentences below.

1. Basic features of a _____ are protagonist, antagonist, suspense, surprise, complication, crisis, and denouement.
2. The rising or escalation of action accompanied by suspense and surprise in a novel is called_____.
3. The _____ is the "unknotting" of all the knots—mysteries, misunderstandings, questions—in a work of literature.
4. The complication in the plot of a piece of literature leads to a climax which becomes a_____.

Test Yourself: Write the letter next to the number to match word and meaning.

1. crisis   a. the clearing up of everything unexplained at the end
2. plot   b. the turning point or arc in a story in which the hero's fortune reverses
3. complication   c. the escalation of conflict leading to a climax
4. denouement   d. the structure of the action in a novel or play

On a separate sheet of paper, write a sentence using each of these new words.

> **DID YOU KNOW?**
> British poet and satirist Hilaire Belloc (1870–1953) wrote as his epitaph: *When I am dead, I hope it may be said, "His sins were scarlet, but his books were read."*

epiphany	A breaking through of the divine or a manifestation of God's presence. James Joyce used the word to mean a fleeting moment in time when a special insight occurs in a mundane setting. **WORDS IN CONTEXT:** *Epiphany is a term in Christianity meaning that God has been made visible. It is also a yearly Christian festival, held on January 6. In James Joyce's first draft of* A Portrait of the Artist as a Young Man, *the author used* **epiphany** *to mean a sudden spiritual manifestation. Joyce's novels and short stories teem with* **ephiphanies.**
catharsis	Literally, this means a purging or a purification of the body. In literature, it means a purifying of the emotions or a relieving of emotional tensions. Cartharsis was originally used by Aristotle to mean a purging of pity or terror which resulted from viewing a tragedy in Greek drama. **WORDS IN CONTEXT:** *Aristotle, in his* Poetics, *said that a tragic figure in drama will evoke our pity and terror if he is neither wholly good nor wholly bad. He said that tragedy is a serious drama that incorporates "incidents arousing pity and fear, wherewith to accomplish the* **catharsis** *of such emotion." This is thought to mean that the suffering and defeat of the tragic figure leave the audience relieved and uplifted.*
tragic flaw	Aristotle's tragic figure suffers from a **tragic flaw**—an error of judgment (Aristotle called this hamartia). The tragic figure in drama or literature is led by an error in judgment to a reversal: Because of his or her own doing, fortune changes from happiness to suffering. Sometimes a strength is also a person's weakness: a paradox. **WORDS IN CONTEXT:** *Tragic figures in literature move us to pity them because they are not wicked; they simply suffer from a* **tragic flaw** *that leads them to use poor judgment. Such figures move us to terror or fear, because we can see some of the same flaws in ourselves. The* **catharsis** *comes from that recognition.*
hubris	Again Aristotle, who gave us the definition of tragedy, says that a common tragic flaw is **hubris**—overweening pride or stubborn self-confidence that causes a tragic figure to ignore warnings, divine or otherwise, or disregard moral law. **WORDS IN CONTEXT:** *In Greek drama, Oedipus's* **hubris** *leads him to ignore warnings and clues and pursue a course that brings him to disaster. Likewise, King Lear, in his* **hubris,** *ignores obvious truths, clings stubbornly to his own path, and brings misery on himself. The scene of reversal, in which Lear enters the stage carrying the dead body of his beloved Cordelia, is one in which both audience and Lear undergo a* **catharsis.**

After studying the definitions above, use these new words in the sentences below.

1. An element found in much of James Joyce's work, a sudden manifestation of unearthly radiance illuminating a special insight in a common object or scene is an _____.
2. _____ is the purging of pity and terror in the emotions of an audiences after viewing the reversal in a tragic figure.
3. Overweening pride that leads a tragic figure to disaster is_____.
4. The protagonist's error in judgment or_____led to his or her downfall.

Test Yourself: Write the letter next to the number to match word and meaning.

1. catharsis   a. the bad call that brought the tragic figure down
2. epiphany   b. stubborn self-confidence and pride
3. tragic flaw   c. spiritual radiance seen in an ordinary thing
4. hubris   d. purging the emotions of pity and terror

On a separate sheet of paper, write a sentence using each of these new words.

DID YOU KNOW?
The difference between a utopia and a dystopia: A *utopia* is an ideal world, political state, or way of life. Plato's Republic was the first utopian work. Sir Thomas More wrote *Utopia* (1516). Samuel Butler wrote *Erewhon* (1872)—a name that is an anagram of "nowhere." Utopia means "a good place." A *dystopia*, in contrast means "a bad place," the opposite of utopia. This is an unpleasant imaginary world such as George Orwell wrote of in *1984* and Aldous Huxley in *Brave New World*.

Words for Discussing Poetry

Learning the words in this section will give you the ability to read, write about, and discuss poetry.

DAY 1

| epic poetry | lyric poetry | ode | elegy |

DAY 2

| ballad | sonnet | dramatic monologue | haiku |

DAY 3

| denotation | connotation | epithet | euphony |

DAY 4

| prosody | synesthesia | caesura | portmanteau |

DAY 5

| metaphysical poets | romantic poets | Victorian poets | pre-Raphaelite brotherhood |

DAY 6

| symbolism | surrealism | imagism | free verse |

DAY 7

| aestheticism | decadence | beats | black aesthetics |

epic poetry	Long, narrative poetry on a grand and serious subject, spoken or written in an elevated style, focusing on a heroic figure on whose actions rest the fate of a people—nation, tribe, or race. The material comes from history or legend and grew out of oral traditions. The first **epic poems** were Homer's *Iliad* and *Odyssey* and the Anglo-Saxon epic *Beowulf*. **WORDS IN CONTEXT:** *Literary epics* are written but follow the conventions of the oral tradition: Virgil's *Aeneid*, Milton's *Paradise Lost*, Keats's *Hyperion*, and Blake's *The Four Zoas*. **Epics** begin in medias res (in the middle of things) with formality, cover a grand scale, and speak grandly of a superhuman hero.
lyric poetry	Fairly short poems that do not tell a story but express a thought or feeling. Originally poets accompanied their **lyric** on a lyre, thus the name. The **lyric** is written in the first person, but the poet often takes on a persona and is not speaking for or of himself or herself. Subclasses of **lyric poems** are **odes**, **elegies**, *sonnets*, and *dramatic monologues*. **WORDS IN CONTEXT:** *Examples of **love lyrics**:* Ben Jonson's "Drink to Me Only with Thine Eyes," Robert Herrick's "To the Virgins, to Make Much of Time," Richard Lovelace's "To Lucasta, Going to the Wars," Andrew Marvell's "To His Coy Mistress." *Examples of **meditative lyrics**:* Matthew Arnold's "Dover Beach," John Milton's "On His Blindness," and Dylan Thomas's "Do Not Go Gentle into That Good Night."
ode	A long, serious **lyric poem** with complex stanzas and elevated style. Originated by the Greek poet Pindar, early odes were based on songs sung by the chorus in Greek dramas, and stanzas moved in a dance rhythm, left and right, as the chorus did. They were written to praise someone, such as Olympic game winners. **WORDS IN CONTEXT:** *English odes dropped the elaborate stanza schemes of Pindaric odes; for example, Keats's "Ode on a Grecian Urn," Wordsworth's "Ode on the Intimation of Immortality," and Shelley's "Ode to the West Wind."*
elegy	To Greek and Roman poets, the **elegy** had a special meter, alternating eight lines and five lines. Later, the **elegy** became a solemn, sustained poem of lament for a dead person or dead persons. **WORDS IN CONTEXT:** *Examples of **elegies**:* W. H. Auden's "In Memory of W. B. Yeats," Tennyson's "In Memoriam," and Gray's **elegy** for the dead in general, "Elegy Written in a Country Churchyard."

After studying the definitions above, use these new words in the sentences below.

1. _____ were originally poems written to glorify and praise someone; later they became meditations.
2. Short poems of love, thought, or feeling expressed in a first-person voice and originally written as songs to be accompanied by a lyre are _____.
3. _____ poems are those written in memory of the dead.
4. Long, narrative _____ poems with elevated languge, based on history.

Test Yourself: Write the letter next to the number to match word and meaning.

1. lyric poetry	a. long narrative poems that grew out of oral traditions
2. elegy	b. short, first-person poems of love or meditation
3. ode	c. written in memory of a deceased person
4. epic poetry	d. originally written to praise or glorify someone

On a separate sheet of paper, write a sentence using each of these new words.

DID YOU KNOW?
In Christian elegies, the lyric poet makes a reversal from despair to joy when the poet recognizes that death is only in this life and a heavenly life waits beyond.

ballad	A song that tells a story, usually composed in four-line stanzas (*quatrains*). There are basically two kinds of **ballads**: **folk** and **literary**. **Folk ballads** were passed along orally, and because they were transmitted by word of mouth, the words were often changed, so several versions of the same ballad frequently exist. **Literary ballads** were written down, composed by one person reworking the folk ballad form.

WORDS IN CONTEXT:

Following is one stanza of the **folk ballad** "Lord Randal":

O where hae ye been, Lord Randal, my son?
O where hae ye been, my handsome young man?
I hae been to the wild wood; mother, make my bed soon,
For I'm weary wi' hunting, and fain would lie down.

Here is one stanza from the **literary ballad** "A Ballad of Hell":

A letter from my love today!
Oh, unexpected, dear appeal!
She struck a happy tear away
And broke the crimson seal.

sonnet	Fourteen lines of *iambic pentameter* (five beats of one unstressed syllable followed by one stressed syllable: example—"The curfew tolls the knell of parting day"), written in a single stanza. There are basically two kinds of **sonnets**: **Italian** (or *Petrarchan*) and **Shakespearean** (or *English*).

WORDS IN CONTEXT: *The* **Italian sonnet** *has two main parts—an octave (8 lines) and a sestet (6 lines). The octave rhymes abbaabba, and the sestet rhymes cdecde, or a variant. Petrarch, a fourteenth-century Italian, used this form. Later British poets including Milton, Wordsworth, and Shakespeare adapted it. The* **Shakespearean sonnet** *has three 4-line stanzas and a concluding 2-line stanza. This sonnet rhymes ababcdcdefefgg. Other variants exist, but these sonnet forms are basic.*

dramatic monologue	A poem in which a single persona in a specific situation speaks, addressing and interacting with one or more people whom we never hear (but can take clues from what the speaker says), and the speaker inadvertently reveals himself or herself—temperament, values, character—in what he or she says.

WORDS IN CONTEXT: *Dramatic monologue is a poem of character revelation. The reader or listener reads between the lines of what the speaker tells us to determine what the real story is. Robert Browning was a master of* **dramatic monologue.** *Two of his more notable dramatic monologues are: "My Last Duchess" and "The Bishop Orders His Tomb." A modern example is T. S. Eliot's "The Love Song of J. Alfred Prufrock."*

haiku	A Japanese verse form of three unrhymed lines in 5,7,5 syllables totalling 17 syllables. The subject is most often nature, and the verse evokes a season, a color, or an emotion. Example:

The face of the moon
Crumples in the midnight lake
The boat passes on.

WORDS IN CONTEXT: *Matsuo Basho (1644–1694) established the rules for* **haiku,** *which captures the essence of the moment.*

After studying the definitions above, use these new words in the sentences below.

1. Two kinds of_____are folk and literary; they are meant to be sung.

2. Lyrical poetry with a complex metrical and rhyming system is the_____; Shakespeare excelled at writing one kind.

3. _____is a poem in which one person speaks, telling listeners about a situation, but doing so gives away much about his or her own character.

4. A form of Japanese poetry based on lines, syllables, and nature is_____.

Test Yourself: Write the letter next to the number to match word and meaning.

1. ballad   a. two kinds are Italian and Shakespearean

2. sonnet   b. two kinds are folk and literary

3. haiku   c. brief poem, captures the moment, has 17 syllables

4. dramatic   d. through his or her words, you learn about the psyche
   monologue   of the speaker

On a separate sheet of paper, write a sentence using each new word.

DID YOU KNOW?

American poet Robert Frost wrote a very brief, though moving, poem called "The Span of Life" that approaches, but is not quite, a haiku:

The old dog barks backward without getting up, I can remember when he was a pup.

denotation	The ordinary, everyday, dictionary definition of a word. For example, the **denotation** of the word *river* is "a natural stream of water larger than a creek and emptying into an ocean, a lake, or another river."
	WORDS IN CONTEXT: *The **denotation** of river is described above. There are other ways that we use the word—in idioms and figures of speech: "sell down the river," meaning to betray; "send up the river," meaning to send someone to prison.*
connotation	There are ideas and visual and other sense images that the word *river* brings to mind. These are the **connotations.** What does a river connote? Boats, swimming, fishing, summer, floating, moving on swiftly or slowly.
	WORDS IN CONTEXT: *As the Greek philosopher Heraclitis said, "You can't step in the same river twice." The word brings up different, maybe contradictory, thoughts: What is the river of no return? Drowning? Is life a river? James Joyce, in his stream-of-consciousness novel Ulysses, uses the River Liffy in Dublin to suggest the stream of life, or riverrun. Every word has a **connotation**: those ideas and images that it evokes. Poets take advantage of them.*
epithet	You think this means a swear word, a taboo word? In poetry it has another meaning derived from the Greek *epitheton*, which means "something added."
	WORDS IN CONTEXT: *Homer used **epithets** as a kind of shorthand—descriptions in The Odyssey and The Iliad he used in a formulaic way: "the wine-dark sea,"" fleet-footed Achilles," " bolt-hurling Zeus." Perhaps these were the clichés of the Homeric age.*
euphony	Language that flows smoothly and musically. Poets use a number of technical and linguistic skills to make their poetry **euphonious**, but sometimes they let their subconscious do that work for them.
	WORDS IN CONTEXT: *Samuel Taylor Coleridge wrote a poem called Kubla Khan, which seems to make no rational sense, but the words are so **euphonious** and the poem so lovely to read aloud that no one seems to mind. It begins:* *In Xanadu did Kubla Khan* *A stately pleasure-dome decree:* *Where Alph, the sacred river, ran* *Through caverns measureless to man* *Down to the sunless sea.*

After studying the definitions of the words above, use the new words in the sentences below.

1. The literal, dictionary definition of a word is called its_____.
2. In Homeric epics, adjective-noun combinations (add-ons) used to describe a character or an object are_____, not swear words as we use the term today.
3. All the thoughts, feelings, impressions that hover around a given word are called its_____.
4. _____ is the musical quality of words, as heard in this passage from Ralph Hodgson's "Eve":

> *Eve, with her basket, was*
> *Deep in the bells and grass,*
> *Wading in bells and grass*
> *Up to her knees.*
> *Picking a dish of sweet*
> *Berries and plums to eat,*
> *Down in the bells and grass*
> *Under the trees.*

Test Yourself: Write the letter next to the number to match word and meaning.

1. epithet   a. what the dictionary says about a word
2. euphony   b. the wine-dark sea
3. denotation   c. smooth, musical quality of language
4. connation   d. home: family, security, warmth, familiarity, food, welcoming

On a separate sheet of paper, write a sentence using each of these new words.

DID YOU KNOW? Rhyme in a poem affects the movement of the poem. The more a poem contains rhyme, whether internal rhyme or rhyme at the end of the line, the more the words tend to accelerate in pace. For this reason, poets tend to avoid rhyme in serious poetry: cleverness and fast pace tend to lighten the poem rather than add to its somberness.

prosody	The systematic study of creating poetry. For example, the study of the principles and use of meter, rhyme, stanza, and sound elements (such as *euphony* and *cacophony*—word choices that create harshness, roughness, and discord). **WORDS IN CONTEXT:** *In **prosody**, one learns how a poem comes to be, how it works, the components and techniques that go into it: Compare the harsh language in Robert Browning's "Pied Piper" at right to the euphonious language in Hodgson's "Eve":*	*Rats!* *They fought the dogs and killed the cats . . .* *Split open the kegs of salted sprats,* *Made nests inside men's Sunday hats.*
synesthesia	The describing of one sense impression in terms of another. The poet sometimes attributes colors to smells, or sounds to tactile impressions, playing on our five senses, such as in these words: "The bitter, hard, black of the night." **WORDS IN CONTEXT:** *In Percy B. Shelley's "The Sensitive Plant," there is an example of **synesthesia:***	*And the hyacinth purple, and white, and blue,* *Which flung from its bells a sweet peal anew* *Of music so delicate, soft, and intense,* *It was felt like an odor within the sense.*
caesura	Pauses within a long line of poetry dictated by speech rhythm. Poets use the **caesura** (sez-yoo'-rah) to give variety to the sound or to emphasize a thought. **WORDS IN CONTEXT:** *An example of **caesura** is this passage from Alexander Pope's "Of the Characters of Women":*	*See how the world its veterans rewards!* *A youth of frolics, an old age of cards;* *Fair to no purpose, artful to no end,* *Young without lovers, old without a friend.*
portmanteau	Literally a **portmanteau** is a suitcase that opens like a book and has storage compartments on both sides. Poets have used the concept by creating **portmanteau words,** words that can carry two meanings at once. A common example is *smog,* meaning *smoke* and *fog;* others are *dumbfounded* (*dumb* and *founder*), *twirl* (*twist* and *swirl*). **WORDS IN CONTEXT:** *Humpty Dumpty is the authority on **portmanteau words**. About the word "slithy" in Lewis Carroll's "Jabberwocky," Mr. Dumpty says to Alice, "Slithy means 'lithe and slimy'. . . . You see it's like a portmanteau—there are two meanings packed up into one word." James Joyce was a master of **portmantau language,** which allowed him to layer words with many meanings, denotations, and connotations, from many languages. For example, he said in* Finnegans Wake, *"Wipe your glosses with what you know." (Gloss—polished surface; words of explanation or translation inserted between lines of a text; a tongue; definitions of difficult words; glasses—spectacles, aids to vision.)*	

After studying the definitions above, use these new words in the sentences below.

1. The systematic study of the components and techniques of poetry is called _____.
2. _____ is attributing one sense impression to another.
3. A pause in the middle of a long line of poetry is a _____.
4. A word that can carry two or more meanings at the same time is a _____.

Test Yourself: Write the letter next to the number to match word and meaning.

1. caesura
2. portmanteau
3. prosody
4. synesthesia

a. a furry smell, for example, or a hot color.
b. a pause that refreshes in the middle of a line
c. two-in-one word
d. study of *how* a poem comes to be

On a separate sheet of paper, write a sentence using each of these new words.

DID YOU KNOW? Lewis Carroll (1832–1898) was writing a satire of pompous Victorian poetry in his nonsense verse "Jabberwocky." Carroll delighted in deflating pomposity with ridicule, and those who were aware of the posturing of poets of that age understood that his verse was a send-up of much of the poetry written during that period.

metaphysical poets	Poets of the seventeenth century who used colloquial tone, irony, paradox, tight syntax, and far-fetched, extended analogies called **metaphysical conceits.**
	WORDS IN CONTEXT: *Some metaphysical poets were Andrew Marvell, George Herbert, and John Donne. An example of a metaphysical conceit is found in Donne's "A Valediction Forbidding Mourning," in which he compares two lovers to the legs of a mathematical compass:*

> *If they be two, they are two so*
> *As stiff twin compasses are two;*
> *Thy soul, the fixed foot, makes no show*
> *To move, but doth, if th' other do.*

romantic poets	Poets of the late eighteenth and early nineteenth century in England. These included Robert Burns, William Blake, Sir Walter Scott, William Wordsworth, Samuel Taylor Coleridge, George Noel Gordon, Lord Byron, Percy Bysshe Shelley, and John Keats.
	WORDS IN CONTEXT: *Romantic poets had a particular aesthetic called romanticism. Their work stressed imagination, individualism, and as Coleridge said, "The spontaneous overflow of powerful feelings."*
Victorian poets	The period of **Victorian poets** dated arguably from 1837 when Queen Victoria took the throne until her death in 1901. The writing of the period reflected the culture, which included the Industrial Revolution, Darwin's theory of evolution, and various social and economic reforms.
	WORDS IN CONTEXT: *Notable Victorian poets were Alfred Lord Tennyson, Robert Browning, and Matthew Arnold. Novelists and essayists included Charles Dickens, George Eliot, William Makepeace Thackery, Thomas Hardy, Thomas Carlyle, and John Ruskin.*
pre-Raphaelite brotherhood	A mid-nineteenth-century movement in English art and literature, in which artists returned to the art before Raphael for their inspiration—realism with symbolic overtones, religiousness combined with sensuousness, a certain medieval quality in painting and word images. D. G. Rossetti, both a painter and a poet, was a leader of the movement. His poem, "The Blessed Damozel," is representative of the work of the **pre-Raphaelites.**
	WORDS IN CONTEXT: *In turning for inspiration to Italian art pre-Raphael and the High Renaissance, the pre-Raphaelite brotherhood spurned the English academic style of painting. The literary movement followed the art movement. D. G. Rossetti's sister Christina and other poets including Algernon Swinburne, and William Morris were part of the brotherhood.*

After studying the definitions above, use these new words in the sentences below.

1. Social and economic issues, such as the Industrial Revolution, were typical subjects for the poets and other writers of the _____ period.
2. Keats, Byron, Shelley, Wordworth, Tennyson, and others were _____ poets who stressed imagination and emotion.
3. Seventeenth century _____, of whom John Donne was one, often used bizarre comparisons called *conceits.*
4. The _____ turned its back on the dominent art of England in the mid-nineteenth century and found inspiration in the spirit and flesh imagery that existed before Raphael.

Test Yourself: Write the letter next to the number to match word and meaning.

1. romantic poets
2. metaphysical poets
3. pre-Raphaelites
4. Victorian poets

a. wrote of social reform and cultural issues
b. emphasized emotion and imagination
c. admired the religiosenuous imagery of the era before the High Renaissance
d. Andrew Marvell and John Donne were two

On a separate sheet of paper, write a sentence using each of these new words.

DID YOU KNOW?
What makes a "bad" poem? Poet and critic John Ciardi has suggested a place to begin looking: "An obviously derivative, cliché-studded, rhyme-forced poem in which the poet mangles his metaphors *without seeming to know what he is doing*" may be "flatly declared to be a bad poem." Ciardi adds that there must be a "sympathetic contract" between the reader and the poet; that is, the reader must sympathize with the way the poet takes himself (tone), and the way he takes his subject (attitude).

symbolism	A **symbol** is based in mystery, something hard to define but not hard to grasp through the thoughts and feelings it evokes in context. A **symbol** is a thing that stands for itself but also stands for something else. One might say a **symbol** is the combination of denotation and connotations of a word—and something beyond as well. Consider Robert Frost's familiar poem about "two roads diverged in a yellow wood." The reader comes to know that the poet is talking about more than the choice between two literal roads, but that his choice of one road over another stands for any choice in life between equally attractive alternatives, and that choice can make "all the difference" in the kind of life one experiences. Long before Frost wrote his poem, the **symbolist movement,** which began in France in the 1880s, claimed that literature must be based in mystery; therefore, it must be **symbolic.** **WORDS IN CONTEXT:** *Leader of the **symbolists** was Stephane Mallarmé, who said that a poet should suggest, not state: "To name a thing is to suppress three-quarters of the joy of the poem, which consists in guessing, little by little; suggestion makes the dream." Other important **symbolists** were Maurice Maeterlinck, Paul Verlaine, W. B. Yeats, T. S. Eliot, and Wallace Stevens.*
surrealism	**Surrealist** techniques have always been used in poetry, but in 1924 Andre Breton in France wrote *Manifesto on Surrealism,* which launched a movement that proposed to go deeply into the unconscious to capture in literature the "logic" of dreams. This was an artistic move against the restraints of bourgeois morality and artistic conventions. This revolutionary movement spread through Europe and America in painting, sculpture, and other arts. **WORDS IN CONTEXT:** *Guillaume Appollinaire invented the term **surrealism.** Writers influenced by this experiment with free association and the juxtaposition of unrelated images were Federico García Lorca, Dylan Thomas, Henry Miller, Thomas Pynchon, William Burroughs, and others.*
imagism	A literary movement that caught on in England in about 1910 led by T. E. Hulme and Ezra Pound. Tenets of the **imagists'** faith: direct treatment, subjective or objective, of a thing; the use of no unnecessary word; the use of rhythm as in a musical phrase. Common speech was mandatory, and the image should be hard, clear, and concentrated. **WORDS IN CONTEXT:** *Imagists included H.D. (Hilda Doolittle), and Amy Lowell. Greatly affecting the work of W. B. Yeats, T. S. Eliot, and Wallace Stevens, **imagism** influences poetry to the present day. Pound's two-line **imagist** poem "In a Station at the Metro" is an example: "The apparition of these faces in the crowd, /Petals on a wet, black bough."*
free verse	"Poetry Fetter'd Fetters the Human Race," wrote William Blake in *Jerusalem.* Some other writers seem to think so, too, including Matthew Arnold and Walt Whitman. **Free verse** released poets from the constraints of strict meter and freed them of traditional rhythm written in regular line lengths. **WORDS IN CONTEXT:** *Blake often wrote lyrics in very short lines; Whitman often wrote in long lines in which the rhythmic effects were based on repetition and balance. French **symbolist** poets as well as English and American poets began writing in **free verse** that suspended syntax and meter and allowed the poet more control over time, pause, and pace. T. S. Eliot, William Carlos Williams, and e. e. cummings wrote in **free verse.***

After studying the definitions above, use these new words in the sentences below.

1. _____, beginning in France in the 1880s, was a movement in literature that suggested rather than stated.
2. Dreamlike, sometimes nightmarish poetry that delves into the unruly unconscious for its imagery is_____.
3. Hard, clear, concentrated poetry, influenced by Japanese *haiku,* which wastes no words, uses common speech, and transforms an objective scene into a subjective image is_____.
4. Poets who control the pace of their poems not through conventional meter and syntax but through cadences they can create through varying line length and other visual and aural techniques write in_____.

Test Yourself: Write the letter next to the number to match word and meaning.

1. symbolism   a. nonlogical, nonchronological poetry from the unconscious
2. surrealism   b. suggestive poetry based in mystery
3. free verse   c. clear, concentrated, objective images transformed subjectively
4. imagism   d. short or long lines, poets give up restraint of meter for rhythm

On a separate sheet of paper, write a sentence using each of these new words.

DID YOU KNOW?

Robert Frost disdained free verse and once said that writing in free verse was like playing tennis without a net.

aestheticism	*Art for art's sake*—the motto of poets and other artists of the **aesthetic movement** in France in the late nineteenth century. The **aesthetes** flared after Theophile Gautier claimed that art lacks all utility, and they were led by Baudelaire, Flaubert, and Mallarmé. These writers renounced the values of the day for what Flaubert called,"the religion of beauty." **WORDS IN CONTEXT:** *Led by Walter Pater and Oscar Wilde in England,* **aestheticism** *spurned middle-class morality and self-righteousness. The l'art pour l'art attitude led to a highly self-conscious style of life and presentation of self as well as of poetry, which soon devolved into the period called the* **decadence**.
decadence	The term came from late Greece and Rome when the arts had fallen into decay. Gautier and Baudelaire saw Europe in the same situation. Nature and art were divorced, and artists played on that concept in extreme ways: they dressed and spoke in highly artificial ways, wearing, as Oscar Wilde did, green carnations in their elaborate costumes, flouting the norms of morality and sex. The era was called the *fin de siècle*—the end of the century. **WORDS IN CONTEXT:** *J. K. Huysmans in 1884 wrote Au Rebours (Against the Grain) giving voice to the* **decadent** *sensibility.* **Decadence** *in England was exemplified by poets and writers Wilde, Arthur Symons, Ernest Dowson, and artist Aubrey Beardsley. Wilde wrote The Picture of Dorian Gray (1891). Later, in the United States* **decadent** *precepts were adapted by the* **beat poets.**
beats	This American counterculture movement in the 1950s expressed alienation from conventional society by adopting "cool," detached, and ironic attitudes and vocabulary from jazz musicians. **Beat poets** such as Allen Ginsberg, Gary Snyder, and Lawrence Ferlinghetti liberated poetry by bringing it "back to the streets." They tried to capture immediacy by free writing, without plan. **WORDS IN CONTEXT:** *Beat—the name came first from weariness at "having been used" in a materialistic society and later took from Buddhism the idea of "beatific." Derisively called "beatniks," the poets created work that ranged from undisciplined to powerful. Ginsberg's Howl (1956) influenced other writers such as novelist William Burroughs (Naked Lunch, 1959) and Jack Kerouac. (Kerouac's best-known novel, On the Road, was published in 1957 but early drafts date back to 1951.)*
black aesthetics	African-American writers have produced work in the United States since Jupiter Hammon wrote in 1760 and Phillis Wheatley in the eighteenth century, but in the 1920s, the so-called Harlem Renaissance saw dozens of black artists and writers, including Zora Neale Hurston, Langston Hughes, Jean Toomer, and many musicians flourish in what novelist Ralph Ellison called "our own home-grown version of Paris," in Harlem. Later, black American artists in the 1960s and 1970s sought an art form to promote pride in black identity. Their literature, sometimes written in black vernacular, addressed interracial and sociopolitical tensions and brought African-American history and culture into American arts. Some theorists were Houston A. Baker, Henry Louis Gates, Jr., Addison Gayle, and Hoyt Fuller. **WORDS IN CONTEXT:** *Poets LeRoi Jones (later known as Amiri Baraka) and Don L. Lee (later Haki R. Madhubuti) of the* **black aesthetic movement** *became well known in several genres. The movement was eventually absorbed into the mainstream of American literature, and its notable writers such as Alex Haley, Eldridge Cleaver, Angela Davis, Ishmael Reed, Ntozake Shange, Alice Walker, Toni Morrison, and Sonia Sanchez went on to win major acclaim.*

After studying the definitions above, use these new terms in the sentences below.
1. _____ disdained art as being useful and proclaimed that art was for art's sake.
2. Artists of the _____ saw the culture as having divorced nature from art and so emphasized a life of high artifice in poetry, style, dress, and manner.
3. Weary of conventional culture and hopeful of living a life of quest and spiritual discovery, these _____ artists of the 1950s and 1960s set off *On the Road*.
4. Claiming that _____ had been ignored, they sought to set themselves apart by using a cultural vernacular in their writing and emphasizing their history.

Test Yourself: Write the letter next to the number to match term and meaning.
1. beat   a. claimed beauty was its own excuse for being and had no utility
2. aesthetes   b. drew attention to their history and language and eventually were drawn into the mainstream of art
3. decadence   c. thought nature was divorced from art so emphasized artifice
4. black aesthetic d. howled about the banality of their culture and looked for spiritual highs in sex and drugs

On a separate sheet of paper, write a sentence using each of these new words.

DID YOU KNOW? John Clellon Holmes, in the November 16, 1952, *New York Times Magazine*, wrote an essay explaining the beat philosophy: The beats were "raw"; they had been used; they felt a "loss of God" in the conforming culture but had a "will to believe," though not in conventional terms. They saw a "failure of most orthodox and social concepts" that do not reflect the life they know. Therefore, they felt "stirrings of a quest."

Words for Discussing Classical Mythology

Myths are stories that help explain mysteries. In ancient Greece and Rome, myths were tales about the wonders performed by gods and heroes. They were passed from generation to generation and often recited at public festivals. In this chapter you will find words, concepts, and an outline of some of these stories to help you read, discuss, and write about classical mythology.

DAY 1

Hesiod	Chaos	Gaea	Uranus

DAY 2

Chronus	Aphrodite	Titans	Zeus

DAY 3

Hera	Hades	Poseidon	Athena

DAY 4

Dionysius	Apollo	Medusa	Heracles

DAY 5

Atlas	Prometheus	Tiresius	Delphic oracle

DAY 6

Theseus	Amazons	Oedipus	Antigone

DAY 7

Trojan War	Odysseus	Aeneas	Thebes

Hesiod	This eighth-century B.C. poet brought order to the chronology and genealogy of the hundreds of gods in classical mythology, who interacted and interbred with one another and with mortals, and around whom were built hundreds of myths. WORDS IN CONTEXT: *Hesiod, with the help of Homer, codified and organized the lives of the gods and goddesses of Greek mythology in the* Theogony, *a genealogical map from which the information in this chapter derives.*
Chaos	According to **Hesiod**, in the beginning there was **Chaos**. Sometimes located in the underworld, **Chaos** was vague, undifferentiated matter out of which came *Erebus* (Darkness) and *Nyx* (Night). WORDS IN CONTEXT: *Chaos appears to be the parent of them all, for Darkness and Night had offspring: Hemera (Day) and Aether (Light). Night gave birth to a number of other elements as well, including Death and Sleep, and Eris, the goddess of Strife, who in turn bore Lethe (Forgetfulness.)*
Gaea	Earth Mother, "broad-bosomed . . . the solid and eternal home of all." Earth Mother seems to have begat herself by spontaneous generation, and then came *Eros* (Love), though **Hesiod** does not tell us that Eros was begat by Earth Mother. WORDS IN CONTEXT: *Gaea did, however, give birth to* **Uranus** *(Sky), among others, and then she turned around and mated with him.* **Gaea** *also is mother to Ourea (Mountains), Pontus (Sea), Echo, Rumor, and a host of others.*
Uranus	Father Sky (Uranus) and Mother Earth (Gaea) celebrated the birth of 12 *Titans*, who are the ancestors of almost all the major gods in Greek mythology. WORDS IN CONTEXT: *But* **Uranus** *was not a good father; he hid his children in the crevices of the earth as soon as they were born. When another son, Chronus, was about to be born,* **Uranus** *tried to prevent his birth by pushing him back into the earth womb. Chronus, as we will see, did not react well to that.*

After studying the definitions above, use these new words in the sentences below.

1. _____wrote the genealogy of classical mythological figures in the Theogony.
2. In the beginning, there was_____, out of which came all the elements of the earth.
3. _____gave birth to Sky, Mountains, Sea, and at least twelve strong children.
4. Father Sky was_____who, with Mother Earth, produced the Titans and Chronus, to whom he was not a good father.

Test Yourself: Write the letter next to the number to match word and definition.

1. Gaea   a. tried to prevent one son from being born
2. Uranus   b. the Earth Mother who gave birth to the father of her children
3. Chaos   c. wrote a chronology and genealogy of the gods
4. Hesiod   d. vague, amorphous matter from which many elements came

On a separate sheet of paper, write a sentence using each of these new words.

DID YOU KNOW?
Night, daughter of Chaos, gave birth to many unpleasant offspring, such as the Fates, Hunger, Quarrels, Sorrow, and Righteous Indignation.

Chronus	The son of Gaea and Uranus pushed his way out of the earth womb and took a scythe and cut off the penis of his father, Uranus, thus separating Earth and Sky. **Chronus** tossed the body part into the sea, but drops of blood fell onto the ground, and from the blood sprang the Furies, along with several giants and some nymphs.
	WORDS IN CONTEXT: *The severed organ that* **Chronus** *threw into the sea gathered foam, and from it was born* **Aphrodite**. **Chronus** *became chief of the* **Titans**, *married his sister Rhea, and fathered Hestia, Demeter, Hera, Hades (also known as Pluto), Poseidon, and* **Zeus**.
Aphrodite	The goddess of love, beauty, and fertility. She is youthful and nude in Botticelli's famous painting, *The Birth of Venus*, 1482. (Venus is the Roman name for **Aphrodite**.) She arose from the sea on the island of Cypress and married the crippled blacksmith god Hephaistos but bore children to several other gods including Dionysis and Ares.
	WORDS IN CONTEXT: *The goddess of love loved everyone:* **Aphrodite** *fell for the handsome Adonis. Then she helped start the Trojan War: To get Paris, the Trojan prince, to name her the most beautiful goddess, she promised him the most beautiful mortal woman, who turned out to be Helen, who, alas, had a husband, Menelaus, king of Sparta. This caused a problem.*
Titans	The twelve offspring of Earth and Sky, most of them gods of nature—water, sun, fertility, moon, and so forth. They intermarried, and the men went to war with **Zeus**.
	WORDS IN CONTEXT: *Hesiod described the* **Titans** *in his* Theogony. *The poet John Keats spoke extensively of the fallen* **Titans** *in* Hyperion *and* The Fall of Hyperion *(1818–1819).*
Zeus	A son of **Chronus**. Warned that one of his sons would overthrow him, **Chronus** swallowed his children as they were born. But his wife Rhea hid **Zeus,** who grew to manhood and overthrew his father in a 10-year war with the **Titans**.
	WORDS IN CONTEXT: *Stories about* **Zeus** *abound, but basically he became supreme ruler of the gods and was recognized by the thunderbolt he carried and hurled when agitated. After* **Zeus** *overthrew the* **Titans**, *he and his brothers divided the universe:* **Zeus** *took the sky, his brother Poseidon took the sea, and another brother, Hades, took the underworld.* **Zeus** *also had a startling amorous life.*

After studying the definitions above, use these new words in the sentences below.

1. _____ was the goddess of love, beauty, and fertility whose actions were instrumental in starting the Trojan War.
2. The supreme ruler of the gods_____ was recognizable by the thunderbolt he carried.
3. _____ were the twelve offspring of Earth and Sky, most of them gods of nature.
4. _____ emasculated his father with a curved knife and later became head of the Titans.

Test Yourself: Write the letter next to the number to match word and definition.

1. Chronus
2. Aphrodite

3. The Titans
4. Zeus

a. children of Gaea and Uranus who intermarried
b. he tossed a body part into the sea and from it was born the goddess of love, beauty, and fertility
c. she fell in love with Adonis and helped start the Trojan War
d. took the sky when brothers divided the universe

On a separate sheet of paper, write a sentence using each of these new words.

DID YOU KNOW?
Aphrodite had a magic girdle of love power, which in some stories Hera borrowed to turn Zeus's mind to thoughts of love when he was ready to fight a battle.

Hera	Daughter of Chronus and Rhea, and wife of her brother Zeus. Queen of the Olympians (the gods of Mount Olympus), she was a nag and a jealous wife—as well she might have been. **WORDS IN CONTEXT:** *Hera persecuted her husband's lovers, especially Semele, mother of Dionysus. She also hated Hercules, her husband's bastard son. With Zeus, **Hera** had Ares (god of war) and Hebe (goddess of youth). Without Zeus's help, she had Hephaestus (god of the forge)—in retaliation for Zeus's producing Athena from his own forehead.*
Hades	King of the underworld, also known as Pluto—the part of the universe he got when it was divided with his brothers, *Zeus* and **Poseidon**. **Hades** was not a devil and not a place in classical mythology. **Hades** was bearded and grim. He was married to *Persephone (daughter of Demeter, the goddess of grain)*, whom he abducted. **WORDS IN CONTEXT:** ***Hades's** realm, the underworld, was a dark, barren place inhabited by shades of the dead. Its deepest, blackest place of punishment was Tartarus into which Zeus hurled the Titans after overcoming them. Charon, the ferryman, took the dead across the river Styx into **Hades's** underworld, guarded by Cerberus, a three-headed dog.*
Poseidon	The major god of the sea. Depicted as an old man with a beard who holds a trident (a three-pronged fish spear); he was also god of earthquakes. He entered a contest with *Athena* to see who would be god of Athens. **Poseidon** struck a rock of the Acropolis and a horse sprang out. Athena's strike produced an olive tree. She was judged to be the winner. **WORDS IN CONTEXT:** ***Poseidon's** love affair with Medusa produced Pegasus (the flying horse), and he was father of the one-eyed Cyclops, Polyphemus. **Poseidon** took a stallion's form, mated with Demeter, and Arion, a talking horse, was born.*
Athena	The goddess of wisdom (having sprung full blown from the brow of *Zeus*), and the protector of cities. Depicted with helmet, spear, and shield (on which was the head of *Medusa*), Athena was a virgin. **WORDS IN CONTEXT:** *Stories abound about **Athena**. In one, Hephaestus tried to rape her and failed, but his semen hit the earth and Erichthonius sprang up. She put the baby in a basket and forbid anyone to look at it. Two girls did, and a furious **Athena** caused them to fling themselves to their deaths from the Acropolis. The baby, it seems, was hidden because it had snake legs.*

After studying the definitions above, use the names in the sentences below.

1. Zeus's bad-tempered wife, and queen of the gods of Mount Olympus was_____.
2. _____ was god of the sea, which he chose when three brothers divided the universe.
3. _____was not a devil, but king of the underworld, his part of the universe.
4. The goddess of wisdom who sprang full blown from Zeus's forehead was_____.

Test Yourself: Write the letter next to the number to match word and meaning.

1. Poseidon   a. wears armor and carries a shield with the face of Medusa on it
2. Hades   b. carries a three-pronged spear for fishing
3. Athena   c. queen of the gods and a nag
4. Hera   d. does not look like a devil but a mature, grim man

On a separate sheet of paper, write a sentence using each of these new words.

DID YOU KNOW? Demeter, daughter of Chronus and Rhea, was the goddess of grain and the mother of Persephone, who plucked a flower and found under it a huge hole to the underworld from which Hades emerged and abducted her. Demeter was so doleful that crops refused to grow. Hades finally consented to let Persephone return to earth for two-thirds of the year and live the other third below with him. This created the cycle of the seasons: the time Persephone spent below being when the fields were barren.

Dionysus	God of wine, vitality, sexuality, and animal instinct. Patron of music, art, and drama. Usually depicted as young with flowing hair, followed by a band of frenzied nymphs and satyrs drunk on wine and sexual excitement. **Dionysus** was connected with strange worship rituals. **WORDS IN CONTEXT:** *Dionysus held grudges. Often punishment for those who had done him wrong was being torn to pieces by wild animals.* **Dionysus** *and his followers represent unbridled emotions and instincts run amok.*
Apollo	Half-brother of **Dionysus, Apollo** was his opposite: calm, orderly, a balance of vitality and reason. He was the god of music, poetry, archery, and prophecy, and he had a temple at Delphi. Later he came to be associated with the sun. Many stories surround **Apollo**, who had catastrophic love affairs. **WORDS IN CONTEXT:** *Apollo pursued Daphne, who became a laurel tree to escape him. He also loved the Trojan princess Cassandra and gave her the gift of prophecy. When she rejected him, he added a penalty: no one would believe her.*
Medusa	One of three hideous sisters. She had hair made of snakes, and whoever looked into her face would turn to stone. **WORDS IN CONTEXT:** *Perseus set out to kill* **Medusa,** *a difficult feat without facing her. But Perseus tricked her: he saw her reflection in his shiny shield and was able to cut off her head as she slept.* **Medusa's** *head was placed on Athena's breastplate, and one look at it would paralyze men in battle.*
Heracles	Son of *Zeus* and *Alcmene,* he was the greatest Greek hero. (The Romans called him *Hercules.)* Giant and monster killer, **Heracles** wore a lion skin and carried a club. He is best known for performing Twelve Labors ranging from slaying fierce beasts to cleaning the Augean stables. **WORDS IN CONTEXT:** *Heracles was married to Theban princess Megara, but took many lovers and sired many children. Hera, in her jealousy of him, struck him mad. He died when the blood of a man he had killed consumed his flesh. His body was placed on a lighted pyre, his mortal part burned away, and he rose to heaven.*

After studying the definitions above, use the names in the sentences below.

1. God of wine, women, and song, followed by a frenzied band of satyrs, _____ represents unbridled emotions.
2. Every day for _____ was a bad hair day, and her face turned men to stone.
3. Calm, wise _____ was god of prophecy, poetry, and archery, but the nymph he pursued preferred to be a tree rather than surrender to him.
4. The great Greek hero, _____, slayer of giants and monsters, had Twelve Labors to undergo.

Test Yourself: Write the letter next to the number to match word and definition.

1. Heracles   a. if you got on his bad side, you would be torn to pieces
2. Medusa   b. he carried a club and wore a lion's skin
3. Dionysus   c. Perseus cut off her head without having to face her
4. Apollo   d. he got back at Cassandra when she rejected him

On a separate sheet of paper, write a sentence using each of these new words.

DID YOU KNOW?
Leda became the mother of the beautiful Helen and three other children when Zeus fell in love with her. He took the shape of a swan and seduced her. Several versions of this story exist, but one of the most memorable is W. B. Yeats's poem, "Leda and the Swan," in which, after the coupling of god and mortal, the poet asks: "Did she put on his knowledge with his power/ Before the indifferent beak could let her drop?" Clytemnestra in some versions hatched from the same egg as her sister Helen, became the wife of Agamemnon, king of Mycenae, leader of the Greeks in the Trojan War.

Atlas	A giant whose chore it was to hold the sky on his shoulders. In one of his labors, *Heracles* persuaded **Atlas** to fetch some golden apples for him; meanwhile Heracles offered to hold up the sky. **Atlas** produced the apples but planned to leave Heracles holding up the sky permanently. **WORDS IN CONTEXT:** *Heracles agreed to hold up the sky, but asked **Atlas** to take the sky for a moment while he got himself a cushion for his shoulders. Once **Atlas** took the sky, Heracles made off with the golden apples, leaving **Atlas** holding the sky.*
Prometheus	Son of a Titan, **Prometheus** stole fire from the heavens and brought it back to earth to humans. Zeus punished him by binding him to a mountain, where he hung for eons as an eagle devoured his liver. **WORDS IN CONTEXT:** *In Aeschylus' drama* Prometheus Bound, ***Prometheus** is noted for bringing most of the arts of civilization to mortals. He suffered for ages bound to the rock (part of the time in Tartarus, the depths of hell). Eventually, Heracles set him free.*
Tiresias	The greatest mythological prophet. Born a man, he came upon two snakes mating and killed the female. He immediately turned into a woman. Seven years later, he came upon another couple of snakes mating; this time he killed the male and was turned immediately back into a man. **WORDS IN CONTEXT:** *Because **Tiresias** had lived both as a man and a woman, when Zeus and Hera had an argument about sex—Hera saying that men enjoyed sex more, and Zeus saying the opposite—they called on **Tiresias** to settle the argument. He said that women enjoyed sex more. Angry, Hera struck him blind. But Zeus, hearing what he wanted to, gave him the gift of prophecy.*
Delphic oracle	On a side of Mount Parnassus in central Greece the **Delphic oracle** was established by Apollo. This was a prophetic shrine, a hole in the ground, out of which vapors arose. *Pythia*, priestess of Apollo at **Delphi,** spoke prophecies in verse from the shrine. **WORDS IN CONTEXT:** *Visitors went to the **Delphic oracle** for guidance, asking questions and seeking advice. The hidden **oracle** chanted prophesies. Here too the Omphalus was located—a stone that marked the navel or center of the earth.*

After studying these definitions, use these new words in the sentences below.

1. _____was destined for life to have a backache because he had to hold up the sky.
2. _____lived as both man and woman and learned the sensibilities of each.
3. A hole in the ground from which a voice gave prophecies was the _____.
4. This god,_____, was the mortal's advocate; he stole fire from heaven for humanity.

Test Yourself: Write the letter next to the number to match word and definition.

1. Atlas   a. settled a sex spat between Zeus and Hera and got a mixed reward
2. Prometheus   b. vapor and voice rose from this near the navel of the earth
3. Tiresias   c. ever since his theft, mortal people can cook dinner and stay warm
4. Delphic oracle   d. was tricked into holding a heavy burden forever

On a separate sheet of paper, write a sentence using each new word.

DID YOU KNOW?
The twin sister of Apollo, Artemis, was goddess of the hunt who protected animals. Because she protected the young, she became goddess of birth and women. Artemis (called Diana in Rome) dressed for the hunt in high boots and tunic and carried a bow and quiver.

Theseus	Son of Aegeus, king of Athens, and Aethra. The king hid a sword and sandals under a stone and instructed his son to get them and head for Athens. **Theseus** began his journey, and on the way he met six difficult challenges.
	WORDS IN CONTEXT: *The adventures of* **Theseus** *roughly parallel the labors of Heracles: He encountered Procrustes, who had a plan: if a guest did not fit precisely into the bed he offered, Procrustes lopped off limbs to make him fit.* **Theseus** *gave Procrustes his own treatment.* **Theseus** *also confronted the ferocious minotaur—half bull, half man—in the Labyrinth, a tunnel of winding passages on the island of Crete. Ariadne, daughter of King Minos of Crete, gave* **Theseus** *a ball of string to unwind behind him, so after he killed the minotaur, he would be able find his way out. Ariadne wanted to marry him, but he quickly sailed away.*
Amazons	A tribe of women warriors who cut off their right breasts to more easily use their bows. The **Amazons** reputedly did not care for men and cared only for their female offspring.
	WORDS IN CONTEXT: *In mythology, the* **Amazons** *appeared in stories in which they fought against Perseus, Heracles, and others. As allies of the Trojans, they turned up at the siege of Troy.*
Oedipus	The son of Laius, king of Thebes, whom the king had left out for the wolves because it had been prophesied that **Oedipus** would kill him and marry his wife. **Oedipus** was rescued and later went to the Delphic oracle for news of his parents. The oracle gave no straight answer, but warned him that he would kill his father and marry his mother.
	WORDS IN CONTEXT: *As he left,* **Oedipus** *had a road incident with an old man who made him so angry that he killed the old man. At Thebes he answered the riddle of the Sphinx, a creature with a lion's body and woman's face, and the grateful Thebans made him king. As a gift, they gave him Jocasta—the widow of the man he had killed, the king Jocasta (are you surprised?)—who turned out to be his own mother.*
Antigone	The truth about Oedipus' background came out after he had sired four children with his mother, *Jocasta,* one of whom was **Antigone. Oedipus** was so mortified at what he had done that he blinded himself, prompting Jocasta to commit suicide.
	WORDS IN CONTEXT: **Antigone** *insisted on burying her dead brother, Polynices, whom Creon, king of Thebes, refused burial. For punishment,* **Antigone** *was entombed in a cave to starve, where she took her own life. Her fiancé, Haemon, the king's son, found her dead and killed himself, whereupon his mother, Eurydice, hanged herself.*

After studying the definitions above, use these new words in the sentences below.

1. These tall women,_____, had only one breast and used bows and arrows.
2. This man_____had a father who abandoned him, and in trying to escape his prophecied fate, he ran right into it: his mother, whom he married.
3. This man,_____, escaped having his limbs cut off to fit a bed, and then he escaped a Labyrinth.
4. This daughter of Oedipus,_____, escaped starving in a tomb by killing herself.

Test Yourself: Write the letter next to the number to match word and definition.

1. Theseus   a. she was only trying to bury her dead brother so wolves wouldn't eat him
2. Amazons   b. had no use for men and reared only their daughters
3. Antigone   c. a truly sad life: he blinded himself, and his mother hanged herself
4. Oedipus   d. his adventures roughly paralleled the labors of Heracles

On a separate sheet of paper, write sentences using each of these new words.

DID YOU KNOW?
The Argonauts were sea-goers whose ship Argo was led by Jason in search of the Golden Fleece. Like Odysseus, these mariners wandered and ran into many dangerous situations. Jason and wife Medea had a tragic relationship in which he abducted their children, and Medea slayed them to punish him.

Trojan War	Began with a beauty contest among Hera, Athena, and Aphrodite, all claiming to be the "fairest." *Paris*, the Trojan prince, was called to arbitrate. He gave the prize to Aphrodite, who promised him the most beautiful mortal woman in the world, Helen, married to the king of Sparta. Paris kidnapped Helen, setting off the war. The story is told in the *Iliad* and the *Aeneid*. **WORDS IN CONTEXT:** *Greek warriors rallied to the king's side, among them **Odysseus**, Achilles, Ajax, Patroclus. On the Trojan side, prominent figures were Hector and Paris. Many battles ensued. Finally, a great wooden horse filled with Greek warriors was rolled inside the gates of Troy. At night the Greeks emerged and slaughtered the Trojans.*
Odysseus	The great Greek warrior spent 10 years wandering after the fall of Troy before he reached his home in Ithaca and his wife Penelope. During this time he had many adventures, which are recounted in the *Odyssey*, in Dante's *Divine Comedy*, in Tennyson's poem "Ulysses," and in James Joyce's novel *Ulysses*. **WORDS IN CONTEXT:** *On his journey home, **Odysseus** encountered Lotus-Eaters, the Cyclops, a bag of wind that blew him off course, a sorceress Circe, a monster whirlpool that sucked in ships, sirens to seduce him, a beautiful nymph Calypso—all of which make wonderfully exciting stories.*
Aeneas	The son of Aphrodite and the Trojan prince Anchises, Aeneas was the founder of the Romans and hero of Roman stories as well as of Virgil's *Aeneid*. After the Trojan War, **Aeneas** wandered as **Odysseus** did; unlike **Odysseus** he was not shrewd and clever, but sober and responsible. **Aeneas** was a homebody, forever in search of a home. **WORDS IN CONTEXT:** ***Aeneas** left Troy with his father on his back and leading his son by the hand. In his wanderings, **Aeneas** captivated Dido, who committed suicide when he left her. In Sicily, the Sibyl guided **Aeneas** to the underworld. In Latium, near Rome, he married Lavinia and founded the city of Lavinium. His visit to the underworld is recounted in Dante's* Divine Comedy. *His affair with Dido is recounted in Purcell's opera,* Dido and Aeneas.
Thebes	The location in which many important Greek myths took place: the stories of *Dionysus* and *Heracles*, *Oedipus* and *Antigone*. Other great literature is set here: Sophocles's *Oedipus Tyrannus*, *Oedipus at Colonus*, and *Antigone*; the play by Aeschylus *Seven against Thebes*, and Ovid's *Metamorphosis*. **WORDS IN CONTEXT:** *The story of Niobe was set in **Thebes**. Niobe had seven sons and seven daughters; she bragged that her children were superior to Apollo and Artemis. Apollo killed all her sons, and Artemis killed her daughters. Finally Niobe left **Thebes**, returning to her father in Lydia, where she was turned to stone and became Mount Sipylus. There, her tears in streams of water flow eternally.*

After studying the definitions above, use the words in the sentences below.

1. _____began with a beauty contest and ended with a fake horse and many dead men.
2. The site of many mythological stories including those of Oedipus, Antigone, and Niobe was_____.
3. This man looking for a home,_____, was founder of the Roman people and hero of many Roman myths.
4. On his 10-year journey home to Ithaca_____underwent dangerous and exciting adventures with water, wind, giants, witches, seductresses and more, but he finally made it home to Penelope, his wife.

Test Yourself: Write the letter next to the number to match word and definition.

1. Trojan War   a. the site of many mythological stories
2. Odysseus   b. a wandering Greek of many adventures
3. Aeneas   c. a wandering Roman searching for a home
4. Thebes   d. it was all Paris's fault

On a separate sheet of paper, write a sentence using each new word.

DID YOU KNOW? These are only a few of the words, characters, concepts, and stories in classical mythology—all of them colorful, dramatic, layered, and textured and still exciting reading today. By the way, what was that riddle of the Sphinx that Oedipus answered? THE RIDDLE: "What goes on four legs in the morning, on two at noon, and on three at night?" OEDIPUS'S ANSWER: "Man—in infancy, he crawls; in his prime, he walks; in old age, he leans on a staff."

Words for Discussing the Bible

The Bible is the most widely read, most published, and most influential book in the history of the world. No other book has been so studied and analyzed. This chapter will give you some words, concepts, and outlines of history that will help you read, discuss, and write about the Bible.

DAY 1

| polytheism | monotheism | deism | dualism |

DAY 2

| Jesus Christ | Holy Trinity | heaven | hell |

DAY 3

| Hebrew Bible | Septuagint | Latin Bible | Apocrypha |

DAY 4

| Roman Catholic Bible | Protestant Bible | Pentateuch | versions |

DAY 5

| apostles | Sermon on the Mount | beatitudes | Second Coming |

DAY 6

| Decalogue | Satan | eschatology | apocalypse |

DAY 7

| predestination | original sin | purgatory | indulgences |

polytheism	The belief in many gods, or more than one god. Early beliefs were **polytheistic**; **monotheism** was a late development in the history of ideas.
	WORDS IN CONTEXT: *As classical mythology has shown, ancient Greeks and Romans were **polytheists.** They believed in multiple gods who intervened on behalf of mortals and sometimes cursed them and intermarried with them.*
monotheism	The belief that there is only one god, from the Greek *mono* (one) and *theos* (god). Also called *theism*.
	WORDS IN CONTEXT: *The Bible is the sacred book of Jews and Christians who believe in the one God described therein; this belief is **monotheistic**—a legacy the Jews, the first **monotheists**, passed on to the Christians.*
deism	Belief in the existence of God as a creative force on rational grounds, but the **deist** form of belief rejects formal religion and doctrines of revelation and divine authority.
	WORDS IN CONTEXT: *Deism was the doctrine prevalent among rationalists in the seventeenth and eighteenth centuries: God created the world and its natural laws but takes no further part in its functioning. **Deism** denies miracles and God's intervention.*
dualism	The doctrine that two mutually antagonistic principles exist—good and evil—and that humankind has two natures, physical and spiritual.
	WORDS IN CONTEXT: *Though Christianity is a **monotheistic** religion, it is **dualistic** in its inclusion of righteousness and sin, God and the devil.*

After studying the definitions above, use these new words in the sentences below.

1. _____ is the doctrine that there is only one god.
2. The worship of many or more than one god is _____.
3. The idea of mutually antagonistic forces in the universe is _____.
4. A rationalist's view that God is a creative force no longer acting is _____.

Test Yourself: Write the letter next to the number to match word and meaning.

1. deism   a. good and evil are antagonistic forces in the universe
2. monotheism   b. the belief in more than one god, as the Greeks did
3. dualism   c. the belief that God created the world and then withdrew
4. polytheism   d. the belief in one god, the God of the Bible

On a separate sheet of paper, write a sentence using each of these new words.

DID YOU KNOW?
Another "ism" is pantheism, from the Greek pan (all) and theos (god), the doctrine that God is not a personality but is everything in the universe. God is inseparable from everything—nature, laws, forces—that exist. God is all things. The pantheistic nature of God is found in Hinduism in which God (Brahmin) is all reality, and everything else is illusion.

Jesus Christ	Believed by Christians to be the son of God and the mortal Mary. In the eighth century B.C., the Jewish prophet Micah foretold that a "ruler" would come from Bethlehem (Mic. 5:2). Jesus Christ was born between 6 and 3 C.E., and Luke recorded it about 65 C.E. (Luke 2:4–5). When Jesus was baptized (24 to 27 C.E.), Luke wrote that "the Holy Spirit" descended in the form of a dove, and a voice from heaven said, "Thou art my beloved Son, in thee I am well pleased." (Luke 4: 21–22) **WORDS IN CONTEXT:** *In the eighth century B.C., the prophet Isaiah warned that "He shall be led as a sheep to the slaughter," and Luke later confirmed, "They crucified him there" (Luke 23:33-34). These are key events in the origins of the Christian belief in* **Jesus Christ** *as the son of God. Many other prophecies in the Old Testament were fulfilled in the New Testament, pointing to Jesus, according to Christians, as the son of God.*
Holy Trinity	Three gods in one. Though Christianity is a monotheistic religion, it came to worship God the Father, God the Son, and God the Holy Spirit (also known as the Holy Ghost) in one Godhead. This link was established by a church father, *Tertullian*, from evidence he found in Matthew 28:19. **WORDS IN CONTEXT:** *There, Tertullian discovered that Jesus said, "Go, therefore, and make disciples of all nations, baptizing them in the name of the Father and of the Son and of the Holy Spirit." He also found in Luke 1:35 the angel Gabriel announcing Jesus in Mary's womb: " The Holy Spirit will come upon you, and the power of the Most High will overshadow you; therefore the child to be born will be called holy, the Son of God." After much controversy, late in the fourth century A.D., Christian fathers wrote the final Nicean Creed linking the three in a* **Holy Trinity** *"of the same essence." Thereafter, Christians have worshipped three gods in one.*
heaven	The definition of **heaven** appears to have evolved with the needs of people in various cultures. Most Jews believed in the immortal soul, but not in a physical resurrection of the dead. Early Christians' images of **heaven** included a city of "pure gold, clear as glass" with precious stones (Rev. 4:2–8). Later Christians envisioned an everlasting life where God "will wipe away every tear … and death shall be no more, neither shall there be mourning nor crying nor pain…" (Rev. 21:4). **WORDS IN CONTEXT:** *The Old Testament makes no reference to* **heaven.** *Today, for most Jews,* **heaven** *is reward for taking care of life's obligations. Christian* **heaven** *is life with God, pain-free and peaceful, surrounded by loved ones. Roman Catholic* **heaven** *has tiers of bliss, depending on the degree of sanctifying grace each person has at the moment of death.*
hell	Basically, hell is for other people. And we don't know what it is. The Old Testament does not mention **hell.** It mentions Sheol, a lower world where all souls exist as thirsty ghosts. This was **hell** for early Jews, but most today do not believe in **hell**. **WORDS IN CONTEXT:** **Hell** *is mentioned in the New Testament (Matt. 13:23, 25), and here Christians got the idea of "the furnace of fire" and the "wailing and gnashing of teeth." The book of Revelation paints* **hell** *as even worse, with cosmic forces in combat.*

After studying the definitions above, use these new words in the sentences below.

1. According to Christianity, _____ is the son of God, born to a human woman, Mary.
2. The Father, the Son, and the Holy Spirit comprise the_____
3. _____ is the final resting place of the virtuous, though it has several definitions depending on one's religion.
4. In some religions, _____ is the place the wicked are consigned to after death.

Test Yourself: Write the letter next to the number to match word and meaning.

1. Jesus Christ   a. Christians see this as a place of everlasting life with God
2. hell   b. the three-person Godhead of Christianity
3. Holy Trinity   c. *Sheol*, fire and wailing, or cosmic forces in combat
4. heaven   d. according to the Bible, the son of God born in Bethlehem

On a separate sheet of paper, write a sentence using each of these new words.

DID YOU KNOW?
The ancient Israelites did not know how to define *soul*. In fact, the concept never occurred to them. But it did to Plato in the fourth century B.C. He said that the soul was the vital essence of a person; that it was light as air and floated high above the stars to the Isle of the Blest. This vital essence Plato called the psyche, which means "to blow." In Genesis we find, "Then God formed man out of the dust of the ground and breathed into his nostrils the breath of life, and man became a living being" (2:7).

Hebrew Bible	The sacred text of the Jews that consists of the Old Testament. Accounts here began about 4000 B.C. and are the first continuously recorded history of humankind.
	WORDS IN CONTEXT: *The **Hebrew Bible** is arranged thus: I. The Law (Torah); II. The Prophets; III. The Writings. The Prophets are divided into "Former Prophets" and "Latter Prophets." Present-day Jews use the **Hebrew Bible** arrangement of content but use the individual book names of the Christian Bible.*
Septuagint	The Greek version of the Old Testament used by Greek-speaking Jews of the ancient world and by early Christians. It had its roots in the **Hebrew Bible** composed in the third to first centuries B.C. and differs somewhat from the **Hebrew Bible** of today. (Note that *Septuagint* means *70* and is called this because it is thought to have been translated by 70 men.)
	WORDS IN CONTEXT: *Though ancient manuscripts of the **Septuagint** offer varied ordering of the books, most agree that the arrangement was I. books of Law and History and II. Poetic and Prophetic books.*
Latin Bible	Christian translators between the second and fifth centuries brought the **Latin Bible** into existence. *St. Jerome (d. 410), who translated from the **Hebrew Bible** rather than the Greek, was instrumental in this.*
	WORDS IN CONTEXT: *The **Latin Bible** since 1545 (the Council of Trent that established the canon for Roman Catholics) has contained the Old Testament and 27 books of the New Testament, but it cast two books of Edras (which Christians call Ezra and Nehemiah) and The Prayer of Manasseh into the index as **apocryphal**.*
Apocrypha	Literally meaning "hidden, as in a crypt." These are writings of dubious authenticity or authorship as judged by scholars or translators of the time. Specifically, these are 14 books of the **Septuagint** that Judaism rejected and Protestantism regarded as not a part of the canon (including the three books rejected by the Roman Catholics).
	WORDS IN CONTEXT: *Eleven books that Jews and Protestants rejected and thus relegated to the **apocrypha** were accepted by the Roman Catholics. The **Apocrypha** are composed of various writings that some thought were falsely attributed to Biblical characters or were not the result of revelation.*

After studying the definitions above, use these new words in the sentences below.

1. St. Jerome translated the_____from the Hebrew Bible.
1. The_____is composed of writings whose authenticity Jews and Protestants doubt.
1. The Greek version of the Old Testament translated by 70 men is the_____.
1. The first recorded history of humankind in which the belief system of the Jews is grounded is the_____.

Test Yourself: Write the letter next to the number to match word and meaning.

1. Apocrypha — a. the Greek Bible, sometimes called "Seventy"
1. Hebrew Bible — b. writings Protestants and Jews reject
1. Latin Bible — c. in 1564 it became the canon of Roman Catholics
1. Septuagint — d. I. The Law (Torah), II. The Prophets, III. The Writings

On a separate sheet of paper, write a sentence using each of these new words.

DID YOU KNOW?
The following expressions that people use every day originally came from the Bible. "Eat, drink, and be merry" comes from Ecclesiastes 8:18: "A man hath no better thing under the sun, than to eat, and to drink, and to be merry." The "skin of our teeth" is taken from Job 19:19: "My bone clings to my skin and to my flesh, and I have escaped with the skin of my teeth." "A stumbling block" can be traced to Romans 14:13: "Judge this rather, that no man put a stumbling block or an occasion to fall in his brother's way."

Roman Catholic Bible	This, The New American Bible, which appeared in 1970 and was translated by 50 scholars, is very like the Latin Bible with a few organizational changes; it incorporates the books of Ezra and Nehemiah but does not include the Latin Bible appendix. **WORDS IN CONTEXT:** *Of the 15 books that Protestants found apocryphal (during the Reformation, Martin Luther put them in an appendix to the Old Testament, writing that they are "not held to be equal to holy scripture and yet are profitable and good to read"), the **Roman Catholic Bible** accepts 12.*
Protestant Bible	The Old Testament in **Protestant Bibles** contains only the books that appear in the Hebrew Bible. Other books of the Greek and Latin Bibles are omitted or added in a separate section, the Apocrypha. **WORDS IN CONTEXT:** *The **Protestant Bible** contains both Old and New Testaments. The content and arrangement of the New Testament are identical in the **Protestant Bible** and the Roman Catholic Bible.*
Pentateuch	This term (Greek for "five scrolls") is the name for the first five books of the Old Testament. Hebrew-speaking Jews called the five books the Law (Torah). **WORDS IN CONTEXT:** *The **Pentateuch** explains how the Israelites became the chosen people of God and outlined the people's relationship to God. The five books are the following: Genesis, Exodus, Leviticus, Numbers, and Deuteronomy. Long thought to have been written by Moses, the **Pentateuch,** scholars now believe, was put together in stages over a period of 700 years.*
versions	Translations of the Bible into languages different from the ones in which it was originally written (Hebrew, Aramaic, and Greek). The original manuscripts were written on papyrus (a water plant from which a kind of paper was made) and animal skins. **WORDS IN CONTEXT:** *By the time the printing press was invented (mid-fifteenth century), the Bible had been translated into 33 languages or **versions.** In the nineteenth century, an additional 500 **versions** were available. Today, more than 2000 **versions** have been translated and printed.*

After studying the definitions above, use these new words in the sentences below.

1. The first five books of the Old Testament, which Jews call The Law is_____.
2. Translations of the Bible from the original Hebrew, Aramaic, or Greek are called _____.
3. The New American Bible, which is very like the Latin Bible, is the_____.
4. _____contains Old and New Testaments, the Old from the Hebrew Bible.

Test Yourself: Write the letter next to the number to match word and meaning.

1. Pentateuch   a. translations of the Bible into languages other than the original
2. Catholic Bible   b. accepts 12 books rejected by the Jews and Protestants
3. versions   c. Genesis, Exodus, Leviticus, Numbers, and Deuteronomy
4. Protestant Bible   d. contains the Hebrew Old Testament and the New Testament

On a separate sheet of paper, write a sentence using each of these new words.

DID YOU KNOW?
John Wycliff (1320–1384) did the first complete translation of the Bible into English. After the Reformation (sixteenth century) the following translations were produced: Tyndale's Bible (1525), Coverdale's Bible (1535), the Great Bible (1539), the Geneva Bible (1561), the Bishops' Bible (1568), the Douay Bible (English Catholic version, 1582–1610), and the King James version (1611). Several revised standard versions have been issued since the first in 1946.

apostles	The 12 men chosen by Jesus to follow him and spread his gospel after his death. From the Greek *apostolos* meaning "one who is sent away"; today we might call them missionaries devoted passionately to a special cause. Also known as *disciples*. In the New Testament, an **apostle** has a teacher, in this case Jesus, with whom he studies. Then the **apostle** travels, preaching the message of that teacher. **WORDS IN CONTEXT:** *The 12 apostles of Jesus were Simon (called Peter), Andrew (Peter's brother), James, John (James's brother), Philip, Bartholomew, Thomas, Matthew, another James, Thaddaeus, and Judas. Judas became Jesus's betrayer. Paul also became an apostle. He never met Jesus but took up his mission after Jesus died.*
Sermon on the Mount	In the New Testament (Matt.), the first sermon of Jesus, which he spoke in Aramaic. It contains the central message of the new age that he had come to proclaim. "Be perfect … even as your Father which is in heaven is perfect," he said. This sermon includes the beatitudes, the Lord's Prayer, and the Golden Rule ("Whatsoever ye would that men should do to you, do ye even so to them.") **WORDS IN CONTEXT:** *In the Sermon on the Mount, Jesus also introduced teachings that have since become familiar: Turn the other cheek; cast not pearls before swine; love your enemies; you cannot serve God and Mammon (riches or the pursuit of wealth); judge not that you be not judged; ask and it shall be given unto you.*
beatitudes	The word comes from the Latin *blessed*. Each line of the eight **beatitudes** begins with the word *blessed*. (Matthew lists eight, but Luke lists only four.) These are promises by Jesus to those who behave in godly ways. **WORDS IN CONTEXT:** *The beatitudes contain these lines and others: Blessed are the merciful; for they shall obtain mercy. Blessed are the clean of heart; for they shall see God. Blessed are they that hunger and thirst after justice; for they shall have their fill.*
Second Coming	After Jesus was crucified, it was prophesied in the New Testament that he would return to judge the living and the dead and to see that good triumphed over evil. On this Judgment Day, Christians believe, Jesus will judge the conduct of both the living and the dead and will consider the way they have treated other people as if they had done these deeds, both good and bad, to him. **WORDS IN CONTEXT:** *The apostles, writing in the New Testament after Jesus' death, wrote as if they expected the Second Coming to occur within a generation of their own time. In the Book of Revelation, this Judgment Day and Second Coming are described in visionary terms with symbolic meanings.*

After studying the definitions above, use these new words in the sentences below.

1. _____ are the men that Jesus chose to learn from him and carry his message to others.
2. _____: the word means *blessed*, and each line begins with it.
3. The prophecy of the_____ foretold that Jesus would return to judge the living and the dead.
4. The first sermon that Jesus preached was the_____, in which he spoke about what he expected of his followers and presented the Golden Rule.

Test Yourself: Write the letter next to the number to match word and meaning.

1. beatitudes   a. the return of Jesus on Judgment Day
2. Sermon on the Mount   b. Christ's 12 missionaries
3. Second Coming   c. contains the Golden Rule and the Lord's prayer
4. apostles   d. Christ's promises to his followers in his sermon

On a separate sheet of paper, write a sentence using each of these new words.

DID YOU KNOW?
The Bible contains almost every literary genre: songs—those of Solomon, Deborah, Lamech, and Miriam. Folk tales, legends, romances, tragedies, short stories. It even contains a novel, the ironic story of Esther. The Bible gives us poetry—love lyrics, odes, hymns, dramatic monologues—and it contains wildly visionary drama in Revelation. It tells of crooked kings, mad men, fallen women, lost children, and heroic people of all races.

Decalogue	Meaning "ten words," this is the moral law inscribed on two stone tablets that God gave to Moses. We call the **Decalogue** the Ten Commandments. These were the laws according to which God's chosen people were to conduct themselves. **WORDS IN CONTEXT:** *Jewish tradition considers the First Commandment to be "I am the Lord your God who brought you out of the land of Egypt, out of the house of bondage." Buddhism has Ten Precepts much like the **Decalogue**, though it adds: "Thou shalt not eat after midday." Similarly, the Islamic Koran has a **decalogue**, the tenth law being "Do not strut about the land with insolence."*
Satan	The evildoer in Christian theology. In the New Testament, St. Paul writes that God's forces are clothed in an "armor of light," but **Satan** rules "the dominion of darkness." This dualist view is reinforced in **Satan's** being "below" in "hell," while God lives "above" in "heaven." **WORDS IN CONTEXT:** *In the book of Revelation, as well as in the books of Matthew, Mark, Luke, and John, **Satan** is God's archenemy and the personification of evil. Other names for him in the world of Western literature are Beelzebub, Devil, Lucifer, Baal, Prince of Darkness, Evil One, Antichrist, Mephistopheles, Abaddon, and Apollyon.*
eschatology	The branch of theology that deals with "end things": death, resurrection, judgment, and immortality. The word comes from the Greek meaning *further out*. **WORDS IN CONTEXT:** *An **eschatological** passage in the Bible occurs in the epistles of John. John writes: "Dear children, it is the last time; and as you have heard that anti-christ is coming, so now many anti-christs have arisen; whereby we know that it is the last hour" (1 John 2:18). Here John the apostle warns Christians that the increasing presence of false prophets heralds the end of the world.*
apocalypse	Deriving from the Greek *to disclose*, **apocalypse** means a disclosure regarded as prophetic, or a revelation. **WORDS IN CONTEXT:** ***Apocalyptic*** *writings are those that depict symbolically the ultimate destruction of evil and triumph of good. The book of Revelation, the last book of the New Testament written by John (thought not to be the apostle John), holds out a bewildering, phantasmagoric picture of the end of the world in which a bleeding lamb breaks seven seals on a scroll and unleashes the wrath of God.*

After studying the definitions above, use each new word in the sentences below.

1. Meaning *ten words*, the_____is what we call the Ten Commandments.
2. _____is God's archenemy, the evildoer, an anti-christ.
3. Concepts dealing with "the end," such as death, resurrection, and redemption are called_____.
4. Prophesies or revelations symbolically describing the death of evil and the triumph of good are called_____writings.

Test Yourself: Write the letter next to the number to match word and meaning.

1. apocalypse   a. God gave this to Moses on two stone tablets
2. Satan   b. other names for this creature are Beelzebub, Devil, Baal
3. eschatology   c. in which good wins out over evil in the end
4. Decalogue   d. branch of theology that deals with end things

On a separate sheet of paper, write a sentence using each of these new words.

DID YOU KNOW?
The Bible should watch its language. Errors occur even there—a scary thought when some readers take its words entirely literally. In the Geneva Bible: "Christ condemns the poor widow." (correction: commends) In another version: "Let the children first be killed." (correction: filled) In the "Breeches Bible" in the story of Adam and Eve, the word "apron" was mistranslated, so the good book has our first parents covering their nakedness with "breeches." The worst blooper: in a London Bible of 1631, "Thou shalt commit adultery." (Oops!)

predestination	Early Christians thought that God predetermined the fate of a person, then led the person into that fate. (Not unlike the way Greek gods dealt with Oedipus.) Others who considered this were St. Paul (Rom. 8-11), Matthew (20:23), and John (6:44-45, 66). In the fourth century, St. Augustine concluded that God "elected" some people, so that an "elected" person's salvation came only through the mercy of God. **WORDS IN CONTEXT:** *In 529, the Council of Orange determined that God does indeed "elect" certain people, but thereafter each person must, by choices granted by God through free will, create his or her own destiny or salvation. The Council of Trent in 1545 declared that God does not* **predestine** *any person to go to heaven or hell.*
original sin	Sex was a real problem in early Christianity. Because Adam and Eve disobeyed God, ate from the tree of knowledge in Eden, saw they were naked, and presumably had sex, humankind has been tainted ever since. The fall of man, as described in Genesis (3: 1–23) brought the wrath of God—pain, death, and suffering—on humanity. **WORDS IN CONTEXT:** *Psalms (51:5):"Behold, I was brought forth in iniquity, and in sin did my mother conceive me" appears to be ameliorated by Jesus' coming in Romans 5: 12–19: "Then as one man's trespass led to condemnation for all men, so by one man's act of righteousness leads to acquittal and life for all men." These passages seem to suggest that Christ redeemed Adam's* **original sin.**
purgatory	The notion of a place somewhere between heaven and hell to which one is consigned to "burn off" minor (or *venal*) sins is not supported, most scholars agree, by Biblical scripture. The Council of Trent in the sixteenth century, in reaction to the Protestant Reformation's opposition to Roman Catholicism's doctrine of **purgatory,** defined the location and function of such a place. **WORDS IN CONTEXT:** *This definition of* **purgatory,** *by which family or loved ones could release dead souls to heaven through prayer, fasting, and* **indulgences**, *opened the way to abuse.*
indulgences	Release of a loved one from **purgatory** by paying money. **WORDS IN CONTEXT:** **Indulgences,** *or cash to get into heaven, was not an idea that reformer Martin Luther could tolerate. Luther changed the course of religious history in 1520 by standing before officials of the Church at the Diet of Worms in total defiance, saying, "Here I stand. I can do no other." Thus was born the Protestant Reformation.*

After studying the definitions above, use each new word in the sentences below.

1. _____is a place between heaven and hell where people with trifling sins are consigned.
2. The paying of money to Catholic church officials to spring loved ones from purgatory is called the buying of_____.
3. The idea that God predetermines one fate is called_____.
4. Adam and Eve committed the_____and thus caused the fall of man.

Test Yourself: Write the letter next to the number to match word and meaning.

1. predestination   a. the disobedience in the Garden of Eden that tainted humans
2. purgatory   b. innovative fund-raising by the Church
3. original sin   c. hovered somewhere between heaven and hell
4. indulgences   d. God decided your life and salvation in advance

DID YOU KNOW?
Dante's famous Purgatorio (1319) gave people of that era their first images of purgatory, which is itself not depicted in the Bible. Lying between hell (inferno) and heaven (paradisio), Dante's cone-shaped region, structured as a steep mountain, is divided into seven circles, each illustrating one of the seven deadly sins: pride, envy, wrath, sloth, avarice, gluttony, and lust. Dante and his guide Virgil crawl on all fours up the mountain, becoming more and more purified as they ascend.

PART II

A World of Words

Cool Words

The words in this chapter are old words that have been revived today and are often used by people in casual talk or by media commentators. Their old meanings are sometimes used in new ways. Study the boldface words in the paragraphs that follow.

DAY 1

| misogynist | sycophants | hubris | gravitas |

DAY 2

| pompous | soporific | modus operandi | symposium |

DAY 3

| cacophony | eponymous | vernacular | kvetched |

DAY 4

| lucid | esoteric | ambiguous | coterminous |

DAY 5

| quixotic | insouciance | derided | imprimatur |

DAY 6

| concupiscence | ribald | chided | pulchritude |

DAY 7

| panache | yenta | demure | demurred |

WORDS IN CONTEXT: *The candidate was praised for his **gravitas**, because he quoted Shakespeare, but others criticized him for his **hubris**, accusing him of being arrogant. Still others saw his boorish treatment of women as **misogynist**. Only his **sycophants** saw him as an appropriate candidate for the office.*

Brief Definitions

misogynist	one who dislikes women
sycophants	people who flatter those of wealth or influence to gain favor
hubris	insolence or arrogance, excessive pride
gravitas	grave, solemn, sedate, earnest, weighty

After studying the new words in context, use them in the sentences below.

1. Their critics called his followers _____ because they appeared to agree with every word their leader said.
2. Some accused the politician of _____ because he seemed to overestimate his own positive qualities.
3. The man who had no regard for women's opinions and openly dismissed them was called a _____.
4. The professor who lectured us on the theory of relativity carried himself with _____.

Test Yourself: Write the letter next to the number that matches the definition.

1. gravitas
2. misogynist
3. sycophants
4. hubris

a. someone who hates of women
b. those who flatter to gain favor
c. serious, earnest, weighty
d. pride and arrogance

On a separate sheet of paper, write a sentence using each of these new words.

DID YOU KNOW?
Pyrrhic victory: This is a classical allusion that you may come across in history, literature, or philosophy. It is also used today to mean too many losses, a victory too costly. It refers to victories of Pyrrhus, King of Epirus, who fought the Romans in 280 and 279 B.C. EXAMPLE: The candidate won the election, but it was a Pyrrhic victory for him, given that many unsavory details from his past were exposed to the public.

WORDS IN CONTEXT: *At the **symposium**, the atmosphere was so **soporific** that some people snored in their chairs. Those who left early complained about the **modus operandi** and the **pompous** attitude of the speakers.*

Brief Definitions

pompous	exaggerated, pretentious, overbearing
soporific	causing or tending to cause sleep
modus operandi	mode of operating; procedure
symposium	a conference organized for the purpose of discussing intellectual subjects

After studying the new words in context, use them in the sentences below.

1. His words were so pretentious and his delivery so self-important that many in the audience called him _____.
2. Speaking of the program, the group leader said that the _____ would be two speakers followed by breakout groups for discussion.
3. The air was so warm and the speech was so boring, that the drowsy audience found the experience _____.
4. The _____ had many distinguished speakers addressing various serious topics.

Test Yourself: Write the letter next to the number that matches the definition.

1. soporific   a. mode of operation or procedure
2. symposium   b. something that puts one to sleep
3. pompous   c. overbearing and ostentatious
4. modus operandi   d. a meeting in which weighty subjects are discussed

On a separate sheet of paper, write a sentence using each of these new words.

DID YOU KNOW?
The word symposium actually derives from a Greek word meaning "drinking together." In ancient Greece a drinking party at which intellectual discussion took place was called a symposium. We use the word today to indicate any kind of meeting, conference, or social gathering where opinions are freely exchanged. Example: She read her research paper about Eastern religions at the symposium.

WORDS IN CONTEXT: *Jonathan Rimmer, owner of the **eponymous** marketing agency in Chicago, spoke in the **vernacular** to the students. But the group did not understand his point and **kvetched** in a **cacophony** of voices.*

Brief Definitions

cacophony	dissonance; harsh and jarring sounds
eponymous	an institution, state, or nation the name of which derives from a person or persons
vernacular	the language commonly spoken by a group or in a country, or place
kvetched	complained in a nagging and whining voice

Use these new words in the sentences below.

1. The argument in the street brought forth a _____ of harsh comments.
2. The Duke family established the _____university in North Carolina.
3. The country and western singer spoke in the _____ to his fans in Nashville.
4. The tourists were so unhappy about their accommodations on the trip that they _____ loudly to their guide.

Test Yourself: Write the letter next to the number that matches the definition.

1. vernacular
2. cacophony
3. eponymous
4. kvetched

a. harsh and jarring sounds
b. language common to a group
c. name that derives from a person or persons
d. nagged and whined

On a separate sheet of paper, write a sentence using each of these new words.

DID YOU KNOW?
Kvetch is a Yiddish word that, when used as slang, means "to pinch or squeeze." It is used more often to describe an urgent or insistent person who presses his or her point—a kvetcher, one who complains, nags, or whines. **EXAMPLE: The teacher said: "Stop *kvetching* about the assignment and just do it!"**

WORDS IN CONTEXT: *Some sophomores considered the speaker* **lucid***, but others said his examples from the eighteenth century were too* **arcane***, and his words, which could be interpreted in more than one way, were* **ambiguous***. Others wished for examples more* **coterminous** *with their own lives.*

Brief Definitions

lucid	clear, bright, shining, transparent, readily understood
esoteric	understood by only a few; arcane; hidden or secret
ambiguous	having two or more possible meanings; vague; indefinite
coterminous	bordering on; having the same boundaries, edges, or ends

use these new words in the sentences below.

1. Because his testimony was brief and _____, the jury believed him.
2. The textbook was filled with language too _____ to be understood by contemporary students.
3. His words were so _____ that you could take them in any way you wanted to.
4. The listeners were younger than the speaker, whose illustrations were from another era and not _____ with their own thinking.

Test Yourself: Write the letter next to the number that matches the definition.

1. ambiguous
2. lucid
3. esoteric
4. coterminous

a. vague and unclear
b. having a hidden or secret meaning
c. clear, rational, transparent
d. having the same boundaries or limits

On a separate sheet of paper, write a sentence using each of these new words.

DID YOU KNOW?
The word sophomore comes from the Greek: sophos (wise) and moros (foolish). This "wise fool" is in the tenth grade of high school or the second year of college. The word has come to be used for a person who is opinionated and self-assured, though immature. Did you ever hear a sophomoric joke? **ANOTHER TIP FOR YOU:** The words coterminous and conterminous have exactly the same meaning. They are synonyms.

WORDS IN CONTEXT: The *quixotic* behavior of the politician caused many to call him a visionary, but his *insouciance* was *derided* by others, who refused to put their *imprimatur* on his candidacy.

Brief Definitions

quixotic	romantically idealistic; visionary; impractical
insouciance	carefree attitude; thoughtlessness; indifference
derided	laughed at or ridiculed; made fun of; scorned
imprimatur	a license or permit providing approval

Use the new words in the sentences below.

1. Charles was intelligent but so extravagantly idealistic that many mistrusted what they called his _____ actions.
2. The article in the college paper _____ the actions taken by the administration.
3. The majority of the students had a(n) _____about dress and fashion.
4 College officials allowed the students to publish what they wished in the school paper, but the officials would not put their _____on the content.

Test Yourself: Write the letter next to the number that matches the definition.

1. insouciance
2. quixotic
3. derided
4. imprimatur

a. to laugh at and mock
b. indifference, thoughtlessness
c. give permission or to approve
d. idealistic and impractical

On a separate sheet of paper, write a sentence using each of these new words.

ANOTHER TIP FOR YOU: The word *quixotic* is derived from *Don Quixote* (ke-hoht'-ee), the Spanish writer Cervantes' early seventeenth-century satirical novel about a man who tried in idealistic ways to fight evil and rescue the oppressed, but realistic barriers thwarted him. The name of the romantic hero is generally pronounced differently from the adjective that comes from his name: kwik-sot'-ik.

DID YOU KNOW? Imprimatur derives from a Latin phrase meaning "let it be printed," a stamp of approval of censors in the Roman Catholic Church. (This sanctions or sanctifies.) The word has come to be used as a metaphor today in the sense of giving permission to a specific act.

WORDS IN CONTEXT: *The inebriated man made **ribald** comments about the **pulchritude** of the women at the party until the host **chided** him for his ungentlemanly **concupiscence** and asked him to leave.*

Brief Definitions

concupiscence	strong or abnormal desire or appetite; lust; sexual desire
chided	scolded; mildly reproved
ribald	coarse or vulgar joking or mocking; making direct and earthy sexual remarks
pulchritude	physical beauty

Use the new words in the sentences below.

1. The teacher _____ the students for their late homework.
2. The song's _____ lyrics annoyed some of the radio audience.
3. All the Miss America contestants showed off their_____.
4. Many of Shakespeare's male characters revealed their _____ by their remarks about women.

Test Yourself: Write the letter next to the number that matches the definition.

1. ribald	a. physical beauty
2. chided	b. shamed, scolded, rebuked
3. pulchritude	c. common, vulgar remarks
4. concupiscence	d. overtly lustful

On a separate sheet of paper, write a sentence using each of these new words.

DID YOU KNOW?
The idiom to *gild the lily* means "to paint, adorn, or embellish an object that is already perfect in itself." Actually, this is a misquotation from Shakespeare's *King John*, in which a character complains about the "wasteful and ridiculous excess" of King John's coronation. This, he said, is "To gild refined gold, to paint the lily, / To throw a perfume on the violet. / To smoothe the ice, to add another hue / Unto the rainbow." EXAMPLE: She did not wear the sparkling accessories with her elegant dress because she did not want to gild the lily.

WORDS IN CONTEXT: *The young man presented himself with* **panache,** *but the* **demure** *young woman* **demurred**—*a hesitation that agitated the local* **yenta,** *who was eager to see a love match.*

Brief Definitions

panache	dashing elegance of manner; spirited style; carefree; flamboyant
yenta	a gossip or busybody
demure	modest; reserved; affectedly coy and shy
demurred	hesitated because of one's doubts or objections

Use the new words in the sentences below.

1. The actor was handsome and dashing and filled with_____.
2. The neighborhood busybody, was called a_____ because she seemed to know everyone's business.
3. Miss Marian was the _____ librarian in the Broadway show *The Music Man*.
4. When Professor Harold Hill in that show tried to win the hand of Miss Marian, she initially_____.

Test Yourself: Place the appropriate letter next to the number.

1. yenta   a. spirited style; dashing
2. demure   b. a busybody
3. demurred   c. modest; shy; reserved
4. panache   d. hesitated; objected

On a separate sheet of paper, write a sentence using each of these new words.

DID YOU KNOW?
Panache originally referred to a plume of feathers in one's helmet, which lent a dashing style to soldiers. It has come to mean "rather flamboyant in style."

Yente is the alternate spelling of the Yiddish word yenta.

Demure, from the Old French, originally meant "ripe and mature." (Not to be confused with *demur*, which means "to hesitate because of one's doubts"; it also has a legal meaning: "an objection raised or an exception taken.")

Hot Words

This chapter contains some old words that have been resurrected (often corrupted) to be used in a trendy way. Some are new words and phrases (neologisms) that will likely not outlast the current usage.

In the Words in Context for Week 12, the listed words are sometimes used the way you hear them used—but the usage is not necessarily correct or preferable. Use them in the correct ways given in the definitions.

DAY 1

| repurposed | synergies | iconic | parameters |

DAY 2

| pursuant | teleconference | interface | relevant |

DAY 3

| über | relate to | dichotomy | forte |

DAY 4

| myriad | affective | dialogue | incentivize |

DAY 5

| per | user-friendly | less | viable |

DAY 6

| hit on | come on | hook up | lech |

DAY 7

| unique | businesswise | decimated | ephemeral |

WORDS IN CONTEXT: *We **repurposed** the product to create **synergies** and expand its **parameters**. Now we need a new marketing plan with an **iconic** logo and theme.*

Brief Definitions

repurposed	Actually, this is a *neologism*, or new word, in this case composed of a prefix (**re-**) attached to an established word (**purpose**). There is nothing really wrong with it, except that it has become a kind of jargon of business talk. Too much of this kind of thing tends to degrade the language. What's wrong with saying, "We've found a new purpose for the product"?
synergies	The combined or correlated action of different organs or parts of the body, as of muscles working together. This is a fairly new way of using a word with a very specific biological definition. It's not a bad metaphor. Just don't overdo it.
iconic	This word has to do with an *icon*—a fixed image in a conventional style (the first icons were religious: Jesus, Mary, saints). In the use above, the speaker is asking for a logo or marketing label that is now recognized, or will be recognized; it's hard to tell exactly, because the intent of the speaker is not clear.
parameters	This word is used frequently in this way in business and bureaucrat-speak, but it has a very specific meaning that is often not appropriate for the situation in which it is used. *Parameters* is actually a term in mathematics, difficult to grasp and more difficult to adapt to use outside math. It means "a quantity or constant whose value varies with the circumstances of its application, such as the radius line of a group of concentric circles, which varies with the circle under consideration." All clear? The more appropriate word for the Context paragraph above would be *perimeter* (the outer boundary of a figure or area). The words *perimeter* and *parameter* are frequently confused.

After studying the words in context, use them in the sentences below.

1. This word, _____, is a neologism, a new word coined by adding a prefix to an established word; using too many of these degrades the language.
2. _____, a word that originally had to do with the organs of the body working together, is now used as a metaphor in describing the coordinated workings of any complex body, organization, or mechanism.
3. Originally an image or statue of a religious figure, the word _____ has come to be used for any standard, recognizable image from Madonna to the labels on soup cans.
4. Almost everyone who uses the word *parameters* outside of mathematicians, actually means to use the word_____.

Test Yourself: Write the letter next to the number to match word and meaning.

1. synergies
2. parameters
3. repurpose
4. iconic

a. an image immediately recognizable
b. the parts of a complex organism working together
c. a neologism or invented word
d. a term in math often misused to mean "boundaries"

On a separate sheet of paper, write a sentence using each of these new words.

DID YOU KNOW?
The word *bureaucracy* comes from the French *bureau*, which means "a coarse woolen material" used to cover writing desks. A lot of writing desks existed in government departments. English took from the French the words *bureaucrat* and *bureaucracy*—words patterned after the example of *autocrat* and *autocracy*.

WORDS IN CONTEXT: *Pursuant* to our *teleconference* yesterday, I expect you to *interface* with the *relevant* parties to complete the project.

Brief Definitions

pursuant	following upon or in accordance with. This word is legal jargon, though in other cases, such as the above, it is inflated prose meant to sound impressive or authoritative. Instead, it sounds pretentious—as does the entire sentence. Say **following** or **regarding** instead.
teleconference	a discussion among more than two people held by telephone. A legitimate new word brought to us by technology. The language changes and expands to meet new needs, and in the current era nothing changes language more quickly than technological innovations.
interface	a plane forming the common boundary between two parts of matter or space; a point or means of interaction between two individuals systems, disciplines, or groups; material sewn between the outer fabric and the facing, which gives body to a collar, lapel, etc. As you can see, this word has three distinct meanings, none of which fits the preceding Context sentence exactly. The word **interface** is a noun, but in the example above, it is used as a verb. (One does not **interface**; one creates an **interface**.)
relevant	bearing upon or related to the matter; pertinent; to the point. The word is used correctly in the Context sentence, but this is a word that is often overused in organizations. If it did not follow **pursuant to** and **interface** here, it would not sound so pretentious. Try the entire sentence this way: *Following our phone conversation yesterday, please be in touch with the parties we discussed to complete the project.* Doesn't that sound more precise—and agreeable?

After studying the words in context, use them in the sentences below.

1. _____ means "following." People often use this word to make them sound important, but it does just the opposite.
2. A _____ is a phone conversation among more than two people.
3. The word _____ is a noun, and it means "a point of interaction between two groups or individuals."
4. _____ means "related to the matter at hand," or "pertinent."

Test Yourself: Write the letter next to the number to match word and meaning.

1. relevant   a. at least three people talking on the phone together
2. pursuant   b. individuals or groups coming together for discussion
3. teleconference   c. following, or in accordance with
4. interface   d. pertinent, or related

On a separate sheet of paper, write a sentence using these new words.

DID YOU KNOW?
A *palindrome* is a word or phrase that is identical when read it both forward and backward. For example, Otto, Bob, Ava, Toyota. One of the the most famous palindromes is "Madam, in Eden, I'm Adam" (a joke about what Adam said when he first beheld Eve).

WORDS IN CONTEXT: *Our **über** publicist cannot seem to **relate to** the national media and so is creating a **dichotomy** between our client and the press. National media outreach does not appear to be this publicist's **forte**.*

Brief Definitions

über   This word is a shortened form of *übermensch*, from the German meaning "superman." Here the word is used in a bit of a *snarky* (snide) voice to describe an employee or colleague who is not working successfully. The word is trendy and a bit slangy but can be effective in informal conversation.

relate to   This word has several meanings—all closely **related** (showing a connection or association with). An overused phrase that, as in the Context sentence above, can be vague and general. When you can, be more specific.

dichotomy   A division into two parts, groups, or classes, especially when these are sharply distinguished or opposed. This is a good word when you need a synonym for *division*, but be aware that used in a string of multisyllabic words, it can sound inflated.

forte   a strong point; a special accomplishment. This word, from the Old French, is used accurately here in written form. The danger, however, is that in conversation many people mispronounce it. It is pronounced exactly like the word *fort* in both French and English. The e is silent. (Only the word **forte** from the Italian, meaning "loud"—a direction to a musician—is pronounced *for-tay'*.)

After studying the words in context, use them in the sentences below.

1. A synonym for a division of something into two parts that oppose each other is_____.
2. _____ is a word for a person's special talent or strong point. It has one syllable.
3. A shortened name for a superman is _____.
4. A vague term that means "connection" is_____.

Test Yourself: Write the letter next to the number to match word and meaning.

1. forte   a. It's a bird! It's a plane! No, it's _____! (Smile.)
2. relate to   b. The chasm you find between Democrats and Republicans.
3 dichotomy   c. In French and English it means "strong point." Say it correctly.
4. über   d. One is associated with the other.

On a separate sheet of paper, write a sentence using each of the new words.

DID YOU KNOW? *Bridal* is a combination of two Old English words that meant "bride" and "ale." Once ale or mead was drunk at wedding feasts, and the compounded word referred to that feast but later came to refer to the ceremony itself.

WORDS IN CONTEXT: *Our sales department has a **myriad** of problems that are beginning to affect our profits. Please **dialogue** with the manager there and try to **incentivize** him and his staff to do a better sales job by paying closer attention to the **affective** side of persuasion .*

Brief Definitions

myriad	Originally this word from the Greek meant "ten thousand." It has come to mean "a great number of" or "a great number." It would be less wordy in the Context sentence to say *Our sales department has **myriad** problems,* but **a myriad of** is not actually incorrect.
affective	Pertaining to the emotions as opposed to the intellect. In the context used above, the word is close to being jargon.
dialogue	talking together; a conversation; an interchange; a discussion. This word is a noun. You should not try to make it into a verb by saying "**dialogue** with." The speaker in the Context sentence above should say, "Please talk with (have a conversation with, or discuss this with) the manager."
incentivize	This is not a word. **Incentive** is a noun meaning "something that motivates or stimulates one to take action." The speaker in the context above should say, "try to motivate him," or "try to give him an **incentive** to do a better sales job." Too often in business- or bureaucrat-speak, nouns are turned into awkward (and inaccurate) verbs.

After studying the words in context, use the new words in the sentences below.

1. The critic needed to pay more attention to the _____, or emotional, aspect of the playwright's character development.
2. On a clear night, you can see _____stars.
3. The candidate means *motivate* when he says _____.
4. The two women had a _____ about how to solve the problem.

Test Yourself: Write the letter next to the number to match word and meaning.

1. myriad　　　　　a. relating to the emotional side of a person"
2. dialogue　　　　b. a great number
3. incentivize　　　c. a discussion between two people
4. affective　　　　d. a made-up word that means nothing

On a separate sheet of paper, write a sentence using each of these new words.

DID YOU KNOW? *Alibi* is a legal term meaning "elsewhere." This is the "plea of having been elsewhere at the time when any alleged act took place." We use it informally to mean "excuse."

WORDS IN CONTEXT: *As **per** your instructions, I am making the office more **user-friendly** by putting **less** people in the reception area and creating more **viable** conditions.*

Brief Definitions

per	through; by means of; according to. The writer of the memo in the Context sentence above is using **per** to mean "according to." It is incorrect (and incoherent) to use *as* before **per.** Just "**per** your instructions" will do. Or one might write, "**Per** this letter, I am informing you . . .," meaning *through this letter* or *by means of this letter.*
user-friendly	easy for the user to use. This is a neologism often heard in organizations and businesses and is frequently used when describing an innovation in technology such as a computer or computer software. There is nothing wrong with the use of this adjective, but don't overwork it. In the Context sentence, the writer's office seems to be cluttered, and removing some of the desks might make it "more welcoming to visitors or **user-friendly.**"
less	not so much. As you can see, **less** does not mean "not so many"—**fewer** means "not so many." It would not make sense, then, to say "not so much people." You would say "not so many people." Use **less** when you are discussing an amount—something you can't count: "Put **less** salt in the potatoes." "The tank has less gas in it today." Use *fewer* when speaking of something you can count: "Put *fewer* desks in the room." "I have *fewer* pennies than you do." "We had *fewer* roses than we did last spring and **less** rainfall."
viable	This word actually means "something able to live, to take root and grow." People often use it to mean "workable," but when used that way, the context must have the sense of growth or the likelihood of surviving. In the Context sentence above, the way the word is used does not quite contain those meanings. Be careful to use **viable** appropriately.

After studying the words in context, use them in the sentences below.

1. I weigh_____than you do, but you have fewer wrinkles than I.
2. The bulb you planted in the fall, looks _____ and will probably bloom in the spring.
3 His new digital camera is _____, and he should not have trouble operating it.
4. ____ your instructions, I am booking you into the Pierre Hotel.

Test Yourself: Write the letter next to the number to match word and meaning.

1. per
2. less
3. user-friendly
4. viable

a. easy to use, or welcoming
b. capable of growth or survival
c. according to the boss's wishes
d. use this with weight or amount

On a separate sheet of paper, write a sentence using each of these new words.

DID YOU KNOW?
You could be noisome without being noisy? The word has nothing to do with noise. It means "offensive," "disgusting," and "harmful." Noisome comes from a Middle English word meaning "annoy" and ultimately from a Latin phrase meaning "harmful" and "odious."

WORDS IN CONTEXT: *Did you see how that guy **hit on** me? I certainly wasn't giving him the **come-on**. He told a friend that he was trying to **hook up** with me. What a **lech.***

Brief Definitions

hit on	flirt with; seduce. All the expressions above are those you might hear when one teenager or college student talks to another. These are trendy, slangy expressions, but the young people understand each other.
come-on	an invitation to flirt; a display of openness to romantic attention. These words are student jargon today. Perhaps the expressions will change by tomorrow.
hook up	meeting and establishing an intimate relationship, usually temporary. This expression at one time meant simply *meet, connect*. Old friends or relatives might **hook up** before a social event and go together. In current, trendy-speak, this term usually suggests that the people who **hook up** were not acquainted before but make an immediate, temporary connection.
lech	the shortened form of *lecher*, a predatory person, usually male, who gives unwanted attention to another person. Again, this is slang usage of young people.

After studying the words in context, use them in the sentences below.

1. The girls were upset because a lot of the boys at the party had _____ them.
2. Let's go to the fraternity party and find someone to _____ with.
3. I'm never going back to that place; there was just one _____ after another.
4. She stood there with that _____ attitude and then was surprised that he approached her.

Test Yourself: Write the letter next to the number to match word and meaning.

1. come-on   a. an unwanted move that one person makes on another
2. lech   b. a predatory person—short form
3. hit on   c. an attitude that says "I'm available"
4. hook up   d. they meet, they like each other, they leave together

On a separate sheet of paper, write a sentence using each of these new words.

DID YOU KNOW?
Making a fist and pushing your thumb between your first and middle finger is an obscene gesture in Mediterranean countries? It's called "the sign of the fig," and a fig has been considered something worthless since about 1400. Dante used it in the Inferno section of *The Divine Comedy*. Poet John Ciardi said the gesture's meaning is comparable to the obscene hand gesture we see rude drivers giving each other in the United States.

WORDS IN CONTEXT: *A very **unique** thing occurred to me **businesswise;** the stock market collapsed and **decimated** my savings. My adviser said it was **ephemeral,** however.*

Brief Definitions

unique	one and only; single; sole; having no like or equal; unparalleled. As you can see by the definition, this word can properly take no qualifier: it means "the only one of its kind." So "**a very unique** thing" would be incorrect usage. Nor can you have "**a kind of unique** thing." Simple: "**A unique thing** occurred. There are no degrees of **uniqueness.** Anything **unique** is sui generic. It would, however, be correct to describe something as **almost unique,** or **possibly unique** if there is a degree of uncertainty.
businesswise	Any word with **–wise** tacked onto it is a neologism—an awkward attempt to stretch an established word: moneywise, healthwise, familywise. This addition is meant to convey "in the way of," so why not just say that and be more elegant in speaking and writing? "A **unique thing** occurred to me **in the way of** business (or having to do with business, etc.)."
decimated	This often-used word originally meant "to select by lot and kill every tenth one of." It has come to mean "to destroy or kill a large part of." Examples: *Famine **decimated** the population. The stock market crash **decimated** my savings.* The word is used correctly in the Context sentence, but be smart and remember what the word originally meant.
ephemeral	transitory; impermanent; short-lived. The word is used correctly in the Context sentence. **Ephemeral** also describes many of the words and expressions in this chapter. Trends—even word trends—are **ephemeral**—not long lasting.

After studying the new words in context, use them in the sentences below.

1. The drought in the Midwest _____ the crops.
2. The lovely evening was _____, but we knew that our love was not.
3. It is not good form to say _____, when you mean "having to do with business."
4. This word, _____, is sui generis and means only, sole, one of a kind.

Test Yourself: Write the letter next to the number to match word and meaning.

1. ephemeral
2. unique
3. decimate
4. businesswise

a. once meant killing every tenth one of something
b. an awkward neologism
c. does not take a qualifier because it is the only one of what it is
d. passing, short-lived, impermanent

On a separate sheet of paper, write a sentence using each of these new words.

DID YOU KNOW?
A "Luddite" is a person opposed to any machine, labor-saving device, or technological innovation. The name came from a dim-witted worker in the eighteenth century, Ned Ludd. He smashed some machinery out of anger, probably not at the machines, but at some tormenting boys. Nevertheless, a person today who will not use a computer or other high-tech equipment is often called a "Luddite."

Not Words

This chapter focuses on words or expressions that are not necessarily nonwords, but words that have been so misused that they have little meaning. Some are words or phrases that are not used in Standard English, and some just cause confusion. But first, some definitions.

DAY 1

| Standard English | slang | regionalisms | colloquialisms |

DAY 2

| jargon | neologisms | idioms | pretentious diction |

DAY 3

| being that | preventative | enthused | centered around |

DAY 4

| hopefully | alot | irregardless | firstly, secondly, thirdly, fourthly |

DAY 5

| ahold | alright | reason is because | should of |

DAY 6

| might of | real | major-type | 'til |

DAY 7

| suppose | towards | utilize | anyways |

Standard English	established words, expressions, grammar, and sentence structure that intelligent, educated people use.
	WORDS IN CONTEXT: *Standard English is the language in which books, magazines, and newspapers are written and is the accepted usage in American English.*
slang	Vivid, informal use of language that usually has a generational or cultural base: rock musicians (*hip hop*), teenagers (*cool, hot, clueless*), African-American performers (*bling bling*), politicians (*policy wonk, right winger*), business people (*downsize, upscale*).
	WORDS IN CONTEXT: *Slang is colorful and often humorous, but it tends to go in and out of fashion quickly.*
regionalisms	Words, idioms, and expression common to a particular region. For example, in the South, carbonated beverages are called *cokes*; farther north, they're called *soft drinks*; in the Northeast, they're called *sodas*.
	WORDS IN CONTEXT: *Just as fashions and tastes are **regional**, so too is language.*
colloquialisms	the ordinary, informal language of everyday speech: contractions (*you're, won't, shouldn't*) and expressions such as *bye-bye, ciao, see ya, so long*, all meaning "good-bye," are colloquial. Other examples: *TV* for *television; cell* for *cell phone; whazzup?* or *zup?* for *what is going on in your life?*
	WORDS IN CONTEXT: *Often colloquial words are colorful and provide a shorthand way of communicating. The book you are reading uses Standard English, but in some cases, in an attempt to be informal and user-friendly, it uses **colloquialisms**.*

After studying the terms above, use the words in the sentences below.

1. _____ is informal language that often has a general and cultural base and changes frequently.
2. Informal, everyday language used by most of us is_____.
3. Words, expressions, and idioms influenced by a geographic location are called
   _____.
4. _____ is the established usage of American speech.

Test Yourself: Write the letter next to the number to match word and meaning.

1. slang   a. the language of educated people
2. colloquialisms   b. expressions of a region
3. Standard English   c. informal, generational, cultural speech
4. regionalism   d. informal, everyday speech

On a separate sheet of paper, write a sentence using each of these new words.

DID YOU KNOW?
The only times that nonstandard language, slang, and regionalisms are appropriate are in conversation, personal correspondence, personal essays, and fiction. All these uses of the language are effective if you are creating a character in a play, quoting other people, or writing dialogue. Otherwise, use the standard and sometimes the colloquial stuff.

jargon	specialized words, expressions, and concepts used by people in particular professions, trades, or academic disciplines. Some of the words and concepts you learned in the first section of this book are those of people working in or studying the liberal arts or humanities (For example, *chiaroscuro, perspective, etching,* and *mezzotint,* in the first chapter on art.) **WORDS IN CONTEXT:** *You are not expected to know the* **jargon** *of every group, but the more you read and listen, the more you will become familiar with specialized words.*
neologisms	new words or phrases brought into the language out of necessity because of technological or other advances: high-tech, outsource, e-mail, fax. If you don't know whether to hyphenate neologisms consisting of more than one word, look them up in a current dictionary. If the word is not there, hyphenate it. (Such verbs tend to be hyphenated less often than nouns.) **WORDS IN CONTEXT:** *Neologisms tend to drop their hyphens as they are absorbed into the language. Other* **neologisms**—*for example,* concretize or developmentwise—*are awkward hybrids usually invented by lazy minds. Learn to spot the authentic (lasting) and the fake (sloppy and clumsy)* **neologisms.**
idioms	common phrases, constructions, or expressions embedded in our language from many sources that often do not make much sense if taken literally: *raining cats and dogs, the apple of his eye, forty winks, jump on the band wagon.* **WORDS IN CONTEXT:** *You will find many* **idioms** *in this book with their historical or etymological explanations. (That last word,* etymological, *means the tracing of a word or phrase back as far as possible or to its source.)*
pretentious diction	Inexperienced writers, or those who are trying to make an impression (wrongheadedly) sometimes use **pretentious diction.** This is the use of pompous and flowery words and phrases. Excellent writers use concrete words that call up sense impressions (sight, sound, smell, touch, taste), strong verbs that move the pace along quickly. **WORDS IN CONTEXT:** *Pretentious words or general words (like clothes) are not as strong as specific words (red, cotton shirt). This is not to say that a good writer cannot use long or unfamiliar words that will stretch the reader—but she or he must know exactly what the words mean and how to use them.*

After studying the definitions above, use each in the sentences below.

1. Words used by people who have a particular specialty, such as science, medicine, computer science, and architecture, comprise the _____ of that group.
2. Words, phrases, and expressions that we hear constantly but do not take literally because they are so embedded in our language are called_____.
3. People who are more interested in impressing others than in communicating in clear, graceful, concrete prose often use _____.
4 _____ are new words brought into the language when necessitated by new developments in technology or new ideas.

Test Yourself: Write the letter next to the number to match word and meaning.

1. idioms   a. pompous and flowery words
2. neologisms   b. expressions not to be taken literally
3. jargon   c. new words occasioned by advances
4. pretentious diction   d. specialized words

On a separate sheet of paper, write a sentence using each of these new words.

DID YOU KNOW? The reason wine or champagne drinkers clink glasses in a toast before taking the first sip has to do with our senses. Drinking a glass of wine engages every sense—sight, taste, touch, smell—except that of sound. So when the glasses are clinked together, the act of drinking wine engages all our senses. Salud!

WORDS IN CONTEXT: *Being that* he wanted to study **preventative** medicine, he was **enthused** when he found that his classes **centered around** chemistry and biology.

Brief Definitions

being that	This is not standard usage; that is, educated, intelligent people do not speak or write this way. (Another common error is the use of *being as*. This, too, is incorrect.) Say *since* or *because* he wanted to study. . .
preventative	This is not a choice word. The word is *preventive*. No matter how many speakers or announcers on television you hear use this nonword, remember that it not *Standard English*. Use the correct word.
enthused	This is a colloquial form of *enthusiastic*—language you hear in everyday, informal speech. The proper word is *enthusiastic*. Use it.
centered around	You can't "center around" anything, unless you are running in circles. The proper phrase is *centered on*.

CORRECTED SENTENCE: *Because* he wanted to study **preventive** medicine, he was **enthusiastic** when he found that his classes **centered on** chemistry and biology.

After studying the correct forms of these words, use the correct words in the sentences below.

1. He took the medication as a _____ measure when he felt a cold coming on.
2. Her interest _____ music, so she went to the conservatory to study.
3. The class was _____ about the approaching field trip.
4. _____ he had heard it was going to rain, he took his umbrella.

Exercise: Mark an X through the incorrect word and write the correct word next to it.

1. centered around _____
2. preventative _____
3. being that_____
4. enthused_____

On a separate sheet of paper, write a sentence using each correct word.

DID YOU KNOW?
Texas Congressman Maury Maverick invented the word *gobbledygook*. He got fed up with pretentious, long-winded speeches and government documents and said, "Be short and say what you're talking about. Stop the gobbledygook. Stop 'pointing up' programs. No more 'finalizing,' 'effectuating,' or 'dynamics.' Anyone using the words 'activation' or 'implementation' will be shot." *Gobbledygook* took hold and is now in dictionaries. We are all grateful!

WORDS IN CONTEXT: *Hopefully,* you will all learn **alot** from this book, **irregardless firstly** *of your age,* **secondly** *of your sex,* **thirdly** *of your ethnic background, and* **fourthly** *of your geographic location.*

Brief Definitions

hopefully	This *is* a word, but one from which we advise you to stay away. Why? Because almost no one uses it correctly. It is an adverb meaning "in a hopeful manner." It should modify a verb, an adjective, or another adverb. That's not too hard. Do not use **hopefully** as a sentence modifier meaning "it is hoped." (As it is used above. *Who* is doing the hoping in that sentence?) Say, **"**He tossed the basketball toward the basket **hopefully.**" (That is, in a *hopeful* manner.) Do not say, "**Hopefully,** it will not snow." (No one is doing the hoping there.) Say rather, "I *hope* it will not snow." If you can't remember that, forget the word.
alot	This is *not* a word. This is so much *not* a word that the computer will hardly allow it to be typed. **Alot** is corrected each time. **A lot** is *two* words, but it is better to say "many" or "several."
irregardless	This is *not* a word. The correct word is **regardless.** Use that instead.
firstly, secondly, thirdly, fourthly	These are *not* words. Say **first, second, third, fourth.** Or vary your language. Or use numerals. Just don't use these nonwords.
	CORRECTED SENTENCE: I **hope** you will all learn **a number** of things (or **a lot**) from this book **regardless** of your age, sex, ethnic background, or geographic location. (Now, isn't that better? You may say first, second, third, and fourth, but who needs them?)

After studying the correct forms of these words, use the correct words in the sentences below.

1. The gambler at the casino spun the wheel _____.
2. _____ of how you interpret it, *Ulysses* is a rich and astonishing book.
3. They got _____of money for their house; but then they had to pay _____ for the new one.
4. _____ he was apprehensive, _____ he was scared, _____he was sure he would never get the job, and _____he was overjoyed with the offer.

Exercise: Mark an X through the incorrect word and write the correct word next to it.

1. irregardless _____
2. hopefully_____
3. firstly, secondly, and so on _____
4. alot _____

On a separate sheet of paper, write a sentence using each of the correct words.

DID YOU KNOW?
The expression "cut the red tape" (an idiom) came from English kings who put their royal decrees on rolls of parchment bound with red silk ribbons. Governmental bureaus that followed did the same thing, and then lawyers followed suit with their petitions. Soon, anything official was bound in red ribbon or tape. Thomas Carlyle and Charles Dickens used the phrase red tape when they wrote about bureaucratic and legal delays.

WORDS IN CONTEXT: *I got **ahold** of the book in the campus bookstore, **alright**, and the **reason is because** I got there first. I **should of**; I got up before dawn.*

Brief Definitions

ahold	This is not a word. Like *a lot*, it is *two* words: *a hold*. Simple. Just separate the words, if spell-check doesn't do it for you. It's even better to drop the *a* and just say *hold*.
alright	This is not a word either. It, too, is two words: *all right*.
the reason is because	All these words are legitimate, but the phrase is simple-minded, which you do not want to be. Say "the reason is that." Simple as that.
should of	Now, everyone all together: what should this say? Yes, of course, *should have*. You'd be surprised how many people write "could of, would of, should of." They're wrong. You're right. All right?

CORRECTED SENTENCE: *I got **hold of** the book in the campus bookstore **all right**, and **the reason is that** I got there first. I **should have**; I got up before dawn.*

After studying the correct forms of these words, use the correct words in the sentences below.

1. I found the perfect plasma TV, and_____. I looked in 12 stores.
2. We _____found a better place to have a picnic, one without ants.
3. _____, I don't like this movie either; let's go home.
4. Did you get _____of your brother on the phone today?

Exercise: Mark an X through the incorrect word and write the correct word next to it.

1. alright_____
2. the reason is because _____
3. should of _____
4. ahold _____

On a separate sheet of paper, write a sentence using each correct word.

DID YOU KNOW?
The Greek god Zeus had a lover (or wife) named Mnemosyne, who happened to be the goddess of memory. Ever wonder where the term mnemonic device—those fabled tricks such as tying a string around a finger to help you remember—came from? Look no further for an aid to memory than the goddess Mnemosyne (Ne-mos'-e-nee). The word came from her name. Remember that.

WORDS IN CONTEXT: *My friend said he **might of** had a **real** good time at the party **'til** one of the guys got **real** sick and had a **major-type** problem. Then they had to get out of there **real** quick.*

Brief Definitions

might of	You think nobody talks like this? Listen to some college students talk among themselves. **Might of** is not a correct expression—especially when written in a class paper. The expression is **might have**. Like *could of, should of,* and *would of,* this expression does not transfer well from mumbled conversation to written prose.
real	A perfectly good word when you're talking about the **real** world. But a weak substitute for *very* (which itself is a weak word). Be specific. Write something concrete and colorful. Don't use **real** for *very,* and don't use *very* very often. Put some vigor in your prose.
major-type	Remember *moneywise, familywise,* and all those other *wises* that don't cut it? **Type** as a tacked on word doesn't cut it either. It adds nothing, and it subtracts a good deal of sophistication from your speech and writing. Just say **major.**
'til	Say **until**. In informal speaking or writing, it's acceptable to say **till..'Til** has been frowned upon in good writing since the Romantic poets died—at least. Till the end of time, say **till.**

CORRECTED SENTENCE: *My friend said he might have had quite a good time at the party, till one of the guys nearly passed out and had a major problem keeping his food down.*

After studying the correct forms of these words, use the correct words in the sentences below.

1. My roommate said I couldn't go _____ I had cleaned up my half of the room.
2. It's the end of the semester, and I have a _____test tomorrow.
3. The day was_____(not *real,* not *very,* think of a more descriptive word) gorgeous, so we decided to go for a hike.
4. I think I _____ got an A on my history exam!

Exercise: Mark an X through the incorrect word and write the correct word next to it.

1. might of _____
2. 'til _____
3. real _____
4. major-type _____

On a separate sheet of paper, write a sentence using the correct form of each new word.

DID YOU KNOW?
Dr. Thomas Bowdler, an editor in England, decided, in 1818, to clean up what he considered indelicate language in the works of Shakespeare. He omitted words and expressions "which cannot with propriety be read aloud in a family," to make "these invaluable plays fit for the perusal of our virtuous females." Not everyone appreciated his efforts, and ever since then the word bowdlerized has been used for priggishly censored literature.

WORDS IN CONTEXT: *I knew I was **suppose** to stay on the main road as I was driving **towards** the highway, but I decided to **utilize** a little side road and got lost. **Anyways**, I finally found my way.*

Brief Definitions

suppose	This word should end in a *d*, **supposed**, when used in this way to indicate the past tense. (Use *used to* in the same way—with a final d.) When you are saying something like, "Do you suppose . . .?" or, "Suppose it rains that day," the word does not require a final *d*.
towards	This word in American English does not take a final *s*. Say **toward**. In British English, the final *s* is sometimes used, just as in British English the word *among* is often spelled *amongst*. Know the difference, and use what is common in your own language.
utilize	Although not incorrect, this is a pretentious way of saying *use*. (Avoid *-ize* words when you can. *Democratize, personalize, politicize* are standard, but *incentivize*? No; don't make up words to try to sound impressive.)
anyways	This is simply an ignorant way of saying **anyway**. Perhaps in some regions it's colloquial, but it is not standard American English. Drop that final s—or sound like a hick!

CORRECTED SENTENCE: *I knew I was **supposed** to stay on the main road as I was driving **toward** the highway, but I decided to **use** a little side road and got lost. **Anyway**, I finally found my way.*

After studying the correct forms of these words, use the correct word in the sentences below.

1. I veered_____the left and careened_____the right, then straightened out the car and avoided an accident.
2. I hope you will _____each of these words correctly, without using –ize unnecessarily.
3. The weather was lousy, but we decided to go to the ballgame_____.
4. We were_____to go to the movie, but the theater was closed.

Exercise: Mark an X through the incorrect word and write the correct word next to it.

1. utilize _____
2. towards _____
3. anyways_____
4. suppose _____

On a separate sheet of paper, write a sentence using each of the correct words.

DID YOU KNOW?
The currently trendy word *funky* is really an old word dating back to 1784. It referred to the smell of cheese—old and moldy—and later to stale body odor. Some trace *funky* back to the Latin *fumas* (smoke). It has also been associated with jazz. For these reasons, downtown New York nightclubs are often described as *funky*.

Weird Words

This chapter covers unusual, funny, goofy words that have somehow endured and kept (or lost or changed) their meanings.

DAY 1

| quakebuttock | wedbedrip | defenestration | sesquipedalian |

DAY 2

| oology | groak | flapdoodle | bunkum |

DAY 3

| galoot | Mayday | tintiddle | crambazzle |

DAY 4

| goeduck | taradiddle | slubberdegullion | hobbledehoy |

DAY 5

| wampum | abracadabra | eleemosynary | spoonerism |

DAY 6

| teetotaler | posh | swillbellies | fysigunkus |

DAY 7

| foof | eggtaggling | thripping | xertzing |

quakebuttock	A scornful word for a coward.
	WORDS IN CONTEXT: *The crowd thought him a quivering, quaking coward and so called him a* **quakebuttock.**
wedbedrip *rent*	A full day's reaping from a tenant's land that feudal lords demanded from tenants.
	WORDS IN CONTEXT: *If the sharecropper had known the word* **wedbedrip**, *he would have said that that was what he owed the owner of the land he worked.*
defenestration	Tossing someone or something out the window.
	WORDS IN CONTEXT: *The couple was having such a fight in the small apartment that neighbors were afraid one of them would suffer* **defenestration.**
sesquipedalian	A word a foot and a half long, or one who uses long words.
	WORDS IN CONTEXT: *Sesquipedalian people love to use* **sesquipedalian** *words. One of the words they love to use is* sesquicentennial, *which means 150th anniversary.*

**After studying the words above, use them in the sentences below.
Use the part of speech that applies.**

1. The boys in the playground were fighting, but one _____ held their coats.
2. After eating the orange while driving her car, she_____ the peel.
3. The language expert spoke to the scholars in _____ words.
4. After working all day in the fields, he owed the owner a _____.

Test Yourself: Write the letter next to the number to match word and meaning.

1. wedbedrip   a. a trembling coward
2. defenestration   b. words a foot and a half long
3. quakebuttock   c. toss out the window
4. sesquipedalian   d. a day's reaping owed to the lord

On a separate sheet of paper, write a sentence using each of the new words.

DID YOU KNOW? The word *schmaltz* means "liquid chicken fat." Actually, it derives from the Yiddish word *schmalts*—grease, fat, or lard—but it has come to be used in the sense of overly sentimental or corny, as in, "The Mother's Day card was sweet but schmaltzy," or, "The elevator music was the epitome of schmaltz."

oology	The branch of ornithology (the study of birds) that deals with birds' eggs.
	WORDS IN CONTEXT: *Almost all words like **oology** that begin with "ool" have something to do with eggs of one kind or another, either animal or human.*
groak	Staring at other people's food, hoping they will offer you some of it.
	WORDS IN CONTEXT: ***Groak, groaked, groaking**—all of these activities are fairly rude, unless, perhaps, you are a homeless person in real need of the food a passerby is eating. Then it might be permissible to **groak** at it.*
flapdoodle	Nonsense; rubbish; meaningless talk.
	WORDS IN CONTEXT: ***Flapdoodle** calls up some other weird words, such as its synonyms poppycock and balderdash. Closely related in sound to **flapdoodle** is fopdoodle, meaning a vain, affected dandy (fop) and a fool (doodle).*
bunkum	A politician's long-winded, insincere speech made to impress a crowd. Closely allied with **flapdoodle.**
	WORDS IN CONTEXT: *Buncombe, North Carolina, was the town represented by a politician Felix Walker who, in 1820, dragged out a tedious speech addressing what was to become the Missouri Compromise in the Sixteenth Congress. He was not the last politician to spout **bunkum**, a corruption of his hometown's name.*

After studying the words above, use them in the sentences below.

1. The boring old man's nonsensical talk was nothing but piffle, twaddle, poppycock, and _____.
2. I was so hungry that I stood in line _____ at the plates of food of the people in front of me in the cafeteria.
3. The politician's long, drawn-out speech was simply_____.
4. The ornithologist's special interest was _____ or the study of birds' eggs.

Test Yourself: Write the letter next to the number to match word and meaning.

1. flapdoodle
2. bunkum
3. groak
4. oology

a. staring at other people's food
b. tedious political speech
c. empty, meaningless words
d. eggs, eggs, and more eggs: the study of

On a separate sheet of paper, write a sentence using each new word.

DID YOU KNOW?
Xmas is not just the lazy person's way of writing Christmas. The X in Xmas is the Greek form of *chi*, and *chi* is the first letter of the Greek form of *Christ*. The symbol x or X is the ancient abbreviation for *Christ;* thus, the Xmas (or Christday) holiday has a long tradition.

galoot	A clumsy, dimwitted oaf; a show-off; a likable simpleton; amusing person with loutish though well-meaning behavior. **WORDS IN CONTEXT:** *The town clown loved to hold forth on the corner of Main Street with what he thought were great ideas, but everyone in town thought him a silly **galoot**.*
Mayday	Aside from the obvious meaning, May 1—May Day—this is the international distress signal radioed during World War II when someone was in immediate need. **WORDS IN CONTEXT:** ***Mayday** derives from the French m'aider (Help me! Come to my aid!). It was a wartime emergency call.*
tintiddle	A clever reply that one thinks of too late. **WORDS IN CONTEXT:** *Few things are more frustrating than thinking of a **tintiddle** to another person's remark after he has left the room.*
crambazzle	A dissipated old man. **WORDS IN CONTEXT:** *The young girls were made uncomfortable by the **crambazzle** on the corner who mumbled at them as they passed.*

After studying the words above, use them in the sentences below.

1. The crazy _____ behind me kept talking back to the movie in a loud voice.
2. After I got home, I thought of a dozen _____ with which I could have responded to the man's rude comment.
3. The _____ was thin, pale, and disheveled and looked as though he had been hitting the bottle.
4. The call "_____! _____!" came from the boys in the sinking boat.

Test Yourself: Write the letter next to the number to match word and meaning.

1. crambazzle
2. tintiddle
3. galoot
4. Mayday

a. I wish I'd thought to say that!
b. The old guy had had too much to drink.
c. Help me! Help me!
d. the dimwitted village idiot

On a separate sheet of paper, write a sentence using each of these words.

DID YOU KNOW?
The word *quisling* has something in common with Judas, Brutus, and Benedict Arnold. All these words refer to traitors. Major Vidkun Quisling was a Norwegian, a former minister of defense (1931–1933), and head of a Norwegian fascist party responsible for the deaths of hundreds of Jews. When Norway was liberated from the Nazis, Quisling was charged with treason and murder and was executed in 1945. His name has become associated with traitors and collaborators ever since. In a speech in London in 1941, Winston Churchill used the term, "A vile race of quislings—to use the new word which will carry the scorn of mankind down the centuries."

goeduck	A big clam, weighing up to 12 pounds, found in Puget Sound and other West Coast waters. Pronounced "goo'-ee-duk."
	WORDS IN CONTEXT: *They ordered goeduck from the menu and found the dish neither gooey nor a duck, but a delicious seafood.*
taradiddle	A petty lie; a fib. Also spelled **tarradiddle.**
	WORDS IN CONTEXT: *When the girl said she admired her friend's new spiky haircut, she told a taradiddle.*
slubberdegullion	A slob; a boor; a rude, crude, and socially unacceptable person.
	WORDS IN CONTEXT: *The fraternity boys lolled around the television set drinking beer and dropping chips on the floor like a bunch of slubberdegullions.*
hobbledehoy	A gawky teenager, more than a boy, not quite a man.
	WORDS IN CONTEXT: *He's a man! No, he's a boy! No, he's an awkward hobbledehoy!*

After studying the definitions above, use the words in the sentences below.

1. She committed a_____: she told the professor she was sick, when she actually just needed to sleep instead of going to class.
2. The rude, boorish boy conducted himself like a_____.
3. The clammers hauled in a _____ and joked about having a big dinner.
4. On his 13th birthday, his father teased him about becoming a_____.

Test Yourself: Place the letter next to the number to match word and meaning.

1. taradiddle   a. between boy and man
2. goeduck   b. a slobbish and crude person
3. hobbledehoy   c. an enormous clam
4. slubberdegullion   d. a petty lie

On a separate sheet of paper, write a sentence using each of these words.

DID YOU KNOW?
Originally the word *nickname* in Middle English was *ekename*, meaning an additional name. The word and its article *an* were later telescoped producing a *nekename*; then *neke* became *nick*—creating the word we use today.

wampum	Slang for "money," **wampum** was literally a string of beads, sometimes made of shells, that Algonquian Indians used as money or for ornaments. Black or dark purple wampum was more valuable than white wampum.
	WORDS IN CONTEXT: *The Indians in the movie demanded **wampum** for the deerskins.*
abracadabra	We use the word to mean foolish or unintelligible mutterings, but **abracadabra** was originally a magic word whose letters were arranged in an inverted pyramid. One less letter appeared in each line of the pyramid, until only the letter "a" remained at the bottom. The word was worn, like a piece of jewelry, around the neck as an amulet to ward off trouble or disease.
	WORDS IN CONTEXT: *The idea behind **abracadabra** was that as each letter disappeared from the inverted pyramid, so also did trouble and disease disappear.*
eleemosynary	An institution or corporation devoted to charitable purposes or supported by charity.
	WORDS IN CONTEXT: ***Eleemosynary** comes from a Latin word meaning "alms" and can be traced back to the Greek word eleos meaning "pity," or "mercy."*
spoonerism	The accidental transposing of sounds or letters in words, for example, "trig bubble" for "big trouble." The word comes from the name of an Oxford professor and cleric, the Rev. W. A. Spooner (1844–1930), who frequently scrambled his words, much to the amusement of his students.
	WORDS IN CONTEXT: *Rev. Spooner is said to have committed the following **spoonerism** in church when addressing a person who had come to pray: ""Excuse me, madam, but aren't you occupewing the wrong pie?" And after performing a wedding ceremony, Rev. Spooner told the nervous groom: "It is kisstomary to cuss the bride."*

After studying the definitions above, use the words in the sentences below.

1. He meant to say "the three little pigs," but he got his tongue tangled and said, "the pee little thrigs," thereby using a _____.
2. The Red Cross is an _____ institution.
3. The magician waved a silk handkerchief across the box and said _____, after which the box became a ball.
4. "We want _____ for the land," the American Indian told the settler.

Test Yourself: Place the letter next to the number to match word and meaning.

1. eleemosynary   a. makes magic happen
2. wampum   b. an amusing tongue tangler
3. abracadabra   c. an early American term for money
4. spoonerism   d. a charitable foundation

On a separate sheet of paper, write a sentence using each of these words.

DID YOU KNOW?
The word *nice* originally meant ignorant. It comes from the Latin *nescius*, meaning "not very smart," and moved through Middle English and Old French carrying the meaning "foolish." By the fifteenth century, it had picked up the uncomplimentary sense of "just too-too-refined and delicate." Today, it means "pleasant," "welcoming," "a sweet demeanor." But remember the background of the word the next time you call someone "nice."

teetotaler	A **teetotaler** abstains from all alcoholic beverages. The word is said to have come from *teetotal abstainer*, a phrase coined by temperance workers in the 1830s. It has nothing to do with the fact that **teetotalers** drank only tea.
	WORDS IN CONTEXT: *The tee in **teetotaler** is there for emphasis: as in a total abstainer with a capital T, or an absolutely total nondrinker. A character in George Bernard Shaw's play* Candida *says, "I'm only a beer **teetotaler**, not a champagne **teetotaler**," which is meant to be amusing.*
posh	We use this word to mean "elegant" or "fancy," as in a **posh** party or **posh** affair. The word is said to come from travel arrangements on British ships sailing to India. Important passengers were assigned cabins on the shady side of the ship, which means the *portside* on the way out, and the opposite side, or *starboard,* on the way in. Thus, the tickets of these preferred passengers were stamped **P.O.S.H.—** **p**ort **o**ut, **s**tarboard **h**ome.
	WORDS IN CONTEXT: *The smart set in F. Scott Fitzgerald's novels came from **posh** homes in **posh** areas and always had **posh** accommodations on cruises.*
swillbellies *fat*	A crude word with which to abuse obese people: too much swill in the belly. An equally crude synonym is *greedygut.*
	WORDS IN CONTEXT: *The **swillbellies** on the cruise came rolling along the deck after their fifth meal of the day.*
fysigunkus	A person with absolutely no curiosity.
	WORDS IN CONTEXT: *In the classroom there was one brilliant student, three very bright ones, and one **fysigunkus,** who drove the teacher crazy.*

After studying the definitions above, use the words in the sentences below.

1. The shoppers on our class trip spent all their time in the stores, while the _____ spent their time in restaurants.
2. The wedding was a _____affair in an ornate private club.
3. One reporter said that the candidate's utter lack of curiosity made him a_____.
4. At the party, the wine drinkers were in the library, the beer drinkers were on the porch, and the _____were in the living room.

Test Yourself: Place the letter next to the number to match word and meaning.

1. posh
2. fysigunkus
3. swillbellies
4. teetotaler

a. does not spend much time in bars
b. high-end accommodations
c. prefers soap operas on TV to books
d. like menus with many courses

On a separate sheet of paper write a sentence using each of these words.

DID YOU KNOW? Some time ago, girl could be a boy. From the thirteenth to the fifteenth century, *girl* in Middle English was a word denoting either sex. It gradually lost its meaning to include "boy" (much as "he" in Modern English no longer includes a girl or woman).

foof	To wail, howl, or whine like a wounded animal.
	WORDS IN CONTEXT: *The tired man collapsed on the bed and let out a foof.*
eggtaggling	Wasting time in bad company.
	WORDS IN CONTEXT: *My mother said to come directly home from school without any eggtaggling.*
thripping	Snapping the fingers. (A synonym is *lirping*.)
	WORDS IN CONTEXT: *On the dance floor, the teenagers were thripping and lirping to the music.*
xertzing	Gulping down, swallowing quickly and greedily. (Pronounced *zurtzing*.)
	WORDS IN CONTEXT: *The swillbellies and greedyguts were xertzing their food and drink.*

After studying the definitions above, use the words in the sentences below.

1. The less motivated students liked _____ on the corner rather than attending classes.
2. The _____ coming from the nursery let us know the baby wanted attention.
3. When she got a bright idea, you could hear her fingers _____.
4. After running the marathon, he began _____ water.

Test Yourself: Place the letter next to the number to match word and meaning.

1. thripping
2. foof
3. xertzing
4. eggtaggling

a. hanging out with questionable people
b. snapping a part of the anatomy
c. to wail or whine
d. swallowing greedily

On a separate sheet of paper, write a sentence using each of these words.

DID YOU KNOW?
What do a lot of raucous noise and the game of tennis have in common? Answer: The word *racket*. The word comes from the Old French *raquette*, which meant both "the palm of the hand" and "the sole of the foot"—in other words, clapping and stomping. Tennis was once played using the palm of the hands as a racket. In French, tennis is still called *le jeu de paume*, or the hand game.

Surprising Words

The words in this chapter do not mean what you think they do—or they mean what you think they do and something more.

DAY 1

| swastika | fulsome | canard | penultimate |

DAY 2

| restive | enervate | boondoggle | canary |

DAY 3

| enormity | meretricious | toothsome | cupidity |

DAY 4

| consummate | aquiline | presently | votary |

DAY 5

| friable | risible | opera | attic |

DAY 6

| bootless | salary | sardonic | atlas |

DAY 7

| tantalize | bonfire | logos | bedlam |

swastika	A design or ornament in the form of a cross with four equal arms, each bent at a right-angle extension. This design with the arms bent back clockwise was used, as we know, in Nazi Germany and by other Nazi fascists as a party emblem and a symbol of anti-Semitism.
	WORDS IN CONTEXT: *Not so well known is that this design was an ancient mystic symbol in both the Old and New Worlds. The* **swastika** *with its arms bent back counterclockwise has been found as a symbol used by early Native Americans. Another word for it is fylfot.*
fulsome	Disgusting; offensive; excessive or insincere.
	WORDS IN CONTEXT: *Fulsome praise is mistakenly used as meaning great praise or full of praise, but it actually has a negative meaning: excessive, insincere praise.*
canard	A false or malicious report, fabricated and spread; nasty gossip. This word also has an aeronautical meaning: an airplane whose horizontal stabilizer is located in front of the wings; and the word can be used to describe the stabilizing force in such an aircraft.
	WORDS IN CONTEXT: *Canard is actually the French word for duck, and its derivation is from the duck's quack: rumor, false words.*
penultimate	Next to last, second to the last, as in, "His **penultimate** words were, 'Thank you for everything.' His ultimate words were, 'I love you.'" **Penultimate** is often used to mean final, last, highest. That is a mistake.
	WORDS IN CONTEXT: *Penultimate derives from the Latin paene ("almost") and ultimus ("last"). The* **penult** *is the next-to-last syllable in a word.*

After studying the definitions above, use these words in the sentences below.

1. To John, who appreciates simplicity, the ballroom with all its gilt statues, pillars, and swag draperies was decorated in a _____ manner.
2. "That was a base_____," Jim said, after someone told a fabricated anecdote about him.
3. On the side of the wall, the archaeologists found a_____, an ancient symbol.
4. The _____ meeting—there would be only one more—was last Tuesday.

Test Yourself: Write the letter next to the number to match word and meaning.

1. canard	a. next to last
2. fulsome	b. overdone, exaggerated, offensive
3. penultimate	c. adopted by the Nazis from ancient mystics
4. swastika	d. nasty, malicious remark

Write a sentence using each of these words.

DID YOU KNOW?
The expression, "I could care less," as in the sentence "I could care less about what she said about me," actually means the opposite of what the speaker logically seems to be saying. What the speaker means is "I couldn't (or could not) care less."

restive	Refusing to go forward; balky; unruly; as a horse, nervous under pressure; hard to control. Some people mistakenly use **restive** to mean restful or at rest. The word means quite the opposite.
	WORDS IN CONTEXT: *The crowd in the street demonstration was restive.*
enervate	To weaken; to deprive of strength, force, or vigor, debilitate. Too often **enervate** is used as a synonym for energize.
	WORDS IN CONTEXT: *This weather enervates me; makes me slow and sluggish.*
boondoggle	To do trifling pointless work for which one may get payment or other advantages.
	WORDS IN CONTEXT: *The word is sometimes heard used as in "he made a boondoggle" meaning an error or "boo-boo." No. Getting paid for doing trifling work is not a boo-boo—to some it might seem a smart move!*
canary	**Canary** does describe a singing bird of the finch family, as we all know, and it also refers to the bright yellow color typical of that bird we see in a cage—canary yellow. But there are some surprising aspects to that word: it also refers to a yellow variety of carnelian stone, a light orange-colored wood grown in Brazil, to an island called the Isle of Dogs, to a group of islands in the Atlantic off the coast of North Africa, the Canary Isles, to a lively Spanish dance, and to a light, sweet wine imported from the Canaries.
	WORDS IN CONTEXT: *The most surprising thing about the canary bird, given the fact that it has various yellow-colored words associated with it, is that the wild canary is typically green.*

After studying the definitions above, use the words in the sentences below.
Use the form of the word that applies here.

1. The racehorses in the chutes, eager to run, grew _____.
2. Tweetie Pie of cartoon fame was yellow, as are many such household pets, but in the wild a _____ is more commonly green.
3. Reading this long, bureaucratic document _____ me, and I can't stay awake.
4. The brief speech the politician made was a_____, given the private aircraft and the first-class hotel offered him by his sponsors.

Test Yourself: Write the letter next to the number to match word and meaning.

1. canary   a. trivial, pointless work for payment or advantages
2. enervate   b. associated with birds, an isle, islands, wine, yellow, and green
3. boondoggle   c. nervous under pressure; hard to contain
4. restive   d. debilitate, make tired

On a separate sheet of paper, write a sentence using each of the words above.

DID YOU KNOW?
A "near miss" means a collision. A "near hit" would be more accurate if the speaker meant a narrow escape.

enormity	So you think this means enormous or huge? So you would be wrong. **Enormity** actually means *outrageousness, excessive wickedness, monstrous offense.*
	WORDS IN CONTEXT: *The **enormity** of the serial killer's action was staggering.*
meretricious	Merit? No. This word has nothing to do with merit. In fact, it means quite the opposite. It means attracting attention in a vulgar manner; pertaining to or resembling a prostitute. Less meretriciously, it means a false argument; lacking in sincerity.
	WORDS IN CONTEXT: *The candidate made a **meretricious** statement about his opponent.*
toothsome	This word suggests something about teeth. Right? Well, maybe half right. **Toothsome** means delicious or savory, which may suggest "tooth." But it also means pleasant, attractive, and seductive, as in a **toothsome** offer; and it can mean voluptuous and sexually enticing, as in a **toothsome** woman.
	WORDS IN CONTEXT: *The petit fours at the celebrity party were **toothsome** little morsels—and so were the models who served them.*
cupidity	Cupid aiming at a heart? No, but the word derives from the same root as the cute little guy with the bow and arrow. **Cupidity** means desire for great wealth; avarice; greed.
	WORDS IN CONTEXT: *His **cupidity** led him into excessive gambling.*

After studying the definitions above, use the words in the sentences below.

1. The _____ of the convict's crime had been believed by the jury.
2. The gossip in the tabloid was _____ and believed by no one.
3. The tray at the party held a variety of _____ items I passed up.
4. Her _____ led her to marry the wealthy man, rather than the man she loved.

Test Yourself: Write the letter next to the number to match word and meaning.

1. toothsome   a. marked by greed, avariciousness, motivated by desire
2. cupidity   b. insincerity, false argument
3. enormity   c. attractive, seductive
4. meretricious   d. outrageousness, wicked beyond imagination

On a separate sheet of paper, write a sentence using the words above.

DID YOU KNOW?
Bimonthly means every two months. (Often confused with *semimonthly*, which means twice a month.) *Biannual* means twice a year. (Often confused with *biennial*, which means every two years.) Clearly we need clearer words for these concepts.

consummate	Yes, it means to bring to completion or fulfillment, as in "the marriage was consummated." (That's *con'-sum-māt-ed;* accent on the first syllable.)
	WORDS IN CONTEXT: *Consummate (con-sum'-mit; accent on second syllable), means the highest form; supremely accomplished; utter, as in Bach was the* **consummate** *example of a child prodigy.*
aquiline	Ever hear of an aquiline nose? You think that's a beautiful nose? Maybe so, if you're an eagle. **Aquiline** actually means a hooked or curved beak, like an eagle's.
	WORDS IN CONTEXT: *The Roman warrior had an* **aquiline** *profile.*
presently	Many people use this word to mean "now" or "currently." Actually, it means soon.
	WORDS IN CONTEXT: *He will arrive* **presently.** *(Not he is presently here—use currently or now for that.)*
votary	This word has nothing to do with a ballot box. It means one bound by a vow—to a religious life (a monk or nun) or to an activity, a leader, or an ideal.
	WORDS IN CONTEXT: *He was a* **votary** *of attending church and of supporting his favorite charity, the Heart Foundation.*

After studying the definitions above, use the words in the sentences below.

1. His stately carriage and _____ nose made the man imposing.
2. Currently, she is not here, but we have been told that she will _____ deliver her speech before Congress.
3. Their _____ desire was to _____ their marriage on their wedding trip.
4. He was a _____ of the Catholic Church.

Test Yourself: Write the letter next to the number to match word and meaning.

1. presently   a. a person bound by a vow, an enthusiast
2. aquiline   b. soon, but not now
3. consummate   c. hooked or beaked
4. votary   d. to make complete or fulfilled; alternately the highest

On a separate sheet of paper, write a sentence with the words here.

DID YOU KNOW?
The largest book in the Library of Congress is literally for the birds. It's a special edition of Birds in America by the ornithologist John James Audubon. The book contains several original life-sized illustrations of birds and measures nearly 40 inches tall.

| **friable** | So you think potatoes are friable? Well, maybe they are after they've been fried. But **friable** actually has nothing to do with frying. **Friable** means easily crumbled, brittle—possibly as in crisp French fries, which, by the way, did not originate in France but in Belgium.

WORDS IN CONTEXT: *It was not practical to pack the cookies for mailing because they were **friable**.* |
|---|---|
| **risible** | And dough is not **risible**—unless it makes you laugh. **Risible** means "apt to excite laughter," "ludicrous"; "capable of laughing" or "inclined to laugh."

WORDS IN CONTEXT: *The man made a **risible** comment, and the **risible** child could not stop giggling.* |
| **opera** | This word does mean exactly what you think: a theatrical presentation in which a dramatic performance is set to music. But **opera** is also the plural of *opus*, which means merely a work.

WORDS IN CONTEXT: *So **opera**, in addition to what you think it means, means more than one work. (An **opus** is usually accompanied by a number—**Opus 10**, for example—to designate the order of a composer's works.)* |
| **attic** | This word, too, means exactly what you think it does: a small room or story directly below the roof of a house. But the word has an interesting history. It comes from *Attic story*—in architecture, a small top story having square columns in the **Attic style**.

WORDS IN CONTEXT: *And this **Attic style** means "pertaining to ancient Attica or Athens, Greece." Usually, when used this way, **Attic** is capitalized, and it often refers to classical purity and simplicity. (So much for your grandmother's cluttered **attic**!) Another thing: **Attic** is also the ancient Greek dialect of Athens, in which much of classical Greek literature is written.* |

After studying the definitions above, use the words in the sentences below.

1. The remark made by the defendant was_____, so all we could do was laugh.
2. His "works," or his_____ are in the music library.
3. _____: Granny has one, and so did the Greeks. In fact, they once spoke it.
4. These pie shells, because_____, were packaged carefully with tissue between them.

Test Yourself: Write the letter next to the number to match word and meaning.

1. attic
2. risible
3. friable
4. opera

a. you can't call potatoes this, unless they are already brittle
b. a country, a dialect, and that place above where you store those old love letters and lamp shades
c. *Madame Butterfly* is one of these
d. don't tell that joke again; it makes me laugh too hard

On a separate sheet of paper, write a sentence using each of these words.

DID YOU KNOW? There is a difference between a "podium" and a "lectern." You stand on a podium, a raised platform (which comes from the Greek meaning "small foot"). A lectern is the upright desk behind which a speaker stands. You can't pound a podium to make a point, unless you stomp on it, but many preachers have been known to pound the lectern.

bootless	You think that **bootless** describes bare feet? Well, it can. But Shakespeare didn't use it that way in his line from *Julius Caesar,* when he wrote, "Doth not Brutus bootless kneel?" **Bootless** comes from Anglo-Saxon *bot,* meaning profit, so **bootless** means "without profit"; "fruitless."
	WORDS IN CONTEXT: *My trip to the bank proved **bootless**, since the bank was closed.*
salary	You know what this word means: money in payment for work done. But it originally came from Latin *salarium,* meaning money for salt—maybe sweat or salt from the worker's brow or body.
	WORDS IN CONTEXT: *From **salary** we get the idioms "salt for his labors," and "worth his salt."*
sardonic	A **sardonic** facial expression or a **sardonic** comment is one with a sneer—made with twisted mouth, curled lip; a sour, bitter look as if one had tasted something unpleasant—like a poisonous herb from Sardinia (*herba Sardonia*).
	WORDS IN CONTEXT: *Consuming herba Sardonia contorts one's face in a **sardonic** death grimace, and then, alas, one dies of poisoning. One hopes the person who makes death masks is not around.*
atlas	This means what you think it does: a book of maps, and the name **Atlas** refers to the Titan **Atlas** in Greek mythology who held the heavens on his shoulders. Early books of maps usually carried a picture in the front of **Atlas** doing his heavy lifting, whence came the shortened form of the name of the map book.
	WORDS IN CONTEXT: *The **Atlas** Mountains in northwest Africa were so powerful-looking and formidable that they were thought to support the heavens; their name comes from **Atlas,** the Greek Titan, too.*

After studying the definitions above, use the words in the sentences below.

1. _____could mean you're unshod and also that you did some unprofitable thing.
2. His _____expression made us think he'd taken an exotic poison.
3. _____was a strong god, so strong a book of maps was named for him.
4. So when you went back to the salt mines, did you earn a good_____?

Test Yourself: Write the letter next to the number to match word and meaning.

1. sardonic   a. that book with a picture of a hard-working god in front
2. salary   b. your contorted face reminds me of a plant in Sardinia
3. atlas   c. pass the salt; no pepper
4. bootless   d. no profit, no luck, no shoes

On a separate sheet of paper, write a sentence using the words above.

DID YOU KNOW?
The Greek mathematician Pythagoras added a fifth essence to the four essences already established philosophically: earth, air, fire, and water. This fifth essence or "quint essence" was "ether," or that which most defines a body, thing, or idea: She is the quintessence of grace; he is the quintessence of health; her act was the quintessence of generosity.

tantalize	To motivate by something desired but not attainable. Speaking of Greek mythology, **Tantalus,** a wicked king of Lydia, was sent to the Underworld. His punishment was to stand in a lake with water up to his chin, under a branch on which hung delicious fruit. When **Tantalus** tried to eat the fruit or drink the water, they receded from his grasp—remaining always just out of reach.
	WORDS IN CONTEXT: *From the myth of* **Tantalus** *came the word* **tantalize,** *"to torment with something desired but ever unattainable."*
bonfire	We think we know what this is: that fun fire in which we roast marshmallows, or around which we celebrate after a victorious ballgame. No such luck for people back in the Middle Ages, who gave us the word *banefyre* meaning "fire of bones."
	WORDS IN CONTEXT: *Our jolly* **bonfire** *originated with the burning of victims of the plague and of religious persecution.*
logos	You think this refers to the letters or illustrations—such as GAP, or DKNY—on your T-shirt? Well, you're half correct. **Logos** are those corporate and other symbols. But the word to ancient philosophers meant "reason" and "word." And Christian theologians saw the word "Word" in the way it was used in the New Testament: to mean Jesus Christ.
	WORDS IN CONTEXT: *If you have an old T-shirt sporting the* **logo** *of the musical theater production* Jesus Christ Superstar, *then you can display on your chest your complete knowledge of* **logos.**
bedlam	A scene of confusion; babbling, erratic behavior. Actually, the word refers to the hospital of St. Mary of Bethlehem in London, called **Bedlam**—once a lunatic asylum, a madhouse.
	WORDS IN CONTEXT: *The* **bedlam** *surrounding the student demonstration upset the college administrators.*

After studying the definitions above, use the words in the sentences below. Use the form of the word that applies.

1. He was_____by the job just out of his reach.
2. We don't think about bones burning when we sit before a cozy_____.
3. The company proudly displayed its _____ —without knowing the religious background of the word.
4. When I was moving from one state to another and one house to another, my disorganized life seemed like_____.

Test Yourself: Write the letter next to the number to match word and meaning.

1. bonfire   a. the thing most desired is unobtainable
2. logos   b. what Londoners called that madhouse
3. tantalize   c. refers to both Jesus Christ and the swoosh on your Nikes
4. bedlam   d. burning bones

On a separate sheet of paper, write a sentence using the words above.

DID YOU KNOW?
Shakespeare had a wicked sense of humor. The word petard, which Shakespeare made famous when he had Hamlet say, "The engineer was hoist on his own petard," had a double meaning. It means "blown up by his own bomb," or "caught in his own trap." But raunchy old Will wrote for commoners, who would have known the word also means "fart." (Hoist, of course, means "raised" or "lifted off the ground.")

Trick Words

The words in this chapter have for centuries tripped up speakers of English because they are exceptions to the rules, particularly the homonyms and other words that are simply confusing.

DAY 1

| continual/ continuous | altogether/ all together | foregoing/ forgoing | a while/ awhile |

DAY 2

| censor/ censure | disinterested/ uninterested | elicit/ illicit | compliment/ complement |

DAY 3

| farther/ further | everyone/ every one | imply/ infer | eminent/imminent/ immanent |

DAY 4

| bad/ badly | differ from/ differ with | back up/ backup | emigrate/ immigrate |

DAY 5

| respectfully/ respectively | maybe/ may be | allusion/ illusion | immoral/ amoral |

DAY 6

| adverse/ averse | affect/ effect | ingenious/ ingenuous | passed/ past |

DAY 7

| adapt/ adopt | burst | coarse/ course | explicit/ implicit |

continual	Repeated regularly and frequently.
	WORDS IN CONTEXT: *She was annoyed when her computer suffered* **continual** *breakdowns. I was* **continually** *being interrupted by the telephone.* **TIP:** Think off and on, particularly in terms of nuisances.
continuous	Extended or prolonged without interruption.
	WORDS IN CONTEXT: *The car alarm wailed continuously for 15 minutes. Her migraines became* **continuous.** **TIP:** A good mnemonic device to help you remember this is to think of a siren, which has a sustained sound. Siren—sustained—sound. The word you want for that has an *s* in it: **continuous.** (The goddess Mnemosyne will look fondly on your good memory.)
all together	Everyone gathered.
	WORDS IN CONTEXT: *We want to get our family* **all together.**
altogether	Completely or entirely.
	WORDS IN CONTEXT: *We are not* **altogether** *sure we can get our family* **all together** *for the holidays.*
foregoing	Previously said or written; preceding.
	WORDS IN CONTEXT: *Please ignore the* **foregoing** *instructions. The* **foregoing** *is an alert to watch for a memo.*
forgoing	This means "giving up," "abstaining from," "doing without."
	WORDS IN CONTEXT: *He said he would be* **forgoing** *dessert. I think I will* **forgo** *the party and get a good night's sleep.*
a while	This is a noun with its article "a."
	WORDS IN CONTEXT: *We can stay for* **a while.** **TIP:** If you use *for* or another preposition, use the two-word version: *a while.*
awhile	This is an adverb modifying a verb meaning "some time."
	WORDS IN CONTEXT: *We can stay* **awhile.** *Stick around* **awhile** *and meet the gang. Walk* **awhile,** *and test these shoes.*

After studying the words above, use each in the appropriate sentence below.

1. I am _____the trip during spring break to work on my paper for history class.
2. She said she would be ready in _____, so we will wait for her.
3. I am not _____convinced that his policies are the best ones.
4. The car horns honked off and on _____all night long.
5. Will we be_____ in the same cabin on our trip?
6. She called me _____ago, wanting my opinion.
7. The _____is a preamble to the document I am writing.
8. The siren sounded _____for ten minutes and drove me crazy.

Test Yourself: Write the letter next to the number to match word and meaning.

1. continual — a. preceding, going before
2. continuous — b. means a small amount of time, an adverb
3. foregoing — c. abstaining from, giving up
4. forgoing — d. sustained, extended, or prolonged without interruption
5. awhile — e. repeated regularly and frequently
6. a while — f. gathering together
7. altogether — g. a noun and its article; usually used with a preposition
8. all together — h. completely, entirely

On a separate sheet of paper, write a sentence using each of these words.

DID YOU KNOW?
Where does the word for your *denim* pants called *jeans* come from? From the Italian city of Genoa. In the Middle Ages, Genoa was called Jene or Gene. Our jeans were first made there from *denim,* the name of which comes from the city of Nimes in Southern France where the cloth was made. *Denim* was first called *serge de Nimes* and later simply *de Nimes.* The two words were collapsed into *denimes* and then into *denim.* (So you wear khakis? Tough luck. *Khaki* means "sandy pants; dust-colored!")

censor	To remove or suppress material considered objectionable.
	WORDS IN CONTEXT: *The bishops tried to censor the books that parishioners wanted to read.*
censure	To criticize severely.
	WORDS IN CONTEXT: *The official who committed fraud was censured by the public.*
disinterested	Objective and impartial.
	WORDS IN CONTEXT: *The journalist was a disinterested observer.*
uninterested	Has no interest.
	WORDS IN CONTEXT: *I did not join the club because I was uninterested in its programs.*
elicit	To evoke, or to bring out.
	WORDS IN CONTEXT: *The telephone pollster tried to elicit my opinion.*
illicit	Unlawful.
	WORDS IN CONTEXT: *He was arrested for selling illicit drugs.*
compliment	A flattering remark; to compliment means to flatter.
	WORDS IN CONTEXT: *She gave the speaker a compliment on his presentation; he complimented her for her program notes in return.*
complement	To complete, or something that completes.
	WORDS IN CONTEXT: *As a complement to the turkey, she served dressing. The cranberries also complemented the meal.*

After studying the words above, use each in the appropriate sentence below.

1. His sigh suggested that he was _____ in the details of her shopping adventures.
2. To be fair, judges have to have a _____ view of each case.
3. Through her questioning, the teacher tried to _____ the correct answer.
4. He was tried for _____ use of the corporation's funds.
5. She _____ her friend on the decor of her apartment.
6. Her cape and jewelry were a great _____ to her ball gown.
7. The library board attempted to _____ the materials in the library.
8. She was _____ for her part in the mismanagement of the firm's money.

Test Yourself: Write the letter next to the number to match word and meaning.

1. compliment	a. something that completes another thing
2. complement	b. admiring remarks
3. censor	c. to suppress or remove objectionable material
4. censure	d. critical remarks
5. uninterested	e. objective or detached
6. disinterested	f. simply not engaged in the subject
7. illicit	g. to evoke or bring out
8. elicit	h. not legal

On a separate sheet of paper, write a sentence using each of the words.

DID YOU KNOW?
The term *hoi polloi* is used by masses of journalists, pundits, and others who don't know any better as a term meaning the upper classes or fancy people. It means nothing of the sort. *Hoi polloi* actually means "the masses." *Hoi* is a Greek plural definite article, and *polloi* is Greek for *many*. So if you say "the hoi polloi," you are actually saying *the the many*. If you use the term, drop the first "the."

farther	Use this to refer to linear distance. If you can measure something—in miles, footsteps, or with a tape measure—use **farther**.
	WORDS IN CONTEXT: *You live **farther** from the stadium than I do. **Farther** down the road is a restaurant. You came the **farthest** distance.* TIP: Not fartherest! Farthest.
further	Use this for everything else—degree, depth, quantity.
	WORDS IN CONTEXT: *You read **further** into the book than I did. Think about it **further**. Let's talk about this **further**.*
everyone	Think of *everyone* as a solid body of people. It's an indefinite pronoun.
	WORDS IN CONTEXT: ***Everyone** was there. **Everyone** wanted to go. **Everyone** had a great time.*
every one	Think of *every one* as a group of individuals.
	WORDS IN CONTEXT: ***Every one** of us was there. **Every one** of them wanted to go. **Every one** of the people who came was invited.* TIP: Notice how every one of the people *was* invited. *One* takes the singular verb *was*. The same goes for *everyone* when written as one word. Singular.
imply	This means to state indirectly or to suggest.
	WORDS IN CONTEXT: *His attitude meant to **imply** that the party was over, so the guests should go home. She **implied** that she did not want to see me again. Her **implication** was clear. Are you **implying** that I don't know what I'm talking about?*
infer	This means to draw a conclusion.
	WORDS IN CONTEXT: *I **inferred** from his implication that I was not welcome. She **inferred** that the two were a couple. They **inferred** that the party was winding down, so they should leave.* TIP: Think of a baseball game: *imply* is the pitcher and *infer* is the catcher. He *implied* (pitched), so I *inferred* (caught).
eminent	This means "distinguished or outstanding."
	WORDS IN CONTEXT: *The speaker was an **eminent** scholar of the classics. At the gallery, we met an **eminent** painter.*
imminent	This means "about to happen."
	WORDS IN CONTEXT: *The White House press secretary said that an announcement was **imminent**. The doctor said the birth of the child was **imminent**.*
immanent	There is a third, less frequently used, homonym here: *immanent*. This word, used in a theological sense, means "everywhere present" and is said of God.
	WORDS IN CONTEXT: *God is **immanent** in the universe. His spirit is **immanent**. His **immanence** is present in all humankind. The saints felt His **immanency**.*

After studying the words above, use each in the appropriate sentence below.

1. _____ on our block is coming to the barbeque.
2. The teacher said, "I want _____of you to sit down now!"
3. Are you _____that I did not do my homework?
4. I _____from what you said that I should spend more time studying.
5. Dr. Kerry is the most _____professor in our department.
6. The moderator said that the speaker's appearance was_____.
7. You live _____from the university than I do.
8. Read _____into the text; then we will discuss it_____.

Test Yourself: Write the letter next to the number to match word and meaning.

1. every one	a. seen as a group of people
2. everyone	b. each person seen as an individual
3. imply	c. to suggest or state indirectly
4. infer	d. to draw a conclusion
5. eminent	e. outstanding or distinguished
6. imminent	f. about to happen
7. further	g. suggests degree, depth, or quantity
8. farther	h. suggests linear, measurable distance

On a separate sheet of paper, write a sentence using each of these words.

DID YOU KNOW?

The word *boycott* is derived from the name of a man in Ireland who was despised. Captain Charles C. Boycott, a land agent in County Mayo, raised the rent of land tenants in 1880 when he knew they had suffered a crop failure and could not pay. The tenants banded together, refused to pay, and harassed Capt. Boycott until he was forced to flee to England. "Boycotts" have worked much like that ever since.

bad	Many people use the words bad and **badly** incorrectly. Remember this: **Bad** is an adjective. You should use **bad** as in the examples following.
	WORDS IN CONTEXT: *I feel **bad** about her accident. They felt **bad** about his losing the game. Everyone felt **bad** about his hard luck. She got a **bad** break.* **TIP:** You cannot say, "I feel **badly**" unless you mean that you literally have no feeling in your fingers or sensitivity in your body. (Similarly, if you felt poor, you would not say "I feel poorly." If you felt rich, you would not say, "I feel richly." If you felt happy, you would not say, "I feel happily." Get it?)
badly	This word is an adverb.
	WORDS IN CONTEXT: *My head hurt **badly** after I hit it on the doorframe. She injured herself **badly** when she fell. His injury **badly** affected his ability to play ball.*
differ from	To be unlike.
	WORDS IN CONTEXT: *My house **differs from** yours in that mine is a colonial and yours is a contemporary. His long hair **differs from** her short hair.*
differ with	To disagree.
	WORDS IN CONTEXT: *I beg to **differ with** you over the pronunciation of that word. He **differed with** her in that he wanted a sedan and she wanted a convertible.*
back up	A verb phrase.
	WORDS IN CONTEXT: *You will have to **back up** to get the car out of the driveway. Watch out when you're **backing up**! Get the truck out of the way before you **back up**.*
backup	A neologism created by technology; this means making a duplicate of material stored electronically.
	WORDS IN CONTEXT: *Put your **backup** disks where you can find them easily. Do your **backup** before you forget.*
emigrate	To leave one country and settle in another.
	WORDS IN CONTEXT: *They **emigrated** from Poland.*
immigrate	To enter another country to live.
	WORDS IN CONTEXT: *His parents **immigrated** to the United States from Russia.* **TIP:** A mnemonic device: Both *immigrate* and *in* begin with i. Also think of bonding the words with prepositions: "**immigrate to**" and "**emigrate from**."

After studying the words above, use each in the appropriate sentence below. Use the form of the word that applies.

1. I _____with him about how to handle the sale of the property.
2. The manuscript _____the edited version.
3. Don't try to _____the Jeep until you move the other vehicles.
4. I forgot my _____ disk.
5. I certainly feel _____about the grade I had to give him, but he was lazy.
6. She was _____hurt in the skiing accident.
7. My parents _____to the United States to escape the pogroms.
8. They _____from Russia, which has given them a new life.

Test Yourself: Write the letter next to the number to match word and meaning.

1. badly
2. emigrate
3. bad
4. immigrate
5. differ with
6. backup
7. differ from
8. back up

a. an adjective that describes the way he feels about the problem
b. an adverb that describes how my finger hurt after I cut it
c. leaving one country to live in another
d. a duplicate of electronically stored data
e. to be unlike
f. to disagree
g. a verb phrase referring to an action
h. entering a country to reside there

On a separate sheet of paper, write a sentence using each of these words.

DID YOU KNOW?
In a sense, the word *bikini* —that skimpy swimsuit worn on beaches—should actually be capitalized. Why? Because legend has it that it is modeled on the attire worn by girls on the Bikini atoll in the Marshall Islands. Another tale leads us to believe that the effect on males on the beaches of France in 1947, when the scanty items first appeared, was comparable to the atomic test blasts on the Bikini atolls. Either way, a purist would capitalize this word.

respectfully	Showing or marked by respect.
	WORDS IN CONTEXT: *He spoke to his father **respectfully**. She had a **respectful** attitude toward her professor.*
respectively	Means each in the order given.
	WORDS IN CONTEXT: *John, Carl, and Sam were an A student, a B student, and a C student, **respectively**. Whitney, David, and their father, Craig, ordered, **respectively**, steak, hamburger, and pasta.*
maybe	An adverb meaning "possibly."
	WORDS IN CONTEXT: *The kids begged their father to let them use the car, but all he would say was "**Maybe**." **Maybe** the Red Sox will win tomorrow.*
may be	A verb phrase suggesting doubt or lack of conviction.
	WORDS IN CONTEXT: *It **may be** that our friends will come tomorrow. Our fate **may be** to have rain on our parade day.*
allusion	An indirect reference.
	WORDS IN CONTEXT: *Did you catch the biblical **allusion** in Hemingway's title,* The Sun Also Rises? *Her novel,* Against the Setting Sun, *is an **allusion** to a line in* King Lear.
illusion	A fantasy, a dream, a false impression, a misconception.
	WORDS IN CONTEXT: *He thought it would work, but he was suffering from an **illusion**. In her Cinderella dress, she was an **illusion**. ("Cinderella dress" here is an **allusion** to the fairy tale.)*
immoral	Morally wrong.
	WORDS IN CONTEXT: *Murder is **immoral**; sleeping with your neighbor's wife is **immoral**. Christians tend to take their definition of **immorality** from the Ten Commandments (the Decalogue to you!)*
amoral	Being unconcerned with moral judgments; neither moral nor immoral.
	WORDS IN CONTEXT: *His answers came from an **amoral** perspective. Her philosophy was basically **amoral**.*

After studying the words above, use each of them in the appropriate sentence below.

1. The judge said that it was sometimes hard to make a distinction between what was illegal, what was unethical, and what was_____.
2. She was under the_____ that she was a fair boss, so her employees' boycott surprised her.
3. Not being guided by a religious faith, he made his decision from an _____point of view.
4. In the poems of William Blake, you can find many historical, political, regional, and biblical_____.
5. At the resort, Charles, Dan, and Jacy played badminton, basketball, and tennis _____.
6. In church, he bowed his head_____.
7. Her grandmother _____coming to see her on Monday or Tuesday.
8. _____ her grandfather will come, too.

Test Yourself: Write the letter next to the number to match word and meaning.

1. respectively
2. immoral
3. may be
4. allusion
5. respectfully
6. illusion
7. amoral
8. maybe

a. possibly
b. misconception, fantasy
c. verb phrase expressing uncertainty
d. definitely wrong by most standards
e. in the order given
f. showing honor or respect
g. an indirect reference
h. unconcerned with moral judgment

On a separate sheet of paper, write a sentence using each of these words.

DID YOU KNOW?
The phrase "bell, book, and candle" was a curse. The term was used as a form of excommunication from the church: a bell was tolled (as if a person had died), the priest closed the book (symbol of life), and the candle (symbol of soul) was extinguished. This ritual is described in a Latin text of the fourteenth century, but it is mentioned in many early writings including those by Cervantes and Shakespeare.

adverse	Unfavorable.
	WORDS IN CONTEXT: *His policies are having an **adverse** effect on the economy. The sun affected her rash **adversely**. The drought had an **adverse** impact on farming.* **TIP:** *Adverse* is usually followed by *effect* or *impact*.
averse	Opposed to or reluctant.
	WORDS IN CONTEXT: *He is **averse** to the idea of climate control. Those policies are **averse** to our best interests.* **TIP:** *Averse* is usually followed by *to*.
affect	Usually a **verb** meaning "to influence" or "to produce a change in" (emphasis on the second syllable).
	WORDS IN CONTEXT: *The sun **affected** her rash adversely. My sleep patterns were **affected** by jet lag. The presence of the new baby **affects** the dog's behavior.* However, to complicate matters, **affect** when used in psychology (emphasis on the first syllable, af'-fect), is a **noun** meaning "emotional response or feeling." *When the psychologist mentioned her childhood, the woman's **affect** did not change. When his father walked in, the patient's **affect** was altered.*
effect	Usually a noun meaning "result."
	WORDS IN CONTEXT: *The sun had no **effect** on her rash. Your plans had an **effect** on our schedule. His tax cuts had no **effect** on the economy.* But to compound the complication further, **effect** can also be a verb meaning "to bring about." *The mayor **effected** a change in the school system. Her mother's return **effected** a change in her behavior. The medication **effects** no change in his illness.* When **effect** is used as a verb, the word *change* often follows it. **TIP:** All clear? To aid your memory, when you write your sentences with these words (in the exercise below), it's advisable to write a sentence showing *both* ways in which you can use each of these confusing words.
ingenious	Clever; creative.
	WORDS IN CONTEXT: *She came up with an **ingenious** plan for exchanging her New York apartment for one in Paris for the summer. He invented an **ingenious** device for lighting coals in the barbeque.*
ingenuous	Naive, frank, open, candid.
	WORDS IN CONTEXT: *She has an **ingenuous** manner that encourages people to trust her. He is startlingly **ingenuous** for a politician.*
passed	This is simply past tense of the verb *pass*.
	WORDS IN CONTEXT: *The waiter **passed** the tray of cheeses. We **passed** six white cars in a row. The time to make the call has **passed**.*
past	In a period before this one; beyond a time or place.
	WORDS IN CONTEXT: *In the **past**, these street lamps held candles. My house is just **past** his. We sat up till **past** midnight.*

After studying the words above, use each of them in the appropriate sentence below.
1. On the street, she _____ a man in a clown's outfit.
2. For a corporate boss, his manner was open and _____.
3. His wife said after the argument that she thought the _____ should be forgotten.
4. Arranging the flowers in a cowboy boot was an _____ theme party idea.
5. Her friend's death had a devastating _____ on her.
6. The writer said that he grew up under _____ circumstances.
7. Planting the bulbs a few days early should not _____ their growth.
8. I'm not _____ to vacationing in the mountains, but I'd prefer the seashore.

Test Yourself: Write the letter next to the number to match word and meaning.

1. ingenuous	a. unfavorable
2. affect	b. opposed to or reluctant
3. ingenious	c. the past tense of pass
4. effect	d. in a former time or beyond a time or place
5. adverse	e. influence (or emotional response)
6. averse	f. result (or a verb that usually precedes *change*)
7. past	g. naive, candid, frank
8. passed	h. clever or creative

On a separate sheet of paper, write a sentence using each of these words.

DID YOU KNOW? The idiom "tooth and nail" or to fight as hard as you can, biting and scratching, appears to date back to the sixteenth century. Certainly, Charles Dickens used the phrase in 1850 in *David Copperfield*: "I go at it tooth and nail."

adapt	To make a shift, or to become accustomed to.
	WORDS IN CONTEXT: *He could not **adapt** to the cold weather, so he moved south. She always **adapted** her speeches to her audience. They had a difficult time **adapting** their strong individual personalities to marriage.*
adopt	To take in as one's own.
	WORDS IN CONTEXT: *They decided to **adopt** a Vietnamese child. When I moved south, I tried to **adopt** a southern accent, but I was a failure.*
burst	There is really only one word for coming apart or flying open violently. That word is **burst.** Its basic present, past, and participle forms are identical. (You need to add *s* only for the third person singular present tense form, **bursts**.) All the other words you've ever heard (*bust, busted, bursted*) are slang or incorrect. Remember that something, say a balloon, **bursts** today, it **burst** yesterday, and it will **burst** tomorrow.
	WORDS IN CONTEXT: *I **burst** into laughter at this very moment. I **burst** into laughter three times last night. I will **burst** into laughter tomorrow if you do that again. I have **burst** into laughter four times so far. I had **burst** into laughter seven times before I learned to restrain myself. Forget everything else you've ever heard.*
coarse	Rough in texture, unrefined, or crude.
	WORDS IN CONTEXT: *The homespun fabric of colonial Americans was **coarse**. The language in the film was **coarse** and embarrassing.*
course	This word has many meanings, as shown in the sentences following.
	WORDS IN CONTEXT: *I took a **course** (class, unit of study) in anthropology. The hiking **course** (path) was uphill and tiring. They played on a **course** (playing field) that was wet and soggy. Of **course** (certainly) I was willing to work long hours on the project.*
explicit	Directly expressed or clearly defined.
	WORDS IN CONTEXT: *I got lost, even though his directions were **explicit**. His mother told him **explicitly** not to leave before she arrived.*
implicit	Implied or unstated.
	WORDS IN CONTEXT: *When he did not respond, I assumed his **implicit** approval. She looked away, **implicitly** suggesting that she was displeased.*

After studying the words above, use each in the appropriate sentence below.

1. The texture of the rug was_____, a complement to the informality of the room.
2. I asked for _____instructions on what would be expected of me at the event.
3. The _____was long and difficult, but the bike tour of Ireland was educational.
4. _____ in her words was the message that I should call her as soon as possible.
5. As he bent over, the seams in the clown's pant_____ with a loud noise.
6. I tried to _____ to its way of thinking, but I found Zen Buddhism incomprehensible.
7. When I was in Africa, I _____the natives way of dress and found it exciting.

Test Yourself: Write the letter next to the number to match word and meaning.

1. coarse   a. to explode or fly open violently
2. adopt   b. clearly stated
3. implicit   c. a unit of study, a path, a way of saying "certainly"
4. adapt   d. unrefined texture or language
5. burst   e. to take as one's own
6. explicit   f. to suggest
7. course   g. to adjust or become accustomed to

On a separate sheet of paper, write a sentence using each of these words.

DID YOU KNOW? The saying, "Pull our own weight" is a rowing term. In rowing, each crew member must pull on an oar hard enough to propel his or her own weight. This expression was used in a speech by Theodore Roosevelt in 1902: "The first requisite of a good citizen . . . is that he shall be able and willing to pull his weight."

Slick Words

This chapter deals with contronyms—words that mean the word itself and also its opposite, or very close to its opposite. Other slick, or confusing, words are introduced here, too.

DAY 1

| sanction | dust | bolt | commencement |

DAY 2

| temper | handicap | cleave | mortal |

DAY 3

| critical | qualified | trim | strike |

DAY 4

| buckle | screen | oversight | clip |

DAY 5

| left | dress | weather | fast |

DAY 6

| gave out | hold up | wear | certain |

DAY 7

| founder/ flounder | discreet/ discrete | flout/ flaunt | gauntlet/ gantlet |

sanction	This word means both "give approval to" and "restrain or censure."
	WORDS IN CONTEXT: *The university officials **sanctioned** the idea of street dances for the students, but they put **sanctions** on the use of alcohol. The first use of the word means "approved"; the second use means "disallowed or censured."*
dust	Here's an easy one: we all know that **dust** collects on our furniture when we leave the windows open. So what do we do about it? We **dust,** of course—to get rid of it.
	WORDS IN CONTEXT: *The first meaning of the word **dust** is "material spread about." The second meaning of **dust** is "remove materials that have spread about."*
bolt	One meaning of **bolt** is "to hold in place." Another meaning of **bolt** is "to dash away."
	WORDS IN CONTEXT: ***Bolt** the barn door so the horses will not **bolt!***
commencement	One meaning of this word is "a beginning." Another meaning is "an ending."
	WORDS IN CONTEXT: *One can hardly attend **commencement** exercises at a high school or college without a speaker reminding us that in **commencement** we are witnessing both an ending to the current school days and a beginning of a new life.*

After studying the definitions above, use the words in the sentences below. Use the form of the word that applies.

1. Please _____the door before you leave; yesterday, when it was left open, the dogs_____.
2. The government _____the United Nation's plan, but it refused to impose _____on importing oil.
3. Before too much _____collected on his car in the garage, he _____ the car and then washed it.
4. As she _____on a life after college, she put a _____to her student years.

Test Yourself: Write the letter next to the number to match word and meaning.

1. dust
2. commencement
3. bolt
4. sanction

a. to secure in place; to dart away
b. a beginning and a conclusion
c. material that gathers; remove that material
d. to approve; to disallow

On a separate sheet of paper, write sentences using both meanings of these words.

DID YOU KNOW?
Contronyms, like the words above, are sometimes called Janus words because the Greek god Janus had one head with two faces. The faces looked in opposite directions. (The name of the month, January, which looks backward to the old year and forward to the new year—a commencement of a sort—is derived from that two-faced god.)

temper	One meaning of **temper** is "to soften, make less strong." Another meaning is "to strengthen." (Of course, there is also the meaning that describes emotional proclivities, as in **bad temper, good temper, even temper, foul temper, controlled temper.**)
	WORDS IN CONTEXT: *I tried to* **temper** *my anger when I argued with my father. The factory* **tempered** *the steel to make it stronger.*
handicap	Two opposing meanings again: One, "a disability or having a disadvantage"; the other, " advantage."
	WORDS IN CONTEXT: *The man found his wheelchair a* **handicap** *when he approached a long flight of stairs. His horse carried only 112 pounds, 12 pounds less than the favorite, in the* **handicap** *race.*
cleave	One meaning: "to cut in two; to separate." Another: "to cling to or adhere firmly."
	WORDS IN CONTEXT: *She picked up the meat* **cleaver** *to* **cleave** *the large steak. The Bible tells us to leave our parents and* **cleave** *to our new spouses when we marry.*
mortal	One meaning: "deadly, causing certain death." Another: "live, but subject to dying."
	WORDS IN CONTEXT: *The soldier suffered a* **mortal** *wound on the battlefield and died in the hospital. Human beings are mere* **mortals;** *we cannot live forever.*

After studying the definitions above, use the words in the sentences below.

1. She said she would _____ to her husband, who is now outside _____ wood with his ax.
2. The man did not feel that his broken arm was a_____; he could still play golf with a 10_____.
3. "What fools we _____ be," declared Shakespeare, who, in another play, had a character receive a _____ blow.
4. The worker _____ the metal to harden and strengthen it by heating and cooling it alternately; meanwhile he sought to _____his anger at his nasty boss.

Test Yourself: Write the letter next to the number to match word and meaning.

1. mortal	a. cling to firmly; cut apart
2. temper	b. subject to death; deadly
3. cleave	c. disadvantage and advantage
4. handicap	d. decrease strength; increase strength

On a separate sheet of paper, write sentences using both meanings of these words.

DID YOU KNOW?
Downhill could mean getting easier— "It was all downhill after we won the election." And downhill could mean getting worse— "It was all downhill after we lost the election."

critical	Means both "opposed" and "essential to."
	WORDS IN CONTEXT: First meaning: *The leader was strongly critical of Item 12 in the report and finally rejected it.* Second meaning: *The others thought that Item 12 in the report was critical to the case they were attempting to make.*
qualified	One meaning: "competent." Another meaning: "limited."
	WORDS IN CONTEXT: *Both lawyers pronounced seven of the potential jurists qualified to hear the case, but their endorsement of the eighth candidate was qualified.*
trim	One meaning: "add something to." Another: "to cut away."
	WORDS IN CONTEXT: *After the house was built, the carpenters added the trim. He went to the barber to get a trim. Also, we trimmed the Christmas tree with lights and bright balls, after we trimmed the branches to get it into the house.*
strike	First meaning: to hit or secure in place. Another: to remove.
	WORDS IN CONTEXT: *He hit the nail hard to strike it into the wood. The coach said, "After the game, we'll strike the goal posts." Also, the union went on strike (work stoppage) to strike a deal with management (get a new work agreement).*

**After studying the definitions above, use the words in the sentences below.
Use the form of the word that applies.**

1. We are planning to _____the Christmas tree with silver bells, and then we will ____the fat from the turkey.
2. The teacher made several _____remarks on my first draft that made the final paper better. She said it was _____that I learn to punctuate better.
3. _____ the handle hard when putting together the croquet mallet. _____ that phrase from the contract, please.
4. He said my résumé indicated that I was _____for the job, though he was _____in his comments about my management experience.

Test Yourself: Write the letter next to the number to match word and meaning.

1. trim   a. to hold in place; to remove
2. qualified   b. to add something to; to cut something away
3. strike   c. competent; limited
4. critical   d. opposed; essential

On a separate sheet of paper, write sentences with both meanings of these words.

DID YOU KNOW?
Who causes panic? Pan, of course, the mythological satyr with the body of a man and the legs, ears, and horns of a goat. He was assumed to cause weird things to happen—noises and bumps in the night, strange sounds in the woods. Pan caused panic—and panic was pandemic. (*Pandemic* means "widespread," from the Greek for "all the people.")

buckle	The two meanings: "to fasten together" and "to break apart."
	WORDS IN CONTEXT: *Buckle* up your overcoat, when the wind is free, but don't **buckle** when the pressure becomes too intense.
screen	To hide from view; to view.
	WORDS IN CONTEXT: *Put a heavy* **screen** *on the window to* **screen** *our movements from the neighbors' view. We're invited to* **screen** *a new film that is opening next week.*
oversight	One meaning: "supervision." Two: "failure to supervise; neglect."
	WORDS IN CONTEXT: *The director has* **oversight** *of three divisions. Because of his* **oversight** *regarding the deadline, the team lost the account.*
clip	One meaning: "fasten, hold." Another: "cut, remove, separate."
	WORDS IN CONTEXT: *If you will* **clip** *your hair back from your face, you will be able see better when the wind blows. On the other hand, if you will just* **clip** *your hair into bangs, you'll see better all the time.*

After studying the definitions above, use the words in the sentences below.
Use the form of the word that applies.

1. We _____ the ugly alley by putting up a fence. Please _____ the new version of the film and reply to me as soon as possible.
2. She put a new _____ on her belt so she could _____ it more securely. He hoped he wouldn't _____ when his boss demanded explanations for the financial loss.
3. My new job gives me _____ of the advertising area. Please don't try to excuse the _____ in the budget plan you presented.
4. _____ all these paper together after you copy them, but don't forget to_____ off the ragged edge before you bind them.

Test Yourself: Write the letter next to the number to match word and meaning.

1. screen   a. fasten; fall apart
2. buckle   b. hide from view; look at, view
3. clip   c. supervise carefully; neglect
4. oversight   d. secure, hold; cut off

On a separate sheet of paper, use both meanings of these words in sentences.

DID YOU KNOW?
Laconic means "brief, blunt, concise, and succinct." The word derives from the ancient Laconians whose capital was Sparta. A story illustrates their grace with words. Philip of Macedon sent a message of invasion to the Laconians: "If we come to your city, we will raze it to the ground." Their laconic response: "If."

left	One definition: departed. Another: remaining.
	WORDS IN CONTEXT: *They **left** for the beach for a vacation. When the family finished the picnic, the only thing **left** was one chicken wing.*
dress	Here's one: Put something on. And another: Clean and prepare for cooking.
	WORDS IN CONTEXT: *It's nearly time to **dress** for Thanksgiving dinner, but we have time to **dress** the turkey for cooking.*
weather	One: withstand. Another: wear down or wear away.
	WORDS IN CONTEXT: *It was an ordeal, but we **weathered** the storm. We let the shingles on the house **weather** to a lovely gray tone.*
fast	Stay firmly in one place. Move rapidly to another place.
	WORDS IN CONTEXT: *A hurricane took down the trees, but the house held **fast**. We should get out of here **fast** because it looks as if another hurricane is coming.*

**After studying the definitions above, use the words in the sentences below.
Use the form of the word that applies.**

1. The hunters who brought home the birds for dinner,_____ them before they_____themselves for the evening.
2. The Cliffs of Dover had _____from gray to white, but that they were still there showed they had _____many centuries.
3. We will stand _____against the enemy because our armies know how to move_____.
4. I _____the meeting early, but there were only a few minutes_____ in the final presentation.

Test Yourself: Write the letter next to the number to match word and meaning.

1. fast   a. adding something to; removing feathers from
2. left   b. withstand; wear away
3. dress   c. departed from; remaining
4. weather   d. stay firmly in place; rapidly move

On a separate sheet of paper, write sentences with both meanings of these words.

DID YOU KNOW?
The symbol of health and healing is the caduceus. That's the staff with two intertwined snakes that you often see as a medical emblem. This derives from Greek mythology. Hermes, the messenger of the gods, carried a caduceus, and with it he could put to sleep anyone he wished. Snakes have very long lives (a good medical symbol), and they shed skin to renew themselves (a good healing symbol).

gave out	This means both "worked or produced" and "discontinued working or producing."
	WORDS IN CONTEXT: *The furnace gave out enough heat to keep six rooms warm all winter. The old car gave out just as we were ready to buy a new one.*
held up	Two meanings. One, "supported," and two, "hindered."
	WORDS IN CONTEXT: *The beams held up the roof, even though the snow was three feet deep. The traffic held up our arriving for dinner on time.*
wear	Two meanings. One, "endure," and two, "deteriorate."
	WORDS IN CONTEXT: *He bought the lawnmower because he thought it would wear well, even though he used it each week. We noticed some wear on the roof of the house, even though it was only a couple of years old.*
certain	One definition: "definite." Another: "hard to specify."
	WORDS IN CONTEXT: *They were certain that they could be here by March, but I have a certain feeling that it will be April before they make it.*

After studying the definitions, use the words in the sentences below.
Use the form of the word that applies.

1. We_____ during the ordeal because of our friends' support, though the air traffic _____our family's arrival until just before the services.
2. The teacher _____the semester grades, and then my car _____on me on my spring break to Florida.
3. I didn't know this jacket would _____ so well when I bought it ten years ago, but it still shows very little _____.
4. I'm _____that we can finish this project by the end of the month, but John has this equally _____feeling that we should put the deadline off until later.

Test Yourself: Write the letter next to the number to match word and meaning.

1. hold up   a. work, continue to produce; fail to work
2. certain   b. support and hinder
3. wear   c. definite; difficult to specify
4. gave out   d. continue to hold up; decay over time

On a separate sheet of paper, write sentences using both meanings of these words.

DID YOU KNOW?
Only women can become hysterical. It seems that Greek men (full of hubris) thought that being emotional was unique to women and that this affliction must surely be caused by some bodily organ men did not possess. That would be the uterus, or in Greek, *hustera*. Since only women can have hysterectomies, those old Greek guys must have been right!

founder	To fail utterly; collapse; break down. When said of horses, **founder** means "to become disabled, to go lame."
flounder	To proceed clumsily and in confusion; trying to regain balance.
	WORDS IN CONTEXT: *Founder: The stock I bought yesterday* **foundered** *today, and I lost all the money I invested. As an introvert, he* **foundered** *miserably as a salesman.* **Flounder:** *After college, she* **floundered** *around for a while before she found a job. (These two words are often confused. Except when speaking of the fish of this name,* **flounder** *is often followed informally by* around.)
discreet	Respectful of propriety; modest, reserved in speech and behavior; lacking ostentation or pretension; discerning.
discrete	Consisting of unconnected, distinct parts; constituting a separate thing.
	WORDS IN CONTEXT: *Discreet: Though her friends love to gossip, she is* **discreet** *and will not pass rumors. The woman dressed* **discreetly,** *in a modest navy blue dress, when she appeared on the witness stand.* **Discrete:** *Members of Congress gave three* **discrete** *reasons for passing the legislation. The researchers examined five* **discrete** *groups of subjects.*
flout	Scoff at; scorn; show contempt for.
flaunt	To show off; exhibit ostentatious or gaudy behavior.
	WORDS IN CONTEXT: *Flout: The demonstrators* **flouted** *the words of the politician with signs and banners.* **Flaunt:** *The women of the 1920s* **flaunted** *their freedom from social constraints with short skirts and bobbed hair.*
gauntlet	A glove, usually worn with medieval armor.
gantlet	Two lines of men facing each other armed with sticks or other weapons with which to beat a person forced to run between them
	WORDS IN CONTEXT: *These words are often used interchangeably, but the purist will find a* **discrete** *difference between the two.* **Gauntlet,** *the glove, was in medieval times thrown down as a challenge to another person, after which a duel might have been fought.* **Gantlet,** *the line of punishing men, is what one runs—as in he ran the* **gantlet.** *To make it easy: One throws down a* **gauntlet,** *and one runs a* **gantlet.**

**After studying these definitions, use the words in the sentences below.
Use the form of the word that applies.**

1. He _____ around before he found a direction for his life, while she chose to work for a corporation that ultimately_____.
2. They attempted to be _____about the plans for their marriage, but their two _____groups of friends discovered those plans separately.
3. He _____his family's preference for a college for him to _____his own independence.
4. Alexander Hamilton was killed in a duel because Aaron Burr threw down a_____. In covering the story, the reporters ran a _____of people, who did not want the incident relayed to the public.

Test Yourself: Place the letter next to the number to match word and meaning.

1. founder   a. to show off or exhibit ostentatious behavior (not to scorn)
2. gantlet   b. a line of men one must run past (not a glove)
3. discreet   c. modest, restrained (not distinct and separate)
4. flaunt   d. to fail utterly, to go under (not to flop around clumsily)

On a separate sheet of paper, write sentences using both meanings of each word.

DID YOU KNOW? The word *nemesis* comes from the name of Nemesis, the ancient goddess of retribution. Therefore, it means an avenger or the act of vengeance itself. It has, however, come to mean simply the enemy and is often used in sports writing. **EXAMPLE:** The Yankees are the traditional nemesis of the Red Sox.

Phobia Words

Most everyone knows what claustrophobia is—a morbid fear of enclosed spaces—and not a few of us suffer from it to one degree or another. It is one of the most common human phobias. You may be surprised to learn that there are hundreds of phobias abroad in the land, and a word exists for each of them. Some of these terms you can make an educated guess about, such as telephonophobia—fear of using the telephone. Others may defy you: novercophobia—fear of your stepmother. In this chapter, you will find a healthy (or unhealthy) sample of human fears and dreads.

DAY 1

acrophobia	agoraphobia	anthropophobia	xenophobia

DAY 2

androphobia	gynephobia	pentheraphobia	syngenescophobia

DAY 3

cynophobia	aelurophobia	musophobia	arachnophobia

DAY 4

ornithophoia	ichthyophobia	herpetophobia	entophobia

DAY 5

nyctophobia	phengophobia	thalassophobia	xerophobia

DAY 6

gamophobia	anuptaphobia	coitophobia	rhabdophobia

DAY 7

automysophobia	ergasophobia	stygiophobia	glossophobia

acrophobia	A mortal fear of heights. (*Acro-* = heights.) Along with claustrophobia, this is one of the most common human phobias.
	WORDS IN CONTEXT: *Jerry balked at going to the top of the Empire State Building because of his* **acrophobia.**
agoraphobia	Intense fear of the outdoors and open spaces.
	WORDS IN CONTEXT: *The* **agora** *was the Greek marketplace, an open area where many people gathered. From this word we get* **agoraphobia,** *as in, "The child was* **agoraphobic."** *(Another person who stays out of the* **agora** *is the* **ochlophobe**—*one who fears crowds.)*
anthropophobia	Fear of other people.
	WORDS IN CONTEXT: Anthropo- *indicates humankind, and people who fear humankind in general are* **anthropophobic.**
xenophobia	Fear of foreigners.
	WORDS IN CONTEXT: *He avoided the immigrants in his village because of his* **xenophobia.**

After studying the words above, use each in a sentence below.

1. Tom, being_____, tried to avoid other people.
2. Both the twins were _____and would not leave their room.
3. Pete and Marsha refused to leave the United States because of their_____.
4. He avoided the job offer as a roof repairman because he was_____.

Test Yourself: Place the letter next to the number to match word and meaning.

1. xenophobia   a. fear of heights
2. acrophobia   b. fear of people
3. agoraphobia   c. fear of open spaces
4. anthropophobia   d. fear of foreigners

On a separate sheet of paper, write a sentence using each of these words.

DID YOU KNOW?
What phobia did Franklin D. Roosevelt allude to when he said, "We have nothing to fear but fear itself"? It's called *phobophobia*—the fear of being afraid.

androphobia	Mortal fear of men.
	WORDS IN CONTEXT: *If **anthropophobic** people fear everyone, **androphobes** are lucky: they fear only men. Susan knew that the reason she surrounded herself with women was that she suffered from **androphobia.***
gynephobia	Intense fear of women.
	WORDS IN CONTEXT: *Guy's therapist suggested that becoming a gynecologist was not a sound career route, since he had **gynephobia.***
pentheraphobia	Fear of your mother-in-law.
	WORDS IN CONTEXT: *You think you've heard them all? You're just getting started. Bet you never knew there was a word for mother-in-law fear: **pentheraphobia.***
syngenescophobia	Fear of your relatives.
	WORDS IN CONTEXT: *If you suffer from **syngenescophobia,** maybe you should stay away from family reunions.*

After studying the words above, use each in a sentence below.
Use the form of the word that applies.

1. Charles refused to enter the room full of women because of his _____.
2. Charlene told her husband Jim that his mother was scary, so he accused her of_____
3. Penny spoke only to the women at the party because of her_____.
4. When his aunts, uncles, and cousins visited, Ben, suffering from _____, hid in his room.

Test Yourself: Place the letter next to the number to match word and meaning.

1. androphobe   a. hides from his wife's mother
2. gynephobe   b. hides from all the men she sees
3. syngenescophobe   c. hides from his kinfolk
4. pentheraphobe   d. hides from the girls in the neighborhood

On a separate sheet of paper, write a sentence using each of these words.

DID YOU KNOW?
Phobos was the son of Ares, the god of war. His brother was Deimos, god of terror, and his aunt was Eris, goddess of discord. Is it any wonder that Phobos embodied fear? It is from him that we get the word for all our phobias— hatreds and fears.

cynophobia	Fear of dogs.
	WORDS IN CONTEXT: *Why is it that the word cynosure has to do with the dog star, or more specifically, the dog's tail in the constellation Ursa Minor? Because cyno denotes dog. Ergo,* **cynophobics** *fear dogs.*
aelurophobia	Fear of cats.
	WORDS IN CONTEXT: *You could see this one coming, couldn't you? If cats scare you to death—whether lions, tigers, or tabbies—you're* **aelurophobic.** *This has little to do with your dislike of cat hair on your sofa.*
musophobia	Yes, fear of mice.
	WORDS IN CONTEXT: *Those cartoon women who leap onto tables, raising their skirts and screeching—well, there are degrees of* **musophobia.** *Some* **musophobics** *are more dramatic than others.*
arachnophobia	Fear of spiders.
	WORDS IN CONTEXT: *Nobody but* **arachnophiles** *(the suffix -phile means "like" or "love") adores spiders, but those who really, really hate and fear spiders are* **arachnophobic.**

After studying the words above, use each in a sentence below.
Use the part of speech that applies.

1. She screamed when a cat crawled onto her lap because she was_____.
2. After seeing a mouse in the subway, Terry, a _____took a cab.
3. A spider fell into Jamie's hair, and because he was an_____, he had a fit.
4. Suffering from _____,Whitney screamed bloody murder when the neighbor's dog jumped on her.

Test Yourself: Place the letter next to the number to match word and meaning.

1. arachnophobic   a. hates mice
2. aelurophobic   b. hates dogs
3. cynophobic   c. hates spiders
4. musophobic   d. hates cats

On a separate sheet of paper, write a sentence using each of these words.

DID YOU KNOW?
What kind of phobia does a person have who lives in mortal dread of everything? Pantophobia. The very uncomfortable pantophobe has a *pantophobic* **fear of everything.**

ornithophobia	Fear of birds.
	WORDS IN CONTEXT: *Ever see the Alfred Hitchcock film, The Birds? That could give you* **ornithophobia**. **Ornithophobes** *should stay indoors and certainly not live near a nature preserve.*
ichthyophobia	Intense fear of fish.
	WORDS IN CONTEXT: *It's hard to believe that people could be afraid of such benign creatures as fish, unless maybe they saw Jaws, which plays on our* **ichthyophobia**—*as well as our good sense about swimming in the ocean in general.*
herpetophobia	Dread and fear of snakes.
	WORDS IN CONTEXT: *Many people fear snakes, unless they know a great deal about them and can distinguish the harmless from the harmful. A little* **herpetophobia** *is not a bad thing to have when you're not sure what kind of snake is in front of you.*
entophobia	Fear and hatred of insects.
	WORDS IN CONTEXT: *An* **entomologist** *studies insects. (Not to be confused with an etymologist, who studies words.) An* **entophobe**—*maybe a person who finds cockroaches in the kitchen—hates insects in an exaggerated manner.*

After studying the words above, use them the sentences below.
Use the part of speech that applies.

1. The _____ never went fishing for fear he would catch one.
2. When the wrens and sparrows gathered around his window, the _____ felt weak.
3. A victim of _____, she fainted at the sight of a harmless garter snake.
4. "There's a fly in my soup!" shouted the _____ as she fell out of her chair.

Test Yourself: Write the number next to the letter to match word and meaning.

1. herpetophobia   a. fear of insects
2. entophobia   b. fear of snakes
3. ornithophobia   c. fear of fish
4. ichthyophobia   d. fear of birds

On a separate sheet of paper, write a sentence using each of these words.

DID YOU KNOW?
What do you call someone who is scared to death of the number 13? (Maybe those hotel owners who skip floor 13 when they're numbering the floors.) Are you ready for this? A *triskaidekaphobe.* **No kidding. This is how it breaks down:** *tris* **(three),** *kai* **(and),** *deka* **(ten),** *phobe* **(one who fears). See how simple phobias are?**

nyctophobia	Fear of darkness.
	WORDS IN CONTEXT: *Many children are afraid of the dark, but it takes an extreme fear of darkness for someone to be described as* **nyctophobic.**
phengophobia	Fear of daylight.
	WORDS IN CONTEXT: *History has recorded* **phengophobes** *who have made their homes in caves or underground tunnels.*
thalassophobia	Fear of the sea.
	WORDS IN CONTEXT: **Thalassophobes** *can be distinguished from* **aquaphobes** *in that the former fear is the sea itself, whereas the last-named fear any stream or body of water.*
xerophobia	Fear of the desert or other dry places.
	WORDS IN CONTEXT: *People with* **xerophobia** *do not move to Arizona or ride a camel in the Sahara.*

After studying the words above, use the words in the sentences below.

1. As Nancy Drew entered the dark house, she screamed and fainted, for overnight she had become a_____.
2. The _____troll that lived in the dark shadows under the bridge passed out when he saw the daylight.
3. When Lawrence of Arabia developed_____, his desert buddies called him a sissy.
4. Captain Ahab decided not to follow Moby Dick out to sea when his recessive case of_____ returned.

Test Yourself: Place the letter next to the number to match word and meaning.

1. thalassophobia   a. desert fright
2. phengophobia   b. sea fright
3. xerophobia   c. darkness fright
4. nyctophobia   d. daylight fright

On a separate sheet of paper, write a sentence using each of these words.

DID YOU KNOW?
The popular children's author Hans Christian Anderson suffered from *taphephobia*—the fear of being buried alive. Anderson always carried a note with him with the instructions that if he were found unconscious, no one was to assume he was dead. He also left a note on his bedside table explaining that he may "seem dead," but that he was merely sleeping.

gamophobia	Deathly fear of marriage.
	WORDS IN CONTEXT: *If he doesn't propose after many nudges or if she consistently refuses to accept, you now have an important accusative word:* **gamophobia.**
anuptaphobia	Mortal fear of staying single.
	WORDS IN CONTEXT: *If he proposes to every woman he meets or if she accepts every proposal she gets, then you might accuse these two of* **anuptaphobia.**
coitophobia	Intense fear of sex.
	WORDS IN CONTEXT: *Ever wonder what motivated all those vestal virgins and castrati? Sure, you did. Maybe they had* **coitophobia.**
rhabdophobia	Fear of criticism or punishment.
	WORDS IN CONTEXT: *Some people never finish a project for fear of its being judged critically—yep,* **rhabdophobia.** *And a little* **rhabdophobia** *might change the behavior of a few naughty children.*

After studying the words above, use them in the sentences below.

1. _____ kept Harvey from marrying Marlene, though he loved her dearly.
2. _____ seemed to be responsible for Elizabeth's having six husbands, though she eventually divorced all of them.
3. Though Homer chased Shirley around the bed every night, her _____prevented her from getting into it.
4. Rita avoided finishing her dissertation because her _____made her fearful of the readers' remarks.

Test Yourself: Place the letter next to the number to match word and meaning.

1. gamophobe   a. is dying to get married
2. anuptaphobe   b. is dying to stay single
3. rhabdophobe   c. is dying to stay pure
4. coitophobe   d. is dying with anxiety about being criticized

On a separate sheet of paper, write a sentence using each of these words.

DID YOU KNOW?
Can you guess the name of the phobia that means a deathly fear of words? *Verbaphobia.* A verbaphobe would have a deathly fear of this book.

automysophobia	Morbid fear of being dirty.
	WORDS IN CONTEXT: *Those people you run across occasionally who wash their hands constantly: think automysophobes.*
ergasophobia	Morbid fear of work.
	WORDS IN CONTEXT: *That lazy brother-in-law who won't get off the couch: think ergasophobe.*
stygiophobia	Morbid fear of hell.
	WORDS IN CONTEXT: *Those people who are always trying to find their way to heaven: think stygiophobes.*
glossophobia	Morbid fear of public speaking.
	WORDS IN CONTEXT: *Those people who stammer in front of an audience: think glossophobes. (Some researchers say that glossophobia is the most common phobia of American people. Think: get a good speech coach.)*

On a separate sheet of paper, write a sentence using each of these words.

DID YOU KNOW?
Why should a person who suffers arachibutyrophobia eat his jelly sandwich without peanut butter? What, you didn't know? For shame! Everyone should know this. This particular phobia describes a person who has a deathly fear of getting peanut butter stuck to the roof of his or her mouth. If you're on a diet, you might cultivate this important phobia.

Empty Words

Empty words or phrases simply inflate your prose, and not in a positive way. They can be edited for precision with no loss of meaning. Study these words and phrases and how they can be avoided to help you speak and write more concisely.

DAY 1

| as to whether | each and every | any and all | in the area of |

DAY 2

| due to the fact that | along the lines of | in the neighborhood of | so as to |

DAY 3

| kind of a | at this point in time | in the event of | in spite of the fact that |

DAY 4

| as a matter of fact | at all times | during that time period | due to the fact that |

DAY 5

| came about | until such time as | for the reason that | I think to myself |

DAY 6

| reason is because | come up with | by means of | in order to |

DAY 7

| -type | have the ability to | in the final analysis | impacted on |

as to whether	Use *whether*.
	WORDS IN CONTEXT: (*As to whether*) *Whether* I can come will depend on the weather.
each and every	Use *each* or use *every*, but not both.
	WORDS IN CONTEXT: (*Each and every*) *Each* person in the class needs to listen. Or: *Every* person in the class needs to listen.
any and all	Use *any* or use *all*, not both.
	WORDS IN CONTEXT: (*Any and all*) *Any* of you who wants a ticket must call. Or: *All* of you who want tickets must call.
in the area of	Be specific. Most of the time, simply use *in*. Compare the sentences below.
	WORDS IN CONTEXT: *He is interested **in the area** of science. He is interested **in** science. My paper will be **in the area of** freedom of the press. My paper will **address** freedom of the press. I am not gifted **in the area of** math. I am not gifted **in** math.*

After studying the empty and concise phrases above, use the concise words in the sentences below.

1. He said that _____ he travels abroad again this year depends on _____ he gets a bonus.
2. _____ person in the gym had on white running shoes and _____ had on dark shorts.
3. If _____ of you here has the winning lottery ticket, _____ of you get free drinks.
4. He took his degree _____ environmental studies with a minor _____ agriculture.

Test Yourself: Next to the empty phrase, write a concise word or two to replace it.

1. each and every _____
2. any and all _____
3. in the area of _____
4. as to whether _____

On a separate sheet of paper, write a sentence using these concise words.

DID YOU KNOW?
Many words we use every day are simply "utility words"— words without much meaning or content, but which only convey enthusiasm. We use them because their use keeps us from having to think about word selection. Words such as *wonderful, great, awesome, fine, terrific, marvelous,* and *fabulous* are utility words: useful, but basically colorless and unimaginative. They are better replaced with some fresh, vivid words. Next time you write a thank-you note, remember that.

due to the fact that	*Because.*
	WORDS IN CONTEXT: *I am writing my paper on Greece (**due to the fact that**) **because** I visited there last summer.*
along the lines of	*Like,* or *similar to.*
	WORDS IN CONTEXT: *I want a house (**along the lines of**) **similar to** yours.*
in the neighborhood of	Be specific, or use *about.*
	WORDS IN CONTEXT: *My dad paid (**in the neighborhood of**) **about** $25,000 for his car.*
so as to	Use *so.*
	WORDS IN CONTEXT: *I studied hard for the SATs (**so as to**) **so** I could get into the college of my choice.*

After studying the empty phrases and the concise words, use the concise words in the sentences below.

1. It is _____600 miles to my house in Virginia.
2. _____ he could get his driver's license, he practiced driving with his father.
3. I took a cruise to the Caribbean _____ the one you took this year.
4. _____ she had seen the film before, she declined the invitation to go.

Test Yourself: Place the concise word or phrase next to the empty phrase below.

1. along the lines _____
2. in order to _____
3. in the neighborhood of_____
4. due to the fact that _____

On a separate sheet of paper, write sentences using these words.

DID YOU KNOW?
Beginning a sentence with *there is* or a similar construction delays the reader with annoying empty words. For example: There is a place on the corner where I buy my newspapers. Better: I buy my newspapers at a place on the corner.

kind of a	Use *kind of* without the unnecessary *a*. **WORDS IN CONTEXT:** *I wanted the same **(kind of a) kind of** career that my father had.*
at this point in time	Use *now* or *currently*. **WORDS IN CONTEXT:** ***(At this point in time) Currently**, I am leaning toward voting Democratic.*
in the event that	Use *if* instead. **WORDS IN CONTEXT:** *I told her that **(in the event that) if** my brother comes for a visit , I will not be able to come to the party.*
in spite of the fact that	Use *although* or *though*. **WORDS IN CONTEXT:** ***(In spite of the fact that) Although** I enjoyed The Iliad, my favorite is The Odyssey.*

After studying the empty phrases and the concise words above, use the concise words in the sentences below.

1. You're wearing the same _____ of watch that I am.
2. The evening was lovely _____ the weather was overcast.
3. He said that _____ the car he wanted went on sale, he would buy it right away.
4. _____, she is thinking about moving to North Carolina.

Test Yourself: Place the concise word or phrase next to the empty phrase below.

1. kind of a _____
2. at this point in time _____
3. in the event that _____
4. in spite of the fact that _____

On a separate sheet of paper, write a sentence using the concise words or phrases.

DID YOU KNOW?
The word *only* is extremely tricky. Try this sentence: *The SUV hit the convertible.* Now, try putting only after each word and see how the meaning is changed each time. *The only SUV hit the convertible. The SUV only hit the convertible. The SUV hit only the convertible. The SUV hit the only convertible. The SUV hit the convertible only.* See, it's tricky. Watch where you place *only*.

as a matter of fact	Use *in fact*. **WORDS IN CONTEXT:** *(As a matter of fact)* **In fact**, *I liked* Huckleberry Finn *better than* Tom Sawyer.
at all times	Use *always*. **WORDS IN CONTEXT:** *During my summer vacation I was* **always** *working* **(at all times)**.
during that time period	Use *then*. **WORDS IN CONTEXT:** *It was* **(during that time period)** **then** *that I broke my leg.*
due to the fact that	Use *because* or *since*. **WORDS IN CONTEXT:** *(Due to the fact that)* **Because** *my leg was broken, I couldn't work out in the gym.*

After studying the empty phrases and concise words above, use the concise words in the sentences below.

1. I had a great time at the beach on Saturday; _____, the whole day was fun.
2. _____ during the school year, the girls did homework from 6 to 9 p.m.
3. _____ his mother was visiting, he took the day off to entertain her.
4. _____ the war broke out.

Test Yourself: Place the concise word or phrase next to the empty phrase below.

1. due to the fact that _____
2. during the time period _____
3. as a matter of fact _____
4. at all times _____

On a separate sheet of paper, write a sentence using these concise words.

DID YOU KNOW?
"I can relate to" is a vague expression best to be avoided. Example: *I like Elizabeth Bennett, the character in Jane Austen's novel, because I can relate to her.* Does "relate" here mean identify with, respond to, interact with? Try to find a more specific way of stating your reaction to the character.

came about	Use *occurred* instead.
	WORDS IN CONTEXT: *The best part of the film* **(came about)** *occurred when the two resolved their differences and came back together.*
until such time as	Use *until*.
	WORDS IN CONTEXT: **(Until such time as)** *Until the rest of the family can join us, we can't have the celebration.*
for the reason that	Use *because*.
	WORDS IN CONTEXT: *The members of the group could not be here* **(for the reason that)** *because they were caught in a snowstorm.*
I think to myself	Just use *I think*.
	WORDS IN CONTEXT: **(I think to myself)** *I think I enjoyed that book because it had a character in it who behaved much the way I did in high school.*

After studying the empty phrases and concise words above, use the concise words in the sentences below.

1. As I am driving home, I_____ how much I enjoy my philosophy class and hope to have the same professor next year.
2. _____ we can all get together again, we will stay in touch by e-mail.
3. My stack of new books went unread _____my family and I were packing and moving.
4. The worst part of the storm _____when a tree was uprooted and fell on the house.

Test Yourself: Place the concise word next to the empty phrase below.

1. I think to myself _____
2. for the reason that_____
3. until such time as_____
4. came about when _____

On a separate sheet of paper, write a sentence using these concise words or phrases.

DID YOU KNOW?
Thusly is not a word. Thus, you should never use it. (Thus is already an adverb and therefore needs no adverbial ending.)

reason is because	Use *reason is that* or *reason for*.
	WORDS IN CONTEXT: **The reason** we won the game(**is because**) **is that** our players were faster. **The reason for** his absence was a death in the family.
come up with	Use *arrive at* or *think of*.
	WORDS IN CONTEXT: He couldn't **(come up with)** **think of** the correct answer, so he lost the contest.
by means of	Use *by*.
	WORDS IN CONTEXT: They will arrive in New York from Baltimore **(by means of) by** train.
in order to	Use *to*.
	WORDS IN CONTEXT: **(In order to) To** get my work done on time, I had to stay at my computer all night.

After studying the empty phrases and concise words, use the concise words in the sentences below.

1. They came _____ plane, but they were driving the car back.
2. The two did their math homework together, but they could not _____ the answer to one of the problems.
3. _____ reach the ski resort, we had to drive up a long, winding mountain road.
4. The reason I got an A in the class is _____ I had learned to write clearly in high school.

Test Yourself: Place the concise word or phrase next to the empty words below.

1. in order to _____
2. by means of _____
3. come up with _____
4. the reason is because _____

On a separate sheet of paper, write a sentence using these concise words or phrases.

DID YOU KNOW?
It is better not to use *usage* when *use* will do. *Usage* has a proper meaning: For example, *usage* has changed our language so that we are less strict about the use of *who* and *whom* and *shall* and *will*. *Usage* implies a standard or convention; otherwise, it is a stuffed word for *use*.

-type	Don't use **–type** as a suffix..
	WORDS IN CONTEXT: *She wore a strapless (**-type**) ball gown. It was an organic (**-type**) product.*
have the ability to	Use *can* or *be able to*.
	WORDS IN CONTEXT: *The students (**have the ability to**) **can** work on the project together if they coordinate their schedules.*
in the final analysis	Use *finally*.
	WORDS IN CONTEXT: *(**In the final analysis**) **Finally**, toward the end of the book, all the characters' issues were resolved.*
impacted on	Use *affected*.
	WORDS IN CONTEXT: *His baseball practice schedule (**impacted on**) **affected** his studies negatively.*

After studying the empty phrases and concise words above, use the concise word in the sentences below.

1. Mary was fond of James, but _____she chose Peter as her steady boyfriend.
2. Her shoulder injury _____her tennis game.
3. You may _____to find the directions to her house on the Internet.
4. The teacher gave a Q. and A. exam. (*Not:* The teacher gave a Q and A.-_____ exam.)

Test Yourself: Place the concise word next to the empty words below.

1. impacted on_____
2. boxy-type jacket _____
3. in the final analysis_____
4. have the ability to _____

On a separate sheet of paper, write a sentence using each concise word or phrase.

DID YOU KNOW?
"Needless to say" as an introduction to a statement is illogical. If it is needless to say, why go on to say it? It is better to introduce statements that are "needless to say" with "of course," or "as we all know."

Words for Words

This chapter contains words used to discuss and describe words themselves. You may be surprised how many exist. Notice the subtle differences between them.

DAY 1

argot	lingua franca	lingo	patois

DAY 2

cant	polyglot	orthography	belles lettres

DAY 3

concordance	lexicon	lexicographer	philology

DAY 4

verbiage	chrestomathy	inveigh	glossolalia

DAY 5

platitude	eponym	barbarism	brogue

DAY 6

linguistics	Esperanto	etymology	semantics

DAY 7

syntax	prolix	circumlocution	periphrasis

argot	A specialized vocabulary or set of idioms used by a particular class or group. **WORDS IN CONTEXT:** *The motorcyclists spoke in an* **argot** *not understood by those of us outside the group.*
lingua franca	Any hybrid language used as a medium of communication between people of different languages. Originally, a mixture of Italian, French, Spanish, Arabic, Greek, and Turkish spoken in the Mediterranean area. **WORDS IN CONTEXT:** *The tour group spoke in a* **lingua franca** *of Greek and Arabic.*
lingo	Language that is unintelligible or unfamiliar because it is foreign or is a special jargon. **WORDS IN CONTEXT:** *Their Romany* **lingo** *was charming, if difficult to understand.*
patois	Any regional dialect; any nonstandard or colloquial speech. **WORDS IN CONTEXT:** *The* **patois** *of the street has begun to creep into mainstream teenagers' language.*

After studying the definitions above, use these words or phrases in the sentences below.

1. A special vocabulary of a particular group or class is its_____.
2. The _____one uses is a foreign or special jargon.
3. People of different languages can communicate in_____.
4. _____ is substandard or regional dialect.

Test Yourself: Place the letter next to the number to match word and meaning.

1. patois   a. mixed languages
2. lingo   b. special jargon of a group
3. lingua franca   c. substandard or illiterate language
4. argot   d. specialized idioms or vocabulary

On a separate sheet of paper, write a sentence using each of these words or phrases.

DID YOU KNOW?
What does *paranomasia* **mean? It's wordplay—punning for comic effect; also a punster or anyone who likes to play witty games with words.**

cant	Discourse recited monotonously or mechanically. Hypocritically pious language; trite, unimaginative speech.
	WORDS IN CONTEXT: *Cant can also include the special vocabulary peculiar to a group on the fringes of society (argot) and the special terminology understood among those in a profession or class, but obscure to outsiders (jargon). **Cant** is also the whining language of beggars. It comes from the French, "to sing."*
polyglot	Spoken, written, or composed of several languages. **Polyglot** comes from the Greek *poly* ("mixture") and *glotta* ("tongue"). A person with a reading, writing, or speaking knowledge of several languages. A book, especially the Bible, containing several versions of the same text in different languages.
	WORDS IN CONTEXT: *A **polyglot** of languages may be heard on the streets of any major international city.*
orthography	The art or study of correct spelling according to established usage. The aspect of language study concerned with letters and their sequences in words. Any method of representing the sounds of language by literal symbols.
	WORDS IN CONTEXT: *He was an expert in **orthography** and was therefore asked to judge the National Spelling Bee.*
belles lettres	Literature regarded for its aesthetic value rather than for its didactic or informative content.
	WORDS IN CONTEXT: *Belles lettres is refined literature; its name comes from the French, "fine letters." It is a plural form, but in one of those remarkable twists of language, we use it with a singular verb: **Belles lettres** is beautiful writing.*

After studying the words above, use them in the sentences below:

1. Because he was able to speak and write six languages, he was known as a_____.
2. She could correctly spell more words than anyone because she was an_____.
3. A master of_____, his writing was so graceful that people read it for its beauty alone.
4. The mechanical, trite speeches of many politicians can be called_____.

Test Yourself: Place the letter next to the number to match word and meaning.

1. belles lettres   a. good spelling
2. cant   b. fine writing
3. orthography   c. the stuff of boring, predictable speeches
4. polyglot   d. a profusion of languages

On a separate sheet of paper, write sentences using each of these words.

DID YOU KNOW?
What is the difference between *oral* and *verbal*? Something spoken is both oral and verbal, but that which is written is verbal only. *Verbal* refers to words, and *oral* relates to the mouth. To be safe—and stay out of court—acknowledge that something agreed to by mouth only is an *oral* agreement. But something agreed to on paper— well, call that a *written* agreement.

concordance	An alphabetical index of all the words in a text or a body of texts, showing every occurrence of a word in that text. **WORDS IN CONTEXT:** *Look in the **concordance** of the book for the word **concordance**.*
lexicon	A dictionary, a stock of terms used in a particular profession, subject, or style; vocabulary. **WORDS IN CONTEXT:** ***Lexicon** comes from Greek via Latin meaning "speech" and "word." Many professions have handbooks that carry the **lexicon**—a list of terms and definitions—conventionally used in that profession. The first section of this book might be called a **lexicon** of terms often used in the liberal arts and humanities.*
lexicographer	One who writes or compiles a dictionary. **WORDS IN CONTEXT:** *A **lexicographer** can write or compile the lexicons of many professions, subjects, or styles. (Even in architecture, different styles are called vocabularies.) The compilers (there were several) of the Oxford English Dictionary were great **lexicographers**.*
philology	Literary study or classical scholarship, love of learning; also the study of written records and literary texts to determine their meaning and authenticity. **WORDS IN CONTEXT:** ***Philologists** (or **philologers**) from the Greek **philo** ("love") and **logos** ("word" and "reason") spend their lives in the pursuit of learning.*

After studying the words above, use them in the sentences below.

1. The scholar looked in the _____ for the word *opismath*, which means "one who learns late in life."
2. The _____ put out a call for lists of words in current use so he could include them in his dictionary.
3. The student asked the librarian for the _____ used by most psychologists.
4. The _____ group met in London to attempt to authenticate the literary text.

Test Yourself: Place the letter next to the number to match word and meaning.

1. lexicon   a. love of learning, scholarship
2. concordance   b. one who compiles dictionaries
3. philology   c. a book of words
4. lexicographer   d. an extended index to a text

On a separate sheet of paper, write sentences using the words above.

DID YOU KNOW?
The sentence you may have memorized when you learned how to type, or at least that you have heard all your life, is a pangram. It's the old sentence that contains every letter of the alphabet: *The quick brown fox jumps over the lazy dog.*

verbiage	Words in excess of those needed for clarity or precision; wordy; the manner in which one expresses oneself; diction.
	WORDS IN CONTEXT: *His long-winded speech was filled with trite, boring, repetitive **verbiage.** The aristocrat's **verbiage** was selected to appeal to the British upper classes.*
chrestomathy	A selection of literary passages used in studying literature or a language.
	WORDS IN CONTEXT: *From the Greek meaning "useful learning," **chrestomathy** is the word for the brief essays and excepts from fiction in the texts students read as examples of effective writing in undergraduate composition courses.*
inveigh	To protest in a vehement, dogged way.
	WORDS IN CONTEXT: *At the school board meeting, a parent **inveighed** against overcrowding in the classrooms.*
glossolalia	Babbling, made-up nonsense speech, especially associated with certain schizophrenic syndromes; also associated with certain religious sects whose members speak in tongues during ecstatic religious experiences.
	WORDS IN CONTEXT: *From the Latin "to speak with tongues," **glossolalia** is private, idiosyncratic speech made up of nonsense words.*

After studying the definitions above, use the words in the sentences below.

1. The protesters at the convention _____ against the candidate's stand on environmental protection.
2. Our writing teacher selected a reading from the _____ for the class to study.
3. The editor worked on cutting some of the _____ from the wordy manuscript.
4. Their religious experience moved the churchgoers to _____.

Test Yourself: Place the letter next to the number to match word and meaning.

1. inveigh   a. excess of words
2. glossolalia   b. instructive readings
3. verbiage   c. protracted protestation
4. chrestomathy   d. speaking in tongues

On a separate sheet of paper, write a sentence using each of these words.

DID YOU KNOW?
The word *matrix,* like the word *parameter* is often misused. *Matrix* means a womb or a mold in which something grows. In mathematics, it means a square or rectangular array of symbols.

platitude	A trite remark; a statement lacking originality. **WORDS IN CONTEXT:** *The speaker's remarks were so filled with* **platitudes** *that the audience grew restless and left early.*
eponym	A real or mythical person whose name is or is thought to be the source of the name of a city, country, era, or institution. **WORDS IN CONTEXT:** *Romulus is the* **eponym** *of Rome.*
barbarism	A specific word or words considered crudely incorrect or nonstandard in a language. **WORDS IN CONTEXT:** Nowheres *and* anywheres *are considered* **barbarisms** *in the English language.*
brogue	A strong dialectical accent, especially a strong Irish accent. **WORDS IN CONTEXT:** ***Brogue*** *comes from the Irish word* bróg *for peasants' shoes, brogues.*

After studying the definitions above, use the words in the sentences below.

1. William Penn is the _____ of Pennsylvania.
2. Huckleberry Finn's use of proper language was so poor that he often spoke in _____.
3. The Dubliners exchanged jokes in an unmistakable _____.
4. The student's paper was so filled with _____ that the teacher asked him to work on using fresher language.

Test Yourself: Place the letter next to the number to match word and meaning.

1. brogue
2. eponym
3. barbarism
4. platitude

a. trite, unoriginal language
b. Irish accent
c. real or mythical person for whom a place is named
d. nonstandard or incorrect use of language

On a separate sheet of paper, write a sentence using each of these words.

DID YOU KNOW?
Catachresis means the misuse of a word. Sometimes this misuse is simply a matter of applying the wrong word to the wrong thing. *Catachresis* can also refer to a change in the word's meaning as users over time misunderstand or are ignorant of its etymology. For example, "cole slaw" has to some become "cold slaw" through catachresis, and the phrase "for all intents and purposes" is sometimes stated "for all intensive purposes."

linguistics	The science of language, or the study of the nature and structure of human speech.
	WORDS IN CONTEXT: *The **linguistics** professor taught the course, The Structure of the English Language.*
Esperanto	An artificial international language invented in 1887 and characterized by a vocabulary based on word roots common to many European languages.
	WORDS IN CONTEXT: ***Esperanto** was invented by Dr. L. L. Zamenhof (d. 1917), a Polish philologist who wrote under the name **Dr. Esperanto**, meaning "one who hopes."*
etymology	The origin, historical development, and evolution of a word.
	WORDS IN CONTEXT: *We have looked at the **etymologies** of many words in this book. **Etymology** is also the branch of linguistics that studies the origin and development of words.*
semantics	The study or science of meaning in language, particularly its historical change; also, the study of relationships between signs and symbols and what they represent—sometimes called *semiotics*.
	WORDS IN CONTEXT: *Though **semantics** refers to the meaning of language, **semantics** is also a branch of philosophy.*

After studying the definitions above, use the words in the sentences below.

1. In class we looked up the _____of words because we were interested in their origin and development.
2. A universal language called _____ was invented by a Polish philologist.
3. The structure and science of language is studied in the field of _____.
4. The study or science of meaning in language is studied in _____.

Test Yourself: Place the letter next to the number to match word and meaning.

1. etymology	a. science of language
2. semantics	b. an international language
3. Esperanto	c. the study of where words came from and how they evolved
4. linguistics	d. the study of meaning in language, also signs and symbols

On a separate sheet of paper, write a sentence using each of these words.

DID YOU KNOW?
Nomenclature is the system or set of names used in a specific activity or branch of learning. For example, there is a specific set of names—or nomenclature—for plants, another for animals, another for parts of a machine.

syntax	The way in which words are put together to form phrases and sentences; also the branch of grammar that deals with this. **WORDS IN CONTEXT:** *The word* **syntax** *comes from the Greek meaning "to put together."*
prolix	Wordy and tedious, tending to speak or write at great length. **WORDS IN CONTEXT:** **Prolix** *derives from the Latin meaning "poured forth or extended."*
circumlocution	The use of prolix and indirect language; evasion in speech or writing; to speak in a roundabout way. **WORDS IN CONTEXT:** *People use* **circumlocution** *to answer unwelcome questions; they speak around the question, rather than addressing the question directly. (In a novel, Charles Dickens had a* **prolix** *bureaucrat working in the Office of* **Circumlocution.***)*
periphrasis	The use of circumlocution; to express in a roundabout way. **WORDS IN CONTEXT:** **Periphrasis** *is related to* **circumlocution** *in that it does not address a topic directly (example: "the word of his father," rather than "his father's word"), and it is more* **prolix,** *in that it is more wordy (example: "his father did say," rather than "his father said").*

After studying the definitions above, use the words in the sentences below.

1. The politician did not wish to answer the reporter's question, so he evaded it through _____.
2. The _____ of an English sentence requires at least a subject and a verb.
3. "He went to stay in the house of his mother" is an example of _____.
4. The professor tended to write in _____ sentences that required editing before his book could be published.

Test Yourself: Place the letter next to the number to match word and meaning.

1. prolix   a. the dog of the boy next door
2. periphrasis   b. wordy, tedious language
3. syntax   c. dancing around the subject
4. circumlocution   d. subject-verb-object = English sentence

On a separate sheet of paper, write a sentence using each of these words.

DID YOU KNOW?
How did the *Rx* that you often see on a doctor's prescription pad come to be? *Rx* is an attempt to create a symbol for the word *recipe*. That symbol is an *R* with a slash through the little foot that sticks out on the right of the letter. Why *recipe*? The word is from the Latin that means "take," as in "Take two tablets with water at bedtime." The word *take* (*recipe*) was usually the first word in a prescription. *Recipe* became a word used in cooking much later.

Foreign Words

This week's work contains foreign words a reader will encounter often in English texts and in informal conversation.

DAY 1

summum bonum	pro bono publico	vox populi	sotto voce

DAY 2

persona non grata	ad hominem	tabula rasa	Weltanschauung

DAY 3

sui generic	terra firma	téte-à-téte	laissez-faire

DAY 4

noblesse oblige	objet d'art	sine qua non	Schadenfreude

DAY 5

Sturm und Drang	quid pro quo	bête noir	de rigueur

DAY 6

tempus fugit	ad hoc	bons mot	caveat emptor

DAY 7

aperitif	a poco a poco	carte blanche	flagrante delicto

summum bonum	(Latin): The highest good, usually from which all other good is derived.
	WORDS IN CONTEXT: *In Christian religions, and in the lives of many people, God is the* **summum bonum.**
pro bono publico	(Latin): For the good of the public.
	WORDS IN CONTEXT: *In planning the city, the planners designed a number of parks* **pro bono publico.**
vox populi	(Latin): The popular voice or sentiment.
	WORDS IN CONTEXT: *In a democracy, the* **vox populi** *has endorsed individualism, self-reliance, and self-determination.*
sotto voce	(Latin): In a whisper; under the breath.
	WORDS IN CONTEXT: *At the meeting, my colleague gave me* **sotto voce** *the name of the person who was speaking.*

After studying the definitions above, use the words in the sentences below.

1. The election is over, and the _____ has let us know the pleasure of the people.
2. So as not to be heard, he complained _____.
3. The plaque on City Hall in its motto let us know why it was built: _____.
4. For many scholars, the last word, or the_____, regarding language use is the *Oxford English Dictionary.*

Test Yourself: Place the letter next to the number to match word and meaning.

1. pro bono publico   a. the highest good
2. vox populi   b. in a low voice
3. summum bonum   c. for the public good
4. sotto voce   d. the voice of the people

On a separate sheet of paper, write sentences using each of the words above.

BONUS WORD

Sui juris (Latin)
In law, people of full, legal standing and responsibility.

persona non grata	(Latin): An unwelcome person; an outcast or pariah.
	WORDS IN CONTEXT: *Because of his behavior at the last party, Fred is **persona non grata** at the next one.*
ad hominem	(Latin): An attack on a person's character; an argument against a person.
	WORDS IN CONTEXT: *Rather than addressing the content of John's argument, George argued **ad hominem**.*
tabula rasa	(Latin): Blankness, total innocence.
	WORDS IN CONTEXT: *In Latin **tabula rasa** means "clean slate." Thus the term has come to mean a blank sheet on which nothing has yet been written, or an innocent person.*
Weltanschauung	(German): The world philosophy of an individual; one's essential world view.
	WORDS IN CONTEXT: *In world affairs, one must understand that the **Weltanschauung** of East and West is substantially different.*

After studying the definitions above, use the words in the sentences below.

1. The mother found herself _____ at the teenagers' party.
2. The candidate used _____ attacks against his rival for office.
3. The elementary teacher loved the _____ of her very young students.
4. The young man's _____ changed over time as he learned more and more about the world and human nature.

Test Yourself: Place the letter next to the number to match word and meaning.

1. persona non grata   a. a blank slate
2. ad hominem   b. a person not welcome
3. tabula rasa   c. an attack on a person
4. Weltanschauung   d. world view

On a separate sheet of paper, write sentences using each of the words above.

BONUS WORD

Semper fidelis
(Latin): Always faithful. The motto of the U.S. Marine Corps.

sui generis	(Latin): In a class by itself, unique, of its own kind.
	WORDS IN CONTEXT: *New York City is **sui generis;** there is nothing like it in the world.*
terra firma	(Latin): Solid ground; firm earth.
	WORDS IN CONTEXT: *After many hours on ship, the crew was happy to be back on **terra firma.***
tête à tête	(French): Face to face; confidential discussion.
	WORDS IN CONTEXT: *The parents of three children were delighted to have the time and privacy for dinner and a **tête à tête** in a quiet restaurant.*
laissez-faire	(French): Noninterference; a let alone policy, especially in economic matters.
	WORDS IN CONTEXT: *The federal government took a **laissez-faire** attitude toward the recent fluctuations in the stock market.*

After studying the definitions above, use the words in the sentences below.

1. The original painting that the artist gave me was _____.
2. She swam five miles in the chilly water and was very glad when _____ in the shape of a small island came into sight.
3. The couple, who had been in a crowd of people all day, was happy to retire to a small coffee shop for a _____.
4. The parents agreed that in the matter of the behavior of their teenaged son they would temporarily pursue a _____ policy with the hope that the problems would correct themselves.

Test Yourself: Place the letter next to the number to match word and meaning.

1. sui generis   a. solid ground
2. terra firma   b. unique
3. tête à tête   c. hands-off; noninterference
4. laissez-faire   d. face-to-face conversation

On a separate sheet of paper, write sentences using each of the words above.

BONUS WORD

sans souci (French): Without worry, care, or sadness.

noblesse oblige	(French): Nobility obliges; thus, people of high positions or social rank are obligated to help those beneath them.
	WORDS IN CONTEXT: *Noblesse oblige also includes the obligation of people of high birth to conduct themselves in the dignified manner suitable to their nobility.*
objet d'art	(French): A small piece of art.
	WORDS IN CONTEXT: *A tapestry displayed as an **objet d'art** hung on the wall of their home.*
sine qua non	(Latin): This expression translates directly to "without which not"; it means a necessary quality or thing; indispensable.
	WORDS IN CONTEXT: *Chocolate was her idea of the **sine qua non** of any dessert.*
Schadenfreude	(German): Pleasure felt at the misfortune of others.
	WORDS IN CONTEXT: *When the arrogant businesswoman was sent to jail for fraud, the gleeful attitude of some people was seen by others as **Schadenfreude**.*

After studying the definitions above, use the words in the sentences below.
1. Miss Manners's words were the _____ of proper etiquette.
2. They brought the small sculpture from Africa as an _____ for their library.
3. When the unpleasant but brainy boy in their class got a C on his final, the rest of the class was overcome with _____.
4. The wealthy donor made the large contribution to the faltering inner-city school out of a sense of _____.

Test Yourself: Place the letter next to the number to match word and meaning.

1. objet d'art   a. pleasure in the suffering of others
2. sine qua non   b. obligations of the higher classes to the lower
3. Schadenfreude   c. an art object
4. noblesse oblige   d. indispensable quality or thing

On a separate sheet of paper, write a sentence using each of the words above.

BONUS WORD

coup d'etat (French): A surprise move to overthrow the existing government or political state.

Sturm und Drang	(German): Storm and stress; in eighteenth-century Germany, a literary movement begun in reaction to neoclassicism—romantic in nature, glorifying the individual.
	WORDS IN CONTEXT: *Sturm und Drang has come to describe romantic natures and volatile temperament, as in: The diva was filled with **Sturm und Drang**.*
quid pro quo	(Latin): This for that,; tit for tat; one thing in exchange for another.
	WORDS IN CONTEXT: *Quid pro quo has come to mean in modern parlance, "You scratch my back, I'll scratch yours."*
bête noir	(French): Black beast; bugbear; a fearsome quality or thing.
	WORDS IN CONTEXT: *She was an excellent student, but she found in theoretical physics her **bête noir**.*
de rigueur	(French): Of strictness; thus, according to rules and manners strictly required by etiquette.
	WORDS IN CONTEXT: *The groom was told by the bride that tuxedos for all the men in the wedding party were **de rigueur**.*

After studying the definitions above, use the words in the sentences below.

1. The students in the ballet class saw that the class drama queen was showing her usual signs of _____.
2. Speaking before an audience was Roger's particular _____.
3. Ordering in French in a French restaurant in Paris is seen as _____.
4. As _____for my taking care of his cat, he let me stay in his apartment.

Test Yourself: Place the letter next to the number to match word and meaning.

1. Sturm und Drang   a. this for that
2. bête noir   b. scary, fearsome thing
3. de rigueur   c. storm and stress
4. quid pro quo   d. required manners

On a separate sheet of paper, write sentences using each of the words above.

BONUS WORD

Cave canem (Latin): *Beware of the dog!*

tempus fugit	(Latin): Time flies. **WORDS IN CONTEXT:** *The words written on the sundial in the garden were **tempus fugit**.*
ad hoc	(Latin): In this case only; for this circumstance, this instance alone. **WORDS IN CONTEXT:** *The president called an **ad hoc** meeting of the board to discuss the employees' demands.*
bon mot	(French): A clever phrase; a witty word; a keen observation. The plural is either **bons mots** or **bon mots**. **WORDS IN CONTEXT:** *His stories were peppered with entertaining **bons mots**.*
caveat emptor	(Latin): Let the buyer beware; the seller does not guarantee the product. **WORDS IN CONTEXT:** ***Caveat emptor** has come to be used in the general sense of "a warning," as in "Yes, he's a good professor and I would recommend him, but **caveat emptor**. He can sometimes get a little long-winded."*

After studying the definitions above, use the words in the sentences below.

1. At the reunion, Caroline said, "It seems like yesterday that we were all seniors in college together: "_____!"
2. The committee met on an _____ basis to deal with the various problems that arose.
3. The book club members enjoyed the novels of John Updike because his stories were filled with _____.
4. I like the way the jeans fit at that store on the corner, but, _____, the sweaters run a little large.

Test Yourself: Place the letter next to the number to match word and meaning.

1. tempus fugit   a. for this circumstance only
2. ad hoc   b. clever or witty phrase
3. caveat emptor   c. time flies
4. bon mot   d. a warning

On a separate sheet of paper, write sentences using each of the words above.

BONUS WORD

bitte (German): "Please." Also used as a response to "thank you" (as in English we would say, "You're welcome" —or as some people say, "No problem.")

aperitif	(French): A drink before dinner; light alcohol to increase the appetite. **WORDS IN CONTEXT:** *Would you like an **aperitif** before we go into the dining room?*
a poco a poco	(Italian): Little by little; a little bit. **WORDS IN CONTEXT:** *We acquired our art collection **a poco a poco**.*
carte blanche	(French): A white paper, a blank sheet with an official signature giving permission and authority to fill it as one pleases; thus, full freedom. **WORDS IN CONTEXT:** *The gift certificate gave me **carte blanche** to select anything in the store.*
flagrante delicto	(Latin): While the crime blazes; in the act; in the middle of the occurrence. **WORDS IN CONTEXT:** *In the movie, his girlfriend came into the room and caught him and another woman in **flagrante delicto!***

After studying the definitions above, use the words in the sentences below.

1. Her father gave her _____ to buy any car she wanted.
2. The burglar was caught in _____.
3. Lacking finances for the entire project, they built their summer home _____.
4. The waiter at the club offered _____ before they dined.

Test Yourself: Place the letter next to the number to match word and meaning.

1. a poco a poco   a. in the act
2. aperitif   b. full permission
3. flagrante delicto   c. a little drink before dinner
4. carte blanche   d. little by little

On a separate sheet of paper, write sentences using each of the words above.

BONUS WORD

Bienvenu (French): Welcome.

Words That Fall Trippingly on the Tongue

The following words are musical or just plain fun to say. Notice how many of the words have "l" in them, a letter one can wrap one's tongue around.

DAY 1

ululation	sublunary	susurrant	oleaginous

DAY 2

colporteur	lapidary	tintinnabulation	nullipara

DAY 3

uxorious	exiguous	chrematophobic	obstreperous

DAY 4

lagniappe	mellifluous	illuvial	crepuscular

DAY 5

xanthodontous	velleity	crystallogenesis	quaquaversal

DAY 6

nummamorous	muliebrity	hurly-burly	ineluctable

DAY 7

highfalutin	gracile	oenophile	onomatology

ululation	Howling or hooting, wailing or lamenting loudly.
	WORDS IN CONTEXT: *The women in the stage play were **ululating** in mock mourning.*
sublunary	Located beneath the moon; earthly; mundane; terrestrial.
	WORDS IN CONTEXT: *Humans are **sublunary** creatures; perhaps that's why we are so flawed.*
susurrant	Humming, whispering, murmuring, rustling.
	WORDS IN CONTEXT: *The breeze through the leaves above us made comforting **susurrant** sounds.*
oleaginous	Oily, greasy, unctuous.
	WORDS IN CONTEXT: *The late-night television pitchman spoke in an **oleaginous** manner.*

After studying the definitions above, use the words in the sentences below.

1. Behind us in the theater, we could hear _____ voices commenting quietly about the film.
2. Sitting around the campfire, we could hear in the distance the _____ of animals calling in the forest.
3. The man in the moon looked down on us as we went about our _____ lives.
4. The salesman with his hair slicked back in an _____ style looked less than trustworthy.

Test Yourself: Place the letter next to the number to match word and meaning.

1. susurrant   a. wailing, howling, lamenting
2. oleaginous   b. murmuring, rustling, whispering
3. sublunary   c. oily and unctuous
4. ululation   d. beneath the moon

On a separate sheet of paper, write a sentence using each of these words.

DID YOU KNOW?
Can you guess how many miles of bookshelves there are in the Library of Congress?
ANSWER: 532 miles of shelves.

colporteur	A person who goes from door to door selling Bibles.
	WORDS IN CONTEXT: *No matter what his name suggests, the song writer Cole Porter never sold Bibles door to door as a **colporteur**.*
lapidary	Having the elegance and precision of inscriptions in stone.
	WORDS IN CONTEXT: *The visiting scholar lectured using **lapidary** phrases.*
tintinnabulation	The ringing sound of bells.
	WORDS IN CONTEXT: *Edgar Allen Poe used **tintinnabulation** in his poem, "The Bells"—maybe the last time the word was used!*
nullipara	A female who has never given birth to a child.
	WORDS IN CONTEXT: *The physician saw several women whose health was declining because of having too many children, and a **nullipara** who wanted a child.*

After studying the definitions above, use the words in the sentences below.

1. In the churchyard, we could hear the _____ of the bells coming from the tower.
2. The student's summer job allowed him to meet a lot of people in their homes as he went door to door as a _____.
3. His unforgettable prose was precise, elegant, and _____ in style.
4. The _____ could focus entirely on her profession, because she had no children.

Test Yourself: Place the letter next to the number to match word and meaning.

1. lapidary   a. sells Bibles
2. nullipara   b. like an inscription on a tombstone
3. tintinnabulation   c. childless
4. colporteur   d. ringing sounds

On a separate sheet of paper, write a sentence using each of these words.

DID YOU KNOW? Can you guess the work that contains the longest sentence in the English language? **ANSWER:** *The Rotter's Club* by Jonathan Cols contains a sentence of 13,955 words.

uxorious	Doting on one's wife; irrationally fond; submissive.
	WORDS IN CONTEXT: *The man was so **uxorious** that he had no social life apart from his wife.*
exiguous	Small, scanty, meager little things.
	WORDS IN CONTEXT: *Her little shop sold nothing necessary and everything expensive and **exiguous**.*
chrematophobia	Fear of money.
	WORDS IN CONTEXT: *The banker thought he has seen everything, but now here was a man with **chrematophobia**!*
obstreperous	Stubborn; defiantly resisting restraint; noisily out of control.
	WORDS IN CONTEXT: *She refused to babysit for the **obstreperous** child again.*

After studying the definitions above, use the words in the sentences below.

1. The _____man talked lovingly about his wife at every opportunity.
2. We bought several _____toys and trinkets for the children's Christmas stocking.
3. His _____ almost paralyzed him when he balanced his checkbook.
4. The man who was _____in his political views made a scene at the party.

Test Yourself: Place the letter next to the number to match word and meaning.

1. chrematophobia   a. stubbornly resistant
2. uxurious   b. meager little items
3. obstreperous   c. inordinate affection for one's wife
4. exiguous   d. scared of money

On a separate sheet of paper, write a sentence using each of these words.

DID YOU KNOW?
Can you guess the name of the longest English-language novel? ANSWER: Samuel Richardson's *Clarissa*—**1,533 pages. (There have been many longer series or sequences of novels, but** *Clarissa* **is the longest individual novel in English to date.)**

lagniappe	A small gift given to a customer with a purchase; a gratuity, a tip. Also spelled: **lagnappe.**
	WORDS IN CONTEXT: *The elegant gentleman left a **lagniappe** for his butler.*
mellifluous	Sounding sweet and smooth; speaking in honeyed tones.
	WORDS IN CONTEXT: *She was a charming, graceful woman who spoke with a **mellifluous** voice.*
illuvial	Relating to soil, especially soil materials that have been leeched from an upper layer and deposited in a lower layer of soil.
	WORDS IN CONTEXT: *The scientist was a geologist whose specialty was **illuvial** matters.*
crepuscular	Pertaining to twilight; dim, indistinct; appearing or acting in twilight.
	WORDS IN CONTEXT: *The couple held hands, strolling in the **crespuscular** evening.*

After studying the definitions above, use the words in the sentences below.

1. As I purchased a greeting card, the shopkeeper handed me a _____: a small calendar for the New Year.
2. As she rocked the baby, she murmured in such a _____ voice that the child soon fell asleep.
3. On the geology field trip, the professor pointed out the _____ qualities in the earth.
4. We heard that the moonflowers began to open during the _____ hours of the day.

Test Yourself: Place the letter next to the number to match word and meaning.

1. mellifluous   a. twilight
2. lagniappe   b. smooth, melodic tones
3. illuvial   c. a small gift or a tip
4. crepuscular   d. leeched soil

On a separate sheet of paper, write a sentence using each of the words above.

DID YOU KNOW? Can you guess the name of the longest book in the Bible? **ANSWER: Psalms, 35,353 words.**

xanthodontous	Having yellow teeth. **WORDS IN CONTEXT:** *The witch's costume consisted of long black wig, peaked hat, black robe, and mouthpiece that was definitely xanthodontous.*
velleity	A small urge, an inclination. **WORDS IN CONTEXT:** *The bachelor was not overwhelmed with the woman he met on his first Internet date, but he did sense a velleity in her direction.*
crystallogenesis	Relating to the natural formation of crystals. **WORDS IN CONTEXT:** *The department of crystallogenesis was in the science building.*
quaquaversal	Pointing or facing in every direction, like a mountain sloping in all directions from the tip. **WORDS IN CONTEXT:** *The viewers remarked on the quaquaversal qualities of the sculpture in the gallery.*

After studying the definitions above, use the words in the sentences below.

1. I was not very hungry but felt a _____ for a small snack.
2. Eric was interested in the field of_____, so went on the field trip to study rocks.
3. The family's A-frame cabin in the woods appears to them _____.
4. The _____ man asked his dentist for some whitening solution.

Test Yourself: Place the letter next to the number to match word and meaning.

1. crystallogenesis   a. facing in every direction
2. velleity   b. interest in crystals
3. quaquaversal   c. a small urge or inclination
4. xanthodontous   d. maybe a good toothbrush would help

On a separate sheet of paper, write a sentence using each of the words above.

DID YOU KNOW?
Can you guess the name of the novel in which the final chapter consists of 45 pages of unpunctuated monologue? **ANSWER: The "Molly Bloom" chapter of James Joyce's Ulysses contains Molly's long, unpunctuated monologue (45 pages in the Vintage/Random House, 1961 edition).**

nummamorous	Love of money.
	WORDS IN CONTEXT: *The student interns gossiped about the **nummamorous** qualities of the investment bankers who had hired them for the summer.*
muliebrity	The quality of being womanly, soft, feminine.
	WORDS IN CONTEXT: *Men of virility appreciate women of **muliebrity**.*
hurly-burly	Confusion, tumult, turmoil.
	WORDS IN CONTEXT: *In the **hurly-burly** of packing to move, I forgot to have the electricity turned off.*
ineluctable	That which cannot be struggled out of; inescapable.
	WORDS IN CONTEXT: *The couple saw the financial situation they had gotten themselves into as **ineluctable**, so they met with a financial counselor.*

After studying the definitions above, use the words in the sentences below.

1. She often dressed in men's clothing, but her _____ gave her away.
2. The tourists in Times Square were awestruck at the _____ on the street.
3. _____ is a near opposite of "chremotophobia."
4. They decided to part because the problems in their relationship were _____.

Test Yourself: Place the letter next to the number to match word and meaning.

1. nummamorous   a. womanliness
2. hurly-burly   b. money lover
3. ineluctable   c. turmoil
4. muliebrity   d. inescapable

On a separate sheet of paper, write a sentence using each of the words above.

DID YOU KNOW?
Can you guess what the shortest verse in the Bible is?
ANSWER:
"Jesus wept."
John 11:35.

highfalutin	High-flown, pretentious. **WORDS IN CONTEXT:** *Joe, who saw himself as a beer and pretzels man, refused to go to Joan's* **highfalutin** *party.*
gracile	Slender. **WORDS IN CONTEXT:** *Her* **gracile** *body was perfectly suited to the dance she performed.*
oenophile	A connoisseur of wine. **WORDS IN CONTEXT:** *Mr. Marcus, an* **oenophile,** *offered a course in wine-tasting.*
onomatology	The science of the formation of names or terms. **WORDS IN CONTEXT:** *He was fascinated with* **onomatology,** *or how terms or names are formed.*

After studying the definitions above, use the words in the sentences below.

1. The purple iris had sleek green leaves and a _____ stem.
2. She spoke in a throaty voice using _____ language.
3. As someone interested in _____, she studied language, words, and terminology.
4. We expected an extraordinary dinner, because the host was an _____ and the hostess a gourmet chef.

Test Yourself: Place the letter next to the number to match word and meaning.

1. oenophile   a. slender
2. onomatology   b. wine connoisseur
3. highfalutin   c. studies names
4. gracile   d. pretentious

On a separate sheet of paper, write a sentence using each of the words above.

DID YOU KNOW? Can you guess whence the quotation in the title of this chapter comes? Answer: In *Hamlet* (Act III, sc. ii), these lines appear: "Speak the speech, I pray you, as I have pronounced it to you trippingly on the tongue; but if you mouth it, as many of your players do, I had as lief the towncrier spoke my lines."

Moving Words

Word maven James Kilpatrick said, "The careful writer will want
to distinguish a lurch from a stop, a plod from a slog, a dash from
a sprint." Careful speakers will too—and you may want to know the
conveyances covered in this chapter.

DAY 1

| conveyance | dray | lorry | tram |

DAY 2

| pontoon | barrow | perambulator | rickshaw |

DAY 3

| litter | palanquin | omnibus | phaeton |

DAY 4

| velocipede | tandem | hansom | landau |

DAY 5

| dromedary | tilbury | equipage | droshky |

DAY 6

| dreadnought | flotilla | pantechnicon | freighter |

DAY 7

| yak | hydroplane | trawler | shank's mare |

conveyence	A device to carry something from one place to another.
	WORDS IN CONTEXT: *After their trip, they counted that they had traveled by six kinds of **conveyances**.*
dray	A low cart with detachable sides for carrying heavy loads; a sled.
	WORDS IN CONTEXT: *The hunters had brought a **dray** on which they could drag the deer.*
lorry	A low, flat wagon without sides, or a truck fitted to run on rails.
	WORDS IN CONTEXT: *The car pulled a **lorry** behind it loaded with lumber.*
tram	An open railway car for carrying loads in mines; also a streetcar or a trolley car, sometimes called a *tramcar.*
	WORDS IN CONTEXT: *The miners loaded the coal on a **tram** to send it aboveground.*

After studying the words above, use each in a sentence below.

1. The long pipes were lifted onto a _____ to be pulled to the fields by a truck.
2. The family used its sled as a _____ to drag home the Christmas tree that had been cut down.
3. The tourists in London jumped on a sightseeing _____ to visit historic buildings.
4. The group assembled by means of a number of _____: private cars, trains, planes, ships and taxicabs.

Test Yourself: Write the word that best fits the meaning given below.

1. a sledlike conveyance on which to drag something _____
2. a streetcar, or a rail car in a mine _____
3. any device that moves something from place to place _____
4. a flat wagon without sides _____

On a separate sheet of paper, write a sentence using each of the words above.

DID YOU KNOW? Where do we we get the expression "raring to go" meaning very eager to get started? This appears to be an American term from the late nineteenth century referring to the behavior ("raring") of a sprightly horse when it stands up on its hind legs in its eagerness to get going. In sports writing, we often encounter, "Both teams are rarin' to go."

pontoon	A flat-bottomed boat or floating hollow cylinders used to hold up a temporary bridge (also called a **pontoon**); **pontoons** can also be attached to an aircraft to help it float on water. **WORDS IN CONTEXT:** *The soldiers could not cross the river until several **pontoons** had been put in place.*
barrow	A small cart with one or two wheels, pushed by hand—a wheelbarrow, handbarrow, or pushcart. (**Barrow** has other meanings, too: a heap of earth or rocks marking a grave, even a castrated pig! Just remember for our purposes that it's a conveyance.) **WORDS IN CONTEXT:** *Joan pushed the **barrow** filled with plants to the end of her garden.*
perambulator	A baby carriage or buggy. (Also, one who perambulates—walks around; also, a mechanism pushed around on the ground to measure distance.) **WORDS IN CONTEXT:** *The couple pushed the baby to the park in a **perambulator**.*
rickshaw	A two-wheeled carriage with a hood pulled by one or two men, especially used in the Orient. (Also called *jinkikisha*.) **WORDS IN CONTEXT:** *The tourists hired a **rickshaw** while in Tokyo, which now is somewhat like hiring a horse and carriage in New York City—colorful and historical, but not a current mode of conveyance.*

After studying the words above, use each in a sentence below.

1. Since the couple had twins, they bought a double _____ to take their babies to the local mall.
2. The woman visiting Japan hired a _____ just to have a new adventure, but she worried about the wear and tear on the small man pulling it.
3. He used the _____ to haul the sod from one end of the yard to the other.
4. He sat in the _____ boat near the _____ bridge.

Test Yourself: Write the word that best fits the meaning given below.

1. A two-wheeled carriage, also called a *jinkikisha* _____
2. A baby buggy _____
3. A small cart used in the garden_____
4. A flat-bottomed boat_____

On a separate sheet of paper, write a sentence using each of these words.

DID YOU KNOW?
Where does the expression *hijack* came from? This was a code word during the days of Prohibition when gunmen stopping trucks filled with illegal liquor was common. When the gunman faced the driver, he said "High, Jack," indicating that the driver must raise his hands above his head in surrender.

litter	A framework having long horizontal shafts near the bottom and enclosing a couch on which a person can be carried; a stretcher. (Other meanings: the young borne by dog, cat, or other animal that bears several young at a time; disorder, untidiness, things lying about; straw, hay, or other protective covering for plants.)
	WORDS IN CONTEXT: *The medics carried the wounded soldier on a **litter**.*
palanquin	A covered litter or cotlike couch, usually holding one person, carried by poles on the shoulders of two or more men—formerly used in East Asia.
	WORDS IN CONTEXT: *A **palanquin** (sometimes called **palankeen**) is sometimes seen in historical pictures bearing royalty.*
omnibus	Same as a bus that carries many people. (Other meanings: a large single volume of published works by a single author or on a related theme; something that has a variety of purposes or uses.)
	WORDS IN CONTEXT: *The group of sightseers rented an **omnibus** to take them to the sights of New York City.*
phaeton	A light, four-wheeled carriage, drawn by one or two horses with front and back seats and usually a folding top.
	WORDS IN CONTEXT: *In the nineteenth century, the wealthy often had a **phaeton** in their carriage house and a driver who lived above.*

After studying the words above, use them in the sentences below.

1. An _____ carried the vacationing people through the historical districts of Paris.
2. Asian royalty were carried about in _____ with bright and luxurious cushions.
3. The wealthy woman in the 1820s called for her _____ to carry her on her social rounds.
4. The injured man was taken from his house to the hospital on a _____.

Test Yourself: Write the word that best fits the meaning below.

1. a stretcher to transport wounded people. _____
2. a bus to transport a number of people _____
3. a luxurious couch mounted on a litter _____
4. a carriage that transported well-to-do people in the nineteenth century _____

On a separate sheet of paper, write a sentence using each of these words.

DID YOU KNOW?
The first book in a foreign language to hit *The New York Times* bestseller list was *Winnie Ille Pu*, a 1960 translation into Latin of the adventures of Winnie and friends.

velocipede	Any of various early bicycles or tricycles; also an old type of handcar for use on railroad tracks. **WORDS IN CONTEXT:** *Her great-grandfather told her that when he was a child he had a horse, but what he really wanted was a **velocipede**.*
tandem	A two-wheeled carriage drawn by horses harnessed tandem—in single file, one behind the other; also a bicycle-built-for-two with two seats and sets of pedals placed tandem. **WORDS IN CONTEXT:** *The nineteenth-century couple graduated from a horse-drawn **tandem** to a wheeled **tandem**.*
hansom	Usually followed by the word *cab*—a two-wheeled covered carriage for two passengers pulled by one horse: the driver's seat is above and the cab behind. **WORDS IN CONTEXT:** *In period movies one often sees elegant ladies riding in **hansom** cabs.*
landau	A four-wheeled covered carriage with the top in two sections, either of which can be lowered independently; also a former style of automobile with a top whose back could be folded down. **WORDS IN CONTEXT:** *The **landau** was named for a town in southwest Germany where it was originally made.*

After studying the words above, use them in the sentences below.

1. Fine ladies in Jane Austen novels often rode with their gentlemen friends in _____ cabs, which were private, since there was room only for them and a driver.
2. One of the first convertibles was a _____, made in Germany as indicated by its name.
3. Here with this _____ are two horses single file, or two bicyclers single file.
4. Early bicycles and tricycles were called _____.

Test Yourself: Write the word that best fits the meaning given below.

1. pulled by two horses, single file _____
2. a driver sat above, and the couple sat behind _____
3. bikes and trikes _____
4. its top could fold down _____

On a separate sheet of paper, write sentences using each of these words.

DID YOU KNOW?
Have you ever wondered about the source of the word *aspirin*? The first letter of the word comes from acetylsalicylic acid. *Spir* comes from *Spiraca ulmaria*, the meadowsweet plant, the original source of the compound. The *in* was a common suffix for medications in the late nineteenth century, when aspirin was named. Now, take two with water and go to bed.

dromedary	The one-humped or Arabian camel, occurring from North Africa to India and trained especially for fast riding.
	WORDS IN CONTEXT: *The colonialists often rode* **dromedaries.**
tilbury	A nineteenth-century London coach builder who invented a light, two-wheeled carriage for two people.
	WORDS IN CONTEXT: **Mr. Tilbury** *built one of a number of different kinds of carriages that were precursors to automobiles.*
equipage	Equipment, the furnishing or outfit of a ship, army, expedition; a traveling case for toilet articles; a carriage with horses and liveried servants.
	WORDS IN CONTEXT: *The ship was outfitted with the usual* **equipage** *to make the passengers comfortable.*
droshky	A low, open, four-wheeled Russian carriage with a long, narrow bench that the passengers straddle (also called *drosky*).
	WORDS IN CONTEXT: *The* **droshky** *was not very comfortable, but it carried several people.*

After studying the words above, use them in the sentences below.

1. The early visitors to the North Pole carried _____ to allow them to endure the cold and altitude.
2. The carriage called the _____ was named for its inventor.
3. In the _____ the Russian men straddled the narrow bench and were pulled along by the horse.
4. _____ with one hump, bend your knees, so we can jump!

Test Yourself: Write the word that best fits the meanings below.

1. Used for travel in Moscow before cars _____
2. Lawrence of Arabia rode one _____
3. He gave his name to a light coach _____
4. The soldiers had jeeps following them, carrying their _____

On a separate sheet of paper, write a sentence using each of these words.

DID YOU KNOW?
What does the ZIP in Zip Code stands for? It stands for Zoning Improvement Plan. Who would have thought it?

dreadnought (or dreadnaught)	The first of a class of British battleships built in 1906, which gave its name to all large, heavily armored battleships with many powerful guns. (Also, this word is used for a blanket or a coat of thick woolen fabric.) **WORDS IN CONTEXT:** *The name of the first ship of this kind was* **Dreadnought;** *now it refers to all big, armored battleships.*
flotilla	A fleet of boats or small ships; in the U.S. Navy, a unit consisting of two or more squadrons. **WORDS IN CONTEXT:** *The* **flotilla** *of informal boats rescued the young men after a sailing accident.*
pantechnicon	A furniture van; also a van (warehouse) out of which all kinds of things are sold as at a bazaar. **WORDS IN CONTEXT:** *The* **pantechnicon** *pulled into the swap meet and opened its doors to customers on the street.*
freighter	A ship or aircraft for carrying freight; also the person who loads the ship or sends goods by freight. **WORDS IN CONTEXT:** *My writer friend took a trip on a* **freighter** *to Tahiti to see life on such a boat and get away from tourists.*

After studying the words above, use them in the sentences below.

1. In the movie *Mrs. Miniver* a _____ of small boats rescued the soldiers.
2. The _____ carried supplies to the large ship.
3. They shipped their furnishings by _____.
4. The _____, heavily armored, stood ready for battle.

Test Yourself: Write the word that best fits the meanings below.

1. a van from which things may be sold _____
2. a large ship bearing many guns _____
3. a fleet of boats or ships _____
4. this ship carries freight _____

On a separate sheet of paper, write a sentence using each of these words.

DID YOU KNOW? English contains more words than any other language. It has about 455,000 active words and 700,000 dead ones.

yak	A stocky, long-haired wild ox of Tibet and Central Asia often domesticated as a beast of burden—to carry things. **WORDS IN CONTEXT:** *On our trip to Asia, we saw **yaks** carrying supplies for the villages.*
hydroplane	A small, light motorboat with hydrofoils or with a flat bottom so that it can skim along the water's surface at high speeds (a seaplane); an attachment for an airplane that enables it to glide on the water. **WORDS IN CONTEXT:** *For a new experience, they took a **hydroplane** from France to England.*
trawler	A boat used in trawling—dragging a large, baglike net along the bottom of a fishing bank to catch fish. **WORDS IN CONTEXT:** *In Newfoundland, we saw **trawlers** using a **trawl** to bag cod.*
shank's mare	To go on shank's mare is to walk; the shank is the lower part of the leg between the knee and ankle (and a corresponding part of an animal); can also refer to the whole leg. **WORDS IN CONTEXT:** *After all our adventures on other conveyances, we thought we'd do the final lap home on shank's mare.*

After studying the words above, use them in the sentences below:

1. The fishermen used a _____ with a net to drag for fish.
2. The _____ skimmed along the ocean's surface.
3. The _____ carried wood for the villagers' fires.
4. Tired of conventional means of travel, they took the last five miles the old fashioned way: on _____.

Test Yourself: Write the word that best fits the meaning below.

1. a boat with a net for fishing _____
2. a beast of burden in Asia _____
3. hoofing it _____
4. a flying boat _____

On a separate sheet of paper, write a sentence using each of these new words.

DID YOU KNOW? What do the words *Annuit Coeptis* mean on the one dollar bill? **ANSWER:** The words above the eye on the bill mean "He Favored Our Undertakings." The eye represents the all-seeing God. The pyramid, a symbol of strength, is unfinished, suggesting there is work yet to do.

Emotional Words

Happy, sad, morose, impetuous, blasé, bombastic: the words here describe emotions, emotional styles, emotional outbursts, and more. Some of them are even useful.

DAY 1

| impetuosity | perfervid | blasé | bombastic |

DAY 2

| fulminate | lachrymose | lugubrious | morose |

DAY 3

| distraught | impassive | apnea | dudgeon |

DAY 4

| bumptious | sanguine | parsimonious | mordant |

DAY 5

| languorous | lascivious | vitriolic | truculent |

DAY 6

| vacuous | obstreperous | splenetic | fervent |

DAY 7

| caterwauling | whimsical | volatile | slothful |

impetuosity	Acting suddenly with little thought; rash; impulsive.
	WORDS IN CONTEXT: *His **impetuosity** caused him to take risks without thinking.*
perfervid	Impassioned, ardent, fervent, extremely fervid.
	WORDS IN CONTEXT: *Jane's **perfervid** personality caused her to fall in love frequently.*
blasé	Bored, indifferent.
	WORDS IN CONTEXT: *The tourists had seen so many cathedrals that they found themselves **blasé** about the one in Chartes.*
bombastic	Pompous, grandiloquent; using or characterized by high-sounding, but unimportant or meaningless language.
	WORDS IN CONTEXT: *The speaker held forth in a **bombastic** style that drove away the audience.*

After studying the definitions above, use the words in the sentences below.

1. The boys' _____ caused them to drive dangerously, without proper caution.
2. Ronald had a _____attitude about his schoolwork because he thought he knew it all.
3. John's _____interest in airplanes made him a good candidate for flight school.
4. In auditioning for a new minister, the church committee pronounced one candidate too soft-spoken and another's rhetoric too _____.

Test Yourself: Write the word that best describes the meaning given.

1. rash and impulsive _____
2. use of empty, meaningless words _____
3. full of passion _____
4. full of boredom and indifference_____

After studying the words above, write a sentence using each of these words.

DID YOU KNOW? What is considered the oldest full novel in existence? **ANSWER:** *The Tale of Genji,* written in Japanese in the early eleventh century.

fulminate	To explode with sudden violence; to shout forth denunciations; to detonate (originally, to flash or strike with lightning).
	WORDS IN CONTEXT: *The speaker on the corner was **fulminating** about social problems.*
lachrymose	Tearful; inclined to shed or cause many tears.
	WORDS IN CONTEXT: *The audience watching the sad film was **lachrymose**.*
lugubrious	Very sad or mournful, especially in a way that seems ridiculous.
	WORDS IN CONTEXT: *The drunken group sang old songs in a **lugubrious** fashion.*
morose	Peevish, fretful, gloomy, sullen.
	WORDS IN CONTEXT: *After her date cancelled, she wore a **morose** expression all weekend.*

After studying the words above, use them in the sentences below.

1. The overdone funeral scene in the soap opera came off as _____.
2. His _____attitude let us know that he had failed his driver's test.
3. The radio commentator began to _____ about a politician he disliked.
4. The children were _____ as they buried the pet bunny.

Test Yourself: Write the word that best fits the meaning below.

1. exaggerated sadness or mourning _____
2. sullen and pouty _____
3. to shout and carry on _____
4. overcome with tears _____

On a separate sheet of paper, write a sentence using each of these words.

DID YOU KNOW? In Greek tragedies, what is the difference between *hubris* and *harmartia*? *Hamartia* is the fatal flaw that brings the character to ruin. *Hubris* is overweening (extreme) pride that moves the character toward exhibiting that fatal flaw.

distraught	Extremely troubled, mentally confused, driven crazy.
	WORDS IN CONTEXT: *After the car accident, the teenagers were distraught.*
impassive	Not feeling pain or suffering; insensible, placid, calm, serene; not showing emotion.
	WORDS IN CONTEXT: *She was impassive at her friend's funeral, but we sensed the turmoil inside her.*
apnea	Temporary stopping of breathing, originally, a sneeze.
	WORDS IN CONTEXT: *The child in his tantrum turned blue, as if seized with apnea.*
dudgeon	Very angry, offended, or resentful (originally meaning having one's hand on a dagger).
	WORDS IN CONTEXT: *After the argument, she stormed out of the room in high dudgeon.*

After studying the words above, use them in the sentences below.

1. At the announcement, I sat _____, not knowing what to think.
2. For a few days after his girlfriend had dumped him, he felt _____, but after a while he got over it.
3. The scene was so beautiful that I held my breath, as if overtaken by _____
4. After his rival insulted him before the game, he came out in high _____.

Test Yourself: Write the word that best fits the meaning below.

1. Really, really mad; ready to stab someone _____
2. He was practically blue in the face from _____
3. She sat expressionless _____
4. For a few days after not getting into the college of his choice, he was _____

On a separate sheet of paper, write a sentence using each of these words.

DID YOU KNOW?
Humorist/poet
Ogden Nash wrote
the following famous
lines in 1931,
"Candy is dandy/
But liquor is quicker."
He added another
line in 1968:
"Pot is not."

bumptious	Arrogant, forward, disagreeably conceited.
	WORDS IN CONTEXT: *My parents were appalled at the **bumptious** young man who came to see me with my friends from college.*
sanguine	Cheerful, confident, optimistic, hopeful; in medieval physiology, having a warm, passionate temperament and the healthy, ruddy complexion of one in which the blood is the predominant humor.
	WORDS IN CONTEXT: *My doctor said that he was **sanguine** about the way my injured eye was healing.*
parsimonious	Stingy; over-careful in spending; miserly.
	WORDS IN CONTEXT: *My uncle was so **parsimonious** that my aunt did not have a car of her own, though they could well afford one.*
mordant	Biting, cutting, caustic, or sarcastic in speech or wit; originally an acid or other corrosive substance used in etching.
	WORDS IN CONTEXT: *The **mordant** wit of Professor Higgins was not appreciated by Eliza.*

After studying the words above, use them in the sentences below.

1. He was not _____ about the possibility that his candidate would win.
2. He was entertaining and funny, but his _____ wit struck some people the wrong way.
3. She loved to shop, but her roommate, the opposite, was _____
4. He liked them individually, but when together, he thought the boys in the fraternity were _____.

Test Yourself: Write the word that best fits the meaning below.

1. sarcastic guy _____
2. stingy guy_____
3. optimistic guy _____
4. conceited guy _____

On a separate sheet of paper, write a sentence using each of these words.

DID YOU KNOW?
Robert Louis Stevenson's *Dr. Jekyll* and *Mr. Hyde* had counterparts in real people. Apparently, a Scottish man named William Brodie, known by day as a respected cabinetmaker, wore a mask at night and led a group of gangsters. He was hanged in 1788, but his case inspired Stevenson to write about it almost one hundred years later.

languorous	Listless, lack of feeling or vitality, still, sluggish, dull, lethargic.
	WORDS IN CONTEXT: *We spent a pleasantly languorous day at the beach, and on Monday we were back at work.*
lascivious	Wanton, lustful, tending to exhibit lewd desires.
	WORDS IN CONTEXT: *At the comedy club, we heard a number of lascivious jokes, but they were nothing we hadn't heard before.*
vitriolic	Extremely biting, caustic, sharp or bitter; venomous.
	WORDS IN CONTEXT: *The argument we overheard between the two was vitriolic, and we wondered if their relationship would survive it.*
truculent	Fierce, savage, cruel, rude, harsh, mean, scathing; said of behavior, speech, writing.
	WORDS IN CONTEXT: *In the debate, his political opponent was so truculent that he alienated the audience.*

After studying the words above, use them in the sentences below.

1. The show was so _____ that we wouldn't think of taking our children to it.
2. The warm, _____ last days of summer made us reluctant to face the workplace after our vacation.
3. The strikers put up such a harsh and _____ defense that the company officials eventually gave in to their demands.
4. The scene in the office became _____ with everyone screaming at everyone else.

Test Yourself: Write the word that best fits the meaning below.

1. mean, cruel, and savage _____
2. lethargic, listless, sluggish _____
3. sharp, bitter, biting _____
4. lewd and off-color _____

On a separate sheet of paper, write a sentence using each of these words.

DID YOU KNOW?
What does the word *catafalque* **mean? From the French and Italian, it means "a funeral canopy, a scaffolding, or a stage." It is used to describe a wooden framework draped with cloth on which a coffin holding a body lying in state rests during an elaborate funeral. In the Catholic Church, the word indicates a coffin representing the dead used in Requiem Mass after a burial.**

vacuous	Empty, blank, showing lack of intelligence or purpose; stupid, senseless, inane.
	WORDS IN CONTEXT: *The man she met on the Internet sounded interesting, but she found him **vacuous** and left as soon as she finished her coffee.*
obstreperous	Noisy opposition; unruly; boisterous; resisting control.
	WORDS IN CONTEXT: *Most of the children at the birthday party behaved, but one child was so **obstreperous** that someone had to call his parents.*
splenetic	Bad-tempered, irritable, peevish, spiteful.
	WORDS IN CONTEXT: *At the trial, the woman was **splenetic,** which did not help her case.*
fervent	Intensely devoted or earnest; glowing; passionate.
	WORDS IN CONTEXT: *The buyers were **fervent** about the house and made an offer immediately.*

After studying the words above, use them in the sentences below.

1. He was looking forward to the class, but intellectually he found most of the other students_____.
2. He couldn't wait for the game because he was _____ about soccer.
3. In the argument, one of the men was so _____ that he nearly punched the other.
4. Because of the child's _____ behavior, he was judged not a good fit for the kindergarten.

Test Yourself: Write the word that best fits the meaning below.

1. intense, glowing, passionate _____
2. irritable, peevish, hard to get along with _____
3. out of control, noisy _____
4. dumb, empty, vacant_____

On a separate sheet of paper, write a sentence using each of these words.

DID YOU KNOW?
What does the *Ouija* as in *Ouija* board mean? Yes, yes. In French (*oui*) and German (*ja*), so it means "yes, yes." It's bad luck to let anyone answer in the negative when you suggest getting out the Ouija board.

caterwauling	Making a shrill, howling sound like a cat at rutting time; a screech, a wail.
	WORDS IN CONTEXT: *They heard **caterwauling** coming from the woods.*
whimsical	Full of whimsy, fanciful, out of the ordinary, unpredictable.
	WORDS IN CONTEXT: *The entire family was artistic and **whimsical** and, he found, a lot of fun.*
volatile	Unstable, explosive, capricious, fickle, moving from one idea or interest to another unpredictably.
	WORDS IN CONTEXT: *Finally, she left her job because her boss was so **volatile**.*
slothful	Slow moving, lazy, indolent, like the sloth, an animal that exhibits these characteristics.
	WORDS IN CONTEXT: *He needed an assistant, but the ones the agency sent him appeared to be **slothful**.*

After studying the words above, use them in the sentences below.

1. She fell in love with him because of his humorously _____ and fanciful imagination.
2. The political situation was so _____ that he decided not to run for office.
3. He was crisp and organized, and she was _____, so the relationship didn't have a chance.
4. The _____ from the apartment next door was just the neighbor trying to sing.

Test Yourself: Write the word that best fits the meaning below.

1. slow and lazy _____
2. howling, wailing, and screeching _____
3. capricious, fickle, unstable _____
4. fanciful, unpredictable _____

On a separate sheet of paper, write a sentence using each of these words.

DID YOU KNOW?
Do you know what *lunatic* means? Moonstruck, crazy, a lover of the moon.

Tough Words

Here are some good, tough words, both literally and figuratively.
Use them judiciously.

DAY 1

| barn burner | uproot | diabolic | extirpate |

DAY 2

| cavil | ferule | beleaguer | billingsgate |

DAY 3

| tortuous | abominate | jeremiad | inexorable |

DAY 4

| adamantine | puissance | indomitable | refutation |

DAY 5

| tenacious | sepulchral | obstinacy | virulent |

DAY 6

| Herculean | Augean | Sisyphean | uphill work |

DAY 7

| sinewy | brute | tonicity | thews |

barn burner	An inflammatory event, something that could figuratively burn down a barn.
	WORDS IN CONTEXT: *The election in Florida looked as if it would be a **barn burner**.*
uproot	To remove something from a locale, not necessarily eliminating it.
	WORDS IN CONTEXT: *The weeds were **uprooted** from the park, but their airborne spoors allowed the plants to grow in the wild.*
diabolic	Of the devil or devils; very wicked or cruel; fiendish.
	WORDS IN CONTEXT: *Joe's brother took **diabolic** pleasure in keeping his family upset.*
extirpate	To destroy or remove completely; exterminate.
	WORDS IN CONTEXT: *The insurgents in the village were **extirpated**..*

After studying the words above, use them in the sentences below.

1. The bomb_____ the population of the village; there were no survivors.
2. The event was categorized as a _____, but that was just a figure of speech.
3. We could not understand the _____ attitude he had toward the people who did not share his convictions.
4. The war was intended to _____ the enemy, while allowing them to resettle elsewhere.

Test Yourself: Write the word that best fits the meaning below.

1. to remove something from an area _____
2. wiping out entirely _____
3. an incendiary event _____
4. as evil as the devil _____

On a separate sheet of paper, write a sentence using each of these words.

DID YOU KNOW?
What does *stilo nova* mean? It actually means "new style," but it came to mean "newfangled notions." When the Gregorian calendar was issued in 1582, correspondence carried the term to indicate that the letter was written on a certain date on the new style calendar. In time, the term came to indicate any innovation—thus newfangled.

cavil	To object when there is little reason to do so; trivial faultfinding, carping, quibbling.
	WORDS IN CONTEXT: *The chairman of the committee hoped that members would not **cavil** over small points.*
ferule	A stick, whip, or rod made from a giant fennel plant.
	WORDS IN CONTEXT: *Some men fought with their fists, while others fought with **ferules**.*
beleaguer	To beset with difficulties, to harass; in battle, to besiege by encircling with an army.
	WORDS IN CONTEXT: *The gang planned to **beleaguer** its rivals until they left the neighborhood.*
billingsgate	Foul, vulgar, abusive talk (named after a fish market in London, notorious for the foul language used there).
	WORDS IN CONTEXT: *The angry mob shouted **billingsgate** at the crowd.*

After studying the words above, use them in the sentences below.

1. The bullies on the playground plotted to _____ the boys they didn't like.
2. The men in the jungle hit each other with _____.
3. The coarse language on the street turned to _____ when the crowd got out of control.
4. The striking workers began to _____ with management over its offer.

Test Yourself: Write the word that best fits the meaning below.

1. foul, vulgar language _____
2. quibble over small points _____
3. sticks or rods made from a plant _____
4. harass, annoy, besiege _____

On a separate sheet of paper, write a sentence using each of these words.

DID YOU KNOW?
What pen names did the following authors use: Mary Ann Evans, Eric Arthur Blair, Marie-Henri Beyle, Hector Hugh Munro, Charles Dickens?
ANSWER:
George Eliot,
George Orwell,
Stendhal,
Saki,
Boz.

tortuous	Full of twists, turns, curves, or windings; not straightforward.
	WORDS IN CONTEXT: *She gave a **tortuous** argument for why she did not return on time.*
abominate	To dislike extremely; loathe; have feelings of hatred or disgust for.
	WORDS IN CONTEXT: *The preacher said that he **abominated** the sin, but not the sinner.*
jeremiad	A sad tale of woe (an allusion to he Lamentations of Jeremiah in the Bible).
	WORDS IN CONTEXT: *His story of his trip to the Caribbean, with lost tickets, missed flights, poor accommodations, and then a hurricane in the islands, turned out to be a **jeremiad.***
inexorable	That which cannot be defeated or moved by persuasion; unrelenting.
	WORDS IN CONTEXT: *When he saw lighning strike all around him, he felt that his fate was **inexorable.***

After studying the words above, use them in the sentences below.

1. He told us a long story of his troubles, and we sat with sympathy listening to his _____.
2. She had swum out too far in the ocean, and tired, she felt that drowning was her _____ fate.
3. His parents said that they _____ the behavior of his friends when they began to argue loudly and fight.
4. The crooked path up the mountain was tough and _____.

Test Yourself: Write the word that best fits the meanings below.

1. long, sad tale _____
2. not to be overcome _____
3. winding, twisting, and turning _____
4. view with hatred and disgust _____

On a separate sheet of paper, write a sentence using each of these words.

DID YOU KNOW? Someone actually wrote the ditty, "Mary Had a Little Lamb." The author was Sarah Josepha Hale, and the year was 1830. She was inspired by seeing a child being followed to school by a pet lamb. Hale founded the first national women's periodical, Godey's Ladies Book and worked successfully to get Thanksgiving recognized as a national holiday.

adamantine	The hardest metal, stone, or substance; unbreakable.
	WORDS IN CONTEXT: *His opinions were not always popular, but they were **adamantine**.*
puissance	Powerful strength.
	WORDS IN CONTEXT: *The **puissance** of the team intimidated its rivals.*
indomitable	Unyielding; unconquerable; not easily defeated, discouraged, or subdued.
	WORDS IN CONTEXT: *They were not the strongest players in the league, but their spirit was **indomitable**.*
refutation	Proof by argument or evidence that something is false or wrong.
	WORDS IN CONTEXT: *After the scientist delivered his lecture, he had to sit through an hour of **refutation** from his colleagues.*

After studying the words above, use them in the sentences below.

1. The soldiers faced their enemy with _____ courage.
2. The weaker boys felt threatened by the _____ of the stronger boys in camp.
3. The scholars offered a _____ of the thesis the professor presented.
4. His belief about the matter was _____.

Test Yourself: Write the word that best fits the meaning below.

1. hard as a rock _____
2. argument or evidence to the contrary _____
3. cannot be discouraged or overcome _____
4. power and strength _____

On a separate sheet of paper, write a sentence using each of these words.

DID YOU KNOW?
There was once an Adam and Eve's Day. It's true. On the medieval church calendar, Christmas Eve was called Adam and Eve's Day. That day, pageants were performed depicting the couple's fall from the Garden of Eden. One prop was the "paradise tree," which bore the forbidden fruit. Many German families set up this tree in the mid-1500s. The paradise tree was the forerunner of the Christmas tree.

tenacious	Holding firmly, tough, persistent, cohesive, stubborn.
	WORDS IN CONTEXT: *They tried to clear the vines from the sides of the cabin, but the clinging plants were **tenacious.***
sepulchral	Like a tomb for burial; gloomy; dismal; deep and melancholy.
	WORDS IN CONTEXT: *The singing coming from the church burial ground was **sepulchral.***
obstinacy	The quality of being stubborn; unreasonable; dogged; determined to have one's own way; mulish.
	WORDS IN CONTEXT: *The boy was eventually expelled from school because of his **obstinacy.***
virulent	Extremely poisonous or injurious, deadly; bitterly antagonistic, venomous; said of a disease—highly malignant.
	WORDS IN CONTEXT: *One could sense the **virulent** opposition on the two sides of the aisle in Congress.*

After studying the words above, use them in the sentences below.

1. The _____ of the demonstrators aroused the anger of the police.
2. The caves were dimly lit and _____ in feeling.
3. The physician said the disease was _____.
4. During the rope pull at camp, both sides in the competition kept a _____ hold on the ropes.

Test Yourself: Write the word that best fits the meaning below.

1. poisonous, deadly _____
2. tomblike, dark, and gloomy _____
3. holding on firmly, resistant _____
4. stubborn as a mule _____

On a separate sheet of paper, write a sentence using each of these words.

DID YOU KNOW?
Vladimir Lenin was the most translated author in the world for much of the twentieth century. In the Soviet Union, popular works were routinely translated into the dozens of languages used by people of the states that composed the former USSR. Even today, more than 3,000 translations of Lenin's works still exist.

Herculean	Having great size and strength, powerful; of a task—very difficult to do.
	WORDS IN CONTEXT: *A **Herculean task** is a huge job even for a powerful person like Hercules of Greek legend.*
Augean	Very filthy or corrupt; unclean. King Augeas of Greek legend had a stable which held 3,000 oxen and remained uncleaned for 30 years until Hercules cleaned it one day by diverting a river through it.
	WORDS IN CONTEXT: *The litter and waste surrounding the abandoned housing project was of **Augean** proportions.*
Sisyphean	Endless and toilsome; essentially useless. Again, from Greek myth, Sisyphus, a greedy king of Corinth, was doomed forever in Hades to roll uphill a heavy stone that always rolled down again.
	WORDS IN CONTEXT: *Training an army of the unwilling seemed to be a **Sisyphean** task.*
uphill work	A Sisyphean task. Thankless work that never gets done.
	WORDS IN CONTEXT: *The laborers building the Pyramids no doubt thought it was **uphill work**, since no one completed the task in his lifetime.*

After studying the words above, use them in the sentences below.

1. Moving the stones across the river in a rowboat felt like a _____ task to the boys.
2. Cleaning those stables was a _____ job that only Hercules could do.
3. Something_____(even if it's not a stable) is a filthy thing.
4. _____ work, like that of Sisyphus, never gets done.

Test Yourself: Write the word that best fits the meaning below.

1. something truly nasty _____
2. Sisyphus could do it, but it got him nowhere _____
3. Hercules could do it _____
4. difficult, thankless job _____

On a separate sheet of paper, write a sentence using each of these words.

DID YOU KNOW?
Robert Louis Stevenson bequeathed his birthday to a young girl right before he died, saying, "I have no further use for a birthday of any description." The girl was Annie Ide of St. Johnsbury, Vermont, who had complained to him that Christmas Day was her birthday, and it always got lost in the shuffle of festivities. So shortly before his death, Stevenson drew up a legal will carrying signatures of witnesses and bequeathed to Annie November 13, his own birthday.

sinewy	Tough, strong, vigorous, powerful, muscular; having many or large sinews, like a cut of meat.
	WORDS IN CONTEXT: *The muscles on the blacksmith's* **sinewy** *arms were as tight as iron bands.*
brute	Tough, gross, stupid, senseless and irrational; having no capacity to reason; said of person, animal, or force.
	WORDS IN CONTEXT: *In the Amazon, nature seemed a* **brute** *force.*
tonicity	Having good muscle tone (in music, tonicity refers to the keynote of a diatonic scale or tonic chord).
	WORDS IN CONTEXT: *In the gym, she observed that most of the people had good* **tonicity.**
thews	Good, strong qualities; later this came to refer to strong physical qualities, muscular power, bodily strength.
	WORDS IN CONTEXT: *A* **brute** *is clueless (without a clue), and a weak person is* **thewless** *(without* **thews***).*

Test Yourself: Write the word that best fits the meaning below.

1. stupid, gross person, animal, or force _____
2. good body tone _____
3. good qualities plus good body tone _____
4. tough, muscular, like a cut of meat _____

On a separate sheet of paper, write a sentence using each of these words.

DID YOU KNOW?
What made Dr. Seuss repeat himself in *Green Eggs and Ham*? Editor Bennett Cerf bet Dr. Seuss that he couldn't write a book using only 50 words. The author took Cerf up on the bet and wrote what is probably his best-known work. The story contains 851 occurrences of just 50 words, all but the word "if" are repeated. The only multisyllablic word is *anywhere.*

Fighting Words

The following are words that may cause fights as well as words
that describe fights. You don't want any part in any of them, except
to know what to stay away from.

DAY 1

umbrage	virago	aspersions	egregious

DAY 2

belabor	polemic	belligerent	pugnacious

DAY 3

harrow	scurrilous	malign	malevolent

DAY 4

derision	obloquy	termagant	invective

DAY 5

minatory	jackanapes	jackal	booby

DAY 6

bellicose	derogatory	hectoring	effrontery

DAY 7

contemptuous	supercilious	obdurate	soubriquet

umbrage	Offense or resentment; also means shady or shadowy.
	WORDS IN CONTEXT: *The man took **umbrage** at my remark about his haircut.*
virago	A quarrelsome, shrewish woman; a scold; Amazon; manlike woman.
	WORDS IN CONTEXT: *Calling a woman a **virago** would likely cause a fight.*
aspersions	The act of defaming; slander; innuendo; a damaging or disparaging remark; also, the word is used in baptism as a sprinkling of water.
	WORDS IN CONTEXT: *"Do not cast **aspersions** on my wife by calling her a **virago**," the man said. "I take **umbrage** at your remark."*
egregious	Remarkably bad, flagrant, outstanding for undesirable qualities; also, separated from the herd.
	WORDS IN CONTEXT: *She thought the guest's behavior was **egregious** when he spilled red wine on the white chair and did not apologize.*

After studying the words above, use them in the sentences below.

1. Casting _____ on someone's character is not a kind thing to do.
2. A woman does not like to be called a _____.
3. Name-calling of any kind is _____ behavior.
4. People take _____ at being called unflattering names.

Test Yourself: Write the word that best fits the meaning below.

1. outrageous enough to be remarked upon _____
2. disparaging and damaging remarks _____
3. a disparaging name to call a woman _____
4. offense taken _____

On a separate sheet of paper, write a sentence using each of these words.

DID YOU KNOW?
The Lord of the Flies is the Devil himself. In William Golding's novel, the boys stranded on an island are confronted by the Beast, usually interpreted as evil. In Greek, *Beelzebub,* referring to Satan, the Devil, or one of his demons, literally translates as "Lord of the Flies."

belabor	To beat severely, hit or whip; to attack with words, scolding, criticism.
	WORDS IN CONTEXT: *The girl thought her mother **belabored** the issue of the hour that she had come home the night before.*
polemic	Argument, disputation that causes one to tremble or shake.
	WORDS IN CONTEXT: *His father delivered a **polemic** about his son's use of the family car.*
belligerent	Seeking war, warlike; showing a readiness to fight or quarrel.
	WORDS IN CONTEXT: *The child was **belligerent** on the playground, and his teacher took him to the principal's office.*
pugnacious	To punch; eager and ready to fight; quarrelsome; combative.
	WORDS IN CONTEXT: *The boxer was especially **pugnacious** and took on anyone who challenged him.*

After studying the words above, use them in the sentences below.

1. His wife _____the point about his watching football games all day on Thanksgiving.
2. The general told the soldiers they should be _____ in the face of war.
3. They called the combative boy Pug because he was so _____.
4. The overbearing professor had a _____ for every statement the student brought up.

Test Yourself: Write the word that best fits the meaning below.

1. spoiling for a fight_____
2. another one spoiling for a fight_____
3. beat a dead horse in arguing _____
4. beat a trembling dead horse in argument _____

On a separate sheet of paper, write a sentence using each of these words.

DID YOU KNOW?
What does rock and roll have to do with literature? Rockers calling themselves Uriah Heep took the name from Charles Dickens's *David Copperfield;* Steppenwolf took its name from Herman Hesse's novel of that name; Amboy Dukes took its name from Irving Shulman's novel about Brooklyn street gangs, and Collective Soul's name came from Ayn Rand's *Fountainhead.*

harrow	To torment, distress, cut, lascerate. (Also see "Did You Know?" below.)
	WORDS IN CONTEXT: *A **harrow** (noun) is a sharp-edged, spiked tool often pulled by a tractor used for plowing deeply into the ground to level it or root up weeds; as a verb, **harrow** is often used to mean treating a person as if one were metaphorically using a **harrow** on him or her—cutting, tormenting, lacerating.*
scurrilous	being indecent or abusive in language; coarse, vulgar, foul.
	WORDS IN CONTEXT: *One candidate made a **scurrilous** remark about the other.*
malign	To speak evil of, defame, slander.
	WORDS IN CONTEXT: *The witness sought to **malign** the defendant.*
malevolent	Wishing evil or harm to others; showing ill will; malicious.
	WORDS IN CONTEXT: *They thought him to be a **malevolent** person, so they stayed away from him.*

After studying the words above, use them in the sentences below.
Use the part of speech that applies.

1. The bully _____ the new kid, tormenting him with cutting words.
2. The feuding neighbors made _____ remarks to each other.
3. One man was taken to court because he _____ the other.
4. In the Halloween story the children read, a _____ old witch lived in a spooky house on a hill.

Test Yourself: Write the word that best fits the meaning below.

1. to scare someone with acts or threats of violence _____
2. wishing evil or harm to someone _____
3. abusive or vulgar language _____
4. to slander or defame _____

On a separate sheet of paper, write a sentence using each of these words.

DID YOU KNOW?
The word *harrow* has an archaic religious usage as well as the definitions given above. This use means to rob, plunder, or pillage, often used with the word *hell*—as in "the harrowing of hell," which means to enter hell, destroy demons, and rescue the righteous. Harrowing hell is what has been said Jesus will do on Judgment Day.

derision	Contempt or ridicule. **WORDS IN CONTEXT:** *The imaginative woman in the novel was held up to* **derision** *by people of the small town because her ideas were different from theirs.*
obloquy	A turning aside from moral conduct or sound thinking. **WORDS IN CONTEXT:** *The parishioner was accused by the church of committing an* **obloquy.**
termagant	A boisterous, overbearing, scolding woman; a shrew. **WORDS IN CONTEXT:** *The word* **termagant** *derives from an imaginary deity thought by Crusaders to be worshipped by Moslems and represented in medieval morality plays.*
invective	A violent verbal attack; strong criticism; insults; curses. **WORDS IN CONTEXT:** *One contestant used* **invective** *about another causing the game to be called off.*

After studying the words above, use them in the sentences below.

1. The professor refused to allow ridicule or _____ in the classroom, finding it ineffective in teaching and learning.
2. Another fighting word to call a woman besides virago is _____.
3. The _____ he committed was petty, but his strict religion would not tolerate it.
4. The demonstrators at the convention were full of _____ for the politicians.

Test Yourself: Write the word that best fits the meaning below.

1. strong criticism and verbal attack _____
2. a moral error _____
3. do not call a woman this _____
4. use of ridicule as a put down _____

On a separate sheet of paper, write a sentence using each of these words.

DID YOU KNOW?
F. Scott Fitzgerald was named after a distant relative who was also a writer. Yes, F. Scott's second cousin, three times removed, was Francis Scott Key, who wrote the words to *The Star-Spangled Banner* as he watched the bombardment of Fort McHenry, near Baltimore.

minatory	Menacing or threatening.
	WORDS IN CONTEXT: *It was a dark and stormy night—read,* ***minatory.***
jackanapes	A conceited, insolent, presumptuous fellow.
	WORDS IN CONTEXT: ***Jackanapes*** *originally referred to a monkey, and this usage alludes to that.*
jackal	A person who does dishonest or humiliating tasks for another; a cheat or swindler.
	WORDS IN CONTEXT: ***Jackal*** *refers to several species of wild dogs of Asia and North Africa that prey in packs at night, hunting game for the lion and eating the leavings.*
booby	A stupid or foolish person, nitwit; a disparaging name to call a person.
	WORDS IN CONTEXT: *In games, the word* ***booby*** *is not used disparagingly but indulgently: the* ***booby*** *gets the worst score and usually a ridiculous Certain seabirds were called* ***boobies*** *because in anthropomorphic terms they seemed to be awkward, bumbling.*

After studying the words above, use them in the sentences below.

1. _____is one of the nastiest of name-calling terms for a thoroughly dishonest person who preys on others for little gain.
2. Once _____ referred to a monkey; now it refers to a conceited, unlikable fellow.
3. A _____ is a pretty silly and foolish person.
4. _____can be used to describe any threatening, menacing person, place or thing.

Test Yourself: Write the word that best fits the meaning below.

1. a really bad sort you want to avoid _____
2. gets the silly prize for being last _____
3. scary, spooky, and menacing_____
4. a presumptuous monkey _____

On a separate sheet of paper, write a sentence using each of these words.

DID YOU KNOW?
A mockingbird is buried *In Cold Blood.* Truman Capote's research assistant for his book *In Cold Blood* was Nell Harper Lee, who as Harper Lee wrote one book only, *To Kill a Mockingbird.* After the success of her 1960 novel, Lee used her considerable research skills in another way. Nell Lee is one of the people to whom Capote dedicated his book.

bellicose	Of a hostile or warlike nature; ready to fight or quarrel. **WORDS IN CONTEXT:** *The troops were trained to be **bellicose.***
derogatory	Disparaging, belittling, tending to lessen or impair. **WORDS IN CONTEXT:** *The fight started in the bar after one person made **derogatory** remarks about another.*
hectoring	Browbeating; needling; insulting or baiting other people. **WORDS IN CONTEXT:** *The **hectoring** mob yelled insulting words to onlookers.*
effrontery	Shamelessness, boldness, impudence, audacity. **WORDS IN CONTEXT:** *The presumptuous and dislikable man was characterized by his **effrontery.***

After studying the words above, use them in the sentences below.

1. His attitude was _____, and he appeared ready to fight.
2. His _____ about their habits nearly drove the family crazy.
3. Their bantering insults soon slipped over the line into _____ remarks.
4. The audacious _____ of the couple astounded those who met them for the first time.

Test Yourself: Write the word that best fits the meaning below.

1. warlike _____
2. needling, baiting, carping _____
3. words of personal insult _____
4. uncalled for boldness and impudence _____

On a separate sheet of paper, write a sentence using each of these words.

DID YOU KNOW?
Mark Twain was a joker. One story goes that after hearing a sermon in church, he told the minister that he had a book at home that contained every word in that sermon. The shocked minister said that he'd certainly like to see that book. A few days later he found in his mail a package from Twain: an unabridged dictionary.

contemptuous	Full of contempt; scornful; disdainful.
	WORDS IN CONTEXT: *The look he gave them made it clear that he was* **contemptuous** *of the members of the audience he was about to address.*
supercilious	Disdainful, haughty, characterized by pride or scorn.
	WORDS IN CONTEXT: *The word* **supercilious** *means "raised eyebrow," and thus suggests the facial expression of disdain, haughtiness, pride, and scorn.*
obdurate	Hard-hearted; not easily moved to pity or sympathy; inflexible; not giving in readily.
	WORDS IN CONTEXT: *She had an* **obdurate** *personality that often made it difficult for her to get out of her rigid patterns and treat individuals with compassion.*
soubriquet	A nickname or an assumed name.
	WORDS IN CONTEXT: *A* **soubriquet** *can devolve into a fighting word—like Fatty or Muttonhead, or even Booby—but just as likely a soubriquet can be a loving or warm word, such as Honey or Jimbo, or even Big Bob.*

After studying the words above, use them in the sentences below.

1. The students could tell that the professor was _____ of the introductory material he was having to teach, and therefore of them.
2. The curator examined the art in the gallery with a _____ expression on his face, so we knew he would not purchase any of it.
3. She spoke of her sister in an _____ manner, which led us to understand why the two did not get along well.
4. His _____ was P. Diddy, though we didn't know why.

Test Yourself: Write the word that best fits the meaning below.

1. raised eyebrow _____
2. looks down on with disdain _____
3 answers to a pet name _____
4. hard head, hard heart _____

On a separate sheet of paper, write sentences using each of these words.

DID YOU KNOW?
What is the full name that Charles Dickens gave the book we call *David Copperfield?* **Here goes:** *The Personal History, Experience and Observation of David Copperfield, the Younger, of Blunderstone Rookery, Which He Never Meant to Be Published on Any Account.*

Loving Words

After a week of being immersed in nasty, fighting words, we need some loving words here as an antidote. Work on these.

DAY 1

| leman | ineffable | inamorata | osculating |

DAY 2

| epithalamion | troth | platonic | agape |

DAY 3

| ardent | lothario | rapturous | erotic |

DAY 4

| fancy | exigency | penchant | predilection |

DAY 5

| propensity | relish | hankering | amity |

DAY 6

| ardor | avid | amateur | devotee |

DAY 7

| solicitous | desideratum | alluring | amorous |

leman	A sweetheart or lover, man or woman. **WORDS IN CONTEXT:** *The banker and her **leman** managed to get jobs in the same city.*
ineffable	Inexpressible; too overwhelming to be described in words; too awesome to be spoken. **WORDS IN CONTEXT:** *The new mother said that her feelings about her first baby were **ineffable.***
inamorata	Sweetheart or mistress; a woman in relation to the man who is her lover. **WORDS IN CONTEXT:** *The government official made arrangements for his **inamorata** to accompany him on the trip abroad.*
osculating	Kissing. **WORDS IN CONTEXT:** *The work of art in the gallery carried the amusing, though accurate title, "**Osculating.**"*

After studying the words above, use them in the sentences below.

1. In some religions, the name of God is considered too _____ to be spoken.
2. The deceased man's long-time _____ was listed as sole survivor in his newspaper obituary.
3. We saw the couple with their arms about each other _____ on the park bench.
4. The two had been together as _____ for many years.

Test Yourself: Write the word that best fits the meaning below.

1. pressing lips together romantically _____
2. too awesome to express _____
3. lover (man or woman) _____
4 lover (usually woman) _____

On a separate sheet of paper, write sentences using each of these words.

DID YOU KNOW?
What was the first book printed in italics? A 1501 edition of Virgil's works printed by a man named Aldus Manutius who invented the new type. The printer dedicated the book to Italy, thereby giving the new type a name: italic.

epithalamion	A song or poem in honor of a bride or bridegroom or both. Also spelled **epithalamium**. **WORDS IN CONTEXT:** *Poets of the romantic period often wrote* **epithalamia** *(plural, also* **epithalamiums** *or, less preferable,* **epithalami***) for their friends' nuptials.*
troth	One's pledged word; promise of faithfulness and loyalty. **WORDS IN CONTEXT:** *Many marriage vows include the words, "I plight thee my* **troth***," originally meaning to pledge or promise one's truth or one's word.*
platonic	A relationship between two people that is purely spiritual or intellectual and without sexual activity. **WORDS IN CONTEXT:** **Platonic** *also describes the philosophy of Plato; idealistic and visionary.*
agape	(emphasis on second syllable): God's love for humanity; divine love; also, the word has come to mean spontaneous, altruistic love on the part of humankind. **WORDS IN CONTEXT:** **Agape** *was originally a love feast—a meal that early Christians ate together.*

After studying the words above, use them in the sentences below:

1. To make a promise of marriage, some couples include the word _____ in the ceremony.
2. The two friends who had grown up together had a _____ relationship.
3. _____ is divine love, of God for humanity.
4. A wedding song or poem is an _____.

Test Yourself: Write the word that best fits the meaning below.

1. a promise of truth _____
2. an asexual relationship _____
3. love feast _____
4. love song _____

On a separate sheet of paper, write a sentence using each of these words.

DID YOU KNOW?
Can you guess what *The Nothing Book* by Bruce Harris was about? You're right. Nothing. (Not even about cereal, as Jerry Seinfield might have said.) The book held only blank pages. Apparently, it sold well during the 1970s and 1980s. But its major victory was that it survived a plagiarism suit brought by a foreign publisher who claimed he held the copyright on blank books. The court decision, however, declared that emptiness was in the public domain.

ardent	Warm or intense in feeling; passionate; devoted, zealous, glowing, burning.
	WORDS IN CONTEXT: *His **ardent** feelings for her prompted him to call her every day.*
lothario	A seducer of women, a rake. Originally the name of a young rake in Nicholas Rowe's play *The Fair Penitent* (1703).
	WORDS IN CONTEXT: *The seasoned actor was equally convincing as a **lothario** and as a saint.*
rapturous	Ecstatic, greatly joyous, highly pleasurable; being carried away in body or spirit.
	WORDS IN CONTEXT: *Thoughts of the love of God made the nun **rapturous**.*
erotic	Arousing sexual feelings or desires; sexual love or stimulation.
	WORDS IN CONTEXT: *The school board ordered all the **erotic** literature removed from the library.*

After studying the words above, use them in the sentences below.

1. The mother had devoted and _____ feelings for her children.
2. About town, the young man had the reputation as a _____.
3. She felt _____ in the arms of the man she had agreed to marry.
4. The hotel room offered a number of _____videos.

Test Yourself: Write the word that best fits the meaning below.

1. ecstasy of body or spirit _____
2. evoking sexual desire _____
3. a seducer of women _____
4. warm, intense feelings _____

On a separate sheet of paper, write sentences using each of these words.

DID YOU KNOW?
It's a good bet that you cannot guess how the Greek dramatist Aeschylus died. Get this: he was killed by a tortoise dropped on his bald head by an eagle. (According to Valerius Maximus, IX, xii, and Pliny, History, VII, vii.)

fancy	An inclination, liking, or fondness; also, imagination, whimsy, caprice. **WORDS IN CONTEXT:** *Fancy* has several varying definitions; two of them are above. Others include ornamental, decorative, superior quality, extravagant.
exigency	A condition of pressing needs, urgent demands; a situation calling for immediate attention. **WORDS IN CONTEXT:** *His strong desire to have her as his bride put him into* **exigency.**
penchant	Inclined toward something; a strong liking or fondness for. **WORDS IN CONTEXT:** *The women had a* **penchant** *for French cuisine and wine.*
predilection	Preference, preconceived liking, partiality. **WORDS IN CONTEXT:** *The men had a* **predilection** *for steak and beer.*

After studying the words above, use them in the sentences below.

1. She found herself in _____ because of a lack of cash and an urgent need to pay her bills.
2. In the shop window, I see a fancy dress that I _____, but I hope it's not too fancy to wear to the party.
3. Though his brother was partial to blondes, Charles had a _____ for red-haired women.
4. Her sister was fond of muscular men, but Sue had a _____ for intellectual types.

Test Yourself: Write the word that best fits the meaning below.

1. in extreme need _____
2. an inclination for (also imagination) _____
3. preference, partiality _____
4. fondness for, inclination toward _____

On a separate sheet of paper, write a sentence using each of these words.

DID YOU KNOW?
Can you guess (since you did so well with the last death question) how the composer Jean Baptiste Lully died? When beating time with his cane on the floor, while directing a performance of *Te Deum*, Lully struck his foot and subsequently died from the abscess that set in.

propensity	Natural inclination, bias, tendency, bent.
	WORDS IN CONTEXT: *Propensity,* as you can see, means much the same as *predilection* and *penchant. The words can be used interchangeably in most cases, though **propensity** suggests a little less freedom of choice and more instinct.*
relish	Strong liking or craving; a pleasing taste.
	WORDS IN CONTEXT: *Relish has several meanings including the two above; others are anything that gives pleasure, zest, or enjoyment, and foods that add flavor.*
hankering	A craving or yearning.
	WORDS IN CONTEXT: *A **hankering** differs from **relishing** a bit, in that in **hankering** one yearns more and goes after what one wants less aggressively, whereas **relishing** something suggests going for it with zest.*
amity	Friendly, peaceful relations as in friendships among people or nations.
	WORDS IN CONTEXT: *The countries viewed each other with **amity**, which was fortunate, since they were adjacent to each other.*

After studying the words above, use them in the sentences below.

1. She attacked the bowl of ice cream with _____.
2. The first time Harry met Sally, he had a _____ for her, but it took him a while to get around to calling her.
3. We lived next to our neighbors in peace and _____.
4. George had a _____ for falling for the wrong kind of woman.

Test Yourself: Write the word that best fits the meaning below.

1. peaceful relations _____
2. strong inclination (proactive) _____
3. inclination (more passive) _____
4. natural inclination (more instinctive) _____

On a separate sheet of paper, write a sentence using each of these words.

DID YOU KNOW?
What is the origin of the word *pigtail*? Originally, it appeared in the seventeenth century in England as the name of a tobacco that was twisted into a thin rope. Also, when China was conquered by the Manchu in the seventeenth century, the Chinese were required to wear queues or pigtails as a sign of their servitude.

ardor	Emotional warmth, passion, eagerness, enthusiasm.
	WORDS IN CONTEXT: *They raised their son with a great deal of attention and **ardor**.*
avid	Intensely enthusiastic or craving, greedy, eager, enthusiastic.
	WORDS IN CONTEXT: *She was **avid** for power (greedy), and she was also an **avid** reader (eager and enthusiastic).*
amateur	A person who engages in something—art, science, sports—for the pleasure of it rather than as a professional.
	WORDS IN CONTEXT: *The word **amateur** derives from the Latin* amator, *lover or to love. An **amateur** does something purely for the love of it.*
devotee	A person strongly devoted to someone or something.
	WORDS IN CONTEXT: *Don was a **devotee** of the opera.*

After studying the words above, use them in the sentences below.

1. She was an _____ painter but by profession a lawyer.
2. His _____ love of golf took him to the links every Sunday.
3. She entertained friends with grace and _____.
4. Sarah was devoted to her family, but she was a _____ of the ballet.

Test Yourself: Write the word that best fits the meaning below.

1. does it for the love of it _____
2. strongly devoted _____
3. intense, greedy, or eager _____
4. warmth and enthusiasm _____

On a separate sheet of paper, write a sentence using each of these words.

DID YOU KNOW?
Who was the most celebrated early Persian writer after Omar Khayyam? His name was Sadi (1194–ca.1292), and he wrote *Gulistan*—a volume of philosophical musings and stories containing sections on kings, dervishes, love, youth, and old age. In Persian, *Gulistan* means "the garden of roses."

solicitous	Showing care, attention, or concern. **WORDS IN CONTEXT:** *Their friends were* **solicitous** *of the welfare of the family that had lost a child.*
desideratum	Something needed and wanted. **WORDS IN CONTEXT:** **Desideratum** *derives from desire.*
alluring	Tempting with something desirable, attractive, enticing, fascinating. **Allure** is the power to entice or attract. **WORDS IN CONTEXT:** *The girls in their summer dresses were* **alluring.**
amorous	Full of love or fond of making love; enamored. **WORDS IN CONTEXT:** **Amorous** *comes from the Latin* amorosus, *loving.*

After studying the words above, use them in the sentences below.

1. The fund-raising committee declared that the next _____ was a mission statement.
2. The models in the fashion magazine were photographed in _____ poses.
3. Charlotte discovered that her new husband was an _____man.
4. When we moved into the new neighborhood, we found our neighbors _____ of our needs.

Test Yourself: Write the word that best fits the meaning below.

1. something desired and needed _____
2. full of love _____
3. enticing, tempting, fascinating _____
4 showing care and attention _____

On a separate sheet of paper, write a sentence using each of these words.

DID YOU KNOW?
What are a drum and a drum major? Now hear this: A *drum* **was a popular name in the eighteenth century for a noisy, crowded house party (so-called because the boisterousness resembled the drumming up of recruits). The most riotous of these parties were called** *drum majors*—**as in major noisy parties.**

Cross Words

Cross words can save you, work you over, twist your mind, or get you into trouble. Here are some of them.

DAY 1

anathema   misanthrope   deprecate   disgruntle

DAY 2

pique   incendiary   spurious   contumelious

DAY 3

fractious   captious   pettifogger   acerbic

DAY 4

acidulous   discountenance   querulous   disputatious

DAY 5

disparagement   churlish   surly   irascible

DAY 6

cross   crossbones   crosspatch   cross-file

DAY 7

crosstalk   crosswind   cross tie   cross-stitch

anathema	A thing or person accursed, damned, or greatly detested; also, a formal curse or condemnation excommunicating a person from a church or damning something.
	WORDS IN CONTEXT: *The salesman had showed himself to be dishonest so many times that he had become anathema to everyone who had dealt with him.*
misanthrope	A person who hates or distrusts people.
	WORDS IN CONTEXT: *The old misanthrope on the corner was always shouting at the children to stay out of his yard.*
deprecate	To belittle; make something seem trifling or less important; disparage.
	WORDS IN CONTEXT: *Marie, the assistant, complained that her boss often deprecated her work.*
disgruntle	To make peevishly discontented; displease and make sulky.
	WORDS IN CONTEXT: *The child did not mean to disgruntle her teacher by asking her age.*

After studying the words above, use them in the sentences below.

1. The arrogant producer would routinely _____ the work of the actors.
2. Father had a sign on his door that said, "Do not _____ me by entering without knocking."
3. Molliere has a play called *The* _____ about a man who despises people.
4. Shirley was so haughty and rude that she became _____ to anyone making a party list.

Test Yourself: Write the word that best fits the meaning below.

1. to make peevish and sulky _____
2. one who hates people_____
3. a cursed or greatly detested person _____
4. to make seem less important _____

On a separate sheet of paper, write a sentence using each of these words.

DID YOU KNOW?
Why is the highest honor in most of the English-speaking world the blue ribbon? It all started with the British crown and its Order of the Knighthood; the blue ribbon is the garter, the highest honor. In Britain, the Blue Ribbon of the Church is the Archbishopric of Canterbury, that of the Law, the office of Lord Chancellor.

pique	Resentment at being slighted or disdained; offended, provoked, ruffled.
	WORDS IN CONTEXT: *He was offended by her words and left in a fit of **pique**.*
incendiary	Willfully stirring up strife, riot, or rebellion; a person who destroys property by fire.
	WORDS IN CONTEXT: ***Incendiary** refers to anything that causes or is designed to cause fires, such as bombs and dangerous substances.*
spurious	Not true or genuine, false, counterfeit.
	WORDS IN CONTEXT: *She thought the diamond he gave her was the real thing, but at the jeweler she found that it was **spurious**.*
contumelious	Rude in a contemptuous way; insulting and humiliating.
	WORDS IN CONTEXT: *The scientist's **contumelious** attitude drove his interns away.*

After studying the words above, use them in the sentences below.

1. I thought he had given me his word about the job, but I found his word to be _____.
2. In every group, his _____ personality stirred up arguments, and the leader had to put out the fires.
3. *He was mistakenly turned away at the voting booth, so he left in a _____ of resentment.*
4. The director's _____ words left the workers feeling insulted.

Test Yourself: Write the word that best fits the meaning below.

1. not genuine _____
2. rude and humiliating _____
3. causing fires or stirring up strife _____
4. resentment, ruffled feathers _____

On a separate sheet of paper, write a sentence using each of these words.

DID YOU KNOW?
What is Galileo said to have remarked during the Inquisition in Rome in 1633 after he had recanted his belief in the Copernicum system (in which the earth moves around the sun)? "Eppur si muove"—"and yet it [the earth] does move."

fractious	Hard to manage, unruly, rebellious, creating discord.
	WORDS IN CONTEXT: *The inmates in one part of the prison were particularly **fractious**.*
captious	Quick to find fault; fond of catching others in mistakes; remarks made only for the sake of argument or faultfinding.
	WORDS IN CONTEXT: *His **captious** comments stirred up the crowd.*
pettifogger	A trickster, cheater, quibbler, caviler; also a lawyer who handles petty cases and uses unethical, trumped-up charges.
	WORDS IN CONTEXT: *Her first attorney was such a **pettifogger** that she dismissed him after only two days.*
acerbic	Harsh in temper, sour, bitter, sharp, irritating, astringent.
	WORDS IN CONTEXT: *The speaker's voice had an **acerbic** ring, which made us wonder what was bothering him.*

After studying the words above, use them in the sentences below.

1. His _____nature prompted him to write many letters to the editor harping on errors he had found and hoping to stir up an argument.
2. He was a small-time lawyer and _____ who was accused of chasing ambu-lances to get clients.
3. One fraternity was closed down because the members had become _____.
4. Her sharp and _____tongue did not win her many friends in the political party.

Test Yourself: Write the word that best fits the meaning below.

1. sour, bitter, astringent _____
2. trickster, shyster, sleazy lawyer _____
3. loves to play "gotcha!" _____
4. unruly, creates discord _____

On a separate sheet, write a sentence using each of these words.

DID YOU KNOW?
You've heard the term *Shangri La* all of your life, but what is it? Here's the lowdown: Shangri La was the hidden Buddhist lama paradise described in James Hilton's novel *Lost Horizon* in 1933. (According to one source, Shangri La has a counterpart in real life—Hunza, Pakistan, a community where many people live to age 100 or more.) The name was also given to Franklin D. Roosevelt's mountain retreat in Maryland, and it was the code word for the secret base used for the American air raid on Tokyo in 1942.

acidulous	Somewhat sarcastic; acid or sour.
	WORDS IN CONTEXT: *The testy scholar wrote **acidulous** letters to colleagues.*
discountenance	To make ashamed or embarrassed; disconcert; refuse approval or support.
	WORDS IN CONTEXT: *The manager was fired because he **discountenanced** his staff and created pessimism in the workplace.*
querulous	Complaining, inclined to find fault, peevish.
	WORDS IN CONTEXT: *The **querulous** old woman returned the gloves to the department store nattering on about how they were poorly made.*
disputatious	Fond of arguing, contentious, inclined to dispute.
	WORDS IN CONTEXT: *Three of the students in the study group were cooperative, but the fourth one was irritatingly **disputatious**.*

After studying the words above, use them in the sentences below.

1. The manager should have known he could not motivate people through his embarrassing _____ of them.
2. "I don't mean to be _____," her sister said, "but where did you put the blouse you borrowed from my closet?"
3. I told him that I did not appreciate his sarcasm, after he spoke to me in an _____ tone.
4. It seemed that whatever subject I came up with to research for the project, my _____ teacher found in it something to dispute.

Test Yourself: Write the word that best fits the meaning below.

1. loves complaining and finding fault _____
2. loves contentious dispute _____
3. loves sarcasm _____
4. loves to withhold approval and support _____

On a separate sheet, write a sentence using each of these words.

DID YOU KNOW?
Where do we get the expression *the toolies,* meaning "somewhere far, far away"? It probably came from "Ultima Thule"—the end of the world, the last extremity, as mentioned by Virgil in *Georgics,* I, 30. It was also the name the ancients gave to a point of land six days' sail north of Britain and considered to be the extreme northern limit of the world; some think it to be Shetland, and others, to be some part of the coast of Norway. Today it refers to a district in northwest Greenland and also to an area on the planet Mars.

disparagement	To lower in esteem, speak slightingly of.
	WORDS IN CONTEXT: *She felt he had mistreated her, and she spoke of him with* **disparagement.**
churlish	Boorish, surly, hard to manage, gruff.
	WORDS IN CONTEXT: *Churlish has some relationship to surly below: the first derives from churls, rustic laborers who were difficult to manage, and the second derives from sire, referring to the master who couldn't manage the churls. Both got bad names.*
surly	Bad-tempered; brusque and rude; hostile, uncivil, arrogant. The original word was *sirely,* which referred to a master who was all the above as well as imperious.
	WORDS IN CONTEXT: *The salesman who knew he was being laid off was very* **surly** *during his final week on the job.*
irascible	Easily angered, quick-tempered.
	WORDS IN CONTEXT: *Probably both the churls and the sires were* **irascible,** *so a lot of cross words came out of this relationship.*

After studying the words above, use them in the sentences below.

1. The _____ workers were ill-tempered and hard to manage.
2. The rude, uncivil, and _____ bosses made life hard for the rustic laborers.
3. It's not surprising that all these _____ people had difficulty getting along in medieval times.
4. She left the relationship because she could stand his _____ of her no longer.

Test Yourself: Write the word that best fits the meaning below.

1. hostile, arrogant, brusque _____
2. boorish, gruff _____
3. slighting remarks _____
4. irritable, spiteful, probably the spleen at work _____

On a separate sheet of paper, write a sentence using each of these words.

DID YOU KNOW?
How can witches tell what's about to happen? "By the pricking of my thumbs/ Something wicked this way comes," says the second witch in Shakespeare's *Macbeth* (IV, I). Then who enters? Macbeth himself. In popular superstition, thumb pricking was a portent of very bad doings in Elizabethan times.

cross	This word has numerous definitions from "ill-tempered" and "cranky" (earlier entries) to crosswalk (a lane marked off for pedestrians to use in crossing the street). Here is another definition: an upright post with a bar across it near the top, on which the ancient Romans fastened convicted persons to die. And here is another, related definition: a symbol of the crucifixion of Jesus and hence of the Christian relgions.
	WORDS IN CONTEXT: *Christmas is called Xmas because the X stands for the **cross,** or Jesus. The pedestrian was **cross** because it took so long to **cross** the **crosswalk**.*
crossbones	Two thighbones placed across each other, usually under that of a skull, used as a symbol of death or danger.
	WORDS IN CONTEXT: *The historical pirate sign was a skull and **crossbones**.*
crosspatch	A childish, bad-tempered person.
	WORDS IN CONTEXT: *Generally said of a child, but an older person can be a **crosspatch**, too.*
cross-file	To file as a candidate in the primary elections of two or more parties.
	WORDS IN CONTEXT: *The candidate decided to **cross-file** as both a Democrat and a Libertarian.*

After studying the words above, use them in the sentences below.

1. _____: a post with a bar near the top; Romans used it poorly.
2. _____: a post with a bar near the top; a Christian symbol.
3. An old nursery rhyme goes like this: "_____, draw the latch, sit by the fire and spin. Take your cup and drink it up, then call the neighbors in!"
4. The candidate who decided to _____ in the primaries lost; he was accused of waffling.

Test Yourself: Write the word that best fits the meaning given below.

1. danger _____
2. ill-tempered _____
3. a two-party candidate _____
4. childish _____

On a separate sheet of paper, write a sentence using each of these words.

DID YOU KNOW?
What do the brassy actress Mae West and many subtle poets have in common? Both use *chiasmus* in their speech. *Chiasmus* means "a crossing." This crossing occurs when one reverses the order of words in two otherwise parallel statements: Mae said, "It's not the men in my life, it's the life in my men."

cross talk	In radio, interference on one channel from another or others.
	WORDS IN CONTEXT: *The new rooftop antenna helped reduce the **cross talk** when he listened to the distant stations on his radio.*
crosswind	A wind blowing at right angles to the line of flight of an aircraft or the course of a ship.
	WORDS IN CONTEXT: *The plane skidded off the slippery runway as the strong **crosswinds** of the approaching blizzard arose.*
cross tie	A beam, post, or rod placed crosswise to give support; specifically, any of the transverse timbers supporting the rails of a railroad track.
	WORDS IN CONTEXT: *The train's derailment was attributed to some rotten **cross ties** hidden in the mud.*
cross-stitch	A stitch made by crossing two stitches diagonally in the form of an X, or needlework made with this stitch.
	WORDS IN CONTEXT: *The novice seamstress's pace slowed when she attempted **cross-stitches**.*

After studying the words above, use them in the sentences below.

1. The builder placed the _____ in position to hold up the wall.
2. The airplane was caught in the _____, which slowed it down a little.
3. _____ on the radio interfered with our reception.
4. Our grandmother made a _____ wall hanging that said, "Bless Our Happy Home."

Test Yourself: Write the word that best fits the meaning below.

1. beam that holds things up in a structure _____
2. wind that changes the direction of ships _____
3. old-fashioned needlework _____
4. interrupts radio reception _____

On a separate sheet of paper, write a sentence using each of these words.

DID YOU KNOW?
Crux means "cross"—the crossing of two lines. But it refers to the knotty point at which the two lines cross, perhaps a point at which a decision has to be made. It has come to mean the point of trouble or difficulty, as in "the crux of the matter."

Deceptive Words

Some words are deceptive; some words mean deceptive; some speakers just taunt you into having deceptive thoughts. Know the difference.

DAY 1

artifice   cozen   dissimulate   demagoguery

DAY 2

imposture   panderer   duplicity   guile

DAY 3

perfidy   disingenuous   humbug   fallacious

DAY 4

bamboozle   travesty   belie   agitprop

DAY 5

hornswoggle   mendacity   subreptitious   equivocal

DAY 6

prevarication   pretense   malingering   quackery

DAY 7

charlatan   casuistry   misrepresentation   Pharisaism

artifice	A sly or artful trick produced with skill and ingenuity.
	WORDS IN CONTEXT: *The trompe l'oeil on the wall was an* **artifice** *that fooled the eye.*
cozen	To fraud; to trick; to cheat, defraud, or deceive.
	WORDS IN CONTEXT: *The street vendor tried to* **cozen** *me into buying the briefcase, but I could see it was fake leather.*
dissimulate	To hide one's feeling by pretense; to dissemble or lie.
	WORDS IN CONTEXT: *George had a reputation for* **dissimulation,** *so it was very hard to take his words seriously.*
demagoguery	The speech of a leader who obtains power by impassioned appeals to the emotions and prejudices of the populace.
	WORDS IN CONTEXT: *The politician won the election through* **demagoguery**—*telling the people not the truth but what they wanted to hear.*

After studying the words above, use them in the sentences below.

1. The advertising director won the account through the _____ of her proposed ads.
2. The street peddlers knew how to _____ the tourists with faux labels.
3. We knew what she was thinking, but she tried to _____ to hide her thoughts.
4. His _____ finally lost him the election, because the voters saw through it.

Test Yourself: Write the word that best fits the meaning below.

1. to lie or hide one's feelings _____
2. to defraud or cheat by trickery _____
3. the use of skill to trick or gain advantage _____
4. to appeal to emotions and bias through rhetoric _____

On a separate sheet of paper, write a sentence using each of these words.

DID YOU KNOW?
Why do we call excessive patriotism "chauvinism"? The word comes from the name of Nicolas Chauvin, a veteran of the Napoleonic wars with an attachment to Napoleon so exaggerated that he was ridiculed even by his comrades.

imposture	Assumption of a false identity; fraud.
	WORDS IN CONTEXT: *The FBI saw at once that this was an act of **imposture** and that the man was not who he claimed to be.*
panderer	One who caters to the lower tastes and desires of others or exploits their weaknesses.
	WORDS IN CONTEXT: *The **panderer** who handed them the sleazy come-ons attempted to exploit the tourists.*
duplicity	Deliberate deception in behavior or speech; double-dealing.
	WORDS IN CONTEXT: *Her **duplicity** did not fool him; he knew she was seeing another man.*
guile	Insidiousness, treacherousness, cunning, craftiness, dissimulation.
	WORDS IN CONTEXT: *She used her **guile** to get the theatergoers to buy tickets to the failing show.*

After studying the words above, use them in the sentences below.

1. They spotted the _____ and arrested the woman who claimed to be a government agent.
2. The _____ tried to get the tourists into the show that he knew had been cancelled.
3. Through _____ the spy was able to sneak the material to the enemies.
4. She was a master of _____, which helped her in her job with the politician.

Test Yourself: Write the word that best fits the meaning below.
1. insidious cunning_____
2. deliberate deception in speech or behavior _____
3. rips off those with lower instincts_____
4. assumed a false identity _____

On a separate sheet of paper, write a sentence using each of these words.

DID YOU KNOW?
Why do we describe a distraught person as "beside himself or herself"? Because the ancients believed that under great stress the soul would actually leave the body. When this happened, a man would be "beside himself." The expression "out of one's mind" is similar, and in the word *ecstasy*, we find the same idea: in Greek, *ecstasy* literally means "to stand out of."

perfidy	A deliberate breach of faith; calculated violation of trust. **WORDS IN CONTEXT:** *The **perfidy** of the soldiers of fortune astounded the Red Cross volunteers.*
disingenuous	Not straightforward, crafty. **WORDS IN CONTEXT:** *Her words were **disingenuous**, and no one was persuaded by what she said.*
humbug	Something intended to deceive; a hoax; imposture; deceptive nonsense and rubbish. **WORDS IN CONTEXT:** *"This is **humbug**," the lawyer said. "It'll never hold up in court."*
fallacious	Containing or based on fallacy; not real or sound; delusive. **WORDS IN CONTEXT:** *His reasoning was **fallacious** from the start, and few accepted his thesis.*

After studying the words above, use them in the sentences below.

1. The _____ of the traitor was clear to the reporter covering the story.
2. She gave her testimony, but the jury thought she was _____ in her presentation.
3. Some were dazzled by the man's talk, but others thought it was full of _____.
4. The candidate's logic was _____, but nevertheless, some believed him.

Test Yourself: Write the word that best fits the meaning below.

1. rubbish intended to deceive _____
2. based on false reasoning _____
3. not straightforward _____
4. a violation of trust _____

On a separate sheet of paper, write a sentence using each of these words.

DID YOU KNOW?
Why do we say that someone showing insincere emotion is weeping crocodile tears? The expression comes from an old story about travelers being eaten by crocodiles, which concludes that the crocodile weeps, but it isn't sorry at all. We can only speculate about its insincerity, but it's true that a crocodile sheds tears when it eats. Why? This has to do with a biological function of its mouth.

bamboozle	To trick or deceive by elaborate misinformation; hoodwink. **WORDS IN CONTEXT:** *I nearly was **bamboozled** into buying that old lemon of a used car.*
travesty	A broad or grotesque imitation of a lofty work or theme with intent to ridicule. **WORDS IN CONTEXT:** *We thought the production of* Hamlet *would be the real thing, but the acting company had changed it in so many ways that it was a **travesty**.*
belie	To tell lies about; to slander, defame, misrepresent or picture falsely. **WORDS IN CONTEXT:** *Her youth and innocent appearance **belie** her fine, sophisticated mind.*
agitprop	Propaganda; words, not necessarily true, used to convince or persuade the listener to the speaker's point of view. **WORDS IN CONTEXT:** *We listened to the politician's **agitprop** but didn't believe a word of it.*

After studying the words above, use them in the sentences below.

1. The sleekness and design of the automobile _____ its faulty engine.
2. On the house tour we paid to see an original Tudor mansion, but the place was a _____, a modern, shoddy copy of Tudor architecture.
3. The captured soldiers were brainwashed night and day with _____.
4. The street vendors tried to _____ the young girls into buying cheap watches.

Test Yourself: Write the word that best fits the meaning below.

1. propaganda _____
2. misrepresent _____
3. hoodwink _____
4. ridiculous imitation _____

On a separate sheet of paper, write a sentence using each of these words.

DID YOU KNOW?
Why is the Wall Street trader who sells stocks short called a *bear?* **The word goes back to an old folk saying: "He sold the skin before he got the bear." When people sell stocks without having them, hoping that the price will go down so that they can buy what they need at a lower cost, they are selling the skin without the bear.**

hornswoggle	To deceive, bamboozle.
	WORDS IN CONTEXT: *He thought he could **hornswoggle** me into signing the contract.*
mendacity	Falsehood, untruth.
	WORDS IN CONTEXT: *The **mendacity** of the speaker's words astonished the audience.*
subreptitious	Deliberately misrepresenting through concealment of the facts.
	WORDS IN CONTEXT: *At the convention, the politician's **subreptitious** estimate of the cost of the war drew boos from the crowd.*
equivocal	Indeterminate, uncertain, evasive; capable of two interpretations.
	WORDS IN CONTEXT: *He spoke about the economy in **equivocal** terms.*

After studying the words above, use them in the sentences below.

1. Her comments struck me as filled with _____, but I didn't challenge her.
2. The guy _____ the boys into buying a broken-down bike.
3. We felt that the protesters' _____ statements made their claims less than credible.
4. The man said in an _____ voice: "I'm of two minds about that idea."

Test Yourself: Write the word that best fits the meaning below.

1. calculated concealment _____
2. you can take it two ways _____
3. out and out lies _____
4. two funny words with the same meaning: bamboozle and _____

On a separate sheet of paper, write a sentence using each of these words.

DID YOU KNOW?

Why is a college degree called a *bachelor's* degree? Originally a "bachelor" was a soldier so young that he could not lead men into battle. The word was applied to the college degree to imply a rank inferior to that of doctor.

prevarication	A straying from or evading of the truth; an equivocation.
	WORDS IN CONTEXT: Prevarication *derives from a Latin word that means "to walk crookedly"—to straddle, stretch, bend, or walk knock-kneed.*
pretense	The act of pretending; a false appearance or action intending to deceive; a mere show without reality; an outward appearance only; an affectation.
	WORDS IN CONTEXT: *The new government made only a **pretense** of democracy.*
malingering	Pretending to be ill or injured to avoid duty or work.
	WORDS IN CONTEXT: *He told his boss he had the flu, but he was suspected of **malingering.***
quackery	The practice of an untrained person who pretends to have medical knowledge; charlatan, mountebank.
	WORDS IN CONTEXT: *He called himself a doctor and performed several operations, but he was accused of **quackery** when it was found that he had not attended medical school.*

After studying the words above, use them in the sentences below.

1. The man claimed to have served in the armed services, which was a
   _____ because it was untrue.
2. The staff accused the receptionist of _____ the third time she called in sick.
3. He was arrested for practicing medicine without a license and accused of
   _____.
4. She made a _____ of loving animals, but she was actually afraid of dogs.

Test Yourself: Write the word that best fits the meaning below.

1. charlatan, imposter _____
2. pretending to be ill _____
3. false outward appearance _____
4. straying from the truth _____

On a separate sheet of paper, write sentences using each of these words.

DID YOU KNOW?
Where does the word *silhouette* came from? Etienne de Silhouette was French Comptroller General in 1759. He took drastic economic measures, stripping every unnecessary detail from everything, even paintings. In this spirit of economy, portraits in black and white outline—silhouettes—became popular and were so-called to suggest the economist's strict measures. (Some experts disagree with this, but it's a good story anyway.)

charlatan	A person claiming to have knowledge or skill that he or she does not have; a quack.
	WORDS IN CONTEXT: *He was revealed as a **charlatan** when his customers lost money after following his investment advice.*
casuistry	A disparaging term for a person who claims absolute knowledge of right and wrong in matters of conscience and conduct.
	WORDS IN CONTEXT: *His claims to total understanding of right from wrong were seen by others as simplistic **casuistry**.*
misrepresentation	An incorrect or misleading account of fact or truth.
	WORDS IN CONTEXT: *The government official gave a **misrepresentation** of the national economic situation.*
pharisaism	Hypocritical observance of the letter of religious or moral law without regard for the spirit; sanctimoniousness.
	WORDS IN CONTEXT: ***Pharisaism** (written with a capital P) derives from the doctrines and practices of the Pharisees, an ancient Jewish sect that emphasized strict interpretation and observance of the Mosaic law in both its oral and written forms.*

After studying the words above, use them in the sentences below.

1. His _____ in matters of good and evil was annoying to others.
2. The moralizer's _____ could be observed in his hypocrisy about religion.
3. She claimed to be able to tell people's fortunes, but we could see that she was simply a _____.
4. The campus recruiter gave a _____ of the actual scholarships available.

Test Yourself: Write the word that best fits the meaning below.

1. hypocrite _____
2. misleading account _____
3. fake, phony, imposter _____
4. claims of knowledge of right and wrong _____

On a separate sheet of paper, write a sentence using each of these words.

DID YOU KNOW? What is the origin of the word *snob?* It was a town/gown thing. All college students in England at one time were sons of nobility. They used the word *snab*—the Scottish term for "boy'" or "servant"—to refer to townspeople. Then Cambridge in the 1600s began admitting commoners as students, who, when registering, described on the forms their social position as *Sine Nobilitate*, meaning in Latin "without nobility." The students, nasty things, began to refer to the commoner students as *S. Nobs*. This of course sounded too much like *snab* for all to ignore, so the terms were collapsed into *snob*, meaning "a pretender to position."

Noisy Words

How many words might there be for noise or for noisy?
Read on and find out.

DAY 1

| clamorous | racket | ebullition | pother |

DAY 2

| palaver | banshee | jubilation | diatribe |

DAY 3

| pandemonium | rodomontade | strident | bloviation |

DAY 4

| tocsin | braggadocio | uproarious | panegyric |

DAY 5

| sonic | resonance | auditory | aural |

DAY 6

| din | hubbub | fracas | charivari |

DAY 7

| vociferous | hullabaloo | stentorian | rumpus |

clamorous	Jarring, noisily insistent. **WORDS IN CONTEXT:** *She held her ears to close out the* **clamorous** *hoots of the car horns on the streets of New York City.*
racket	A clamor or an uproar; also an illegal or dishonest practice. **WORDS IN CONTEXT:** *The kids playing in the next room were making a* **racket.**
ebullition	A boiling or bubbling up; effervescence; an outburst, as of some emotion. **WORDS IN CONTEXT:** *The* **ebullition** *of the crowd was evident even before the opening kick-off.*
pother	A commotion, disturbance; fuss, trouble, worry, confusion. **WORDS IN CONTEXT:** *Winnie the Pooh said, "Oh,* **pother***!" when in a state of anxiety.*

After studying the words above, use them in the sentences below.

1. A spirit of _____ filled the gym, as the students cheered the team on.
2. His sudden _____ hammering under her window caused her to awaken with a start.
3. A _____ came from the chicken yard on the farm.
4. "Oh, fuss and _____!" Grandpa said, when smoke from the stove filled the kitchen.

Test Yourself: Write the word that best fits the meaning below.

1. bursting excitement _____
2. commotion and confusion _____
3. uproar _____
4. noisily tumultuous _____

On a separate sheet of paper, write a sentence using each of these words.

DID YOU KNOW? Where did we get that sweet word *lollypop?* In northern England, "lolly" means tongue. And what do you do with that sugary stuff on a stick but "pop" it into your mouth—ergo, "lollypop."

palaver	Idle chatter; talk intended to charm or beguile.
	WORDS IN CONTEXT: *The teenagers' **palaver** in the next room kept Dad from sleeping.*
banshee	A female spirit in Gaelic folklore believed to presage a death in the family by wailing outside the house.
	WORDS IN CONTEXT: *The little girl who had fallen in the mud puddle was wailing like a **banshee** in the backyard.*
jubilation	Exultation, or celebration, or other expressions of joy.
	WORDS IN CONTEXT: *The hundredth anniversary of the city called for **jubilation**.*
diatribe	A bitter or abusive criticism or denunciation; invective.
	WORDS IN CONTEXT: ***Diatribe** comes from the Greek for "a wearing away" or to "rub hard, wear out."*

After studying the words above, use them in the sentences below.

1. The _____ from the cocktail party inside drifted out to the balcony.
2. A _____ wail came from the woods where the young people were camping, and we assumed someone had spotted a snake.
3. The man was in the middle of a _____ about local politics.
4. A _____ celebrated the team's win.

Test Yourself: Write the word that best fits the meaning below.

1. bitter criticism _____
2. a state of great happiness _____
3. a legendary spirit that wails outside the house of the dying_____
4. chatter _____

On a separate sheet of paper, write a sentence using each of these words.

DID YOU KNOW?
The expression "she jumped over the broomstick" refers to a woman who began living with a man before they were married. This woman often thought that she would ignore housewifely duties—the broomstick being one of them—so she was said to have "jumped over the broomstick." After the expression became well known, rather than being carried over the threshold like a regular bride, these women sometimes literally jumped over a broomstick.

pandemonium	Wild uproar and noise, or any place filled with that.
	WORDS IN CONTEXT: *Pandemonium came from the name of the capital of Hell in Milton's* Paradise Lost; *it signifies the noise of all demons.*
rodomontade	Pretentious boasting or bragging.
	WORDS IN CONTEXT: *Before the fight, the boxer gave a blustery* **rodomontade** *about his abilities in the ring.*
strident	Loud, harsh, and grating; shrill.
	WORDS IN CONTEXT: *The sailors understood the captain's* **strident** *commands.*
bloviation	Windy commentary by those not necessarily well informed; said of radio and TV talk show hosts.
	WORDS IN CONTEXT: *Helen turned the car radio off because the* **bloviation** *of the commentators was annoying.*

After studying the words above, use them in the sentences below.

1. The mother's _____ yell summoned the boys, who were swimming out too far.
2. They turned off the political _____ on Fox radio.
3. A great deal of _____ was going on inside the roller rink.
4. Mohammed Ali delivered an amusing _____ before the fight.

Test Yourself: Write the word that best fits the meaning below.

1. shrill and grating_____
2. blustery commentary on radio or TV _____
3. bragging and boasting_____
4. wild uproar _____

On a separate sheet of paper, write sentences using each of these words.

DID YOU KNOW?
How did a joke come to be called a "gag"? Originally the word was used by actors who tossed in ad-libs, usually a joke, to throw another actor off his or her lines. These were called "gags" because they so surprised and stopped the other actor that he or she might as well have been gagged.

tocsin	An alarm sounded on a bell; sometimes viewed as an omen or a warning.
	WORDS IN CONTEXT: *The **tocsin** sounded, and we knew it was another fire drill.*
braggadocio	A braggart with a swaggering manner; cockiness; empty bragging.
	WORDS IN CONTEXT: *In the play, the **braggadocio** tried hard, but the more modest man won the heart of the heroine.*
uproarious	Loud and full, as laughter; boisterous; causing hearty laughter; hilarious.
	WORDS IN CONTEXT: *We went to a comedy club and heard some **uproarious** jokes.*
panegyric	A formal eulogy intended as a public compliment; elaborate praise lauding a person or persons; encomium; public speech.
	WORDS IN CONTEXT: *From the lectern, the speaker gave a lengthy **panegyric** to the founding members of the organization.*

After studying the words above, use them in the sentences below.

1. The men at our "Wild Tales" club told _____ stories.
2. The _____ for the beloved woman spoke of her many good deeds.
3. Some thought the candidate for the presidency was a swaggering _____.
4. We heard the _____ when we were in a Mexican village, and knew it was time for a parade.

Test Yourself: Write the word that best fits the meaning below.

1. bell alarm _____
2. cocky braggart _____
3. hilarious _____
4. elaborate public compliment _____

On a separate sheet of paper, write a sentence using each of these words.

DID YOU KNOW?
Have you heard the naked truth about gymnastics? In Latin the word means "naked"—the condition in which athletes of early Greece competed with one another.

sonic	Relating to an audible sound. (A sonic wave, having a speed of or approaching that of sound in the air, is about 738 miles per hour at sea level.)
	WORDS IN CONTEXT: *We heard a **sonic** boom and looked up to see an airplane.*
resonance	The intensification and prolongation of sound, especially of a musical tone produced by sympathetic vibrations.
	WORDS IN CONTEXT: ***Resonance** has several definitions having to do with acoustics, chemistry, medicine, and phonetics. The above definition refers to acoustics.*
auditory	Pertaining to the sense organs or experience of hearing.
	WORDS IN CONTEXT: *The hearing test showed that the child had no **auditory** problems.*
aural	Having to do with the ear.
	WORDS IN CONTEXT: *The driving test showed that the senior citizen had no visual or **aural** difficulties.*

After studying the words above, use them in the sentences below.

1. The concert hall had a perfect _____ for the symphony.
2. The class was studying the _____ wave, determining the speed of sound in the air.
3. The room proved a good _____ environment.
4. The physician determined that her _____ senses were not impaired by the accident to her ear.

Test Yourself: Write the word that best fits the meaning below.

1. anything about the ear _____
2 anything about the experience of hearing _____
3 anything about the vibrations of sound _____
4. anything about the speed of sound in the air _____

On a separate sheet of paper, write a sentence using each of these words.

DID YOU KNOW?
Why did the ancient Greeks call foreigners "barbarians?" Because to Greeks, foreign languages sounded like "baba," and who would speak in such nonsense words but "barbarians"?

din	A combination of resounding and discordant noises; a continuing cacophony.
	WORDS IN CONTEXT: *There was such a din in the gym that her head began to hurt.*
hubbub	A confused babble of loud sounds and noises; uproar; upheaval.
	WORDS IN CONTEXT: *We stopped to try to find out what was causing all the hubbub at the airport.*
fracas	A disorderly uproar, noisy quarrel, row, brawl.
	WORDS IN CONTEXT: *A fracas broke out on the floor at the political convention, and several demonstrators were escorted from the building.*
charivari	A noisy, mocking serenade to newlyweds.
	WORDS IN CONTEXT: *Charivari derives from the French through the Latin for "headache," and from the Greek, meaning "heavy head."*

After studying the words above, use them in the sentences below.

1. We saw that the _____ was a noisy quarrel between two rival fraternities.
2. Her sorority sisters organized a group to present a surprise_____ on the night of their wedding.
3-4. The _____ was so loud that we couldn't figure out what the _____ was all about.

Test Yourself: Write the word that best fits the meaning below.

1. noisy quarrel, brawl _____
2. mocking serenade to newlyweds _____
3. confused babble of sound _____
4. discord, cacophony _____

On a separate sheet of paper, write a sentence using each of these words.

DID YOU KNOW?
What are we saying when we say, "How do you do?" The last *do* means "fare," and we're asking, "How are you faring?" or "How are things going?"

vociferous	A vehement, demanding outcry. **WORDS IN CONTEXT:** *The vociferous cry at the football game was, "Hit 'em again, hit 'em again, harder, harder!"*
hullabaloo	A great noise or excitement. **WORDS IN CONTEXT:** *At the family reunion, there was a great hullabaloo when the parents of the bunch arrived.*
stentorian	Extremely loud. **WORDS IN CONTEXT:** *His voice was so stentorian that we could hear him in the back of the room with no trouble.*
rumpus	A noisy clamor. **WORDS IN CONTEXT:** *When the children arrived at the birthday party, there was such a rumpus that we didn't get all their names.*

After studying the words above, use them in the sentences below.

1. The chairwoman was _____ in her demands to the committee.
2. We needed no microphone for his _____voice.
3. The boys caused a _____when they brought the frogs into the house.
4. We enjoyed the _____ of the class reunion.

Test Yourself: Write the word that best fits the meaning below.

1. a really loud voice _____
2. noisy clamoring _____
3. demanding outcry _____
4. excitement and noise _____

On a separate sheet of paper, write sentences using each of these words.

DID YOU KNOW? Where does the word *parlor* come from? It comes from the French *parler,* meaning "to speak." The parlor is a room in which you have to have conversation with your guests— you can't just ignore them.

Quiet Words

The following words are quiet. Work quietly, so you won't disturb them.

DAY 1

| succinct | reticent | taciturn | dulcet |

DAY 2

| eremitical | surreptitious | propitiate | euphonic |

DAY 3

| mollify | quiescent | softshoe | modulate |

DAY 4

| somnambulist | somnolent | lull | muted |

DAY 5

| aphonia | sough | stasis | obtund |

DAY 6

| purl | stifle | damper | plash |

DAY 7

| soft sell | sourdine | soft pedal | pianissimo |

succinct	Clearly expressed in few words; terse; brief and clear. **WORDS IN CONTEXT:** *We were impressed with the new director whose **succinct** style kept the weekly meetings short and focused.*
reticent	Habitually silent or uncommunicative; disinclined to speak readily; reserved; understated. **WORDS IN CONTEXT:** *She was **reticent** about her past life.*
taciturn	Almost always silent; does not like to talk. **WORDS IN CONTEXT:** *My grandfather was **taciturn**, but kind.*
dulcet	Soothing or pleasant to hear; sweet-sounding; melodious. **WORDS IN CONTEXT:** *My grandmother spoke in **dulcet** tones—and could talk for hours.*

After studying the words above, use each in a sentence below.

1. His words were _____, but thoughtful and often humorous.
2. Because she was reserved, she was_____ to speak personally.
3. The men sat in a _____silence, none of them willing to speak.
4. Her soothing voice, with its _____tones, eventually put the baby to sleep.

Test Yourself: Write the word that best fits the meaning below.

1. sweet-sounding, melodious _____
2. simply does not want to talk _____
3. brief, to the point _____
4. reserved _____

On a separate sheet of paper, write a sentence using each of these words.

DID YOU KNOW?
What is the derivation of the expression "Peeping Tom"? Tom was the name of the tailor who peeped at Lady Godiva as she rode naked through the streets of Coventry. (It's said that her ride was an attempt to get taxes reduced for the townspeople—well, anything to reduce taxes.) Tom tried to get a look at the lady. (It's said that he was struck blind.) Do we believe any of this? Have another chocolate and consider the matter....

eremitical	Living reclusively, like a hermit.
	WORDS IN CONTEXT: *He lived an* **eremitical** *life, collecting entries for a new dictionary.*
surreptitious	Done in a secret, stealthy way; clandestine.
	WORDS IN CONTEXT: *She courted her new friend* **surreptitiously**, *and then all of a sudden asked him to move into the dorm with her.*
propitiate	Pacify, appease, or conciliate.
	WORDS IN CONTEXT: *The young man hoped to* **propitiate** *himself for his sins by talking to a priest.*
euphonic	The quality of having a pleasant sound; musical; sweet-voiced.
	WORDS IN CONTEXT: *Her* **euphonic** *voice came to me from across the room, so I knew she had arrived.*

After studying the words above, use each in a sentence below.

1. The voices of the choir were _____.
2. The minister asked the members of the congregation to _____ for their past behavior.
3. The woman lived an _____life in the woods with her dog and six cats.
4. He crept up in a _____way, then grabbed her and said, "I gotcha!"

Test Yourself: Write the word that best fits the meaning given below.

1. lives alone and likes it _____
2. appeasing, conciliatory _____
3. musical voiced _____
4. sneaky _____

On a separate sheet of paper, write a sentence using each of these words.

DID YOU KNOW?
Why do we call raucous, silly comedy *slapstick*? Because it's named for a prop used by actors in low comedy. This device is two pieces of wood nailed loosely together, so that when one comedian spanks another with it, the thing produces a loud whack. Pretty silly, right? Well, what can you expect? The thing is called a *slapstick*.

mollify	To soothe the temper; pacify; to make less intense, severe, or violent.
	WORDS IN CONTEXT: *John tried to **mollify** his mother when he broke her chandelier.*
quiescent	To become quiet, still, inactive.
	WORDS IN CONTEXT: *The **quiescent** atmosphere in the room led him to believe he had said something wrong.*
softshoe	A kind of tap dancing done without metal taps on the shoe soles.
	WORDS IN CONTEXT: *At the recital, the dancers did a **softshoe** before the tap dancers came on.*
modulate	Said of the voice or musical instrument, to vary the pitch in intensity to a lower degree; the shift from one key to another; regulate; adjust.
	WORDS IN CONTEXT: *The singer asked the pianist if he could **modulate** to a slightly lower key.*

After studying the words above, use each in a sentence below.

1. The girls sat _____, afraid to speak.
2. The mime did a funny routine and danced a _____.
3. Penny could not _____her sister, who had lost the competition.
4. As we entered the quiet room, I asked my companion to try to _____ her voice.

Test Yourself: Write the word that best fits the meaning given below.

1. a soft, shuffling dance _____
2. a shift from one key to another _____
3. a quiet environment _____
4. an attempt to comfort _____

On a separate sheet of paper, write a sentence using each of these words.

DID YOU KNOW?
Why do we call a *taxi* by that name? It's because a taximeter used to measure the fare (or tax), and early cabbies were so proud of having a taximeter that they printed "Taximeter" on their cabs' doors. Soon it was shortened to "Taxi." (Call me a taxi. OK, you're a taxi. See *slapstick* earlier.)

somnambulism	The act or practice of sleep-walking; a trancelike state.
	WORDS IN CONTEXT: *At camp, we heard someone walking in the night and learned that one of our roomies was a **somnambulist**.*
somnolent	Sleepy; drowsy; inducing drowsiness.
	WORDS IN CONTEXT: *He tried hard to read his book on economics, but he became **somnolent** at page 46.*
lull	To calm or soothe by gentle sound or motion; reassure; allay; a short period of quiet or inactivity.
	WORDS IN CONTEXT: *To **lull** the baby, the mother begin singing to him.*
muted	Softened or muffled sound; subdued intensity.
	WORDS IN CONTEXT: *Her voice became **muted** as she spoke of her life in a foster home.*

After studying the words above, use them in the sentences below.

1. When the hypnotist began speaking, my head dropped and I became _____.
2. The waves gently hitting the shore _____ me to sleep.
3. I thought he was a ghost, but I saw that it was just my guest who was a _____.
4. The _____ sound of a trombone drifted from the party next door into my window.

Test Yourself: Write the word that best fits the meaning given below.

1. a calming and soothing sound _____
2. muffled sounds _____
3. someone is walking in her sleep _____
4. drowsy and nodding _____

On a separate sheet of paper, write a sentence using each of these words.

DID YOU KNOW?
Where did we got the word *thimble*? The thimble was originally worn on the thumb, and it has a bell shape: So, thumb bell—thimble.

aphonia	Loss of voice through organic or functional disorder.
	WORDS IN CONTEXT: *Because of a node on a gland, she suffered from **aphonia**.*
sough	A soft, low, murmuring, sighing or rustling sound; to make a sough (cry).
	WORDS IN CONTEXT: *We heard the **sough** of the wind in the trees.*
stasis	A stoppage, standing still; state of balance or stagnancy.
	WORDS IN CONTEXT: *My mind had been moving this way and that way about the decision, but it finally came to a **stasis**.*
obtund	To make blunt or dull by striking; to deaden.
	WORDS IN CONTEXT: *The carpenter tried to **obtund** the squeaky hinge.*

After studying the words above, use each in a sentence below.

1. The _____ of the leaves in the trees was comforting.
2. Julie Andrews, the singer, lost her voice through _____.
3. I knew I had come to a _____, when I stopped being indecisive.
4. We need to_____ the sound of the air conditioner.

Test Yourself: Write the word that best fits the meaning given below.

1. to deaden_____
2. a balance_____
3. loss of voice_____
4. a rustle or murmur _____

On a separate sheet of paper, write sentences using each of these words.

DID YOU KNOW?
How did we come by the term *limelight*? Once upon a time, lime was necessary to make a spotlight: a stream of oxygen and a stream of hydrogen were burned on a ball of lime to produce a brilliant white light.

purl	to move in ripples or with a murmuring sound; eddy; swirl; the murmuring sound of softly swirling water.
	WORDS IN CONTEXT: *We watched the water **purl** in the pool below.*
stifle	To kill by cutting off air supply; suffocate, smother, choke, suppress; to suffer or die from lack of air.
	WORDS IN CONTEXT: *We walked into the room and felt **stifled** by heat and lack of air.*
damper	Anything that deadens or depresses; a device to check vibrations in the strings of a keyboard instrument.
	WORDS IN CONTEXT: *My father put a **damper** on my evening by telling me that he was cutting off my allowance.*
plash	To dash or splatter a liquid substance; or the sound made when such a thing occurs; splash.
	WORDS IN CONTEXT: *I heard a **plash** in the bathroom, and I knew my toddler had thrown his toy into the toilet again.*

After studying the words above, use each in a sentence below.

1. The _____ of the soft drink on the floor made her call for a paper towel.
2. The closed room was _____.
3. He put a _____ on my day by telling me about my bad grade.
4. I heard the _____ of the water in the drain.

Test Yourself: Write the word that best fits the meaning given below.

1. splatter _____
2. ripples of water _____
3. cut off air supply _____
4. deaden or depress _____

On a separate sheet of paper, write a sentence using each of these words.

DID YOU KNOW? Why do we call a coward "lily-livered"? Because the ancient Greeks thought that the liver was the seat of passion. The more dark bile in the liver, the stronger the passion. Someone whose bile was the color of a lily just didn't have any guts.

soft sell	selling that relies on subtle inducement or suggestion rather than high pressure.
	WORDS IN CONTEXT: *I was grateful that he gave me a **soft sell** about buying a class ring, which I could not afford.*
sourdine	A mute, especially for a trumpet; any of a variety of obsolete musical instruments having a soft, low tone.
	WORDS IN CONTEXT: *At the jazz club, the trumpeter used a **sourdine** to mute his instrument.*
soft pedal	To make less emphatic, tone down, play down, soften or dampen the tone.
	WORDS IN CONTEXT: *When I broke up with him, I tried to **soft pedal** it.*
pianissimo	In music, a direction to play very softly; opposite of fortissimo.
	WORDS IN CONTEXT: *Gerri played the final movement on the cello **pianissimo**.*

After studying the words above, use each in a sentence below.

1. _____ is an unfamiliar word for a mute for an instrument.
2. The teacher tried to _____ the fact that we would have to take three exams during the semester.
3. The music was marked_____, so I played very softly.
4. The timid Girl Scout at the door used a very _____ to get rid of her cookies.

Test Yourself. Write the word that best fits the meaning given below.

1. tone down _____
2. play softly _____
3. used to mute an instrument _____
4. a subtle selling technique _____

On a separate sheet of paper, write a sentence using each of these words.

DID YOU KNOW?
Why do American paratroopers shout "Geronimo!" as they jump? This is the story: Several paratroopers at Fort Benning Georgia, saw the movie *Geronimo,* and, making fun of the souped-up heroics in the film, the men started calling each other by the name of the movie. Soon, in practice, the paratroopers began shouting the word as they leapt.

Healthy Words

Take heart. These exercises won't strain you, and the words are fat-free.

DAY 1

| robust | systolic | diastolic | sphygmomanometer |

DAY 2

| florid | vigorous | buff | fine fettle |

DAY 3

| syngamy | panacea | salubrious | ameliorate |

DAY 4

| eupeptic | hale | flush | staunch |

DAY 5

| longevity | salutary | prophylactic | bracing |

DAY 6

| tonic | sanative | flourishing | hardy |

DAY 7

| salve | salud | rubicund | sanatorium |

robust	Hardy, strong, full of vigor and stamina.
	WORDS IN CONTEXT: *The robust man rode a motorcycle and climbed mountains three months of the year.*
systolic	Describes the pressure of the blood flow when the heart beats.
	WORDS IN CONTEXT: *While listening and watching the gauge of the medical instrument, the health-care professional records two measurements; one of them is systolic pressure.*
diastolic	Describes the pressure between heartbeats.
	WORDS IN CONTEXT: *The second measurement the health-care professional records is diastolic pressure.*
sphygmomano- meter	The medical instrument used to measure blood pressure.
	WORDS IN CONTEXT: *To measure systolic and diastolic pressure, the doctor wrapped the rubber cuff of the sphygmomanometer around the patient's upper arm.*

After studying the words above, use each in a sentence below.

1. The doctor measured the _____ pressure of the woman's blood flow when her heart beats.
2. Jose, who lived a _____ life, jogged five miles a day and on the weekends rode his bicycle twenty miles.
3. The instrument the physician used to measure blood pressure is called a_____.
4. _____pressure is that between heartbeats.

Test Yourself: Write the word that best fits the meaning given below.

1. hale, hearty, healthy, and active _____
2. a medical instrument used in measuring blood pressure _____
3. the pressure between heart beats _____
4. pressure of the blood flow when the heart beats_____

On a separate sheet of paper, write a sentence using each of these words.

DID YOU KNOW?
Where do we get the expression, "get your goat"? It came from horse racing. A goat is sometimes placed in the stall of a nervous horse, which supposedly calms the horse. But if the owner of a rival horse manages to get, or steal, the goat, then the horse becomes even more nervous and might lose the race.

florid	Rosy, ruddy, flushed with red or pink, said of complexion.
	WORDS IN CONTEXT: *One of the sisters was very pale, and the other was **florid**.*
vigorous	Living or growing with full, vital strength; forceful, powerful, energetic.
	WORDS IN CONTEXT: *Even at 50, Paul led a **vigorous**, athletic life.*
buff	In the sense of healthy, buff refers to well-toned muscles, as in a polished body.
	WORDS IN CONTEXT: *Her daily workout had produced a fit and **buff** body.*
fine fettle	High degree of health; quality of being fit and healthy.
	WORDS IN CONTEXT: *The old-timer remarked that he felt in **fine fettle** even after he fell.*

After studying the words above, use each in a sentence below.

1. The professional tennis player led a _____ life off the courts as well as on.
2. He lifted weights every day to keep himself_____.
3. The elderly lady felt in _____, so she picked up her cane and went for a walk.
4. His belly was ample and his face was _____, so the doctor recommended he lay off the beer and pretzels.

Test Yourself: Write the word or phrase that best fits the meaning given below.

1. defined, polished muscles _____
2. feeling groovy _____
3. active and energetic _____
4. ruddy, flushed _____

On a separate sheet of paper, write a sentence using each of these words or phrases.

DID YOU KNOW?
What is that sensation, *neurapraxia*? **Ever have your foot fall asleep? You're suffering from neurapraxia; this generally occurs when a nerve** *(neura)* **is compressed** *(praxia)* **between a bone and another hard object. Blood continues to circulate, but your foot tingles and may function poorly for a few seconds after you get up:** *neurapraxia.*

syngamy	Sexual reproduction.
	WORDS IN CONTEXT: *The twins were conceived in the usual way—syngamy.*
panacea	A cure or supposed remedy; a cure-all.
	WORDS IN CONTEXT: *The physicians reported that there was no panacea for the deadly disease, but there were preventive measures one could take to avoid it.*
salubrious	Promoting health or welfare; wholesome; salutary.
	WORDS IN CONTEXT: *The waters in the hot springs spa were salubrious to those with aches and pains.*
ameliorate	To make better, improve.
	WORDS IN CONTEXT: *The doctor gave her patient an ointment to ameliorate the pain in his neck.*

After studying the words above, use each in a sentence below.

1. No _____ has yet been found to cure cancer.
2. The newly married couple did not know the word, but they found the activity of _____ enjoyable.
3. Drinking eight glasses of water each day is _____ to your health.
4. The aspirin tended to _____ not only her headache but also the pain in her shoulders.

Test Yourself: Write the word that best fits the meaning given below.

1. a cure-all _____
2. the most common way to increase the size of your family _____
3. wholesome _____
4. makes it better _____

On a separate sheet of paper, write a sentence using each of these words.

DID YOU KNOW? Can you guess this: where did the Adam's apple get its name? Yes, legend has it that a piece of that fateful apple got stuck in Adam's throat. (It's really a projection of the thyroid cartilage of the larynx.) Eve didn't have one to speak of.

eupeptic	Conducive to digestion.
	WORDS IN CONTEXT: *She found the sparkling water **eupeptic.***
hale	Sound in body; vigorous; healthy; also, a greeting.
	WORDS IN CONTEXT: *At the beginning of the season, the team felt **hale** in body and spirit.*
flush	As a healthy word, flush means to blush, glow; become excited, animated.
	WORDS IN CONTEXT: *After basketball practice, Susan returned home **flushed.***
staunch	To stop or check the flow of blood or tears; stop or lessen; quell; sometimes spelled stanch; staunch also means strong, firm, solidly made, substantial, loyal.
	WORDS IN CONTEXT: *My mother gave me a bandage to **staunch** the flow of blood after I cut my hand with a kitchen knife.*

After studying the words above, use each in a sentence below.

1. He found that drinking water was _____.
2. The man told his friends he was _____and hearty.
3. He_____ with excitement upon hearing he had won the award.
4. The father _____ the tears of his daughter who had taken a spill.

Test Yourself: Write the word that best fits the meaning given below.

1. blush, glow _____
2. stop or lessen the flow _____
3. vigorous and sound _____
4. helps your digestion _____

On a separate sheet of paper, write a sentence using each of these words.

DID YOU KNOW?
The Greeks had a word for good digestion—*eupeptos;* now we have something better: Pepto Bismol.

longevity	A long duration of life; also a long duration in general, as in an occupation or political office.
	WORDS IN CONTEXT: *The **longevity** of my ancestors is encouraging to me.*
salutary	Conducive to health, healthful, beneficial.
	WORDS IN CONTEXT: *Everyone in the family finds a daily swim **salutary.***
prophylactic	Preventive or protective; guard against disease; a device, treatment, or condom.
	WORDS IN CONTEXT: *His mother told her young son to put on his rubber boots as a **prophylactic** against the rain puddles outside.*
bracing	Invigorating, stimulating, refreshing; also supporting.
	WORDS IN CONTEXT: *Our run around the reservoir in the early fall weather was **bracing.***

After studying the words above, use each in a sentence below.

1. The bracing hike on a fall afternoon was _____ to our constitutions.
2. The old house, which has been in my family for generations, has more _____ than my ancestors.
3. He used a _____ to keep from catching a disease.
4. Virgil's run in the park with his dog, Dante, was _____.

Test Yourself: Write the word that best fits the meaning given below.

1. protective guard or device _____
2. stimulating, refreshing _____
3. beneficial to health _____
4. long life _____

On a separate sheet of paper, write a sentence using each of these words.

DID YOU KNOW? How much is the *lion's share*? Most people think it means "most." But in the Aesop's fable to which it alludes, the lion's share is *all.*

258

tonic	Producing good muscle tone; mentally or morally invigorating; a stimulant.
	WORDS IN CONTEXT: *He sat at his computer all day, so he found his visit to the gym after work a tonic—then he went home and had a gin and tonic.*
sanative	Having power to heal or cure; curative.
	WORDS IN CONTEXT: *I had a headache, so I took a couple of aspirin as a sanative.*
flourishing	To be at the peak of development; a thriving or blooming state.
	WORDS IN CONTEXT: *The teenagers on the tennis court were full of vim and appeared to be flourishing in every way.*
hardy	Robust, vigorous, able to survive; also, bold and resolute.
	WORDS IN CONTEXT: *To survive in the arid West Texas plains, people as well as plants must be hardy.*

After studying the words above, use each in a sentence below.

1. In August, in North Carolina, the roses are _____.
2. Diving into the cool mountain spring proved a _____.
3. The _____old oak tree had outlived all the other vegetation.
4. Awaking with the sniffles, as a _____, I took some cold medicine.

Test Yourself: Write the word that best fits the meaning given below.

1. robust and vigorous _____
2. at its peak _____
3. curative_____
4. invigorating _____

On a separate sheet of paper, write a sentence using each of these words.

DID YOU KNOW?
What did the word *pedagogue* originally refer to? In ancient Rome, a pedagogue was a slave who took children to school; sometimes he taught them as well. The word has come to mean teacher.

salve	Medicinal ointment applied to balm wounds; a soothing substance; smooth over; assuage. **WORDS IN CONTEXT:** *The word* **salve** *derives from "fat, butter"— which is a good description of the consistency of a* **salve** *itself.*
salud	"To your good health"—a toast. **WORDS IN CONTEXT:** *The host raised his wineglass to the newlyweds and said,* **"Salud."**
rubicund	Reddish, ruddy, rosy; indicates health. **WORDS IN CONTEXT:** *The* **rubicund** *condition of the child's skin indicated to the school nurse that he was in good health.*
sanatorium	A quiet resort, usually in the mountains, where people go to regain health; an institution for the care of invalids or convalescents. Sometimes spelled **sanitarium**. **WORDS IN CONTEXT:** *In the novel, the man with tuberculosis was sent to a* **sanatorium** *in Switzerland to recuperate.*

After studying the words above, use each in a sentence below.

1. He toasted our new home with a "_____."
2. She went to a _____ to rest after her surgery.
3. Her fresh face appeared _____ and wholesome.
4. His mother put some _____ on his mosquito bites.

Test Yourself: Write the word that best fits the meaning given below.

1. a quiet place to recuperate _____
2. rosy _____
3. "to your health" _____
4. ointment _____

On a separate sheet of paper, write a sentence using each of these words.

DID YOU KNOW?
Why do we "inaugurate" a person into office? Apparently, because the birds approve. The word in Latin, *inaugurare,* means "to take omens from the flight of birds." The birds had to approve the installation of a Roman official.

Sick Words

William Blake wrote, "Oh, rose, you are sick." Here are some other sick words, some not so poetic.

DAY 1

nepenthe	miasma	lethonomania	narcolepsy

DAY 2

emaciated	malnourished	adynamia	wan

DAY 3

squeamish	phlegmatic	vitiated	etiolate

DAY 4

cankered	iatrogenesis	migraine	syndactyle

DAY 5

allergin	banality	superannuated	neurasthenic

DAY 6

valetudinarian	torpid	insipid	distemper

DAY 7

apoplexy	consumption	prostration	pestilence

nepenthe	Anything causing forgetfulness. **WORDS IN CONTEXT:** *Nepenthe comes from a drug believed by ancient Greeks to cause loss of memory.*
miasma	Unwholesome or befogging atmosphere. **WORDS IN CONTEXT:** *Miasma is literally a vapor rising from marshes or from decomposing animal or vegetable matter.*
lethonomania	Uncommon drowsiness or torpor; loss of power of sensation or motion. **WORDS IN CONTEXT:** *Lethonomania derives from the Latin lethe, "idle": its opposite is ergon "work."*
narcolepsy	A condition of frequent and uncontrollable desire for sleep. **WORDS IN CONTEXT:** *The elderly man dozing as he stands by the fireplace suffers from narcolepsy.*

After studying the words above, use each in a sentence below.

1. His _____caused him to fall asleep at inappropriate times and in inconvenient places.
2. An evil-smelling _____ rose from the stagnant pond.
3 Her _____caused her to become drowsy and lose sensations of power and motion.
4. The couple often forgot where they placed things and found that old age was a drug worse than _____.

Test Yourself: Write the word that best fits the meaning given below.

1. causing drowsiness _____
2. causing one to fall asleep at odd times_____
3. causing one to forget things_____
4. caused by decomposing animals or plants_____

On a separate sheet of paper, write a sentence using each of these words.

DID YOU KNOW? Why do we call a lugubrious or overly sentimental person "maudlin"? The word is a reference to Mary Magdalene; the British pronunciation of Magdalene is "maudlin." She was depicted by medieval painters as weepy and sad.

emaciated	Abnormally lean; loss of too much weight by starvation or disease.
	WORDS IN CONTEXT: *The fashion model looked **emaciated**, and we wondered if she had an eating disorder.*
malnourished	Faulty or inadequate nutrition; insufficient food; improper diet.
	WORDS IN CONTEXT: *During the famine in Ireland, the people were **malnourished**.*
adynamia	Lack of vital force as a result of illness; debility.
	WORDS IN CONTEXT: *The malnourished family suffered from **adynamia**.*
wan	Sickly, pale, pallid, weak, faint, feeble.
	WORDS IN CONTEXT: *After surgery, the patient looked tired and **wan**.*

After studying the words above, use each in a sentence below.

1. The loss of so much weight had _____ him.
2. Many of the people in Africa looked _____ in the photos.
3. Prolonged illness had created a condition of _____ in which his energy was lost.
4. Feeble and _____, she attempted a smile from her hospital bed.

Test Yourself: Write the word that best fits the meaning given below.

1. pallid, sickly _____
2. loss of energy _____
3. poor nutrition _____
4. abnormally skinny _____

On a separate sheet of paper, write a sentence using each of these words.

DID YOU KNOW?
Why do we use the term *nest egg* for something put away for the future? The term derives from a once-common practice of leaving an egg in a hen's nest when collecting the rest; this was thought to encourage the hen to lay more eggs.

squeamish	Having a digestive system that is easily upset; readily nauseated, queasy. **WORDS IN CONTEXT:** *Onboard the ship in the pitching waves, Sam began to feel **squeamish**.*
phlegmatic	Sluggish, dull, apathetic. **WORDS IN CONTEXT:** *Two weeks of the flu had made him **phlegmatic**.*
vitiated	Imperfect, faulty, impure, debased, perverted, morally weakened. **WORDS IN CONTEXT:** *Becoming addicted to prescription drugs had **vitiated** his health.*
etiolate	To cause to be pale and unhealthy; to deprive of strength; in biology, to blanch or bleach by depriving of sunlight. **WORDS IN CONTEXT:** ***Etiolate** has meaning in common with "etiology"—the science of the causes and origins of disease.*

After studying the words above, use each in a sentence below.

1. He had a _____ personality: dull, apathetic, and sluggish.
2. Teddy's drinking was beginning to _____ his health.
3. I felt _____ ' when I had to climb on the roof to get the ball.
4. Too many weeks inside during the cold winter had begun to _____ her normally wholesome complexion.

Test Yourself: Write the word that best fits the meaning given below.

1. pale, weak, unhealthy_____
2. impure, morally weakened_____
3. sluggish and dull _____
4. slightly nauseated _____

On a separate sheet of paper, write a sentence using each of these words.

DID YOU KNOW?
How did we come by the expression "in the nick of time"? Back in the Middle Ages, a wooden stick was notched to record the attendance of those who should be in school and church. The stick was nicked or notched when the person arrived. So to arrive in the nick of time meant that one's presence was duly noted.

cankered	Infected, debased, or attacked by disease or corruption.
	WORDS IN CONTEXT: *Heat and moisture had **cankered** the blister on his heel.*
iatrogenesis	Physician-induced or medically induced illness.
	WORDS IN CONTEXT: *A victim of **iatrogenesis**, he had reacted negatively and violently to the medication the doctor had prescribed.*
migraine	Severe, recurrent headache, usually affecting only one side of the head; characterized by sharp pain and often accompanied by nausea.
	WORDS IN CONTEXT: *The word **migraine** comes from the Greek word for "half a head." It is said that the shrinking and expanding visions Lewis Carroll described in* Alice in Wonderland *were hallucinations he experienced before one of his migraine attacks.*
syndactyle	Having webbed feet, as a duck; having two or more digits united.
	WORDS IN CONTEXT: *The baby was born **syndactyle**, but doctors said that it could be fairly easily remedied with foot surgery.*

After studying the words above, use each in a sentence below.

1. His medicine literally made him sick, and he realized there was a word for that: _____.
2. When she was under great pressure or got emotionally overwrought, she would come down with an incapacitating _____.
3. The cut on her hand had become infected and _____.
4. When she was born, her thumb and forefinger were _____, but this was taken care of through surgery, so she now has a normal hand.

Test Yourself: Write the word that best fits the meaning given below.

1. sick headache _____
2. webbed feet _____
3. my doctor made me sick _____
4. my wound got infected _____

On a separate sheet of paper, write a sentence using each of these words.

DID YOU KNOW? What does the word **pain** actually mean? Literally, it means punishment. The word is from the Latin poena meaning penalty; apparently, our pain is a punishment from someone's original sin—the guy with the Adam's apple.

allergen	Pollen or dust that causes allergic reactions, or allergic rhinitis, in many people.
	WORDS IN CONTEXT: *Allergens*, which can include tree pollens, household dust, molds, and animal dander, cause allergies in more than 15 million Americans.
banality	Dullness or staleness stemming from overuse; triteness, commonplaceness, ordinariness (in a negative sense).
	WORDS IN CONTEXT: *Banalities* are sick words because they have become stale and unwelcome from overuse.
superannuated	Old-fashioned, obsolete, retired from service because of age or infirmity.
	WORDS IN CONTEXT: He called himself a *superannuated*, retired person, but his volunteer work in the library was valuable to hundreds of schoolchildren.
neurasthenic	One with neurosis as a result of emotional conflicts characterized by irritability, fatigue, weakness, anxiety, and often pain without apparent physical causes.
	WORDS IN CONTEXT: Eliza was a smart and creative employee, but she was such a *neurasthenic* that she annoyed our clients, and so unreliable that we had to let her go.

After studying the words above, use each of them in a sentence below.

1. Jerry, a journalist, still has the _____ typewriter that he used in his first job on a newspaper 30 years ago.
2. Sandy discovered that it was the _____ in her house, specifically mold, that was making her sick.
3. When Shirley made a speech, everyone dozed because her statements were so filled with _____.
4. Olivia went from doctor to doctor trying to get a diagnosis for her anxiety, irritability, and fatigue; finally a psychiatrist determined that she was _____.

Test Yourself: Write the word that best fits the meaning given below.

1. neurosis caused by emotional conflicts _____
2. old-fashioned, obsolete_____
3. household dust and tree pollen, among others _____
4. sick, stale, dull, trite words_____

On a separate sheet of paper, write a sentence using each of these words.

DID YOU KNOW?
Why do we say that a rumor travels by "the grapevine"? Here's the story: A Colonel Bernard Bee in 1859 built a telegraph line between Virginia City and Placerville by attaching the wire to trees. Over time, the line fell down, lying in loops on the ground. Some thought it looked like a grapevine. During the Civil War, though, troops constructed similar lines, but the news coming through the grapevine telegraph was often conflicting and unhelpful. Thus, the term "grapevine" is used for dubious information without a reliable source.

valetudinarian	Sickly, infirm person; an invalid; one anxiously concerned about his or her own health. **WORDS IN CONTEXT:** *The physician helped the **valetudinarian** find an assisted living home.*
torpid	Sluggish, dull, having lost temporarily all or part of the powers of sensation or motion. **WORDS IN CONTEXT:** *Living in the heat and humidity of the tropics made Charles **torpid.***
insipid	Without flavor; tasteless, dull, lifeless. **WORDS IN CONTEXT:** *Like banal, **insipid** is a sick word because it describes dull, lifeless, flavorless people, places, and things.*
distemper	In health, distemper is a physical or mental disorder; an infectious viral disease; also, to make bad-tempered, ruffled. **WORDS IN CONTEXT:** *Victor's neighbor suffered from **distemper** and was uncomfortable to be around.*

After studying the words above, use each in a sentence below.

1. The speaker made some _____comments that we'd all heard a thousand times, so we turned her off and focused on our own interests.
2. My aunt, who was a jolly soul, fell into _____ after my uncle died, and she's now not so much fun to be around.
3. The hot afternoon made me _____, and all I wanted to do was lie around and drink ice tea.
4. Uncle Jacob did not become a _____until he was about 85.

Test Yourself: Write the word that best fits the meaning given below.

1. flavorless, colorless, trite, uninteresting _____
2. sluggish, without energy _____
3. excessively worried about his or her health _____
4. The vet said our dog, Woolfe, had a viral disease called _____

On a separate sheet of paper, write a sentence using each of these words.

DID YOU KNOW? Why do we call the person who sits over your shoulder, especially when you play cards, a "kibitzer"? The word comes from the German *kiebitz*, via Yiddish and refers to a bird whose note resembles a human sigh and whose call sounds like a plaintive, "Dear me." This bird, if you really need to know, is called a peewit or lapwing.

apoplexy	A sudden paralysis with total or partial loss of consciousness and sensation caused by breaking or obstruction of blood vessels in the brain; stroke.
	WORDS IN CONTEXT: *Uncle Phillip was hospitalized after a fit of **apoplexy**.*
consumption	Consumption, when we speak of health matters, is a wasting away of the body or a disease causing this.
	WORDS IN CONTEXT: *We read of people years ago dying of consumption; today, we'd probably have more definite diagnoses for their health problems.*
prostration	Utter physical or mental exhaustion or helplessness.
	WORDS IN CONTEXT: ***Prostration** is another word that was used in the eighteenth and nineteenth centuries, which now would have a more specific diagnosis.*
pestilence	Any virulent or fatal contagious or infectious disease, especially one of epidemic proportions, such as bubonic plague; anything harmful or dangerous.
	WORDS IN CONTEXT: *In Albert Camus's The Plague, one can read of a mysterious **pestilence**.*

After studying the words above, use each of them in a sentence below.

1. At the seder, we read of the _____ that swept through Egypt.
2. Women of earlier centuries sometimes died of utter exhaustion, called _____; now we know that bearing 12 children in 14 years would knock anyone out.
3. Several nineteenth-century poets died of _____, a wasting way of the body; today that disease might be diagnosed as "shopping till dropping."
4. An obstruction of blood vessels in the brain resulted in _____, which paralyzed the victim.

Test Yourself: Write the word that best fits the meaning given below.

1. utter physical or mental exhaustion _____
2. a wasting away of the body _____
3. stroke _____
4. fatal infectious or contagious disease _____

On a separate sheet of paper, write a sentence using each of these words.

DID YOU KNOW? Why do we call children "kids"? They often act like baby goats for one thing, but that similarity plus the Anglo-Saxon word for child, *cild*, are credited for this. Apparently, people usually failed to pronounce the *l* and the *c* was hard in *cild*. So the word stuck.

Edible Words

Lots of English words refer to eating and drinking. Here are some words, some of them surprising, that will allow you to eat and drink all you want, using the proper vocabulary.

DAY 1

| voracious | lampoon | postprandial | masticate |

DAY 2

| inebriated | europhageous | canapés | piquant |

DAY 3

| satiety | hors d'oeuvres | cloying | refectory |

DAY 4

| manducation | ruminate | deglutition | esculent |

DAY 5

| mandible | draught | libation | pemmican |

DAY 6

| provender | alimentation | comestibles | viands |

DAY 7

| potage | fricassee | savory | repast |

voracious	Greedy to devour or gorge; ravenous, gluttonous, insatiable.
	WORDS IN CONTEXT: *At breakfast the next day, he demonstrated his usual **voracious** appetite.*
lampoon	"Let us drink"—a refrain in a drinking song; also, a piece of satirical writing, usually ridiculing something or someone. Used as a verb, **lampoon** means "to satirize" or "to ridicule."
	WORDS IN CONTEXT: *In a cheerful book honoring his retirement, colleagues **lampooned** his many idiosyncrasies.*
postprandial	After a meal, especially after dinner.
	WORDS IN CONTEXT: *The **postprandial** pleasantries did not end until after midnight.*
masticate	To chew; to grind or knead to a pulp.
	WORDS IN CONTEXT: *The puppy grabbed the rag doll and **masticated** it.*

After studying the words above, use each of them in a sentence below.

1. They decided to call their irreverent new magazine_____.
2. Short speeches came first in the _____ entertainment.
3. After their long walk, they felt _____ as they headed into the dining room.
4. His false teeth made clicking sounds as he _____ the steak.

Test Yourself: Write the word that best fits the meaning given below.

1. greedy, hungry, ravenous _____
2. chew _____
3. after dinner _____
4. let us drink _____

On a separate sheet of paper, write a sentence using each of these words.

DID YOU KNOW? How did the X-ray get its name? Originally it was called *Roentgen ray* for Wilhelm Roentgen, the scientist who discovered it. But Roentgen wanted to call it *X-ray* because he did not understand the nature of the ray, and X is the algebraic symbol for the unknown.

inebriated	Referring to a person who has drunk too much alcohol.
	WORDS IN CONTEXT: *When he wrecked his car, he was found to be **inebriated**.*
euryphageous	Eating a whole variety of foods (opposite of *stenophageous*—eating only a limited variety of foods).
	WORDS IN CONTEXT: *Because the guests were **euryphageous**, the caterers set out a table containing a variety of foods.*
canapés	Appetizer; small toast, bread, or crackers spread with spiced meats, fish, or cheese.
	WORDS IN CONTEXT: *The waiters delivered **canapés** on silver trays.*
piquant	Agreeably pungent or stimulating to the taste; pleasantly sharp, biting.
	WORDS IN CONTEXT: ***Piquant** actually means "to prick or sting," and so is descriptive of condiments such as salsa made of peppers and onions.*

After studying the words above, use each of them in a sentence below.

1. The _____ guests hovered over the buffet containing a variety of foods.
2. Almost everyone at the bachelor party consumed too much alcohol and became_____.
3. The sharp and _____ dishes pleased the guests.
4. The _____ included my favorite: toast spread with caviar.

Test Yourself: Write the word that best fits the meaning given below.

1. pungent and biting _____
2. appetizer _____
3. eating lots of different stuff_____
4. he didn't turn down a drink all evening _____

On a separate sheet of paper, write a sentence using each of these words.

DID YOU KNOW?
Where did we get the word *tip*, meaning "a gratuity"? It seems that in English taverns patrons often dropped coins into a box on the wall for the waiters. A subtle sign on the box said, "To insure promptness." Later, the even more subtle initial letters to the words remained: TIP.

satiety	The condition of being full, satisfied, sated, stuffed. **WORDS IN CONTEXT:** *He sank into **satiety** after the weekend of feasts.*
hors d'oeuvres	Appetizers such as olives, anchovies, and *canapés* served before a meal. **WORDS IN CONTEXT:** Hors *means "outside," while* oeuvre *means "work"—thus **hors d'oeuvres** are something to eat outside of work, or outside of working on a full meal.*
cloying	Something too sweet or rich that one has indulged in to excess, **WORDS IN CONTEXT:** *One can indulge in **cloying**, sentimental music as well as in cloying, overly rich food.*
refectory	A dining hall in a monastery, convent, or college dorm. **WORDS IN CONTEXT:** *Most students avoided eating at the **refectory**.*

After studying the words above, use each in a sentence below.

1. The waiters passed out the _____ before we sat down to dinner.
2. The dinner offered more than _____; it offered good conversation, too.
3. I found the sweet *postprandial* drinks _____.
4. I have to admit, this sumptuous dinner beats eating in the _____.

Test Yourself: Write the word that best fits the meaning given below.

1. too sweet or rich _____
2. place to dine _____
3. full after dinner _____
4. nibble before dinner _____

On a separate sheet of paper, write a sentence using each of these words.

DID YOU KNOW? Why do we say that something a bit questionable should be taken "with a grain of salt"? Because if you swallow the thing whole, you may not notice how flat it is, since salt brings out the flavor and allows you to test the food's worth.

manduication	Chewing or mastication.
	WORDS IN CONTEXT: *Manduication was difficult because the steak was tough.*
ruminate	To chew (the cud) as a cow does; to turn something over and over in one's mind; meditate; ponder.
	WORDS IN CONTEXT: *The long dinner gave them a chance to **ruminate**, both physically and mentally.*
deglutition	The act or process of swallowing.
	WORDS IN CONTEXT: *A sore throat made even the simple act of **deglutition** challenging.*
esculent	Something fit for food; edible, especially a vegetable.
	WORDS IN CONTEXT: *After spending a year in England, he found brussels sprouts barely **esculent**.*

After studying the words above, use each in a sentence below.

1. _____ was painful after his tonsilectomy.
2. They had to _____ over what they had heard at dinner.
3. While my jaw was numb, I found the_____ of any food awkward but not impossible.
4. Finally, I found something_____: a simple tomato.

Test Yourself: Write the word that best fits the meaning given below.

1. to swallow _____
2. edible, if not tasty _____
3. thinking and chewing at the same time _____
4. simply chewing _____

On a separate sheet of paper, write a sentence using each of these words.

DID YOU KNOW?
Where does the word sandwich come from? It seems that the fourth Earl of Sandwich, John Montague, was so addicted to playing cards that he didn't want to take time out to eat. He found that placing slices of meat between pieces of bread made a good impromptu meal, and he didn't have to leave the card table.

mandible	The jaw, especially the lower jaw of a vertebrate; both jaws of insects or beaked animals. **WORDS IN CONTEXT:** *Examining the large fossil's* **mandible** *suggested to the scientists that it was most likely a vertebrate.*
draught	In reference to edibles and potables, a draught is a draft, a drink, as in beer on draft—out of a beer storage urn rather than a bottle. **WORDS IN CONTEXT:** **Draught** *is the British spelling of the word* draft.
libation	The ritual of pouring out wine or oil upon the ground as a sacrifice to ancient gods; the liquid, an alcoholic drink, or drinking itself. **WORDS IN CONTEXT:** *"May I offer you a* **libation**?*" he inquired.*
pemmican	Dried beef, suet, dried fruit, prepared as concentrated high-energy food used for emergency rations, as on Arctic expeditions. **WORDS IN CONTEXT:** *They secured the* **pemmican** *for the trip with foil and string.*

After studying the words above, use each of them in a sentence below.

1. In the pub, most of the libations were on _____.
2. Because the guests were of all ages, the company offered a variety of _____, from milk to bourbon.
3. Just seeing its_____, the tourists in the Museum of Natural History got a sense of its size.
4. As the days wore on as they climbed the mountain, leaders decided to ration the _____.

Test Yourself: Write the word that best fits the meaning given below.

1. beer on tap _____
2. anything to drink _____
3. big teeth, big animal_____
4. take enough on an expedition to stay alive_____

On a separate sheet of paper, write a sentence using each of these words.

DID YOU KNOW?
The common flavoring vanilla comes from the seedpod found in some tropical American orchids. The seedpod and the orchid are called vanilla, a word that originally came from the Spanish *vainilla*, denoting the flower, the pod, and the flavoring.

provender	Provisions; food; also dry food for livestock.
	WORDS IN CONTEXT: *Before leaving, they made certain to provide enough **provender** for the cattle.*
alimentation	Nourishment or being nourished; nutrition support sustenance.
	WORDS IN CONTEXT: *The recommended diet offered bare **alimentation**.*
comestibles	Food, eats, something edible.
	WORDS IN CONTEXT: *The pantry shelves were loaded with **comestibles**.*
viands	Food of various kinds, especially choice dishes.
	WORDS IN CONTEXT: ***Viands** were abundant at the banquet.*

After studying the words above, use each in a sentence below.

1. In modern supermarkets, choice _____ are only part of the inventory.
2. They assembled _____ for the excursion.
3. Anything, simply sustenance for _____ was all they needed.
4. _____ is an old-fashioned word for food.

Test Yourself: Write the word that best fits the meaning given below.

1. eats _____
2. choice eats _____
3. bare sustenance _____
4. cattle must eat, too _____

On a separate sheet of paper, write a sentence using each of these words.

DID YOU KNOW? Why is taking a drink the morning after a night of debauchery called taking "a hair of the dog"? Weird as it sounds, apparently old folklore had it that any disease you might get after a dog bites you could be cured by taking a hair of the dog that bit you and placing it in the wound. Maybe that's the same principle as fighting fire with fire—which doesn't work either.

potage	Soup or broth.
	WORDS IN CONTEXT: *In Charles Dickens's day, orphans subsisted mainly on thin potage. ("More please," said Oliver Twist.)*
fricassee	To cut up and fry; a dish of meat cut into pieces, stewed or fried and served in its own juices as gravy.
	WORDS IN CONTEXT: *The restaurant served a **fricasseed** version of hanger steak.*
savory	Pleasing to the taste or smell, appetizing, pleasant, agreeable, attractive, respectable; also a small, salty or piquant highly seasoned portion of food served as an appetizer or at the end of a meal.
	WORDS IN CONTEXT: ***Savory** scents wafted from the kitchen.*
repast	Food and drink for a meal; the eating of food; mealtime.
	WORDS IN CONTEXT: *Join us for **repast** and libations," the invitation said.*

After studying the words above, use each in a sentence below.

1. The _____ smell of the Thanksgiving dinner wafted through the house.
2. We enjoyed the delightful holiday _____ with friends and family.
3. An old-fashioned or literary word for soup or broth is _____.
4. We had chicken_____ for dinner with grilled vegetables.

Test Yourself: Write the word that best fits the meaning given below.

1. pleasing smell or taste _____
2. mealtime _____
3. cut it up and fry it; serve in its own juice _____
4. food and drink_____

On a separate sheet of paper, write a sentence using each of these words.

DID YOU KNOW?
Where did we get the term *sour grapes* for something we desire but can't have? From the fable of the fox and the grapes. The fox tried to reach the grapes hanging on a vine, but they were too high for him, and he finally gave up. "Well, they're sour anyway," he said.

Amusing Words

The English language is filled with amusing words. Some of these below have amusing definitions, curious backgrounds, or just—at least to the author—sound funny.

DAY 1

| ecdysiast | tittle | oolong | azygous |

DAY 2

| funny bone | muumuu | purfle | horripulation |

DAY 3

| lummox | berserker | nincompoop | noli me tangere |

DAY 4

| cockamamie | zanana | usufruct | zaftig |

DAY 5

| syzygy | Tartuffe | yashmak | urceolate |

DAY 6

| drollery | frippery | tomfoolery | harlequinade |

DAY 7

| Pantaloon | Columbine | schnozzle | pygidium |

ecdysiast	A stripteaser. **WORDS IN CONTEXT:** *Ecdysiast* is a word that derives from ecdysis—the stripping off or shedding an outer layer of skin as snakes do. Gypsy Rose Lee was an unusually intelligent stripper; she called herself an **ecdysiast.**
tittle	A very small particle; a dot; iota, jot. **WORDS IN CONTEXT:** *Jot and **tittle** were words used for tiny marks in early printing.*
oolong	Dark tea from China or Taiwan, partly fermented from being dried. **WORDS IN CONTEXT:** *The name of this tea recalls an old song that goes, "So long, **Oolong**. How long you gonna be gone?"*
azygous	Unpaired, unwedded; in biology, occurring singly. **WORDS IN CONTEXT:** *Azygous* from the Greek means "without yoke."

After studying the words above, use each in a sentence below.

1. The _____ ordered new tassels from the costume catalogue.
2. _____ a very small thing that usually accompanies another very small thing called a jot.
3. The Chinese guest brought his hostess a tin of _____.
4. Anything _____ has no mate.

Test Yourself: Write the word that best fits the meaning given below.

1. underdressed dancing girl _____
2. dark tea _____
3. has no companion _____
4. tiny bit _____

On a separate sheet of paper, write a sentence using each of these words.

DID YOU KNOW? Where did we get the word *speakeasy* for an illicit saloon? During Prohibition, when the sale and drinking of alcohol went underground, sometimes literally, the drinkers couldn't raise their voices for fear of alerting the police, so the code word came to be "speak easy."

funny bone	A place on the elbow where the ulnar nerve passes near the surface: a sharp impact here causes strange, tingling sensations in the arm.
	WORDS IN CONTEXT: *When we hit our **funny bone** our arm tingles, but also, it is said that people with a **funny bone** have an inclination to laughter.*
muumuu	A full, long, loose garment for women, usually of a bright print as originally worn in Hawaii.
	WORDS IN CONTEXT: ***Muumuus**, shapeless garments, were designed by prudish missionary women to cover the nudity of Hawaiian women who covered themselves with little more than a strategically placed flower or two.*
purfle	To decorate the border of; an ornamental border or trimming.
	WORDS IN CONTEXT: *She added a purple **purfle** to the hem of her white skirt.*
horripulation	Erection of the hair on head or body caused by fear, disease, or goose flesh; hair standing on end.
	WORDS IN CONTEXT: *He was so horrified in the haunted house that he experienced **horripulation.***

After studying the words above, use each in a sentence below.

1. _____ in Hawaiian means literally "cut off," maybe because its introduction cut off the practice of women running around in the altogether. (Actually, it is said that the dresses were so named because, having no yoke, they looked cut off at the neck.)
2. His body reacted in goose flesh at the thought and his hair in _____.
3. A _____ decorated the edge of the pie-crust table.
4. She hit her _____ on the edge of the door, and for an instant little needles attacked her arm.

Test Yourself: Write the word that best fit the meaning given below.

1. hair standing on end _____
2. loose, colorful dress _____
3. decorated border _____
4. so funny it tingles _____

On a separate sheet of paper, write a sentence using each of these words.

DID YOU KNOW?
Where does the expression *son of a gun* come from? Here's the dope: When sailors in the British Navy were allowed to take their wives to sea with them, a child born at sea was called a "son of a gun" because it was born beneath the guns of the ship. (This has nothing to do with a shotgun wedding.)

lummox	An extremely clumsy person. **WORDS IN CONTEXT:** *When he tried to imitate the juggler, he was a real **lummox**.*
berserker	One in a state of destructive rage or frenzy. **WORDS IN CONTEXT:** *The term **berserker** comes from the word for a warrior in a bearskin in an Old Norse legend who worked himself into a frenzy before battle.*
nincompoop	A stupid, silly person; a fool or simpleton. **WORDS IN CONTEXT:** *The **nincompoop** walked into the lake while he was wearing his Sunday suit.*
noli me tangere	A warning against touching, interfering, or meddling: touch me not. **WORDS IN CONTEXT:** ***Noli me tangere** comes from the Latin meaning, "Do not touch me." This was Jesus' warning to Mary Magdalene (Vulgate, John 20:17).*

After studying the words above, use each in a sentence below.

1. "Mother!" she yelled. "Come get my silly little brother; he is acting like a _____!"
2. The sign on the freshly painted wall read: _____, but no one understood it.
3. The _____ was on a rampage, destroying property.
4. The _____ stumbled on the steps, even though they were not at all steep.

Test Yourself: Write the word or phrase that best fits the meaning given below.

1. an uncoordinated person _____
2. do not touch me _____
3. silly person_____
4. person in a rage _____

On a separate sheet of paper, write a sentence using each of these words or phrases.

DID YOU KNOW?
How did the Sphinx get its name? Sphinx means "the strangler" in Greek. According to legend, she strangled people who could not solve the riddle she tossed at them. The name is Greek, but the legend is Egyptian, which just confounds the contradiction: The Greek Sphinx of legend is a woman, but the actual Egyptian Sphinx has the head of a man.

cockamamie	Trifling, ludicrous, nonsensical; poor quality, inferior.
	WORDS IN CONTEXT: *The boys gave their tree house the cockamamie name "Dark Cave."*
zanana	The part of a house in India and Pakistan reserved for the women of the household; sometimes written **zenana**. Sometimes this word refers to a harem.
	WORDS IN CONTEXT: *The word **zanana** comes from the Persian in which* zan *means woman.*
usufruct	The right to use and enjoy the profits and advantages of something belonging to another, so long as the property is not damaged or altered in any way.
	WORDS IN CONTEXT: *A **usufructuary** is a person who holds property by **usufruct**; both words are legal terms.*
zaftig	Full-bosomed; having a comfortably ample figure.
	WORDS IN CONTEXT: *In Yiddish, **zaftig** means plump.*

After studying the words above, use each in a sentence below.

1. Though the strip of land near the water did not legally belong to us, we were given the right of _____ by its owner.
2. The word _____ rhymes with banana and is the area in an Indian home reserved for women.
3. The boys came home telling a _____ story about being chased by an elephant.
4. Her grandmother was _____, so the children liked to cuddle into her lap.

Test Yourself: Write the word that best fits the meaning given below.

1. pleasingly plump _____
2. you may use it, but don't abuse it _____
3. nonsensical, valueless _____
4. no men allowed_____

On a separate sheet of paper, write a sentence using each of these words.

DID YOU KNOW?
How did we get the expression "stole his thunder"? It seems that a playwright named Dennis in about the year 1700 found a way to create the sound of thunder off stage. But someone stole the machine he invented to do this. This idea was so amusing to actors that the expression was adopted to mean that someone had upstaged or gotten out in front of them. (Maybe *thunder* is a code word for applause.)

syzygy	In astronomy, the configuration of the sun, the moon, and the earth lying in a straight line. **WORDS IN CONTEXT:** *Syzygy* comes from the Greek "suzugia," which means union, coupling, yoked, or paired.
Tartuffe	A hypocrite, especially one who displays religious piety. **WORDS IN CONTEXT:** *Tartuffe* is the title character in Moliere's comedy written in 1664. The word comes from the Latin, meaning "truffle of the earth," or potato.
yashmak	A veil worn by Moslem women to cover their face in public. **WORDS IN CONTEXT:** *The Moslem woman was allowed to attend school, but she was required to wear a* **yashmak.**
urceolate	A jug or pitcher that is urn-shaped. **WORDS IN CONTEXT:** *Urceolate* comes from the Latin meaning urn.

After studying the words above, use each in a sentence below.

1. He was always delivering moral lectures to his friends, but we thought he was a

    _____.
2. In the marketplace, the women wore _____.
3. The Greek woman pored water for her bath from an _____.
4. A _____ is an all-star lineup: sun, moon, and earth.

Test Yourself: Write the word that best fits the meaning given below.

1. Scrabble players delight in getting the letters that make up the word_____
2. so self-righteous we don't believe him _____
3. urn-shaped jug _____
4. Moslem veil _____

On a separate sheet of paper, write a sentence using each of these words.

DID YOU KNOW?
Where do we get the word *blockhead*? Apparently a man once kept his wig on a wooden block called a *blockhead*. If he wasn't overly bright, he was called that himself.

drollery	An amusing, odd, whimsical, comical way of acting, talking, or behaving; clowning or joking; something droll, as an odd, amusing anecdote. **WORDS IN CONTEXT:** *We sat around the campfire singing, joking, and telling* **drolleries.**
frippery	Pretentious finery, excessively ornamental dress, ostentation, trivia. **WORDS IN CONTEXT:** *Frippery comes from an Old French word meaning "frill" and from a Medieval Latin word meaning "fiber."*
tomfoolery	Something trivial or foolish, foolish behavior, nonsense. **WORDS IN CONTEXT:** *The chaperone asked the students on the trip to cut out the* **tomfoolery.**
harlequinade	A comedy or pantomime in which Harlequin, a clown or buffoon—dressed in a parti–colored bodysuit with a ruffle around his neck and an eye mask—is the main attraction. **WORDS IN CONTEXT:** *In the* **harlequinade** *we saw a series of farcical sequences based on the characters of Italian commedia dell'arte: Harlequin, Pantaloon, Columbine, and others.*

After studying the words above, use each in a sentence below.

1. The little girls played dress-up in _____ they found in the attic.
2. A lot of _____ goes on in the boys' dressing room in the gym.
3. The stories they told were filled with humor and _____.
4. The grotesquely shaped eyeglasses have slanted, pointy-end frames resembling the mask worn by the clowns in Italian comedies called _____.

Test Yourself: Write the word that best fits the meaning given below.

1. nonsensical behavior _____
2. a comedy featuring farcical clowns _____
3. odd, whimsical, amusing _____
4. fussy finery _____

On a separate sheet of paper, write a sentence using each of these words.

DID YOU KNOW?
How can you become a "high brow"? Knock into some walls; get a few bumps on your head. In phrenology—a system in which an analysis of character can be made by studying the shape and protuberances of the skull— you were known by the bumps on your head. If you had a high brow, you were thought to have great intellect. Phrenology has, fortunately, fallen into disuse.

Pantaloon	A character in commedia dell'arte portrayed as a foolish old man in slippers and billowy trousers called pantaloons.
	WORDS IN CONTEXT: *Pantaloon as a stock character is the butt of a clown's jokes.*
Columbine	The female character in commedia dell'arte.
	WORDS IN CONTEXT: *In farce or pantomime, Columbine is usually young, flighty, and "dovelike"—which is what her name means in Medieval English and Latin.*
schnozzle	The nose.
	WORDS IN CONTEXT: *Schnozzle is probably an alteration of the word "shnoitsl" or snout from Yiddish and the German "Schnauze." The nose or* **schnozzle** *is sometimes called in slangy humor "the old schnozzola."*
pygidium	The posterior body region of certain arthropods.
	WORDS IN CONTEXT: *The* **pygidium** *is, in certain arthropods, sometimes called the rump.*

After studying the words above, use each in a sentence below.

1. _____ is the female character in certain Italian comedy.
2. _____ a cheeky word for nose.
3. _____ wears trousers bearing his name.
4. _____ part of the body of an insect, crustacean, or other arthropods.

Test Yourself: Write the word that best fits the meaning given below.

1. you smell with it_____
2. foolish old man in comedy_____
3. dovelike beauty in comedy_____
4. bug's rear end _____

On a separate sheet of paper, write a sentence using each of these words.

DID YOU KNOW? How you can become a *bigwig*? Get the biggest wig in town. Once all men of importance in England were recognized by the wigs they wore (which they kept on blockheads). Lawyers and judges still do. The bigger the wig, the more important the man.

Growing Words

Growth, growing, increasing, spreading—the English language has a number of words to indicate these activities. A few are below.

DAY 1

burgeoning	pandemic	incipient	rampant

DAY 2

expound	plethoric	rapacious	accretion

DAY 3

conglomerate	agglomeration	congeries	permeating

DAY 4

accession	metamorphosis	magpie	synthesize

DAY 5

augmentation	increment	aggrandizement	accumulation

DAY 6

amplification	pullulation	incubation	turgescence

DAY 7

tumescence	exacerbation	concretion	agglutination

burgeoning	To sprout, grow, blossom, develop rapidly. **WORDS IN CONTEXT:** *The **burgeoning** talent of the cellist was acknowledged by the audience.*
pandemic	Widespread, general, universal; an epidemic over a wide area. **WORDS IN CONTEXT:** *The disease was **pandemic** in several states.*
incipient	In the initial or early stage; just beginning to appear. **WORDS IN CONTEXT:** *The disease that was pandemic in other states was only **incipient** in Washington.*
rampant	Extending unchecked, unrestrained, wide-spreading. **WORDS IN CONTEXT:** *A **rampant** growth of junipers had taken over the property.*

After studying the words above, use each in a sentence below.

1. Every seven years, locusts are _____.
2. The kudzoo ran _____ in the South.
3. The talented young boy was a _____ scientist.
4. The roses were still _____, but the daisies were blooming.

Test Yourself: Write the word that best fits the meaning given below.

1. widespread over an area_____
2. in early stages_____
3 running wild_____
4. develop rapidly _____

On a separate sheet of paper, write a sentence using each of these words.

DID YOU KNOW?
How did we get the word *savvy*? It's a synonym for *knowledge*, and it comes from the Spanish phrase *save usted,* "do you know?" influenced by the French verb *savoir.*

expound	To give a detailed statement, explain at some length, hold forth.
	WORDS IN CONTEXT: *The professor was **expounding** on the history of World War II.*
plethoric	Excessive in quantity, superabundant.
	WORDS IN CONTEXT: *The **plethoric** wealth of the Trump organization allowed it to expand its holdings.*
rapacious	Taking by force, plundering, ravenous.
	WORDS IN CONTEXT: *The **rapacious** greed of the real estate company got its owners into trouble with the law.*
accretion	Any growth or increase in size by gradual, external addition, fusion, or inclusion.
	WORDS IN CONTEXT: *The sediment **accretion** along the coast of Long Island caused the builders problems.*

After studying the words above, use each in a sentence below.

1. The _____ corporation tried another hostile takeover of a company.
2. The _____ addition of homes in the neighborhood was making the area crowded.
3. _____ gains in the stock market delighted investors.
4. The minister _____ on a different book of the New Testament every Sunday.

Test Yourself: Write the word that best fits the meaning given below.

1. ravenously greedy _____
2. gradual growth or increase _____
3. explain at length _____
4. superabundant _____

On a separate sheet of paper, write a sentence using each of these words.

DID YOU KNOW? Why do some people carry an umbrella in sunshine? *Umbrella* is the Latin word for "little shadow." But you would do just as well by carrying a parasol—French: to "ward off the sun."

conglomerate	To collect into an adhering or rounded mass; a cluster; to become a coherent mass. **WORDS IN CONTEXT:** *The small collection of banks steadily grew into a great **conglomerate**.*
agglomeration	A confused or jumbled mass of things clustered together; a heap; a rounded mass of disparate things. **WORDS IN CONTEXT:** *The police officer opened the door to the victim's apartment and found an **agglomeration** of stuff that must have been collected for many decades.*
congeries	A collection of things heaped together, an aggregation. **WORDS IN CONTEXT:** *The student's paper had no focus but was simply a **congeries** of his thoughts.*
permeating	Spreading or flowing out, pervading, diffusing. **WORDS IN CONTEXT:** *The sound of the rock band was **permeating** the lounge and reception area of the building.*

After studying the words above, use each in a sentence below.

1. The boy's closet held an _____ of stuff: sports equipment, shoes, and CDs.
2. The smell of garden flowers_____ the patio.
3. After our move, a _____ of boxes sat in the garage for days.
4. A _____ of libraries, all belonging to the county, were open to anyone.

Test Yourself: Write the word that best fits the meaning given below.

1. spreading, pervading _____
2. confused jumble _____
3. clustered into a coherent mass_____
4. a collection of things_____

On a separate sheet of paper, write a sentence using each of these words.

DID YOU KNOW?
What does "fit to a T" allude to? That would be a T-square, used by architects and builders. A perfect fit, as on the drafting board. (By the way, a T-shirt is spelled this way because when you hold it up, it's shaped like a T.)

accession	An increase by means of something being added.
	WORDS IN CONTEXT: *The accession of new land increased the value of the original property.*
metamorphosis	A change of form, shape, structure or substance; a transformation.
	WORDS IN CONTEXT: *In biology, metamorphosis is the physical transformation undergone by various animals during development after the embryonic state; in medicine, it is the pathological change of form of some tissues.*
magpie	Any number of birds of the jay family with the habit of noisy chattering and collecting odds and ends to build a nest.
	WORDS IN CONTEXT: *A person who chatters or collects odds and ends is sometimes referred to as a magpie.*
synthesize	To combine so as to form a new, complex product; to produce by putting together separate elements.
	WORDS IN CONTEXT: *They synthesized the various reports into one large document.*

After studying the words above, use each in a sentence below.

1. Her aunt was a little dotty and collected bits and pieces like a _____.
2. We worked to _____ the thoughts of the committee members into one statement.
3. The caterpillar underwent a _____ when it changed into a butterfly.
4. By the accession of two neighboring farms, they increased the size of their holdings.

Test Yourself: Write the word that best fits the meaning given below.

1. collects odds and ends _____
2. to combine to form something new _____
3. dramatic transformation _____
4. increase by addition _____

On a separate sheet of paper, write a sentence using each of these words.

DID YOU KNOW?
Where did we get the term *Indian file?* In the woods, Indians were accustomed to walking single file, placing their feet in the footsteps of the Indian walking before. The last Indian would wipe out the footprints, so they could not be tracked by any pursuers. Now we call the pathbreakers Native Americans, and we're pleased to walk in the tracks they first made.

augmentation	The condition of being extended, enlarged, increased; an addition; in music, the repetition of a theme.
	WORDS IN CONTEXT: *The shop advertised what it called "hair **augmentation**," which was essentially weaving long strands of hair into the ends of short hair.*
increment	An increase in number, size, or extent; growth, enlargement; something added or gained.
	WORDS IN CONTEXT: *After the birth of calves in the spring, we had an **increment** in our herd.*
aggrandizement	An increase in the scope of; enlarged, made greater, exaggerated.
	WORDS IN CONTEXT: *Her **self-aggrandizement** made her unpopular in the modest crowd.*
accumulation	The act of amassing or gathering, as into a pile; a mass of something heaped or collected.
	WORDS IN CONTEXT: *At the end of our property, we formed a compost pile with an **accumulation** of trimmings from the hedges and trees.*

After studying the words above, use each in a sentence below.

1. For a major _____ of their art collection, they purchased a Picasso.
2. We found an_____ of old car keys in a box in the garage.
3. Having heard her _____ of her country home, we expected it to be larger.
4. He found that the interest on his money had brought him a substantial _____ this year.

Test Yourself: Write the word that best fits the meaning given below.

1. exaggeration _____
2. addition _____
3. enlargement or extension _____
4. a heap or pile _____

On a separate sheet of paper, write a sentence using each of these words.

DID YOU KNOW?
Why do we use the expression *earmarked* when we refer to something set aside for a particular use? It has to do with cattle and hogs. English farmers once notched the ears of their cattle to identify them. Still, in many places, hogs' ears are earmarked—and sometimes the ears of cattle are tagged.

amplification	The act or result of making something—thought, idea, book, music—larger or more powerful.
	WORDS IN CONTEXT: *With the **amplification** of her ideas in the short story, she turned the concept into a novel.*
pullulation	Indicating rapid and abundant breeding; germination; sprouting; a teeming or swarming.
	WORDS IN CONTEXT: *The **pullulation** of the hydrangeas gave us a yard full of beautiful flowers.*
incubation	Allowing development or foment in a controlled environment; the development or hatching of eggs.
	WORDS IN CONTEXT: *The **incubation** of the hen's eggs produced more and healthier chicks this season.*
turgescence	The process of swelling up, or the condition of being swollen.
	WORDS IN CONTEXT: *The **turgescence** of his ego was noticeable by everyone present.*

After studying the words above, use each in a sentence below.

1. The university added a new program in which the _____ of young businesses in a separate facility could promote their growth.
2. The _____ of winged insects this year brought swarms of bees to the garden.
3. The _____ of his knee after he tore a ligament created a need for surgery.
4. The _____ of the music in the auditorium nearly ruptured our eardrums.

Test Yourself: Write the word that best fits the meaning given below.

1. swelling up or swollen _____
2. germination or rapid breeding _____
3. making larger or more powerful _____
4. environmental conditions to promote development _____

On a separate sheet of paper, write a sentence using each of these words.

DID YOU KNOW? Why do we call the first team of a university the "varsity"? Because it represents the university; the word is simply a shortened form of that word.

tumescence	A swelling or enlarging; a swollen part or organ. **WORDS IN CONTEXT:** *The doctors noted **tumescence** in his brain, which caused them to operate.*
exacerbation	An increase in the severity; an aggravation. **WORDS IN CONTEXT:** *The manager told me that although my behavior had not created the negative situation, it had **exacerbated** it.*
concretion	The act or process of growing together or becoming united in one mass. **WORDS IN CONTEXT:** *The trees that separated the two houses had grown to the point of **concretion**.*
agglutination	Adhesion of parts; a mass formed by combining elements—words, word parts, etc.—as if by glue; a mass or clump caused by adhesion. **WORDS IN CONTEXT:** *The two words, bell and hop, have become one through **agglutination**.*

After studying the words above, use each in a sentence below.

1. Through the process of _____, the six bushes had become one.
2. Her skin condition was _____ by exposure to the sun.
3. _____ in his gland caused him pain.
4. The chewing gum in the package left in the sun in a closed car _____ into one sticky mass.

Test Yourself: Write the word that best fits the meaning given below.

1. stuck together as if with glue _____
2. the act of growing together in one mass _____
3. swelling or enlarging _____
4. an aggravation of an existing condition _____

On a separate sheet of paper, write a sentence using each of these words.

DID YOU KNOW?
What does the word *vaccine* have to do with cows? The first vaccine was made from the virus that causes cowpox, as the derivation from the Latin *vacca* suggests. Edward Jenner in the late eighteenth century discovered that someone who has had cowpox, a mild bovine disease, was usually immune to smallpox. Jenner called the smallpox vaccine, "vaccine virus."

Short Words

Some of the following words are short, while others mean short.

DAY 1

| eke | yegg | yclept | coupé |

DAY 2

| virgule | scintilla | yaw | brachydactylic |

DAY 3

| miff | dollop | mob | luff |

DAY 4

| adze | rue | edgy | tup |

DAY 5

| tyro | wee | zed | cuff |

DAY 6

| tun | trull | cull | rig |

DAY 7

| jot | modicum | iota | whit |

eke	To supplement with great effort; strain to fill out. **WORDS IN CONTEXT:** *He eked out a living working his farmland.*
yegg	A burglar or safecracker. **WORDS IN CONTEXT:** *Yegg is said to derive from the name of safecracker John Yegg.*
yclept	Also known as or AKA; named, called. **WORDS IN CONTEXT:** *Yclept from Middle English is used in this way—Jonathan Smithton yclept J. Smith signed the document.*
coupé	A closed two-door automobile; the end compartment in European railway cars. **WORDS IN CONTEXT:** *Coupé, as in she drives a black coupé, comes from Old French meaning "cut off."*

After studying the words above, use each in a sentence below.

1. The _____ is for style, while the SUV is for drudgery.
2. The Red Sox _____ out a victory with two runs in the ninth inning.
3. In literature, Jimmy Valentine, with his sensitive fingers, was the ultimate_____.
4. His name was Paul Martini, but he used the _____ Paul Martin.

Test Yourself: Write the word that best fits the meaning given below.

1. also known as _____
2. two-door auto and end train compartment _____
3. strain to fill out_____
4. safecracker or burglar _____

On a separate sheet of paper, write a sentence using each of these words.

DID YOU KNOW? Suede, though haute couture in France and the United States, actually comes from Sweden. *Gants de Suede,* a French phrase that means literally "gloves from Sweden," referred to gloves made of undressed kidskin, native to Sweden.

virgule	A slash, as in "either/or," or used at the end of a line of poetry; also used for the word *per* as in 10 miles/hour. Also known as a *solidus* or *diagonal*.
	WORDS IN CONTEXT: *He used a **virgule** when writing "both/and."*
scintilla	A minute amount; a trace; an iota.
	WORDS IN CONTEXT: *Not a **scintilla** of the drug was found in the man's blood.*
yaw	To deviate from the intended course, as with a ship; to move unsteadily; to weave.
	WORDS IN CONTEXT: *The ship pitched and **yawed** as it sailed through the bad weather..*
brachydactylic	Having abnormally short toes or fingers.
	WORDS IN CONTEXT: *The long word **brachydactylic** actually indicated on his medical chart that he had very short toes.*

After studying the words above, use each in a sentence below.

1. Finding not a _____ of evidence of guilt, the judge dismissed the charges.
2. Leaving the bar, he _____ liked a rowboat in a storm.
3. _____ from birth, she never felt comfortable going barefoot.
4. Adopting the _____ form, computer users speak of forward slash or back slash.

Test Yourself: Write the word that best fits the meaning given below.

1. iota, trace_____
2. to weave unsteadily_____
3. stubby toes_____
4. either/or, both/and, for example _____

On a separate sheet of paper, write a sentence using each of these words.

DID YOU KNOW? The English word *pen,* with which we now write, came from the Latin *penna,* which means "feather." The Latin word for a writing instrument was *stilus,* which means "a stake." The ancient Romans wrote on wax tablets and used pointed instruments—ink and inkwells came much later.

miff	A petulant, bad-tempered mood; a huff; also, a petty quarrel or tiff; to offend a person.
	WORDS IN CONTEXT: *She was **miffed** when she learned that the class she wanted in college was closed.*
dollop	A large lump, helping, or portion.
	WORDS IN CONTEXT: *Please put a **dollop** of whipped cream on my cake.*
mob	A large, disorderly crowd; a mass of common people; to crowd, jostle, or attack others.
	WORDS IN CONTEXT: *The **mob** was in the street yelling for changes in the political platform.*
luff	The act of sailing closer to the wind, said of a ship; to flap while losing wind, said of a sail.
	WORDS IN CONTEXT: *As they sailed, they saw the ship's sail begin to **luff.***

After studying the words above, use each in a sentence below.

1. We called it a carefully organized demonstration; they called it a _____scene.
2. Children learning about boats know they need not panic if they see their sails_____.
3. The sundae arrived with a_____ of crushed strawberries on the ice cream.
4. She let him know that she was _____simply by refusing to look at him.

Test Yourself: Write the word that best fits the meaning given below.

1. lump, helping, or portion _____
2. a large, disorderly crowd_____
3. a huff, a bad mood _____
4. flap while losing wind_____

On a separate sheet of paper, write a sentence using each of these words.

DID YOU KNOW?
The word *mob* is a shortened form of the word *mobile,* which in the early seventeenth century meant "the masses." *Mobile* was itself a shortened form of the Latin *mobile vulgus*—"the excitable populace."

adze	An axlike tool with an arched blade set at a right angle to the handle, used on wood.
	WORDS IN CONTEXT: *He picked up the **adze** to strip the bark from the log.*
rue	To feel remorse or sorrow; to regret.
	WORDS IN CONTEXT: *She knew she would **rue** the day she met him.*
edgy	On edge, tense; with an excessively sharp definition; aggressively avant-garde.
	WORDS IN CONTEXT: *The film had an **edgy** quality that disturbed the viewers.*
tup	To copulate with; a male sheep, a ram.
	WORDS IN CONTEXT: *Shakespeare used the Middle English word **tup** to indicate having sex.*

After studying the words above, use each in a sentence below.

1. He wielded the _____ in a frightening manner.
2. Mickey Spillane's _____ style changed American detective stories.
3. He feared that he would _____ his decision, yet he pushed forward.
4. The author Larry McMurtry adopted the word *poke* as a euphemism in his novel *Lonesome Dove*, just as Shakespeare had used_____.

On a separate sheet of paper, write a sentence using each of these words.

DID YOU KNOW?
A *mess* was not always a mess. It did not become "a disorderly jumble" until late in the nineteenth century. Before that, it meant a meal, or a quantity of food, from the Latin *missus* and had the sense of "a group of persons who usually eat togther," as it does now in mess hall.

tyro	An inexperienced person, a beginner, a neophyte.	
	WORDS IN CONTEXT: *He was a **tyro** at golf, but he was willing to practice.*	
wee	Very tiny, a little bit; also, very early.	
	WORDS IN CONTEXT: *He was a **wee** boy to be up until the **wee** hours of the morning.*	
zed	The letter z, chiefly in Great Britain.	
	WORDS IN CONTEXT: *The London inhabitant read the alphabet from a to **zed**.*	
cuff	To strike with an open hand, slap; a blow or a slap; also, a fold or band at the bottom of a sleeve or trouser leg. Also used to mean gratis—without payment.	
	WORDS IN CONTEXT: *A diner in a white shirt with blue **cuffs cuffed** the waiter on the ear, and then demanded that his meal be on the **cuff**.*	

After studying the words above, use each in a sentence below.

1. A _____ in politics, the intern was not the least cynical.
2. He asked for a _____ bit of brandy to soothe his throat.
3. The last letter of the British alphabet, _____, is a variation of the American letter z.
4. Some gentlemen prefer trousers with_____; others find this style to be old-fashioned.

Test Yourself: Write the word that best fits the meaning given below.

1. tiny bit _____
2. z _____
3. a beginner
4 a slap; a band on trouser legs_____

On a separate sheet of paper, write a sentence using each of these words.

DID YOU KNOW?
Kind was not always kind— meaning "possessing qualities usually attributed to those of good birth." The word carries meanings from Old English of thunder and death. In the thirteenth century it came to mean "well-born" and "of good nature."

tun	A large cask for liquids, especially wine; a measure of liquid capacity: 252 gallons.	
	WORDS IN CONTEXT: *The winemakers filled the **tun** to set in the warehouse.*	
trull	A strumpet, harlot.	
	WORDS IN CONTEXT: ***Trull** is an unattractive word to call a woman; it's from Old Norse meaning "troll."*	
cull	To pick out from others, select.	
	WORDS IN CONTEXT: *They **culled** the best berries from the day's pick to eat fresh and whole.*	
rig	To fit out, equip; dress or clothing; to construct in a makeshift manner; to manipulate dishonestly.	
	WORDS IN CONTEXT: *They **rigged** out the boat, while the woman put on her sailing **rig** after **rigging** a line of rope in her closet on which to hang her clothes; meanwhile, the man in the casino **rigged** the game.*	

After studying the words above, use each in a sentence below.

1. A bawdily dressed group of _____ awaited the truckers after they unloaded their wares and left the parking lot.
2. The dishonest politician _____ all the inconsistent words he could find in his opponent's speech, then used them out of context.
3. Gamblers were said to have_____ the 1919 World Series by bribing eight Chicago White Sox players, who were then dubbed "the Black Sox."
4. It takes brawny men to maneuver a _____.

Test Yourself: Write the word that best fits the meaning given below.

1. a large cask _____
2. to equip; manipulate dishonestly—and several more meanings _____
3. to select _____
4. a strumpet _____

On a separate sheet of paper, write sentences using each of these words.

DID YOU KNOW? Back in the eighteenth century, you couldn't have much fun. Well-bred people did not use the word or engage in the activity. The word *fun* may have come from the word *fon*, which meant "to make a fool of or to be foolish."

jot	The smallest bit or particle; also, to write down briefly.
	WORDS IN CONTEXT: *Not a **jot** of ink was left in the pen when he tried to **jot** down his notes.*
modicum	A small or moderate amount or quantity.
	WORDS IN CONTEXT: *The children left only a **modicum** of cereal in the box after breakfast.*
iota	A very small amount, usually used with a negative: "not an iota"; also, the ninth letter of the Greek alphabet.
	WORDS IN CONTEXT: *Not an **iota** of meat was left on the Thanksgiving turkey.*
whit	A particle; least bit; iota.
	WORDS IN CONTEXT: *He did not care a **whit** about the rain hitting his hair, but he did worry about his shoes getting wet.*

After studying the words above, use each in a sentence below.

1. Finding not a single _____ of evidence to sustain the charges, the judge dismissed them.
2. The writer awakened suddenly in the middle of the night and knew he must quickly _____ down the idea for a new story.
3. The president's speech made only a _____ of sense at best.
4. She cared not a _____ about his hurt feelings.

Test Yourself: Write the word that best fits the meaning given below.

1. the least bit _____
2. a very small amount _____
3. the smallest particle, or to write quickly _____
4. a moderate amount _____

On a separate sheet of paper, write a sentence using each of these words.

DID YOU KNOW? Your boss is your "master." The word *boss* goes back to the Dutch word *baas*, meaning "master." As it entered the U.S. lexicon, the word seemed not to haul along its negative connotation. So serve your boss and admit no one as your master!

Long Words

The following words are l-o-o-o-ong. Some are more common than others, but it'll make you feel smarter just knowing that some of the uncommon ones exist.

DAY 1

pusillanimous	nepheligenous	latitudinarian	alembriated

DAY 2

irrefragable	setaceous	tritanopia	sericeous

DAY 3

Brobdignagian	euphuistic	quinquagenarian	mansuetude

DAY 4

hagiographic	penumbra	quinquagesima	antifebrile

DAY 5

etymological	insolation	autotomy	kinesthesia

DAY 6

matelasse	abstemious	xylotomous	gallimaufry

DAY 7

asseveration	troglodyte	galligaskins	furfuraceous

pusillanimous	Cowardly, lacking courage.
	WORDS IN CONTEXT: *The faint-hearted and* ***pusillanimous*** *little boy hid from the bullies.*
nepheligenous	That which sends out clouds of smoke. The word comes from a Greek word meaning "cloud." Nephelology is the study of clouds.
	WORDS IN CONTEXT: *Environmentalists are unhappy with* ***nepheligenous*** *industries that pollute the air and surrounding areas.*
latitudinarian	Favoring freedom of thought and behavior, especially in religion.
	WORDS IN CONTEXT: *As opposed to the fundamentalists, the* ***latitudinarian*** *allowed much latitude in thought and action.*
alembicated	Purified, altered, or transformed by a process like distillation.
	WORDS IN CONTEXT: *The lake water was* ***alembicated*** *to be made potable.*

After studying the words above, use each of them in a sentence below.

1. The _____ cigar smokers were unwelcome in the restaurant.
2. One gang of boys accused the other gang of being _____ and unwilling to fight.
3. The machine _____ the water from the tap.
4. The _____ was proud of his open mind.

Test Yourself: Write the word that best fits the meaning given below.

1. purified_____
2. free and open _____
3. emitting clouds of smoke _____
4. sissy _____

On a separate sheet of paper, write a sentence using each of these words.

DID YOU KNOW?
The title Margaret Mitchell chose for her long novel, *Gone with the Wind,* came from a poem by the British poet Ernest Dowson, *Non Sum Qualis Eram Bonae Sub Regno Cynara.* ("I am not as I was under the reign of the good Cynara.") Dowson's words were, "I have forgot much, Cynara! gone with the wind / Flung roses riotously with the throng, / Dancing, to put they pale, lost lilies out of mind." Dowson's title comes from a line from Horace (IV.1). Both wrote of women who had once mesmerized them.

irrefragable	Unable to be refuted.
	WORDS IN CONTEXT: *The founders intended the U.S. Constitution to be **irrefragable**.*
setaceous	Having or consisting of bristles; bristly; resembling a bristle.
	WORDS IN CONTEXT: *He liked a sturdy and **setaceous** hairbrush.*
tritanopia	A rare visual defect involving the inability to distinguish between the colors blue and yellow.
	WORDS IN CONTEXT: *Uncle Tony said, "That flag is red, white, and what?" and we discovered that he is a sufferer of **tritanopia**.*
sericeous	Silky; in botany, covered with soft, silky hair.
	WORDS IN CONTEXT: *Her long, golden hair was as **sericeous** as corn silk.*

After studying the words above, use each in a sentence below.

1. "I think, therefore I am" is _____.
2. The thistle was_____.
3. Being a victim of _____, he bought a yellow blazer thinking it was blue, a color he could not distinguish.
4. The Persian cat was amber, _____, and mean.

Test Yourself: Write the word that best fits the meaning given below.

1. unable to tell blue from yellow_____
2. hair like Sarah Jessica Parker's _____
3. hair like G.I. Joe _____
4. It's a fact: I was born; you were born _____

On a separate sheet of paper, write a sentence using each of these words.

DID YOU KNOW?
How did a French humanitarian's name became associated with an infamous beheading device? Joseph Ignace Guillotin, a physician, argued that a beheading device would be quicker and less painful than rope or a sword. One was developed and first used in 1792 to execute a highwayman. The nasty guillotine still bears kind Dr. Guillotin's name. But there's more to the story; see the next "Did You Know?"

Brobdingnagian	Giants about 50 feet tall who lived in Brobdingnag in Swift's *Gulliver's Travels*.
	WORDS IN CONTEXT: *The group of huge athletes reminded me of the* **Brobdingnagians**.
euphuistic	High-flown, affected speech or writing.
	WORDS IN CONTEXT: *John Lyly, in his two prose romances* Euphues, *featured a character by this name, from which* **euphuistic**, *the word for a certain stilted style, is derived.*
quinquagenarian	Fifty years old or between the ages of fifty and sixty; a person of this age.
	WORDS IN CONTEXT: *You've heard of septuagenarian? Now you've heard of a younger group of people:* **quinquagenarians**.
mansuetude	Gentleness, tameness.
	WORDS IN CONTEXT: *The nurse treated the ill children with* **mansuetude**.

After studying the words above, use each in a sentence below.

1. He was 50 or 60, a _____, but still vigorous.
2. Her _____ made her a favorite with children and old folks.
3. His elaborate, _____prose put the reader to sleep.
4. The cartoon featured characters as big as_____.

Test Yourself: Write the word that best fits the meaning given below.

1. middle-aged_____
2. gentle _____
3. giant _____
4. highfalutin speech _____

On a separate sheet of paper, write a sentence using each of these words.

DID YOU KNOW?
The guillotine was not always called a *guillotine*. It was designed by a Dr. Anton Louis and was called a *louisette* or a *louison* after its inventor. But because Dr. Guillotin had advocated for its use, his name got stuck to it. A coda to this story: After Guillotin died in the early 1800s, his children campaigned to get the guillotine's name changed. They failed—so they changed their own name.

hagiographic	Biographically idealizing a subject.
	WORDS IN CONTEXT: *Hagiographic was a word originally used in relation to works written about the lives of saints.*
penumbra	The partly lighted area surrounding a complete shadow.
	WORDS IN CONTEXT: *An example of **penumbra** is the light surrounding the moon in full eclipse; a vague, indefinite, or borderline area.*
quinquagesima	The Sunday before Lent or the 50th day before Easter.
	WORDS IN CONTEXT: *Yes, **quinquagesima** means the 50th day, and some cultures do celebrate it.*
antifebrile	Able to reduce fever.
	WORDS IN CONTEXT: *He took the **antifebrile** aspirin to help reduce his fever.*

Study the words above and use each in a sentence below.

1. The biography of Jacqueline Kennedy by her best friend was_____.
2. She stood in front of the light, and a _____appeared around her.
3. They had a special religious feast on_____.
4. The baby was burning with fever, so we gave her an _____.

Test Yourself: Write the word that best fits the meaning below.

1. 50th day_____
2. light surrounding the dark _____
3. admiring book_____
4. aspirin is the best known _____

On a separate sheet of paper, write a sentence using each of these words.

DID YOU KNOW?
How did *grammar* become *glamourous*? Both are derived from a Greek word referring to letters or literature. Its Latin form *grammatical* referred to learning in general and also to magic and astrology. As the word evolved, the first *r* became an *l*, and *grammar* became *glamour*—and kept its association with magic.

etymological	According to the principles of etymology—the tracing of the origin and development of a word, phrase, and so forth.
	WORDS IN CONTEXT: *The etymological origins of some words, phrases, and idioms are found in this book.*
insolation	A treatment of disease by exposure to the sun's rays; sunstroke; the radiation from the sun received by a surface, such as the earth's surface.
	WORDS IN CONTEXT: *Insolation can be a boon sometimes, as in treatments of some diseases and warming the earth's surface; however, it can contribute to sunstroke, too.*
autotomy	In zoology, the spontaneous casting off of a body part, as the tail of certain lizards.
	WORDS IN CONTEXT: *Some living creatures protect themselves by casting off a body part through autotomy.*
kinesthesia	The sensation of position, movement, tension of body parts perceived through nerve end organs in muscles, tendons, and joints.
	WORDS IN CONTEXT: *Practicing yoga made him aware of his body's kinesthesia.*

After studying the words above, use them in a sentence below.

1. Many books are available to trace the_____ development of words.
2. The elderly woman stayed inside during the heat of the day to avoid_____.
3 Humans do not ordinarily use _____ to protect themselves.
4. He exercised because the _____that resulted gave him energy.

Test Yourself: Write the word that best fits the meaning given below.

1. abandoning a body part _____
2. sensation of movement in body party _____
3. sunbath as a treatment _____
4. discovering where a word came from _____

On a separate sheet of paper, write a sentence using each of these words.

DID YOU KNOW?
Although Columbus discovered America in 1492, no speaker of that time would have agreed. Why? Because the word *discover* in the sense of "to be the first to learn of" was not used until 1555. "Discover" in that new sense had not been discovered.

matelasse	Having a surface with a raised design; embossed fabric; highly textured. **WORDS IN CONTEXT:** *The catalog showed several examples of bed coverings made of rich* **matelasse**.
abstemious	Eating and drinking in moderation; sparing. **WORDS IN CONTEXT:** *They were* **abstemious** *people and seldom splurged on dinner out.*
xylotomous	Said of certain insects that can bore into or cut wood. **WORDS IN CONTEXT:** *The exterminator made quick work of the* **xylotomous** *termites.*
gallimaufry	A hash made of meat scraps; any hodgepodge or jumble. **WORDS IN CONTEXT:** *Years ago, women often kept a pot on the back of the stove into which they would throw meat and other leftover scraps to create a new dish sometimes called* **gallimaufry**.

After studying the words above, use each in a sentence below.

1. We inspected the house for _____ insects before we bought it.
2. They enjoyed a rich social life, even though they were _____ at parties.
3. My mother called her delicious stew pantry hash or _____.
4. In our new apartment, we covered the bed in white_____.

Test Yourself: Write the word that best fits the meaning given below.

1. hodgepodge of stuff, or hash_____
2. termites_____
3. moderate eaters_____
4. highly textured fabric _____

On a separate sheet of paper, write a sentence using each of these words.

DID YOU KNOW? How did the Quakers get their name? The founder of The Society of Friends, George Fox, addressed the magistrates of England, telling them that they should "quake" at the word of the Lord. One of the magistrates, Justice Bennett, picked up the word, and it has stuck.

asseveration	A firm declaration or earnest assertion. **WORDS IN CONTEXT:** *He **asseverated** that he in fact did not write the letter to the editor that bore his name.*
troglodyte	A prehistoric cave dweller; a person like a caveman in being reclusive and brutish. **WORDS IN CONTEXT:** *Phoebe referred to the old man who lived back in the hills by himself as a **troglodyte**.*
galligaskins	Loose-fitting breeches, especially those worn in the sixteenth and seventeenth centuries; loose hose. **WORDS IN CONTEXT:** *The characters in the play wore **galligaskins**, which became popular with young people of the time.*
furfuraceous	Like bran; covered with dandruff. **WORDS IN CONTEXT:** *What is that **furfuraceous** stuff on your clothes? Is it dander, or did you spill your cereal?*

After studying the words above, use each in a sentence below.

1. At the end of the day, the proofreader came lumbering out of his cubicle like a_____.
2. Some of Shakespeare's male characters wore_____.
3. The man was rumpled and untidy, and his jacket was_____.
4. His _____were so insistent and repetitive that we wondered whether we should actually believe them.

Test Yourself: Write the word that best fits the meaning given below.

1. baggy pants_____
2. caveman_____
3. earnest statement_____
4. flaky _____

On a separate sheet of paper, write a sentence using each of these words.

DID YOU KNOW?
To crisscross something was once a religious act. The word literally means "the cross of Christ" and indicated a cross made with two crossed lines. This mark was used above teaching material for children; it was also used as a signature (like an X later) by illiterate people. The word lost its religious association in the nineteenth century.

Euphemistic Words

Euphemisms are words or phrases substituted for more offensive and distasteful ones. The word derives from Greek terms meaning "to use words of good omen or good sound." Unfortunately, these good-sounding words often mask disagreeable truths, sometimes unspeakable actions; euphemisms have become tools of propagandists, governments, and corporate managers. The Nazis used *special treatment* for *hanging*, and *resettlement* for *deportation* to concentration camps. Euphemisms are especially effective in wartime by camouflaging reality—for after all, war is heck.

DAY 1

| collateral damage | casualties | subversives/ insurgents | detainees |

DAY 2

| friendly fire | embedded media | incursion | traumatic amputation |

DAY 3

| disinformation | plausible deniability | civil patrols | use of force/ police action |

DAY 4

| proactive downsizing | work reengineering | employee repositioning | outplacing |

DAY 5

| preowned | customer care representative | free gift | special criteria |

DAY 6

| passed on | remains | effects | differently abled |

DAY 7

| misdeeds | sources | irregularities | unethical |

collateral damage	The killing of civilians, and other innocent people.
	WORDS IN CONTEXT: *In the bombing of the city, collateral damage was incurred.*
	TRANSLATION: *Civilians, passers-by, and innocent women and children were killed or wounded in the bombing of the city.*
casualties	Dead or wounded people.
	WORDS IN CONTEXT: *The war produced 37 casualties yesterday.*
	TRANSLATION: *Yesterday, 37 people were killed or wounded in the war.*
subversives and insurgents	People whose political beliefs differ from those in power and who are seen as terrorists, having no right to be in an area.
	WORDS IN CONTEXT: *The subversives and insurgents who survived were detained for questioning.*
	TRANSLATION: *Those people of different political beliefs who remained alive were disarmed, searched, and questioned by methods thought to produce information.*
detainees	Prisoners or hostages.
	WORDS IN CONTEXT: *The detainees are being held in a special compound for further questioning.*
	TRANSLATION: *The prisoners and hostages have been placed in prisons and will continue to undergo harassment by guards and others in order to acquire information.*

After studying the words above, use each in the sentences below.

1. The soldiers discovered several _____ in the swamplands and brought them back to be searched.
2. Yesterday the general announced that there were 37_____ caused by the war.
3. The _____ were held in a prison camp in Guantanamo.
4. Missiles and bombs left much _____ in their wake.

Test Yourself: Place the letter next to the number to match word and meaning.

1. detainees   a. people of different political views
2. collateral damage b. prisoners and hostages
3. casualties   c. killing and wounding of civilians
4. subversives   d. dead or wounded soldiers

On a separate sheet of paper, write a sentence using each of these words.

DID YOU KNOW?
The term *war games* is an oxymoron. Game means "any form of play or way of playing, amusement, recreation, frolic, a sport." And war? "Open, armed conflict between countries, or between factions within a country; hostility, contention, struggle, confusion, strife." What kind of amusement or frolic is war? The term *war games* was originally called *Kriegsspiel* and was introduced by a Prussian officer in 1824, who used maps as small battlefields and little wooden blocks to represent troops. War boardgames became extremely complex in the 1970s, so much so that now war games are usually found in computer format.

friendly fire	Being shot at by your own troops. **WORDS IN CONTEXT:** *Six casualties from **friendly fire** were reported by **embedded media**.* **TRANSLATION:** *Reporters who agreed to go along with the government's program reported that six soldiers were killed by soldiers on the same side of the conflict as their own.*
embedded media	Representatives from newspapers, television, and other news outlets who have agreed with the government in power to observe the war firsthand and report on it from the government's point of view. **WORDS IN CONTEXT:** *Five reporters acting as **embedded media** with appropriate equipment accompanied the armed soldiers in three armored conveyances.* **TRANSLATION:** *Five co-opted reporters equipped with cameras, microphones. and technological equipment rode in three tanks along with the soldiers.*
incursion	Invasion. **WORDS IN CONTEXT:** *The **incursion** took place just outside the occupied territories where armed intervention was deemed necessary to quell suspected resistance.* **TRANSLATION:** *The invasion took place just outside the captured lands where war was thought to be the only response against those who leaders suspected would fight back.*
traumatic amputation	Having a limb blown off. **WORDS IN CONTEXT:** *Several of the troops underwent **traumatic amputation** and were brought into the medical compound for treatment.* **TRANSLATION:** *Three or more of the soldiers had an arm or leg blown off and were taken to the hospital.*

After studying the words above, use them in the sentences below.

1. The _____ took place at midnight.
2. On the battlefield, two soldiers suffered _____ and were tended by medics.
3. The cause of the injuries to the American troops was _____ from an American helicopter.
4. In the jeep, _____ rode alongside the soldiers.

Test Yourself: Place the letter next to the number to match word and meaning.

1. incurson   a. gunshots from friends
2. traumatic amputation   b. reporters along for the ride
3. friendly fire   c. losing a limb in battle
4. embedded media   d. invasion

On a separate sheet of paper, write a sentence using each of these words.

DID YOU KNOW? Robert McNamara, secretary of defense in the mid-1960s, speaking of Vietnam, defined killing as "autocratic methods within a democratic framework."

disinformation	Lies intended to convince listeners of the righteousness of a government. **WORDS IN CONTEXT:** *In confidence, government leaders instructed their communications experts to make public presentations of **disinformation** in language that would appease critics and forestall negative demonstrations.* **TRANSLATION:** *Government leaders secretly told their spokespeople to find a way to spin lies to favor leaders and to avoid criticism and street riots.*
plausible deniability	Lies that will be legally acceptable and seem reasonable to the public. **WORDS IN CONTEXT:** *Leaders further cautioned their communications experts to make sure that government lawyers approved the **plausible deniability** language and make it seem sensible enough for public consumption.* **TRANSLATION:** *Leaders further cautioned their spokespeople to run their lies by government lawyers for approval of the language and to keep it simple enough for the public to understand.*
civil patrols	Armed groups—irregular forces, paramilitary and security forces—that commit terrorist acts for a government and that the government can deny with plausibility. **WORDS IN CONTEXT:** *The government announced that **civil patrols** are keeping the streets safe in the beleaguered city.* **TRANSLATION:** *Armed bands of unofficial fighters are doing secret dirty work for a government.*
use of force/ police action	War. **WORDS IN CONTEXT:** *The government announced that **use of force** was necessary and called for **police action**.* **TRANSLATION:** ***Use of force** and **police action** mean war, no matter how euphemistic they sound.*

After studying the words above, use them in the sentences below.

1. The officers' _____ convinced the citizens that not many soldiers were dying and that the war was about to be won.
2. _____ took over the village and arrested anyone on the street.
3. Rather than negotiate, the leaders demanded _____.
4. The officers accused the spy of misleading them with _____.

Test Yourself: Place the letter next to the number to match word and meaning.

1. plausible deniability
2. use of force
3. disinformation
4 civil patrols

a. unofficial armed groups
b. propagandistic lies
c. war
d. legal lies

DID YOU KNOW?
The word *war* comes from Old English and Old Norse words meaning "worse." Other meanings were "bad, evil, harmful, and unpleasant to a greater degree."

proactive downsizing	An act a company may take—cutting its employees from the payroll and closing some offices—to protect itself when it foresees financial troubles ahead.
	WORDS IN CONTEXT: *It has been decided that the company must close offices in four cities in a **proactive downsizing** attempt.*
	TRANSLATION: *You're fired! The company must let 2,000 workers go. You are one of them.*
work reengineering	The restructuring of jobs and job titles, usually as a result of a perceived need to downsize.
	WORDS IN CONTEXT: *It is regretted that the current economic situation forces us to organize a new **work reengineering** program and ask some people to take other positions in our loyal family of employees.*
	TRANSLATION: *You're fired! Your job is being eliminated.*
employee repositioning	The company is redefining some positions.
	WORDS IN CONTEXT: *The new **employee repositioning** department regrets that it has been determined that some jobs must be redefined.*
	TRANSLATION: *You're fired! Your job as product manager has been redefined to that of groundskeeper.*
outplacing	The company has determined that its resources can be used more profitably.
	WORDS IN CONTEXT: *In our new **outplacing** program, we have hired a consulting firm to help us determine how we can best take advantage of our current resources and staffing.*
	TRANSLATION: *You're fired! The company will try to help you find another job and let you use our phones and e-mail for two months while you look for work.*

After studying the words above, use them in the sentences below.

1. Job redefinition caused _____ in work some employees were not suited for.
2. Twenty men and women lost their jobs in the company's _____, but they stayed on for a couple of months to use the phones.
3. Because of _____ jobs and titles were reshuffled.
4. The company was losing money, so it began _____.

Test Yourself: Place the letter next to the number to match word and meaning.

1. proactive downsizing
2. work reengineering
3. outplacing
4. employee repositioning

a. you're fired, but use our resources to find new work
b. you're fired; jobs are being redefined
c. you're fired; title and positions are being shuffled
d. you were a manager; now you're a file clerk

On a separate sheet of paper, write a sentence using these words.

DID YOU KNOW?
What did Shakespeare mean by "taffeta phrases" in these lines?

Taffeta phrases, silken terms precise, Three-piled hyperboles. Love's Labor Lost, V. ii.

He suggested something like euphemisms—smooth, silk phrases. *Taffeta,* a word that comes from the Persian "to twist," is a smooth, silken fabric.

preowned	These are used cars on this lot.
	WORDS IN CONTEXT: *People who invented this euphemism—**preowned**—must have got really tired of jokes about used car salesmen.*
	TRANSLATION: *Whatever you call this item for sale, look for dings, dents, and any tinkerings with the odometer.*
customer care representative	This is a telemarketer; make no mistake about it.
	WORDS IN CONTEXT: *"I'm your customer care representative with a new offer for you, and I hope you love your new slender-designed, guaranteed, Art Deco toaster, with an extra-wide slot for bagels."*
	TRANSLATION: *Our self-identified **customer care representative** is caring for us by calling again as we sit down to dinner.*
free gift	Be assured, somebody wants your money.
	WORDS IN CONTEXT: *Only advertisers or others who want your business or backing will offer you a **free gift**.*
	TRANSLATION: *Gifts, by definition, are free. When you encounter this redundancy, turn it down. Somebody wants your money.*
special criteria	Restrictions, limitations, and hedges.
	WORDS IN CONTEXT: *"This once-in-a-lifetime offer is worth many dollars to you. (Read the back of this coupon for **special criteria**.)"*
	TRANSLATION: *Read the fine print carefully. The once-in-a-lifetime offer may not apply in 48 states, and anyway it expired last week. (Other **special criteria** in pale or small print to watch for: Blackout dates may apply. Actual results may vary. Subject to availability. Annual percentage rate may vary, and so on....)*

After studying the words above, use them in the sentences below.

1. Only people who want your money offer you a _____.
2. Restrictions on offers are often called_____.
3. With cars, the euphemism is _____; with clothes, it's "gently worn."
4. Our _____called us after we'd already gone to bed.

Test Yourself: Place the letter next to the number to match word and meaning.

1. special criteria	a. your own special telemarketer
2. preowned	b. tiny print hedges
3. free gift	c. somebody else had it first
4. customer care representative	d. a redundant present

On a separate sheet of paper, write a sentence using each of these words.

DID YOU KNOW?
In his novel *1984*, George Orwell coined the words *newspeak* and *doublethink* for language that basically hides the harshness of the truth. Many euphemisms, especially in the hands of propagandists, operate as *newspeak* and *doublethink*.

passed on	Died.
	WORDS IN CONTEXT: *"My grandfather **passed on** a decade ago."*
	TRANSLATION: *My grandfather died a decade ago.*

remains	Corpse or body.
	WORDS IN CONTEXT: *The soldier's **remains** were placed in Memorial Cemetery.*
	TRANSLATION: *The soldier's **body** was buried in Memorial Cemetery.*

effects	The personal belongings of someone who has died.
	WORDS IN CONTEXT: *There is some dispute among his heirs about his **effects**.*
	TRANSLATION: *His children are arguing about his possessions.*

differently abled	Disabled, needs special help.
	WORDS IN CONTEXT: *Johnny's third grade teacher found him to be a **differently abled** child.*
	TRANSLATION: *Johnny's teacher found that Johnny needed special help.*

After studying the words and phrases above, use them in the sentences below.

1. She told me that a friend had _____, so I knew the friend had died.
2. They brought his body home in a flag-draped coffin and placed the _____ in a local cemetery.
3. My grandfather asked the family to go through our grandmother's _____ and help him decide what to do with them.
4. In the social worker's jargon, Pat was _____, but he was only mildly dyslexic.

Test Yourself: Place the letter next to the number to match words and meaning.

1. differently abled	a. euphemism for death
2. to pass on	b. euphemism for needs special help
3. remains	c. euphemism for body or corpse
4. effects	d. the deceased's personal belongings

On a separate sheet of paper, write a sentence using each of these words or phrases.

DID YOU KNOW?
In the nineteenth century, southern politicians substituted *our peculiar institution* for the shameful word slavery.

misdeeds	Crimes. **WORDS IN CONTEXT:** *The politician was indicted for the **misdeeds** he is alleged to have committed while he was in office.* **TRANSLATION:** The politician was indicted for the crimes he is alleged to have committed while he was in office.
sources	Informants. **WORDS IN CONTEXT:** *Highly placed **sources** said that fighting will continue in Falluja.* **TRANSLATION:** ***Informants** said that fighting will continue in Falluja.*
irregularities	Fraud. **WORDS IN CONTEXT:** *The auditors discovered **irregularities** in the financial structures at Enron.* **TRANSLATION:** The auditors discovered **fraud** at Enron.
unethical	Dishonest. **WORDS IN CONTEXT:** *The senator was found to be **unethical** in his financial dealings.* **TRANSLATION:** *The senator was found to be **dishonest** in his use of finances.*

After studying the words above, use them in the sentences below.

1. The investigators found fraud, or what they called_____ in the firm's books.
2. The Ethics Committee found the congressman_____, but his colleagues knew he had been dishonest.
3. The man never said that he lied; he said that he misspoke. He never committed a crime, but he was found guilty of _____.
4. The government said its _____were reliable, but instead the informants deliberately gave it incorrect information.

Test Yourself: Place the letter next to the number to match word and meaning.

1. misdeeds   a. informants
2. unethical   b. crimes
3. irregularities   c. dishonesty
4. sources   d. fraud

On a separate sheet of paper, write a sentence using each of these words.

DID YOU KNOW? The word *agitprop* is a portmanteau word. A portmanteau word is two words put together like a portmanteau suitcase with two compartments. The compartments are *agitate* and *propaganda*. The first word gives plain old propaganda a bit of edge.

Golden Words

Some words here denote golden; some connote golden; and some are here because they're as desirable as gold.

DAY 1

| coruscate | googol | halcyon | jeroboam |

DAY 2

| zenith | sumptuous | surfeit | beatific |

DAY 3

| epiphany | bargain | perquisites | rectitude |

DAY 4

| elixir | numinous | ambrosia | paragon |

DAY 5

| chaytoyant | opulence | incandescence | clairvoyance |

DAY 6

| apotheosis | aura | tranquility | approbation |

DAY 7

| luster | eminence | iridescent | gilt |

coruscate	Glitter, sparkle, shimmer, emit flashes of light.
	WORDS IN CONTEXT: *We watched the jewels in the handle of the ancient sword in the museum **coruscate** in the light.*
googol	Number 1 followed by 100 zeros; 10 to the 100th degree; any very large number.
	WORDS IN CONTEXT: *Googolplex is number 1 followed by a **googol** of zeros—a golden word when preceded by a dollar sign.*
halcyon	Tranquil, happy, idyllic, usually with a nostalgic reference.
	WORDS IN CONTEXT: *We looked back on our wedding trip to Hawaii as the **halcyon** days of our marriage.*
jeroboam	A large bottle of wine or champagne that holds about .8 gallon; a large bowl or goblet.
	WORDS IN CONTEXT: *In the Bible, **Jeroboam** was the first King of Israel; it is unclear how much wine he drank at a sitting, but the very large wine bottle is said to be an allusion to Jeroboam "a mighty man of valour" (I Kings, 11.28) "who made Israel to sin" (xiv.16).*

After studying the words above, use each in a sentence below.

1. As the celebration continued, they finished their _____ of champagne.
2. _____ is one of the largest numbers used in mathematics.
3. On the red carpet, her sequined dress seemed to _____ in the flashbulb pops.
4. To many Americans, the immediate post-World War II years remain the_____ days.

Test Yourself: Write the word that best fits the meaning given.

1. a very large bottle of wine _____
2. happy, nostalgic times _____
3. a very large number _____
4. glitter, sparkle, shimmer _____

On a separate sheet of paper, write a sentence using each of these words.

DID YOU KNOW?
Money was once liquid. The word *currency* can be traced back through several changes to the Latin verb meaning "to run"—as in liquid. The word and meaning changed over the centuries, but it finally took on the sense of coins, much as we use it today. Ben Franklin first recorded the word in this sense in 1729. Too bad the meaning changed: we could use more liquid funds.

zenith	The point in the sky directly overhead; the highest point, culmination, summit.
	WORDS IN CONTEXT: *The man was at the **zenith** of his career when he retired.*
sumptuous	Costly, lavish, magnificent, or splendid in furnishings; involving great expense.
	WORDS IN CONTEXT: *The wedding feast was **sumptuous** as was the hall in which it was held.*
surfeit	Overindulgence, especially in food and drink; too great an amount; to indulge to excess.
	WORDS IN CONTEXT: *At the resort where we stayed, we found a **surfeit** of pleasures.*
beatific	Blissful or blessed; showing happiness, delight, as a creature blessed by heaven.
	WORDS IN CONTEXT: *Dressed in white and singing in the Christmas program, the little girl looked **beatific**.*

After studying the words above, use each in a sentence below.

1. They needed to diet after the _____ of treats over the weekend.
2. He used his company's money to provide the _____ birthday party for his wife—and got into very big trouble.
3. For baseball teams, winning the World Series represents the _____ of their plans.
4. Her _____ smile belied a coarse mind.

Test Yourself: Write the word that best fits the meaning given below.

1. blessed _____
2. overindulgence _____
3. highest point _____
4. lavish _____

On a separate sheet of paper, write a sentence using each of these new words.

DID YOU KNOW?
Young people with a *curfew* might impress their parents if they had knowledge of the word's original meaning. (Recommended use: When you come in late and need to do some fast talking.) *Curfew*, from Old French *cuevrefeu* (*couvir*: to cover) and (*feu*: fire), meant that all fires must be covered at a particular hour when the curfew bell was rung. Presumably, this was to protect the village from night fires. So put out the fires early, and get home on time.

epiphany	An appearance or manifestation of god or other supernatural beings; also (usually capitalized) a Christian religious rite.
	WORDS IN CONTEXT: *In many Christian churches, **Epiphany** is a yearly religious festival occurring on January 6. Also, **epiphanies** are seen as breakthroughs to a spiritual realm that can occur in our routine, daily lives.*
bargain	Something offered, bought, or sold at a price favorable to the buyer; the terms of a mutual agreement; to discuss the details of a transaction.
	WORDS IN CONTEXT: *No list of "golden words" would be complete without the simple word **bargain**— something we all look for, anticipate, and finally expect.*
perquisites	Something added to regular profits or pay resulting from one's position or employment; a privilege or benefit to which a person is entitled by virtue of status. Most commonly used in abbreviated form as **perks.**
	WORDS IN CONTEXT: *One of the first questions a job candidate has when offered a position is: What are the **perks**? **Perquisites**—a company car, or a computer at home—make the job more attractive.*
rectitude	Conduct according to moral principles; strict honesty, uprightness of character, correct judgment.
	WORDS IN CONTEXT: *People rarely doubted the words of the judge, who they felt was filled with **rectitude**.*

After studying the words above, use each in a sentence below.

1. He had an_____, which enabled him to crack the code he had been challenged by for years.
2. We hope for but often don't find _____in our politicians.
3. Lunch in the executive dining room was one of the _____of her new job.
4. Buying gasoline at a discount is always a _____because your car must have gasoline to run.

Test Yourself: Write the word that best fits the meaning given below.

1. moral, honest, upright, good judgment _____
2 a benefit or entitlement_____
3. breakthrough in mundane world to the world beyond _____
4. buyer likes the price_____

On a separate sheet of paper, write a sentence using each of these words.

DID YOU KNOW?
O. Henry took his name from a prison guard. William Sidney Porter (O. Henry's real name) was a private person who didn't reveal much about himself, but he did serve three years in the Ohio Federal Penitentiary for bank fraud. During that time, a guard, Orrin Henry, was particularly influential, and the writer decided to follow the straight and narrow. After he left prison, O. Henry wrote "A Retrieved Reformation"— and many other stories. His life as well as many of his stories had a surprise ending.

elixir	Medieval alchemists sought this hypothetical substance to change base metals into gold; also, a supposed remedy, a panacea, for all ailments. **WORDS IN CONTEXT:** *The elixir of Life, were it ever discovered, is thought to prolong life indefinitely.*
numinous	Supernatural; divine; having deeply spiritual or mystical effects. **WORDS IN CONTEXT:** *The evening, with its fresh air, music, and touching words, had a numinous effect.*
ambrosia	The food of the gods in Greek and Roman myth; anything tasting and smelling delicious; a specific food made with whipped cream, coconut, and pineapple. **WORDS IN CONTEXT:** *The dinner was so perfect that every dish tasted like ambrosia.*
paragon	A model or pattern of perfection or excellence; a large, perfect diamond or pearl. **WORDS IN CONTEXT:** *The student saw her mentor as a paragon she hoped to emulate.*

After studying the words above, use each in a sentence below.

1. Aspirin might be the closest thing to an_____ that we have.
2. The priest was a _____of virtue, or so his congregation thought.
3. Climbing in the Himalayas gave her a _____ feeling, no matter how often she did it.
4. All the restaurant's desserts seemed to be concoctions of _____.

Test Yourself: Write the word that best fits the meaning given below.

1. deeply spiritual or mystical_____
2. a model of perfection _____
3. believed to change base metal into gold; a panacea _____
4. delicious in all ways _____

On a separate sheet of paper, write a sentence using each of these words.

DID YOU KNOW?
The Rockbottom Remainders is a band consisting of 11 American writers, which performs sporadically, without, they claim, ever rehearsing. They take themselves seriously as writers, and they take themselves, well, out in public, as musicians. Everyone has a lot of fun. The writers are Stephen King, Amy Tan, Scott Turow, Ridley Pearson, Mitch Albom, Dave Barry, Roy Blount, Jr., Kathy Goldmark, Matt Groening, Greg Iles, and James McBride. (*Remainders*, by the way, is the term for publishers' overstock offered for sale at a reduced price, usually of books that don't sell, and *rockbottom* is self-explanatory.)

chaytoyant	From a French word meaning "cat-like," pronounced "shat'-way-on." Having a changeable, undulating luster like that of a cat's eye in the dark; also, a type of stone, also known as a cat's eye.
	WORDS IN CONTEXT: *In the poem "The Cat and the Moon" (1918), W. B. Yeats writes these words describing the **chaytoyant** eyes of the cat Minnaloushe:*
	Does Minnaloushe know that his pupils *Will pass from change to change,* *And from round to crescent,* *From crescent to round they range?* *Minnaloushe creeps through the grass* *Alone, important and wise,* *And lifts to the changing moon* *His changing eyes.*
opulence	Having much wealth or property; rich; characterized by abundance, profusion, and luxuriance.
	WORDS IN CONTEXT: *The **opulence** of the palaces we visited in England was overwhelming **ineffable**.*
incandescence	Glowing with intense heat; red hot or white hot; shining brilliantly; gleaming.
	WORDS IN CONTEXT: *The lighting in the ballroom gave an appearance of **incandescence** to everyone and everything there.*
clairvoyance	The supposed ability to see things not in sight or that cannot be seen; keen perception or insight. A specific type of clairvoyance is *precognition*, the alleged ability to actually foresee (as opposed to logically predict) the course of future events.
	WORDS IN CONTEXT: *The woman claimed **clairvoyance**, but the man doubted that such abilities exist.*

After studying the words above, use each in a sentence below.

1. Their country home offered a stunning display of_____.
2. Her performance was nothing short of _____, the critics agreed.
3. Only a gambler with_____ should bet on horse races.
4. In the twilight, the woman's green eyes held a _____ quality, almost feline.

Test Yourself: Write the word that best fits the meaning given below.

1. shining brilliantly, gleaming _____
2. ability to see things not in sight _____
3. abundance, profusion, luxuriant _____
4. like the eyes of a cat_____

On a separate sheet of paper, write a sentence using each of these words.

DID YOU KNOW?
Where is Thomas Hardy's heart? Here's a tale about the heart of the author of *Return of the Native, Tess of the D'Urbervilles, Jude the Obscure,* and more who died in 1928. It seems that he wanted his heart to be buried next to his wife, Emma. But somehow, his remains—minus his heart—were buried in the Poet's Corner of Westminster Abbey. His heart was sent to his family to bury as he wished. (Are you sure you want the full story?) His heart, placed on a kitchen counter to be buried next to Emma, was devoured by the family cat. This story, while not confirmed, is thought to be true.

apotheosis	The act of raising a person to the level of a god; deification, glorification; a glorified ideal.
	WORDS IN CONTEXT: *He saw the opera star as the **apotheosis** of musical excellence.*
aura	Invisible emanation from a person or thing of grandeur; a particular atmosphere surrounding something.
	WORDS IN CONTEXT: *We liked the **aura** of the environment and so decided to camp in the mountains.*
tranquility	A state of calmness and serenity.
	WORDS IN CONTEXT: ***Tranquility** surrounded them as they rowed the small boat down the stream.*
approbation	Official approval, sanction, or commendation.
	WORDS IN CONTEXT: *The scientist enjoyed the **approbation** of his colleagues.*

After studying the words above, use each in a sentence below.

1. His last novel was the _____ of a long career.
2. She exuded an _____ of control every time she entered the stage.
3. The silent and calm Sea of _____ seemed the safest place for a moon landing.
4. One needs the _____ of officious clerks to get a driver's license.

Test Yourself: Write the word that best fits the meaning given below.

1. calmness and serenity _____
2. official approval _____
3. invisible emanation _____
4. raising a human to the level of a god _____

On a separate sheet of paper, write a sentence using each of these words.

DID YOU KNOW?
Is oxygen an acid? French chemist Lavoisier in the eighteenth century thought so when he misnamed "oxygen." The word oxygene meaning "acid-born" was adopted by the chemist who isolated the element because he then thought oxygen was a component of acid. Not true, but we could, and do, breathe a lot worse things.

luster	Shining in reflected light, gloss, sheen, radiance; great fame or distinction.
	WORDS IN CONTEXT: *Being in the presence of the great man seemed to cast a **luster** on us all.*
eminence	Greatness, celebrity, superior in rank, position, character, achievement; a title of honor; a high or lofty place.
	WORDS IN CONTEXT: *The **eminence** of the artist who had invited them to the gallery prompted them to change their plans in order to go.*
iridescent	Showing shifting changes in color or an interplay of rainbowlike colors, when seen from different angles.
	WORDS IN CONTEXT: *The girls shopped for prom dresses together and both were taken by the **iridescent sheen** of the gowns they were shown.*
gilt	Overlaid with a thin layer of gold, making the object appear more attractive or valuable than it is.
	WORDS IN CONTEXT: *The **gilt** candelabra shone in the soft lights of the room, and the **gilt**-edged paper of the leather-bound books looked expensive.*

After studying the words above, use each in a sentence below.

1. The gleaming _____ picture frames of the family's ancestors lined the walls of the dining room.
2. Her eyes changed color in the light and seemed to dance with_____ when she smiled.
3 The university's president had achieved _____in many fields.
4. Her freshly shampooed hair pleased her with its_____.

Test Yourself: Write the word that best fits the meaning given below.

1. showing an interplay of colors_____
2. gold plate or veneer _____
3. greatness in character and achievement_____
4. sheen, gloss, radiance _____

On a separate sheet of paper, write a sentence using each of these words.

DID YOU KNOW?
The true Americanism "pan out" was first used in gold mining. You can guess why. "Pan" as a noun is in one sense a metal vessel used in washing gold from gravel, and "pan out" in all its original senses had to do with washing gold in a pan. It has come to mean that things turned out well, as in "it all panned out in the end."

Legal Words

Legal words are used in our daily conversations and transactions.
Many of these words are used in the original Latin; some have become
so commonplace in our vocabulary that they no longer warrant italics.

DAY 1

| moot | prima facie | ipso facto | pro tempore |

DAY 2

| amicus curiae | brief | restraining order | recidivism |

DAY 3

| paralegal | corpus delicti | defamation | in camera |

DAY 4

| grand jury | plaintiff | defendant | verdict |

DAY 5

| pro bono | class action | fiduciary | habeas corpus |

DAY 6

| conspiracy | de jure | de facto | voir dire |

DAY 7

| tort | subpoena | exclusionary rule | cross-examination |

moot	Subject to or open for discussion or debate; debatable; so hypothetical as to be meaningless. In a legal context, a case is considered moot when there is no reason to decide it. **WORDS IN CONTEXT:**: *After the competing parties agreed to merge, their lawsuit became **moot**.*
prima facie	Evidence that is sufficient to establish a fact in the absence of any evidence to the contrary, but the evidence is not conclusive and is subject to contrary evidence. **WORDS IN CONTEXT:** *He made a **prima facie** case for joining the select group.*
ipso facto	By that very fact itself; speaks for itself. **WORDS IN CONTEXT:** *His arrival showed **ipso facto** that he was not ignoring his old friends.*
pro tempore	For the time being; temporary or temporarily; often shortened to ***pro tem**.* **WORDS IN CONTEXT:** *While the mayor was sick, the president of the City Council became mayor **pro tem**.*

After studying the words above, use each in a sentence below.

1. A 100-year-old man became president_____ of the U.S. Senate.
2. Law students hone their skills in _____court cases.
3. His argument made sense_____, but they had not heard from the other side.
4. That silly statement showed_____that you don't know what you're talking about.

Test Yourself: Write the word that best fits the meaning given below.

1. for the time being _____
2. speaks for itself _____
3. no reason to decide the case_____
4. evidence is sufficient on the face of it, but is not conclusive_____

On a separate sheet of paper, write a sentence using each of these words.

DID YOU KNOW?
The word *sneeze* comes from an Old English word *fneoson*. Somewhere along the line—perhaps in medieval manuscripts where *f* and *s* could easily be mistaken—the word dropped its *f* and became an *s*. So the word developed into a cold sneeze rather than a cold freeze—which makes some sense because the original *fneoson* is related to the Greek term *pneuma*, "breath."

amicus curiae	Friend of the court; a person who is not a party to a case but offers, or is called in, to advise a court on some legal matter.
	WORDS IN CONTEXT: *In major Supreme Court cases, dozens of* **amicus curiae** *briefs are sometimes filed.*
brief	A written argument filed with a court before a trial or appellate hearing.
	WORDS IN CONTEXT: *Again, in major Supreme Court cases, dozens of* amicus curiae **briefs** *are sometimes filed.*
restraining order	An order to prevent some action until a hearing can be held on that action.
	WORDS IN CONTEXT: *The company won a* **restraining order** *against the strike.*
recidivism	Habitual or chronic relapse, or tendency to relapse into crime or antisocial behavior.
	WORDS IN CONTEXT: *Many criminologists believe that serious prison sentences do not curtail* **recidivism**.

After studying the words above, use each in a sentence below.

1. Writing a strong _____requires lengthy research.
2. The _____rate is falling among young male convicts.
3. The actress won a _____ against her alleged stalker.
4. The ACLU frequently files _____briefs in civil rights cases.

Test Yourself: Write the word that best fits the meaning given below.

1. an order to prevent action _____
2. a written argument filed with the court _____
3. habitual or chronic relapse into crime
4. friend of the court _____

On a separate sheet of paper, write a sentence using each of these words.

DID YOU KNOW?
What happened when an ancient army was defeated? It was "subjugated." Survivors were made to walk under two upright spears with another spear as a crossbar on top to form a sort of yoke. The Latin subjugare means "to bring under the yoke." The Romans didn't like that much—just as nobody today likes to be subjugated.

paralegal	A person not formally educated as a lawyer, but who has some experience and knowledge about law and can provide certain basic assistance to lawyers. **WORDS IN CONTEXT:** *She worked as a **paralegal** to earn enough money to attend law school.*
corpus delicti	The person or object against whom a crime has been committed. **WORDS IN CONTEXT:** *No murder charges could be filed until the police found the **corpus delicti.***
defamation	Damaging a person's reputation through written word (libel) or speech (slander). **WORDS IN CONTEXT:** *Some listeners thought his speech contained words of **defamation** about them.*
in camera	Literally meaning "in chambers," this is a judicial proceeding that excludes the public, but it need not be held in the judge's chambers. **WORDS IN CONTEXT:** *The lawyers met with the judge **in camera** to decide if the evidence would be allowed.*

After studying the words above, use each in a sentence below.

1. Some states require police to produce a_____; others do not.
2. _____ of character is considered a tort in the law.
3. The firm fired a number of young associate lawyers and replaced them with_____.
4. What courts call_____, boards of directors may call *executive sessions*.

Test Yourself: Write the word that best fits the meaning given below.

1. a judicial proceeding "in chambers" _____
2. libeling or slandering a person _____
3. performs certain basic assistance to lawyers _____
4 victim of a crime _____

On a separate sheet of paper, write a sentence using each of these words.

DID YOU KNOW? What does the word *testicle* have to do with *testify* and *testimony*? All go back to the Latin word *testis* meaning witness. Some etymologists think that this usage could be as a result of a testicle being a witness to virility.

328

grand jury	A jury composed of 12 to 23 people appointed to review a possible case of criminal activity, to report on it, and to indict a person when it finds evidence that he or she may have committed a crime. **WORDS IN CONTEXT:** *Because no defense evidence can be presented, prosecutors usually get the result they want from a **grand jury**.*
plaintiff	The person or organization that brings the suit. **WORDS IN CONTEXT:** *A father served as **plaintiff** in the suit on behalf of his daughter.*
defendant	The person or organization being sued. **WORDS IN CONTEXT:** *He became a **defendant** in suits from all his neighbors about the hygienic condition of his home.*
verdict	A jury or judge's finding of fact. This is not the final disposition of the case, however, for a judge can overturn a jury's verdict; in addition, many jury verdicts are overturned on appeal. **WORDS IN CONTEXT:** *The businesswoman decided to accept the jury's **verdict** and go to jail before her appeal was heard.*

After studying the words above, use each word in a sentence below.

1. The _____ handed up 14 indictments last week.
2. The lawyer announced immediately after the _____ that he would appeal.
3. The city government is accustomed to being a _____ in lawsuits.
4. As the _____ of record, Linda Brown's father became a historic figure.

Test Yourself: Write the word that best fits the meaning given below.

1. a judge or jury's finding of fact _____
2. the person or organization being sued _____
3. the party or parties that bring the suit _____
4. a jury of 12 to 23 people appointed to review a criminal case _____

On a separate sheet of paper, write a sentence using each of these words.

DID YOU KNOW?
How do you keep a volcano from erupting? Feed it a fish. The word *volcano*, which as we know means a mountain capable of pouring out molten lava, is derived from the name of the Roman god Vulcan, who was responsible for fire. In Rome at the festival of Volcanalia, a burnt offering of fish from the Tiber River was made to Vulcan, perhaps to persuade the god to keep his temper and forgo erupting.

pro bono	A *pro bono* attorney takes a case without a fee, often to back a cause he or she believes in or to help someone who cannot afford a lawyer.
	WORDS IN CONTEXT: *In most large law firms, senior partners do not perform as much* **pro bono** *work as their junior associates.*
class action	A lawsuit brought by a group of people who have a shared interest in it.
	WORDS IN CONTEXT: *The women filed a* **class-action suit** *against the maker of breast implants.*
fiduciary	A trusted person who acts for another person—executor, guardian, agent, or boards of directors, for example.
	WORDS IN CONTEXT: *The board of directors did not fulfill its* **fiduciary** *responsibilities to the shareholders.*
habeas corpus	A judge's order to determine the legality of imprisonment.
	WORDS IN CONTEXT: *They filed a writ of* **habeas corpus** *on behalf of prisoners detained without counsel.*

After studying the words above, use each in a sentence below.

1. The bank served as _____ of the trust.
2. Abraham Lincolm suspended _____ during the Civil War.
3. _____ suits often prove more profitable for lawyers than for the plaintiffs.
4. He charged $600 an hour for his business clients, but he chose to spend many hours doing _____ work for the poor.

Test Yourself: Write the word that best fits the meaning given below.

1. a judge's order regarding legality of imprisonment _____
2. executor or guardian, for example _____
3. an attorney who takes a case without a fee _____
4. a lawsuit brought by a group with an interest in it _____

On a separate sheet of paper, write a sentence using each of these words.

DID YOU KNOW?
What are "cockles"? A lot of strange things. First, cockles are scallops—those mollusks whose muscle is good to eat. Then, there are cockle shells—small boats. Also, there's the cockle hat that English pilgrims wore. Then add these: the game of hot cockles in which players cover their eyes, put their heads in another's lap and guess who gave them a blow on the backside; cockles of the heart—presumably the ventricles; and "to try cockles," meaning to be hanged, gurgling from strangulation. None of these clarify what Mistress Mary had in her garden along with her silver bells and pretty maids all in a row.

conspiracy	A plot among two or more people to break the law.
	WORDS IN CONTEXT: *The corporate officers were not charged individually, but they were accused of* **conspiracy** *to mislead their employees.*
de jure	A practice backed by law.
	WORDS IN CONTEXT: *Until the Brown vs the Board of Education decision in 1954,* **de jure** *segregation of schools by race prevailed in most of the South.*
de facto	A practice backed by custom.
	WORDS IN CONTEXT: *After the Brown decision in 1954 held racial segregation of schools to be unconstitutional, neighborhood housing patterns in many places led to* **de facto** *segregation.*
voir dire	The interrogation of people called to jury duty to determine their qualification as jurors: also a trial hearing without the jury to determine a matter, such as whether a confession is valid. From the French "voir" (true, or the truth) and "dire" (to say). Pronounced "vwar deer."
	WORDS IN CONTEXT: *Her skilled* **voir dire** *of prospective jurors got a sympathetic jury for her client.*

After studying the words above, use each in a sentence below.

1. Some older people are anxious as they face _____ examination.
2. He accused the political opponents of a vast_____.
3. Many universities are _____biased in favor of alumni children.
4. He argued that his position must prevail_____.

Test Yourself: Write the word that best fits the meaning given below.

1. interrogation of those called to jury duty _____
2. a practice backed by custom _____
3. a practice backed by law_____
4. two or more people plot to break the law _____

On a separate sheet of paper, write a sentence using each of these words.

DID YOU KNOW? Where did we get the word *ditto*? It comes from the Latin *dictum*, meaning "that which has been said before; the same or a similar thing." In addition, *dittoes* means a coat, a waistcoat, and trousers all to match.

tort	An act, usually by negligence, that harms a person or a person's property—for example, the result of an automobile accident. **WORDS IN CONTEXT:** *Her expertise in **tort** law won her many clients in traffic-accident cases.*
subpoena	A written order from the court requiring a person to testify at a specific judicial proceeding. **WORDS IN CONTEXT:** *The reporter was issued a grand jury **subpoena**, which attempted to force him to reveal his source for the story.*
exclusionary rule	The preventing of introduction at trial of evidence obtained as a result of unreasonable searches and seizures. **WORDS IN CONTEXT:** *The **exclusionary rule** kept the prosecutor from using the evidence police obtained without a search warrant.*
cross-examination	Interrogation of a witness who has already offered testimony in an attempt to discredit him or her or shed new light on that testimony. **WORDS IN CONTEXT:** *His story collapsed under the withering **cross-examination**.*

After studying the words or phrases above, use each in a sentence below.

1. The most common type of lawsuit falls in the _____ category.
2. Lawyers should never ask a question on _____ that they do not already know the answer to.
3. The _____ spares some defendants because police violated the law in gathering evidence.
4. Anyone would be uncomfortable upon receiving a _____ to appear before a federal grand jury.

Test Yourself: Write the word or phrases that best fits the meaning given below.

1. a court order requiring a person to testify _____
2. usually an act of negligence that injures another party _____
3. prevents evidence in court obtained by unreasonable searches and seizures

   _____
4. interrogation of a witness who has already been questioned _____

On a separate sheet of paper, write a sentence using each of these words or phrases.

DID YOU KNOW?
What does *fee simple* mean? It's a property held by a person in his or her own right, free from limitations. A conditional fee simple is one granted with conditions, which, if unfulfilled, gives the grantor the right to enter.

Dirty Words

Here are some dirty words, both literally and figuratively. It's good to know them, but be careful of when and where you use them!

DAY 1

fetid	chthonic	salaceous	anathema

DAY 2

scatology	bawdy	lubricity	squalid

DAY 3

lurid	coprophagous	prurient	incestuous

DAY 4

venal	turpitude	vinasse	priapism

DAY 5

libidinous	clamjamphrie	feisty	fud

DAY 6

detritus	butt	licentious	calumny

DAY 7

voluptuary	iniquitous	nefarious	eviscerate

fetid	Having a bad smell, as of decay; stinking; putrid. **WORDS IN CONTEXT:** *The airport restroom has a **fetid** smell.*
chthonic	Of or pertaining to the underworld; infernal. From the Greek *chthōn*, meaning "earth." **WORDS IN CONTEXT:** *The unlit caverns seemed frighteningly **chthonic**.*
salacious	Lecherous; erotically stimulating; pornographic. **WORDS IN CONTEXT:** *At one time, many movie theaters near Times Square showed **salacious** films.*
anathema	Anything accursed or assigned to damnation; also, any curse or imprecation. Originally, **anathema** (from the Greek) meant "a thing devoted to divine use"; later, it took on the meaning of a curse. **WORDS IN CONTEXT:** *The Pope condemned the war, but no heed was paid to his **anathema**.*

After studying the words above, use each in a sentence below.

1. During the Civil War, slavery was _____ to the Union soldiers.
2. The book appeared tame to some, but I considered it_____.
3. Peering into the _____ depths, Hercules could not decide whether to enter the gates of Hades.
4. The_____ odor of the decomposed body made the detective sick.

Test Yourself: Write the word that best fits the meaning given below.

1. stinks_____
2. underworldly _____
3. lecherous _____
4. a curse _____

On a separate sheet of paper, write a sentence using each of these words.

DID YOU KNOW? Where does the word *shyster* come from? If you think the word goes with *lawyer*, you may be right. Some experts say the word comes from the name of a Mr. Sheuster, a nineteenth-century lawyer of disrepute. Others claim that the word comes from the German *scheisser*, meaning "one who defecates," a German pejorative. In any case, it's a dirty word.

scatology	Obscenity or obsession with the obscene, especially with excrement or excretion in literature.
	WORDS IN CONTEXT: *Scatology originally referred to the study of feces or of fossil excrement.*
bawdy	Indecent, obscene, salacious, licentious.
	WORDS IN CONTEXT: *Bawdy is characteristic of a **bawd**—a loose woman, or the madam of a brothel.*
lubricity	Trickiness, shiftiness, lewdness.
	WORDS IN CONTEXT: *Lubricity derives from a word meaning "lubricant," indicating slipperiness.*
squalid	Foul or unclean, especially as a result of neglect or unsanitary conditions; wretched; miserable.
	WORDS IN CONTEXT: *The city officials tried to find healthier quarters for people living in **squalid** conditions.*

After studying the words above, use each in a sentence below.

1. Because of official corruption, everyone in the district lived in _____ apartments.
2. The major's _____ enabled him to escape his many lies.
3. The coarse barmaid in Shakespeare's play used _____ language.
4. The novelist Henry Miller was once accused of using _____ to shock readers.

Test Yourself: Write the word that best fits the meaning given below.

1. tricky and slippery _____
2. foul; unsanitary _____
3. indecent, salacious _____
4. obscenity; obsessed with body excrement _____

On a separate sheet of paper, write a sentence using each of these words.

DID YOU KNOW?
Dr. Fell was a real person. The Dr. Fell about whom this famous ditty was written: *"I do not love thee, Dr. Fell/ The reason why I cannot tell / But this alone I know full well / I do not love thee, Dr. Fell."* Yes, he was Dr. John Fell, Dean of Christ Church, and Bishop of Oxford (1625–1686), who expelled the author of the ditty, Tom Brown (1663–1704), but said he would reinstate the student if he translated the following: *"Non amo te, Sabidi, nee possum dicere quare; / Hoc tantum possum, dicere, non amo te."* Brown is said to have given the Dr. Fell translation (with a little twist) on the spot. The literal translation from Martial, *Epigram i.33:* *"I do not love thee, Sabidius, nor can I say why; this only I can say, I do not love thee."*

lurid	Vivid in a harsh and shocking way; characterized by a violent passion or crime.
	WORDS IN CONTEXT: *The pulp magazine was filled with **lurid** tales of crimes of passion.*
coprophagous	Feeding on dung, as some beetles do.
	WORDS IN CONTEXT: *A **coprophagous** person suffers from **coprophilia**, an abnormal interest in feces.*
prurient	Having or expressing lustful ideas or desires; tending to excite lust; lascivious, lewd.
	WORDS IN CONTEXT: *In the film, the man had a **prurient** interest in the woman into whose window he could see across the alley.*
incestuous	A sexual relationship between two people too closely related to be legally married.
	WORDS IN CONTEXT: *Oedipus and Jocasta went mad because they discovered their sexual relationship was **incestuous**: they were son and mother.*

After studying the words above, use each in a sentence below.

1. The peeping Tom had a _____ interest in the women he saw through the windows.
2. Most of us can't imagine who would be interested enough in feces to be_____.
3. The students read _____ passages from pulp fiction to one another at night in the dorm.
4. The Bible describes an _____ relationship between a father and his two daughters.

Test Yourself: Write the word that best fits the meaning given below.

1. an illegal sexual relationship _____
2. lustful and lascivious _____
3. harsh, vivid, and shocking _____
4. one who eats foul matter _____

On a separate sheet of paper, write a sentence using each of these words.

DID YOU KNOW?
To what might "half fac'd groat" have been referring in these lines from Shakespeare's *King John* I, I: "With that half face would he have all my land/ A half fac'd groat five hundred pounds a-year!" The groats (silver coins) issued during the reign of Henry VIII had the king's head in profile. So this is a joke about the king's *head*.

venal	Characterized by corruption or bribery; referring to one who can easily be corrupted or bribed.
	WORDS IN CONTEXT: *Venal originated from a word that meant "sale"; it brought with it the sense of bribery or being corrupted for the right price or payment.*
turpitude	Baseness, vileness, depravity or an instance of this.
	WORDS IN CONTEXT: *The man's contract said that he could be fired from his position for moral **turpitude**.*
vinasse	The sediment left in a still after the process of distillation of wine.
	WORDS IN CONTEXT: *Usually the **vinasse** is discarded; sometimes vintners experiment with it to see whether it is usable.*
priapism	A pathological condition of persistent erection of the penis, especially without sexual excitement; a lascivious attitude.
	WORDS IN CONTEXT: ***Priapism** derives from a Greek and Roman mythological god, Priapus, the son of Dionysus and Aphrodite, who personified the male procreative power. Priapus is sometimes called Phallus.*

After studying the words above, use each in a sentence below.

1. A famous screen star was charged with_____ and went to prison.
2. The boys in *Oliver Twist* were sent out to beg and steal by a _____mentor.
3. Despite that Greek and Roman mythological god, we wonder if _____ is a physical or mental disorder—or maybe both.
4. The sediment left after making wine is_____.

Test Yourself: Write the word that best fits the meaning given below.

1. base, vile, depraved _____
2. corruption and bribery_____
3. walking around like this could be uncomfortable _____
4. at the bottom of the barrel _____

On a separate sheet of paper, write a sentence using each of these words.

DID YOU KNOW?
To what does the *Grand Guignol* refer? This is a series of macabre plays centered on the character *Guignol* (ge'nyol) in a popular eighteenth-century puppet show. A twentieth-century cult movie of that name is sometimes shown on or around Halloween in the United States.

libidinous	Characterized by lust; lewd; lascivious. **WORDS IN CONTEXT:** *The **libidinous** person is ruled by his or her uncontrolled libido—the sexual urge or instinct that can generate loving feelings, but that also can become perverted.*
clamjamphrie	Spoken rubbish, rot, trumpery (trash, deception); canaille (a pack of dogs). **WORDS IN CONTEXT:** *Only a vile person would use **clamjamphrie.***
feisty	Full of spirit; energetic, lively; also, quarrelsome and aggressive. **WORDS IN CONTEXT:** ***Feisty** is included here because it initially described a small, snappish dog that routinely "broke wind." **Feisty** may not necessarily be a flattering thing to call your spirited friend!*
fud	Backside or buttocks; the tail of a hare or rabbit. **WORDS IN CONTEXT:** *"Get your **fud** out of my yard," one rowdy boy shouted to another.*

After studying the words above, use each in a sentence below.

1. His _____ nature endeared him to some women, but offended others.
2. He unleashed a torrent of_____ that angered everyone around him.
3. Insulting, but colorful, words like_____, meaning backside or buttocks, would be used more often if more people knew them.
4. _____ is a word commonly used to describe spirited men and strong-willed women.

Test Yourself: Write the word that best fits the meaning given below.

1. backside _____
2. energetic, quarrelsome, aggressive _____
3. rubbish, rot, trash _____
4. lustful and lewd _____

On a separate sheet of paper, write a sentence using each of these words.

DID YOU KNOW?
What does a "knobstick" wedding refer to? In the eighteenth century, church wardens of a parish could use their authority to enforce the marriage of a pregnant woman. The term "knobstick" alluded to the warden's staff, his symbol of office. (This has nothing to do with a broomstick wedding; it's more like a shotgun wedding.)

detritus	Any accumulation of disintegrated material or debris.
	WORDS IN CONTEXT: *Detritus initially referred to fragments of rock produced by disintegration or wearing away.*
butt	Besides having the meaning of buttock, rump, or the thicker end of anything, **butt** has a number of other meanings, including: a flat fish such as a sole or fluke; a cask or barrel for wine; a measure of wine, usually 126 gallons; a terminal point or boundary mark; a short and stumpy object; a mound, hump, hillock, or promontory; a person made the object of a joke; a hinge or joint; and a bundle or pack.
	WORDS IN CONTEXT: *When used as a verb,* **butt** *means a push, thrust, or shove, usually with the head or horns, and* **to butt in** *is to intrude or meddle.*
licentious	Morally unrestrained, especially in sexual activity; disregarding of accepted rules and standards.
	WORDS IN CONTEXT: *The* **licentious** *man was arrested for stalking a young woman and making lewd remarks.*
calumny	False and malicious representation, to the injury of another; libelous detraction, slander.
	WORDS IN CONTEXT: *"I will not endure this* **calumny**!" *the woman shouted at the man who was accusing her falsely.*

After studying the words above, use each in a sentence below.

1. Sifting through the _____ of his notes, recovered from the fire, the reporter managed to fashion a telling political story.
2. Her disregard for rules and generally _____ behavior embarrassed the entire sorority.
3. In court, the accused felt the witness's lies were heaping _____ on him.
4. The little boy's mother told him that _____ was not necessarily a "bad word," but it was rude to call his sister that.

Test Yourself: Write the word that best fits the meaning given below.

1. libel, slander, false representation _____
2. ignores established rules and is unrestrained in sexual activity _____
3. rump, rear-end, thicker part of anything, and the object of a joke. _____
4. a bunch of debris _____

On a separate sheet of paper, write a sentence using each of these words.

DID YOU KNOW?
The renowned poet Ranier Maria Rilke earned his identity crisis the hard way. His mother lost a baby daughter, so when he came along, she compensated by dressing him in girl's clothes and calling him Sofia. When he was nine, his parents separated, and his father sent him to military school to which he had a difficult time adjusting.

voluptuary	A person devoted to luxurious living and sensual pleasures; a sensualist or sybarite.
	WORDS IN CONTEXT: A **voluptuary** is not necessarily voluptuous, at least in one sense: a voluptuous person usually has a full, shapely body that others find sexually attractive.
iniquitous	Wicked, unjust, vicious; lacking in righteousness.
	WORDS IN CONTEXT: The Bible points out **iniquitous** people as sinners.
nefarious	Base, wicked, villainous, iniquitous.
	WORDS IN CONTEXT: The gang had a **nefarious** way of operating that offended the residents of the neighborhood.
eviscerate	To remove the entrails of; to disembowel.
	WORDS IN CONTEXT: After the hunters killed the deer, they hung it up and **eviscerated** it.

After studying the words above, use each in a sentence below.

1. To remove the viscera or entrails from an animal or a human is to_____it.
2. I'm more than a little tired of his_____ schemes.
3. The preacher railed against _____men and women.
4. It never goes out of fashion—or out of human nature: Medieval kings and modern sheiks share some of the same _____ desires.

Test Yourself: Write the word that best fits the meaning given below.

1. wicked, unjust, vicious _____
2. base and villainous _____
3. a sensualist_____
4. remove entrails or guts

On a separate sheet of paper, write a sentence using each of these words.

DID YOU KNOW? A Mickey Mouse cartoon was banned because of Clarabelle's risqué reading habits. In 1932, Walt Disney's animated film *The Shindig* showed Clarabelle the Cow out in a pasture reading Elinor Glyn's novel *Three Weeks.* Some librarians were scandalized by the sexual nature of the book and removed it from libraries around the country. The film revealed nothing about the book except its cover. (Nor will we.)

Clean Words

Many ways exist to suggest squeaky clean. Try these.

DAY 1

| antimacassar | clarified | fastidious | meticulous |

DAY 2

| ablution | lavation | lustration | purgation |

DAY 3

| immaculate | unsullied | aseptic | cathartic |

DAY 4

| dentifrice | unadulterated | blanch | fumigation |

DAY 5

| wholesome | orderly | rarefied | methodical |

DAY 6

| swabbed | scrupulous | refined | elutriated |

DAY 7

| expurgate | saponify | edulcoration | filtered |

antimacassar	A covering, sometimes an ornamental doily, thrown over the backs of sofas or chairs to protect them from grease in the hair.
	WORDS IN CONTEXT: *"Macassar" was once a proprietary name for hair oil; thus **antimacassar**, to protect furniture from it.*
clarified	made clear, clean, or pure; also made understandable.
	WORDS IN CONTEXT: *After the fire, the fire fighters **clarified** the room of smoke.*
fastidious	Overly nice; easily disgusted, squeamish; also, full of pride, disdainful.
	WORDS IN CONTEXT: *Sarah, like her mother, was a **fastidious** housekeeper.*
meticulous	Overly careful about minute details.
	WORDS IN CONTEXT: *Cindy was so proud of her new P.T. Cruiser that she was **meticulous** in caring for it.*

After studying the words above, use them in the sentences below.

1. It was because of _____ preparation that his lectures went so smoothly.
2. The _____ on every chair gave the furniture a Victorian look.
3. The waiter spread the napkins and rearranged the silver with _____ care.
4. Through the _____ windows, the sun beat down brutally.

Test Yourself: Write the word that best fits the meaning given below.

1. decorative protection _____
2. detailed attention_____
3. showy attention _____
4. made clean, clear, or pure _____

On a separate sheet of paper, write a sentence using each of these words.

DID YOU KNOW?
Who was the first woman to win the Pulitzer Prize in Fiction? Answer: Edith Wharton with her novel, *The Age of Innocence*. After that, women took the prize three of the next four years: Willa Cather for *One of Ours*, 1923; Margaret Wilson for *The Able McLaughlins*, 1924, and Edna Ferber for *So Big*, 1925. (Who won in 1922? Booth Tarkington for *Alice Adams*.)

ablution	The act of washing clean; in religious rites, the washing of the priest's hands during communion; also, the water used in that ritual.
	WORDS IN CONTEXT: *The priest attended to his **ablution** during the ritual.*
lavation	The action or an act of washing.
	WORDS IN CONTEXT: *The cowboy did his **lavation** in a nearby creek.*
lustration	Various acts of purification, spiritual or moral; an inspection or review, sometimes said of an army; in ancient Rome, purification by an offering or sacrifice.
	WORDS IN CONTEXT: *After a great plague, the oracle advised that a **lustration** was needed for the city.*
purgation	The action of purging or clearing away impurities; ceremonial or ritual cleansing from defilement; the purification of the soul in purgatory; the action of clearing oneself from the accusation or suspicion of crime and guilt; the cleansing of one's body with a purgative or cathartic.
	WORDS IN CONTEXT: *The church demanded that the ex-convict go through a ritual **purgation** before he would be welcome back into the community.*

After studying the words above, use them in the sentences below..

1. In the convent, the young women used the water of _____ daily.
2. Her leisurely evening bubble bath was a _____ she looked forward to after a hectic day.
3. In the myth, a sacrificial _____ was called for to purify the city.
4. The need for _____ in a place between heaven and hell was a part of the man's religious beliefs.

Test Yourself: Write the word that best fits the meaning given below.

1. personal cleansing _____
2. showing oneself clean _____
3. purification by offering or sacrifice _____
4. moral or spiritual purification _____

On a separate sheet of paper, write a sentence using each of these words.

DID YOU KNOW?
What famous novelist was also a lepidopterist (a specialist in butterflies)? That would be Vladimir Nabokov, author of *Lolita* and many other novels. He was once a Harvard research fellow and headed the butterfly section of the university's Museum of Comparative Zoology; he discovered and named several species of butterfly.

immaculate	Free from spot or stain; pure, unblemished, undefiled, spotlessly clean.
	WORDS IN CONTEXT: *The bride was dressed in **immaculate** white. Also, the conception of the Virgin Mary was held to have been free from the taint of original sin, thus an Immaculate Conception.*
unsullied	Unpolluted, unstained, unblemished, undefiled.
	WORDS IN CONTEXT: *Her reputation for honesty was **unsullied**.*
aseptic	An antiseptic; preventing putrefaction; also, anything not liable to putrefy.
	WORDS IN CONTEXT: *An **aseptic** can be an important protection against disease.*
cathartic	An event or action that can clear the mind or the emotions; also, cleansing the bowels with a laxative; the purgative that produces the cleansing.
	WORDS IN CONTEXT: *Before the surgery, the patient was instructed by the physician to take a **cathartic** to cleanse his internal body.*

After studying the words above, use them in the sentences below.

1. The candidate's reputation was _____ by rumors of dishonesty or debauchery.
2. The doctor prescribed an _____ to stop germs before they could cause harm.
3. Writing the firm letter to her children was a_____ experience.
4. The little boy was _____ in his new suit until he jumped in the mud.

Test Yourself: Write the word that best fits the meaning given below.

1. absolutely clean_____
2. without flaw _____
3. cleansing the body inside_____
4. guards against illness _____

On a separate sheet of paper, write a sentence using each of these words.

DID YOU KNOW? What famous humorist who hated his name was referred to as "Plum" by his family? That's Pelham Granville (P. G. to you) Wodehouse, who protested about his name to a clergyman at his baptismal.

dentifrice	A paste, powder, or other substance for rubbing and cleansing the teeth. **WORDS IN CONTEXT:** *The dentist prescribed a special **dentifrice** for the man's false teeth.*
unadulterated	Unstained by adultery; undebauched; undebased; uncorrupted by spurious admixture; pure. **WORDS IN CONTEXT:** *The makers claimed their brand of bottled spring water was **unadulterated** by pollutants.*
blanch	To make white by depriving of color; bleach; also, said of almonds, to scald in order to remove skin. **WORDS IN CONTEXT:** *Age had **blanched** her hair, and she used a special cream to **blanch** the brown spots on her hands.*
fumigation	The process of applying smoke or fume to disinfect or purify; in medicine, exposing one to fumes to produce a therapeutic effect. **WORDS IN CONTEXT:** *The old house had sat empty for so long that the buyers felt that **fumigation** was necessary to disinfect it.*

After studying the words above, use them in the sentences below.

1. After the chemical plant explosion, every building in town needed_____.
2. The development of stannous fluoride changed all _____products.
3. Before painting the walls, the crew _____ them.
4. He would use only _____sugar.

Test Yourself: Write the word that best fits the meaning given below.

1. eliminate color_____
2. cleanse disease-producing space _____
3. for brushing teeth _____
4. pure _____

On a separate sheet of paper, write a sentence using each of these words.

DID YOU KNOW?
What nineteenth-century author had a friend in the White House who did him favors? Strange old Nathaniel Hawthorne was a Bowdoin College friend of Franklin Pierce. When Pierce ran for president in 1852, he asked Hawthorne to write his campaign biography. After that, Pierce offered him a job as consul in Liverpool, England, where Hawthorne could continue to write. His last collection of essays *Our Old Home*, 1863, was dedicated to Pierce.

wholesome	Conducive to well-being of health, mind, and character; referring to one who is sound in body and mind and lives in a healthy manner.
	WORDS IN CONTEXT: *The couple moved to the country because they felt it provided a **wholesome** environment for their children.*
orderly	Neat and tidy in arrangement; systematic, well-behaved; law-abiding; peaceful; also, a person in the military or hospital assigned to performing systematic tasks.
	WORDS IN CONTEXT: *The **orderly** was **orderly** in every aspect of his life and thus gained respect in many areas.*
rarefied	To make or become more refined, subtle, or lofty.
	WORDS IN CONTEXT: *Her mother created a **rarefied** atmosphere in her home in which **wholesome** children were encouraged to become ladies and gentlemen and value order and learning.*
methodical	Said of one who closely and regularly follows a definite procedure that is carefully planned in detail.
	WORDS IN CONTEXT: *The researcher made a **methodical** investigation into the background of the people she surveyed.*

After studying the words above, use them in the sentences below.

1. Each evening before she went to bed, she arranged her next day's clothes in an _____fashion.
2. The police conducted a _____ search of the premises.
3. He found in prep school a _____style he had never before known.
4. _____ foods helped them to lose weight.

Test Yourself: Write the word that best fits the meaning given below.

1. classy, refined _____
2. clean living_____
3. painstakingly organized_____
4. step by careful step _____

On a separate sheet, write a sentence using each of these words.

DID YOU KNOW?
What was Dr. Seuss's medical specialty? No, he wasn't a jolly pediatrician. He had no medical degree. He held an honorary doctorate in humane letters from Dartmouth, his alma mater, but his father had always wanted him to be a doctor, so after 1956 he was one—of a sort.

swabbed	Made clean by gentle scrubbing or mopping. **WORDS IN CONTEXT:** *The nurse **swabbed** the child's skinned knees and applied a mild unguent.*
scrupulous	One who lives by scruples—conscience and propriety; characterized by strict and minute regard for what is right and attentive to the smallest detail; meticulous in behavior in moral and nonmoral matters. **WORDS IN CONTEXT:** *For her wholesome living and **scrupulous** behavior, she was nominated for the Woman of the Year.*
refined	Made free from other matter or from impurities; free from crudeness or coarseness; cultivated; elegant; characterized by subtlety and precision. **WORDS IN CONTEXT:** *The women in my book group are intelligent, **refined**, and, above all, curious.*
elutriated	Purified by straining the lighter from the heavier particles of a mixture; separated by washing; decanted. **WORDS IN CONTEXT:** *The scientists **elutriated** the minerals in order to take their measurements.*

After studying the words above, use them in the sentences below.

1. _____sugar is usually less healthy than sugar in its natural state.
2. This was a lawyer, he discovered, _____in every action.
3. The enlisted men _____the decks every morning.
4. The 49ers around Sutter's Mill _____the rocks to find their gold.

Test Yourself: Write the word that best fits the meaning given below.

1. playing by every rule of fairness _____
2. cultivated behavior _____
3. liquid cleansing _____
4. cleaning a surface_____

On a separate sheet of paper, write a sentence using each of these words.

DID YOU KNOW?
Who was the first American to be awarded the Nobel Prize in Literature? Sinclair Lewis in 1930.

expurgate	To purify or amend by removing what is objectionable; often refers to a book that has been edited to remove words or ideas thought to be impure. **WORDS IN CONTEXT:** *The **expurgated** edition of Joyce's Ulysses was not popular with readers.*
saponify	To convert a fat into soap by reaction with an alkali; to undergo conversion to soap. **WORDS IN CONTEXT:** *In the laboratory the chemists undertook to **saponify** the glyceryl esters or fat to produce a new variety of soap.*
edulcoration	To act of freeing, from harsh and acrid properties, purifying, softening, making sweet. **WORDS IN CONTEXT:** *In chemistry, **edulcoration** is the action or process of washing away particles soluble in water.*
filtered	having passed a liquid through a porous substance (paper, woolen cloth, felt) to free it from impurities. **WORDS IN CONTEXT:** *They **filtered** the water they drank with a **filtering** apparatus bought at a health food store.*

After studying the words above, use them in the sentences below.

1. The coffee had been _____ through a paper napkin.
2. The _____ editions of Henry Miller's works are almost worthless.
3. The company making soap found a new way to _____ the ingredients.
4. In the high school lab, students studied _____ of materials by washing away their impurities.

Test Yourself: Write the word that best fits the meaning below.

1. cut out the dirty bits _____
2. cleaned as through a strainer _____
3. separation by liquid _____
4. conversion of fat to cleaning substance _____

On a separate sheet, write a sentence using each of these words.

DID YOU KNOW?
Who was the first American poet laureate? Robert Penn Warren (1986) was both a poet and a novelist. The first English poet laureate was Ben Jonson in 1616. But the title didn't become an official royal office until 1668, when John Dryden was named to the post.

News Words

The media have their own lingo. Here are a few of the major terms used in newspapers, magazines, and news broadcasts.

DAY 1

| layout | dateline | lead | byline | close up |

DAY 2

| jump | masthead | slug | trim | kicker |

DAY 3

| subhead | body type | deadline | op-ed page | spots |

DAY 4

| anchor | caption | head | copy | chromakey |

DAY 5

| proof | managing editor | live | library | cut |

DAY 6

| rewrite | correspondent | copy editor | proofreader | dissolve |

DAY 7

| newsroom | filler | feature | pig | drive times |

layout	In a newspaper, a sheet ruled into columns indicating where the stories and advertisements will be placed on the page. **WORDS IN CONTEXT:** *By checking the **layout**, the editor discovered that the story was too long.*
dateline	In a newspaper, the name of the city or town and the date, which are placed at the beginning of stories not of local origin. **WORDS IN CONTEXT:** *The **dateline** of the story was BAGHDAD, Iraq, Sept. 11. (The year, 2004, along with the full date, usually appears elsewhere in the publication.)*
lead	This has two meanings in journalism. First, *lead* (pronounced "leed" and sometimes spelled *lede*) refers to the opening paragraph or paragraphs of a news story, giving the most important information and the highlights of a story. Second: *lead*, pronounced "led," is less important than in former years. Before electronic typesetting, newspapers and magazines were set into type with hot metal or lead. Thin strips of lead could be added between lines to adjust spacing; thus the terms *leading* or *leaded*, which are still used to refer to spacing between lines of type. **WORDS IN CONTEXT:** *Example one: The **lead** began: "They gathered at a hole in the ground in Lower Manhattan, a lonely patch of earth in rural Pennsylvania and a spot near the healed breach in the seat of military power, the Pentagon." (The New York Times, September 12, 2004). Example two: He **leaded** out the story because it was too short.*
byline	The reporter's name preceding a story. **WORDS IN CONTEXT:** *The top story, "Medicare Costs Are New Focus for Candidates," carried two **bylines**: Robert Pear and Carl Hulse.*
close-up	A picture in broadcast news in which the subject is framed tightly on the screen; generally a close-up shows only head and shoulders of the subject. **WORDS IN CONTEXT:** ***Close-up** is often abbreviated CU in broadcasting. The script might read, "CU: Peter Jennings," or "CU: Diane Sawyer."*

After studying the words above, use each in a sentence below.

1. They hired a new designer to create a more attractive_____.
2. The reporter neglected to use his most dramatic material until the seventh paragraph, which in newspaper parlance is called "burying the_____."
3. The intrepid correspondent filed_____ from all over the world.
4. The two young reporters shared a_____ on Watergate stories.
5. The script read, CU: Tom Brokaw, indicating a_____of the anchor.

Test Yourself: Write the word that best fits the meaning given below.

1. name of city or town from which the story is filed, and the date_____
2. the opening paragraphs of a news story, or the metal strips that affect spacing_____
3. the reporter's name preceding the story _____
4 a sheet ruled into columns _____
5. a tightly framed picture of the subject_____

On a separate sheet of paper, write a sentence using each of these words.

DID YOU KNOW?

What are the pseudonyms or pen names sometimes or usually used by the following authors? (A) Isaac Asimov; (B) Robert Benchley; (C) Agatha Christie; (D) Samuel Clemens; (E) Edna St. Vincent Millay; (F) Gore Vidal; (G) Dorothy Parker. ANSWERS: (A) Dr. A. Paul French; (B) Guy Fawkes; (C) Mary Westmacoff, also Agatha Christie Mallowen; (D) Mark Twain; (E) Nancy Boyd; (F) Edgar Box; (G) Constant Reader.

jump	The continuation of a front-page story on an inside page. **WORDS IN CONTEXT:** *The front-page story, "Chechen Rebels Mainly Driven by Nationalism," **jumped** to page 4.*
masthead	The heading on the editorial page that gives information about the newspaper including the names of the highest-ranking executives. **WORDS IN CONTEXT:** *The **masthead** of the Raleigh, North Carolina, News and Observer, September 14, 2004, carried the titles and names of the president/publisher, senior vice president/executive editor, editorial page editor, and managing editor, along with the titles and names of the business executives of the newspaper.*
slug	Word or words placed on copy to designate the story internally in the news room and production facilities. **WORDS IN CONTEXT:** *The writer gave his story the **slug**, "Medicare controversy."*
trim	To reduce the length of a story; to cut. **WORDS IN CONTEXT:** *To make the story fit the space allotted, the editor had to **trim** five lines.*
kicker	A humorous or light story, fairly brief, run at the end of a newscast. Or, in print journalism, a quote—called a "kicker quote"—or turn-of-phrase closing a story, usually on a light note. **WORDS IN CONTEXT:** *The newscast ended with a **kicker** of college kids on spring break in Florida tossing one another into the swimming pool.*

After studying the words above, use each in a sentence below.

1. Reporters on a paper refer to their bosses as the _____ names.
2. He _____ the story "scandal" and sent it to his editor.
3. The World Series story began on the front page and _____ to the sports page.
4. The senior editor wanted a five-inch _____ on the story.
5. The_____ was a story of a grandfather teaching his grandson how to roller-skate.

Test Yourself: Write the word that best fits the meaning given below.

1. internal designation of the story _____
2. gives information about the newspaper's executives _____
3. story moves from front page to inside page_____
4. to reduce the length of a story_____
5. clever quotation or phrase at the end of a print news story _____

On a separate sheet of paper, write a sentence using each of these words.

DID YOU KNOW?
Do you know or can you guess two African-American women writers who have won the Pulizer Prize in Letters?
ANSWER: Alice Walker, *The Color Purple*, 1983, and Toni Morrison, *Beloved*, 1988.

subhead	Lines of type in boldface or other set-off font (often darker and heavier than the body type), inserted periodically in a long story; they call attention to the paragraphs below them but are used principally to break up long columns of type. **WORDS IN CONTEXT:** *The editor said to use **subheads** every three paragraphs in the story.*
body type	The type size in which most of the newspaper or magazine is set, generally 8-point type. **WORDS IN CONTEXT:** *The **body type** in the paper was 8 point, but the type in the headlines was larger.*
deadline	The time by which all reports for the newspaper or news program must be completed and submitted to the final editor. **WORDS IN CONTEXT:** *The camera operator's car stalled so he missed the **deadline** for the six o'clock news.*
op-ed page	Short for "opposite the editorial page." The op-ed page, opposite the editorial page in many newspapers, is usually devoted to articles of opinion by columnists or others, sometimes but not necessarily in opposition to the opinions of the publication found on the left editorial page. **WORDS IN CONTEXT:** *The Secretary of State wrote an op-ed page article to explain his United Nations speech.*
spots	A television and radio term for commercial advertisements. **WORDS IN CONTEXT:** *The half-hour newscast ran four **spots** for pharmaceuticals.*

After studying the words above, use each in a sentence below.

1. In semiretirement, he became an _____ columnist for the paper.
2. Journalism students must immediately learn the importance of meeting_____.
3. Because many of its readers are older, the paper increased the size of its_____.
4. Some copy editors are especially skilled at inserting bright_____ into stories.
5. The script allowed for several 30-second _____during halftime of the football game broadcast.

Test Yourself: Write the word that best fits the meaning given below.

1. lines of type in boldface that break up columns_____
2. the type size in which most of a newspaper is set_____
3. opposite the editorial page _____
4. got to get finished by this time_____
5. word for commercial announcements on TV and radio _____

On a separate sheet of paper, write a sentence using each of these words.

DID YOU KNOW?
Who won Pulitzer Prizes in Letters for the following works? (A) *Fire in the Lake;* **(B)** *Gandhi's Truth;* **(C)** *Children of Crisis;* **(D)** *The Dragons of Eden;* **(E)** *The Good War;* **(F)** *A Bright and Shining Lie: John Paul Vann and America in Vietnam.* **ANSWER: (A)** Frances FitzGerald; **(B)** Eric H. Ericson; **(C)** Robert Coles; **(D)** Carl Sagan; **(E)** Studs Terkel; **(F)** Neal Sheehan.

anchor	In television, the primary announcer on a news program.
	WORDS IN CONTEXT: *He retired after 30 years as **anchor** of the eleven o'clock news.*
caption	The explanatory lines accompanying a newspaper photograph, illustration, or diagram.
	WORDS IN CONTEXT: *The **caption** under a photo read: "A police officer, left, and a Buckingham Palace official watch a protester dressed as Batman who climbed onto a palace ledge." (The News and Observer, Sept. 14, 2004.)*
head	Abbreviation for headline.
	WORDS IN CONTEXT: *The **head** for the story above read: "'Batman' Scales Wall Near Palace Balcony."*
copy	The term used for written news material, to be printed or read aloud on television.
	WORDS IN CONTEXT: *The reporter rushed to get his **copy** in on deadline.*
chromakey	The electronic merging of two video sources in broadcast journalism.
	WORDS IN CONTEXT: *The pictures behind the weather anchor were produced by **chromakey**.*

After studying the words above, use each in a sentence below.

1. She started as a weather reporter on television, and worked her way to _____.
2. It takes imagination to write _____ for routine photographs.
3. The page-one _____ was in the largest type the paper had ever used.
4. He wrote "clean" on it, which meant the _____ needed little editing.
5. The director used _____ to show both game and crowd action behind the sports anchor.

Test Yourself: Write the word that best fits the meaning given below.

1. short for "headline" _____
2. accompany a photo or other art _____
3. primary announcer on a news program is the_____
4. written news material _____
5. war pictures behind the newscaster were generated by _____

On a separate sheet of paper, write a sentence using each of these words.

DID YOU KNOW?
Can you guess the three American novelists and their novels with documented sales of more than 30 million copies? Hint: They're all women. Answer: Margaret Mitchell, *Gone With the Wind;* Harper Lee, *To Kill a Mockingbird;* Jacqueline Susann, *Valley of the Dolls.*

proof	An early draft of an article or illustration on which corrections and alterations are made.
	WORDS IN CONTEXT: *The photo editor scrutinized the **proof** carefully.*
managing editor	The person in charge of day-to-day operation of a newspaper or television broadcast; usually second in command to the executive editor or executive producer.
	WORDS IN CONTEXT: *She served as both anchor and **managing editor** of the evening news broadcast.*
live	Used in television so that the viewer knows that the broadcast is showing an event or report as it is happening, rather than on tape.
	WORDS IN CONTEXT: *She reported **live** from Baghdad.*
library	The place in a news organization where clippings or tapes of past stories are kept for reference by reporters and editors; this was once called the "morgue" in news rooms.
	WORDS IN CONTEXT: *He called the **library** for background information before writing his report.*
cut	An abrupt change from one video scene to another used in editing television news.
	WORDS IN CONTEXT: *Dan Rather's introduction was followed by a cut to live pictures of the hurricane.*

After studying the words above, use each in a sentence below.

1. The morning news programs feature segments both _____ and on tape.
2. While the executive editor was on vacation, the _____ took over her duties.
3. The tapes in the _____ allow reporters to know which stories on the sewer scandal their station had previously broadcast.
4. Because all the layouts had changed, they called for a new page _____.
5. In a quick _____, the news show moved from shots of the burning building to firefighters with hoses.

Test Yourself: Write the word that best fits the meaning given below.

1. keeps clippings or tapes of past stories_____
2. corrections and alterations are made on this_____
3. event is shown as it is happening _____
4. he or she directs day-to-day operations of the newspaper or television program

_____

5. a sharp shift from one video scene to another_____

On a separate sheet of paper, write a sentence using each of these words.

DID YOU KNOW?
What writer is in the National Wrestling Hall of Fame in Stillwater, Oklahoma? ANSWER: John Irving, who wrestled in prep school and college and used the sport in several of his stories. When his book *The World According to Garp* was made into a film, Irving appeared as a referee at a wrestling match.

rewrite	To change a story drastically.
	WORDS IN CONTEXT: *He had to **rewrite** his story three times before the editor approved it.*
correspondent	Another name for a reporter. It often refers to a person reporting from overseas. In some television organizations, a person called a correspondent may have a higher rank than a reporter.
	WORDS IN CONTEXT: *He has always aspired to be a foreign **correspondent**.*
copy editor	The person responsible for preparing copy for a publication. As an editor, he or she may change only a few words or even rewrite a story. In most newspapers, the copy editor will also write the headlines.
	WORDS IN CONTEXT: *The **copy editor** came up with an original head for a story: "News You Can't Use."*
proofreader	The person who checks the proof against the copy to detect typographical errors; he or she does not edit a story as a copy editor does.
	WORDS IN CONTEXT: *The **proofreader** found a number of typos in the proof.*
dissolve	One video image slowly replaces another image so that one picture or scene fades into the other.
	WORDS IN CONTEXT: *A **dissolve** is a softer form of editing than a cut and is sometimes used to show the passing of time or the changing of a scene.*

After studying the words above, use each in a sentence below.

1. Some reporters become _____; others start on the editing desk.
2. It takes good eyes and superior patience to be a good _____.
3. She was in tears when her producer demanded that she _____ her copy again.
4. He was the London _____ when the war in Iraq began.
5. The audience saw the little girl's face on screen _____ to a view of the flowers she was picking in the garden.

Test Yourself: Write the word that best fits the meaning given below.

1. prepares copy for publication _____
2. checks for typos _____
3. often a reporter who files from overseas _____
4. to change a story drastically _____
5. a slow fading of one image to be replaced by another _____

On a separate sheet of paper, write a sentence using each of these words.

DID YOU KNOW?
Who wrote the top-selling true crime book in history? The name of the book is *Helter Skelter.* **ANSWER:** The author is Vincent Bugliosi, the Los Angeles district attorney who tried the case that involved the Charles Manson murders. The book has sold more than 7 million copies.

newsroom	Operations center of the news organization.
	WORDS IN CONTEXT: *The **newsroom** with its open cubicles and clicking computers was buzzing as the writers drew near deadline.*
filler	In a newspaper, filler may be a short story written and held until it is needed (to fill space); in television, it may be a story prepared earlier and placed on tape until needed.
	WORDS IN CONTEXT: *The producer needed a 3-minute **filler** when the live report ran shorter than expected.*
feature	A story that is timely and interesting but is not, strictly, news. It often has some relationship to the news of the day.
	WORDS IN CONTEXT: *The newspaper used as a **feature** the soldier's letters home to his parents to show the hardships suffered by the troops.*
peg	An event that a news organization hangs a news story on; sometimes called a *hook.*
	WORDS IN CONTEXT: *The soldier's letters were **pegged** to the disturbing news from Iraq.*
drive times	The periods of the day that radio audiences tend to be highest because so many people are driving to and from work.
	WORDS IN CONTEXT: *Peak radio listening periods occur at **drive times** on weekdays (in the mornings from 6 to 10, and in the afternoons from 3 to 7).*

After studying the words above, use each in a sentence below.

1. On weekends, when news is often limited, broadcasts rely on_____.
2. They produced a _____on the curator when the museum opened.
3. The producer used the 40th anniversary as a _____for a long feature.
4. This _____was once dreary and ill-lit; now it's bright and clean, which cynical reporters say is to protect the computers.
5. During_____, radio listeners pay special attention to traffic reports that might affect their commute.

Test Yourself: Write the word that best fits the meaning given below.

1. a news story often hangs on this_____
2. timely and interesting story, but not really news _____
3. for use on a slow news day _____
4. the work space _____
5. busy people catch up on information from the radio during _____

On a separate sheet of paper, write a sentence using each of these words.

DID YOU KNOW?
What prolific writer of stories about a super strong man has a town in California named after his hero? ANSWER: Edgar Rice Burroughs (1875–1950), who wrote more than 26 Tarzan novels, bought a home in California that he named for the hero whose popularity had allowed him to buy it. When the community around him was incorporated nine years later, the denizens chose to call it Tarzana.

Show-Off Words

Here are words that show off themselves or the people they describe.

DAY 1

| ostentacious | pretentious | four-flusher | high-handed | grandiloquisms |

DAY 2

| swank | swagger | claptrap | splendiferous | bedizened |

DAY 3

| attitudinize | connoisseur | affectation | magnification | coxcombry |

DAY 4

| gaudy | punctilious | magniloquent | gasbag | effulgence |

DAY 5

| simoleon | gasconade | overbearing | garish | embellishment |

DAY 6

| blusterer | vaunted | brazen | imperious | fanfaronade |

DAY 7

| cormorant | unabashed | magisterial | theatrical | farthingale |

ostentatious	Said of a person who makes a showy display, as of wealth, knowledge, consumer goods, and so on. **WORDS IN CONTEXT:** *Jay Gatsby made an* **ostentatious** *show of his wealth to impress Daisy Buchanan.*
pretentious	Making claims explicit or implicit, to some distinction, importance, dignity, or excellence; affectedly grand, superior; ostentatious. **WORDS IN CONTEXT:** *They enjoyed the guests at the party, but the host's* **pretentious** *manner annoyed them.*
four-flusher	One who pretends to be, have, or intend something so as to deceive; bluffer; one who gives the impression of having four times as much or as many as he or she actually has. **WORDS IN CONTEXT:** *In stud poker,* **four-flushing** *means to bluff when one holds four cards of the same suit (four flush) rather than five in a true flush.*
high-handed	Acting or done in an overbearing or arbitrary manner. **WORDS IN CONTEXT:** *She took a* **high-handed** *attitude with her friends—and eventually lost them.*
grandiloquisms	Show-off or grand words or phrases used to replace more common terms. **WORDS IN CONTEXT:** *To impress her guests, the highfalutin woman used* **grandiloquisms** *in her conversation.*

After studying the words above, use them in the sentences below.

1. The agreeable young man introduced himself to the wealthy couple as a friend of their daughter in college, but they discovered later that he was not and was merely a _____.
2. The vaunted academic had such an overbearing manner that the students thought him _____ and defected from his classes.
3. The man's house was so enormous in size and so exaggerated in design that the people in his modest neighborhood thought it_____ and rose up against him.
4. The _____newcomer suggested that he came from a grand family in the South, but they found that he actually came from humble origins.
5. The gentleman spoke in such_____that it was hard for us to keep our faces straight.

Test Yourself: Write the word that best fits the meaning given below.

1. overbearing _____
2. a pretender or fake _____
3. showy display _____
4. bluffer, as in poker _____
5. high-flown words and expressions _____

On a separate sheet of paper, write a sentence using each of these words.

DID YOU KNOW?
Do you know about the author who won the Nobel Prize for his work, which included a book that his homeland would not allow to be published and for which his writers'union expelled him? Furthermore, he was forced to decline the award in 1958. Who might the author be, and what was the work? ANSWER: Boris Pasternak, who wrote *Dr. Zhivago,* had to publish his book in Italy. The Soviet Union of Authors expelled him because his book was so popular in the West, and the union considered the award to be capitalist. The book was finally made available in his homeland in 1988—but Pasternak had been dead for 28 years.

swank	Stylish display or ostentation in dress; to act in a showy, pretentious manner.
	WORDS IN CONTEXT: *The actor had a **swank** penthouse in New York City.*
swagger	To walk with a bold, arrogant, or lordly stride; to strut; to boast, brag, or show off in a loud, superior manner.
	WORDS IN CONTEXT: *The rock star **swaggered** to the microphone in his white suit and bling-bling.*
claptrap	Showy, insincere, empty, cheap talk, used only to get applause or notice.
	WORDS IN CONTEXT: *We could hear the barker at the circus speaking **claptrap** over a loudspeaker, urging the crowd into the tent.*
splendiferous	Gorgeous, splendid, often used in a jocularly pretentious way.
	WORDS IN CONTEXT: *Our trip to New York was **splendiferous** from start to finish, filled with plays, concerts, parties, and visits with friends.*
bedizened	All decked out; decorated, ornamented or dressed in an exaggerated way.
	WORDS IN CONTEXT: ***Bedizened** is a fancy way of saying that something is quite fancy itself. For example, at the ball, the women were dressed in designer gowns **bedizened** with ribbons, ruffles, and crystal beading.*

After studying the words above, use them in the sentences below.

1. My mother said she didn't want to hear anymore of that_____ from the hawkers on the street and went home.
2. They described their weekend at Martha's country estate as _____ because they had run out of adjectives.
3. The politician accused of _____, said, "In Texas, that's what we call walking."
4. It was a _____ crowd, but some people seemed a little overdressed.
5. The windows that overlooked the ocean in the celebrity's house were_____ with silk draperies, swags, and tassels.

Test Yourself: Write the word that best fits the meaning given below. right

1. cheap verbiage _____
2. arrogant strutting_____
3. splendid mocking _____
4. stylish but showy _____
5. decorated or ornamented in a fancy manner _____

On a separate sheet of paper, write a sentence using each of these words.

DID YOU KNOW?
From what author did Queen Mary, mother of King George VI, request a play for the queen's birthday in 1947? The author wrote a 30-minute radio play called *Three Blind Mice.* Later, the author revised and lengthened the play, and it went on to become the longest-running play in history. Can you guess the name of the author and the name she finally gave the play?
ANSWER: The author was Agatha Christie, and the play was *The Mousetrap,* which ran in London for more than 50 years. A nice coda to this story: Christie gave all rights to the play to her grandson, then nine-year-old Matthew Pritchard. So far, it's earned him more than $25 million.

attitudinize	To assume a posture or pose, often an affected or theatrical one; to strike an attitude.
	WORDS IN CONTEXT: *At the fashion show, we saw some male models **attitudinizing** just before they stepped onto the stage.*
connoisseur	A person who has expert knowledge and keen discrimination in some field, especially in the fine arts or in matters of taste.
	WORDS IN CONTEXT: ***Connoisseur** comes from the Old French "to judge" and "to know."*
affectation	A taking on or pretending to like, have, know, and so on; a show of pretense; artificial behavior meant to impress others; mannerisms for effect.
	WORDS IN CONTEXT: *One of the sisters was down-to-earth, and the other was filled with **affectation**.*
magnification	An overstatement of size, status, or importance; enlargement, exaggeration; making to appear larger than is really so.
	WORDS IN CONTEXT: *I believe your statement of the problem is a **magnification** of the situation as it actually exists.*
coxcombry	Arrogance and pretension in manner of behavior; foolishness; foppery.
	WORDS IN CONTEXT: *The man's **coxcombry** was on display in the manner of his dress: black evening cape, wine velvet jacket, and patent leather shoes.*

After studying the words above, use them in the sentences below.

1. "Hey, man, you are stylin'!" the guys in the car shouted to the man who had chosen to _____ on a busy corner.
2. When she mentioned her position at the company, it was always a _____ of what she actually did day to day.
3. Vincent was a _____ of wine and art.
4. Shirley's southern drawl was an _____, for she was born in Brooklyn.
5. Oscar Wilde in his dandy attire and with his posturing attitude was accused of _____.

Test Yourself: Write the word that best fits the meaning below.

1. make to appear larger than is the case _____
2. artificial behavior _____
3. discriminating expert _____
4. to strike a pose for attention _____
5. foppishness and arrogance _____

On a separate sheet of paper, write a sentence using each of these words.

DID YOU KNOW? Whose library became the basis for the Library of Congress as we know it? ANSWER: Thomas Jefferson's. After the British in 1812 burned the contents of the Library of Congress, some 3000 volumes then stored in the Capitol building, Jefferson sold Congress his own private library—more than 6000 volumes. A separate Library of Congress was built in 1897.

gaudy	Bright and showy but lacking in good taste; cheaply brilliant and ornate; tawdry.
	WORDS IN CONTEXT: *The teenagers decorated the gym with balloons, crepe paper, and **gaudy** colors to celebrate the team's victory.*
punctilious	Observant of petty formalities; careful of every detail of ceremony; exact.
	WORDS IN CONTEXT: *His grandmother was **punctilious** about the manners of her grandchildren when they visited her.*
magniloquent	Lofty, pompous, or grandiose in speech or style of expression; boastful or bombastic.
	WORDS IN CONTEXT: *The Shakespearean actor gave a **magniloquent** soliloquy.*
gasbag	A person who talks too much. The term **gasbag** derives from the original meaning, "a bag to hold gas, such as a balloon."
	WORDS IN CONTEXT: *When intoxicated he became an obnoxious, long-winded **gasbag**.*
effulgence	Resplendent radiance, brilliance.
	WORDS IN CONTEXT: *The young actress's talent and **effulgence** in the role of Juliet won over the audience.*

After studying the words above, use them in the sentences below.

1. The windows were swagged in a _____ manner with cheap, glitzy fabric.
2. Her _____ manner about details made everyone uncomfortable.
3. The old _____ was talking again, so we excused ourselves.
4. The CEO made a _____ speech at his retirement, outlining his accomplishments at the corporation.
5. The_____ of Versailles with its lighted candlebra made it a magical place for the guests.

Test Yourself: Write the word that best fits the meaning given below.

1. full of hot air _____
2. grandiose speech _____
3. exacting about petty things _____
4. aesthetically tasteless _____
5. radiance and brilliance _____

On a separate sheet of paper, write a sentence using each of these words.

DID YOU KNOW?
Where did the phrase *robbing Peter to pay Paul* originate? Legend has it that in the sixteenth century Edward VI took funds from St. Peter's Cathedral and used them for much-needed repairs to London's St. Paul's Cathedral.

361

simoleon	Old slang for a dollar. **WORDS IN CONTEXT:** *Simoleon is thought to be from the obsolete "simon," meaning a dollar, combined with the name of Napoleon.*
gasconade	Boastful or blustering talk; a big gasbag who talks about himself or herself. **WORDS IN CONTEXT:** *The pundit had a **gasconade** manner when he corrected his visitor's pronunciation.*
overbearing	Acting in a dictatorial manner; domineering, overriding, proud. **WORDS IN CONTEXT:** *The professor was accused of being overbearing when he publicly pointed out students' errors, humiliating them.*
garish	Too bright or gaudy, showy, glaring, overly decorated or overly ornate. **WORDS IN CONTEXT:** *The showroom was beautifully constructed, but we thought the decor was **garish**.*
embellishment	Adornments; additions to make more attractive, both visually and in statement or narrative. **WORDS IN CONTEXT:** *Listeners were struck at the **embellishment** of her story with anecdotes about famous people she had known.*

After studying the words above, use them in the sentences below.

1. The last house on the Decorator's Home Tour was gaudy; this one was_____.
Why do they use every idea they ever had in one small room?
2. W. C. Fields, the actor with a florid face, a bottle of liquor in his hand, and a lot
of bluster, was a_____.
3. Some say the expression_____ tried to elevate a mere dollar by attaching
it to the name of Napoleon
4. She divorced her husband because she thought him an_____ man who would
not listen to her concerns.
5. The _____in the new museum included eighteenth century moldings and wall
hangings.

Test Yourself: Write the word that best fits the meaning given below.

1. a slang expression for dollars _____
2. even more glaring than gaudy _____
3. even more blustering than a gasbag_____
4. even more obnoxious than a high-handed person_____.
5. additions to make something more attractive_____

On a separate sheet of paper, write a sentence using each of these words.

DID YOU KNOW?
Where does this saying come from, "the straw that broke the camel's back"? Read Charles Dickens's *Dombey and Sons*, 1848. There, he writes, "As the last straw breaks the laden camel's back, this piece of information crushed the sinking spirits of Mr. Dombey."

blusterer	One who speaks or conducts himself or herself in a noisy, swaggering, or bullying manner. **Blusterer** derives from the more violent fluctuations of wind—stormy, noisy, and blowy. WORDS IN CONTEXT: *Immediately after his promotion, the junior executive became a terrible **blusterer**, but he soon mellowed.*
vaunted	Overreaching, unduly confident, ambitious. WORDS IN CONTEXT: *The politician had a **vaunted** opinion of himself and his ideas.*
brazen	To act in a bold way as if one need not be ashamed; impudent; brassy. **Brazen** derives from the color and other qualities of brass—bold, ringing, harsh, and piercing. WORDS IN CONTEXT: *The colonel's **brazen** remarks about the prisoners of war provoked a stern reprimand from the commanding general.*
imperious	Overbearing, arrogant, domineering as if imperial. WORDS IN CONTEXT: *The matriarch of the family had an **imperious** manner with her grown children.*
fanfaronade	Any blustering or vaunting behavior; also, a fanfare or short celebratory prelude for trumpets or other brass instruments. WORDS IN CONTEXT: *The lavishly costumed band led off the parade with a crisp **fanfaronade**. The frantic staff sergeant's **fanfaronade** often provoked silent laughter among the troops, especially when his back was turned.*

After studying the words above, use them in the sentences below.

1. He_____ into the room leaving a trail of windy words behind him.
2. She had a _____ opinion of her importance.
3. The bold and impudent woman was _____in her approach to the boss for a job, and that attitude didn't play well in the office.
4. When she became president of the university, she mistook herself for a queen, and her domineering manner was thought to be_____.
5. The actor played Falstaff with robust_____.

Test Yourself: Write the word that best fits the meaning given below.

1. to act out boldly _____
2. to act as though you owned the world _____
3. to have an overly high opinion of oneself _____
4. to conduct oneself as if propelled by a mighty wind_____
5. one whose presence is as noticeable as a fanfare _____

On a separate sheet of paper, write a sentence using each of these words.

DID YOU KNOW?
All three of the Bronte sisters published their most successful novels in the same year—1847. Charlotte, *Jane Eyre;* Emily, *Wuthering Heights,* and Anne, *Agnes Grey.* Emily and Anne died within two years of that date. Charlotte died in 1855; none reached the age of 40.

cormorant	A vain, greedy, gluttonous person. The term is derived from the cormorant, a dark-feathered, long-necked water bird. **WORDS IN CONTEXT:** *Robert asked me not to invite Harry to the party because the guy is a **cormorant** who always wants to be the center of attention and who would likely try to eat every morsel of food in sight.*
unabashed	Shameless; never embarrassed about one's behavior, no matter how outrageous and transparent; not self-conscious or ill at ease. **WORDS IN CONTEXT:** *Many in the audience saw the politician as **unabashed** about the trouble he had gotten his political party into during his term in office.*
magisterial	Authoritative, pompous; of or suitable for a magistrate or master. **WORDS IN CONTEXT:** *The judge was **magisterial**, though several people disagreed with his opinion.*
theatrical	Melodramatic, histrionic, or affected; having to do with the theater—performance, play, and actors. **WORDS IN CONTEXT:** *The **theatrical** manner of the hostess was cause for some smiles and jokes by the younger guests.*
farthingale	A hoop or series of hoops worn beneath a woman's skirts in the sixteenth and seventeenth centuries; also the skirt worn over the hoop device. **WORDS IN CONTEXT:** *A woman in Shakespeare's day often wore a **farthingale**.*

After studying the words above, use them in the sentences below.

1. He was a shameless liar, _____ by his embarrassing behavior.
2. Offstage, we heard a _____ voice announcing the next act.
3. The people elected him to office because he had a _____ manner.
4. Not only was he a boor, but he was also a greedy _____ to boot.
5. Her _____ skirt was held away from her body by a series of hoops.

Test Yourself: Write the word that best fits the meaning given below.

1. shamelessly unself-conscious _____
2. authoritative _____
3. melodramatic _____
4. a hooped skirt _____
5. a self-centered obnoxiously aggressive person _____

On a separate sheet of paper, write a sentence using each of these words.

DID YOU KNOW? Which very popular author born in 1941 has the given name of Howard Allen O'Brien? It's Anne Rice, whose mother thought giving her daughter a masculine name would give her an advantage. Something did, but she's gone by the name Anne since she entered first grade and made it up. She especially likes it now when she autographs books because it's short to write.

Family Words

There are as many descriptions of families and the way they operate as there are kinds of families. Some of the words here may be familiar; others, less so.

DAY 1

| avuncular | en famille | consanguinity | filiation | distaff side |

DAY 2

| matrilineal | patrilineal | cognation | agnate | spear side |

DAY 3

| lineage | affined | progenitor | stirps | uxorial |

DAY 4

| genealogy | matriarchy | patriarchy | tribe | enceinte |

DAY 5

| descendant | pedigree | solidarity | confederate | mamma |

DAY 6

| coterie | clan | domain | patrimony | once removed |

DAY 7

| patronymic | godparent | extraction | phalanx | genitor |

avuncular	Like an uncle in speech, manner, dress, advice. **WORDS IN CONTEXT:** *Avuncular comes from the Latin word for maternal uncle, and less directly, ancestor. The professor had an **avuncular** style as he conversed with the students from the leather chair in his study.*
en famille	In the family circle. **WORDS IN CONTEXT:** *They celebrated the Thanksgiving holiday **en famille**.*
consanguinity	Blood relationship, close affinity. **WORDS IN CONTEXT:** *Their **consanguinity** was evident by the family resemblance between them.*
filiation	The state or fact of being a son or daughter; relation of a child to its parent; in law, the determination by a court of the paternity of a child. **WORDS IN CONTEXT:** *The tests by the court determined the **filiation** of the baby and the father.*
distaff side	The female line or maternal branch of a family. The **distaff** is the part of a spinning wheel that holds unspun flax or wool. Since spinning was habitually women's work, **distaff** came to mean (in Old and later Middle English) women's concerns and eventually woman or women in general; thus the distaff side refers to the woman's side of the family. **WORDS IN CONTEXT:** *Baldness is a trait inherited from the **distaff** side of a family.*

After studying the words above, use them in the sentences below.

1. The irrevocable bond of _____ protected the family against those who would spread rumors in an attempt to drive them apart.
2. The young man capitalized on his _____ to his rich and well-connected father.
3. The small wedding was conducted _____.
4. Although his message to students was harsh, the university president softened the blow with _____ prose.
5. Hank is my uncle on my mother's or the _____ side of the family.

Test Yourself: Write the word that best fits the meaning given below.

1. closest family ties _____
2. a family together _____
3. generational ties _____
4. style suggesting your uncle _____
5. female line of the family

On a separate sheet of paper, write a sentence using each of these words.

DID YOU KNOW?
Where did the Internet search engine Yahoo! get its name? If that's escaped you, here's the dope: The word originated in Jonathan Swift's *Gulliver's Travels.* When Gulliver visits the land of the Houyhnhnms (those people who look like horses and act like humans), their servants are known as Yahoos. They're a brutish bunch having the form and vices of, well, people. Since then, the word *yahoo* has become a dictionary word— and now a search engine. Early in the twentieth century, it also became an interjection, roughly synonymous with "Yippee!"

matrilineal	Designates descent, kinship, or derivation through the mother and not the father.
	WORDS IN CONTEXT: *The young woman of the court was a* **matrilineal** *descendent of the Crown.*
patrilineal	Designates descent, kinship, or derivation through the father and not the mother.
	WORDS IN CONTEXT: *Another young woman at the reception was a* **patrilineal** *descendent of the Crown.*
cognation	Relationship by descent from the same ancestor or source.
	WORDS IN CONTEXT: *The two discovered their* **cognation** *through studying their genealogical charts.*
agnate	A relative through male descent or on the father's side.
	WORDS IN CONTEXT: *In studying the same charts, the young man found that he had an* **agnate** *relationship to the family.*
spear side	Another way of indicating kinship through the male side of the family.
	WORDS IN CONTEXT: *A spear itself is a weapon consisting of a long shaft with a sharply pointed head. In Old and later Middle English, spear took on the sense of male, and the male side of the family came to be known as the* **spear side**—*as opposed to distaff side.*

After studying the words above, use them in the sentences below.

1. The Prince of Wales, the son of Queen Elizabeth, possesses a_____ tie to the British throne.
2. Elizabeth II, whose father was king, became queen through her _____tie.
3. In the early twentieth century, almost all the crowned heads of Europe traced their_____ to Queen Victoria.
4. The Duke of Edinburgh was found to have an _____relationship to the British royal family.
5. Since only the male used this particular weapon, the male side of the family came to be known as the_____.

Test Yourself: Write the word that best fits the meaning given below.

1. paternal, not maternal _____
2. mother's family _____
3. common lineage _____
4. father's line_____
5. male side of the family named for a weapon _____

On a separate sheet of paper, write a sentence using each of these words.

DID YOU KNOW?
What did some people say as they lay dying? Here's a sample, according to legend.
Henry Ward Beecher: "Now comes the mystery."
Beethoven: "I shall hear in heaven."
Anne Boleyn: "The executioner is, I believe, very expert; and my neck is very slender."
Thomas Hobbes: "I am taking a fearful leap in the dark."
Socrates: "Crito, I owe a cock to Aesculapius."
Rabelais: "I am going to seek the great perhaps."

lineage	Line, direct descent from an ancestor, descendants of a common ancestor or breed. **WORDS IN CONTEXT:** *They found documents in the old castle in Ireland that established his **lineage**.*
affined	Joined or connected in some way; related, under obligation; bound. **WORDS IN CONTEXT:** *The servant in the novel had been **affined** to the family for three decades.*
progenitor	A forefather, ancestor in direct line; source from which something develops; originator or precursor. **WORDS IN CONTEXT:** *The couple were the **progenitors** of 12 children, grandchildren, and great-grandchildren.*
stirps	Family or branch of a family, lineage; in law, the person from whom a family or branch of a family is descended. From the Latin *stirps*, literally meaning "a stalk, trunk, or root." **WORDS IN CONTEXT:** *Because of the destruction of records in the village, the family's **stirps** could not be determined with certainty.*
uxorial	Pertaining to, characteristic of, or befitting a wife. **WORDS IN CONTEXT:** ***Uxorial** duties were clearly understood and seldom questioned overtly until the twentieth century. (Mary Shelley's "On the Subjugation of Women" questioned these **uxorial** notions surprisingly early in the nineteenth century.)*

After studying the words above, use them in the sentences below.

1. The Knights of the Round Table elected to be _____ to King Arthur.
2. Einstein was the _____ of the twentieth century scientific revolution.
3. In law _____ designates a branch of a family.
4. The prince was allowed to marry the young woman because she had impeccable _____.
5. The understanding of _____ characteristics of women has changed over time.

Test Yourself: Write the word that best fits the meaning given below.

1. bound to others _____
2. originator, creator _____
3. family tree _____
4. family branch _____
5. pertaining to a wife _____

On a separate sheet of paper, write a sentence using each of these words.

DID YOU KNOW?
What does the phrase "waltzing Matilda," actually mean? It means carrying your backpack as a tramp does, on the hump of your back. "Matilda" is the tramp's bag or "roll," and "waltzing" refers to the pack jogging up and down as you walk. The Australian phrase, "you'll come a-waltzing Matilda with me" may be another way of saying, "I'm taking my bag and hitting the road." The phrase was made famous by the Australian poet A. B. (Banjo) Paterson (1864–1941).

genealogy	Race, stock, genus; a chart of recorded history of the descent of a person or family from ancestors; pedigree, lineage. **WORDS IN CONTEXT:** *The young man was interested in tracing his* **genealogy**, *so he studied the records of his family he found in the courthouse.*
matriarchy	A form of social organization in which the mother is recognized as the head of the family or tribe; descent and kinship being traced through the mother instead of the father; government, rule, or domination by women. **WORDS IN CONTEXT:** *Historically, some cultures have been governed by a* **matriarchy**.
patriarchy	A form of social organization in which the father or the eldest male is recognized as the head of the family or tribe; descent and kinship being traced through the male line; government, rule, or domination by men. **WORDS IN CONTEXT:** *Historically, people in the United States have been governed by a* **patriarchy**, *but that is slowly changing as more women are elected or appointed to local and national office.*
tribe	A group having recognized linked ancestry. **WORDS IN CONTEXT:** *A* **tribe** *was originally one of three groups into which ancient Romans were divided: Latin, Sabine, and Etruscan; also, the twelve divisions of the ancient Israelites were called* **tribes**.
enceinte	Being with child; pregnant. **WORDS IN CONTEXT:** *Pronounced "en-saint'," * **enceinte**, *from the French and Late Latin,* incincta, *means without a girdle. Oddly, as a noun,* **enceinte** *means an encircling fortification around a fort, castle, or town, or that protected by such a fortification—a metaphorical girdle.*

After studying the words above, use them in the sentences below.

1. Some Native American _____ resisted when the U.S. government violated treaties.
2. My grandmother, being the strongest person in the family, created a _____.
3. A _____ is the most common form of royal families.
4. The book *Roots* led to increased interest in _____ not only among African Americans but also among Americans of all races.
5. In biblical accounts, because Mary was _____, Joseph asked for a room in the inn.

Test Yourself: Write the word that best fits the meaning given below.

1. historic governing group _____
2. women-led family _____
3. men-led family _____
4. tracing a family tree _____
5. expecting a child _____

On a separate sheet of paper, write a sentence using each of these words.

DID YOU KNOW?
What is a "warming pan"? Actually, it's a kind of dustpan with hot coals in it that servants ran across the beds of their employers to warm the beds. By extension, it's a person who holds a place temporarily for another while the official holder is being qualified. But in British prep schools, the "warming pan" was the name applied to the underclassman who was forced by an upperclassman to lie in his bed and warm it up until the older student was ready for it.

descendant	A person who is an offspring, however remote, of a certain ancestor, family, group, or so on; something that derives from an earlier form.
	WORDS IN CONTEXT: *I am a **descendant** of strong, pioneer women.*
pedigree	A list of ancestors; record of ancestors, family tree; descent, lineage.
	WORDS IN CONTEXT: ***Pedigree** comes from Middle French pie de grue, literally "crane's foot," which was seen by some to be similar in line and shape to the outline of a family tree.*
solidarity	Complete unity, as of opinion, purpose, interest, feeling.
	WORDS IN CONTEXT: *Our family was close, if not in complete **solidarity** of opinion about everything.*
confederate	A person, group, nation, or state united with another or others for a common purpose but not ruled by a strong central force; ally.
	WORDS IN CONTEXT: *The **Confederate** States of America, composed of people angered by being pushed around by Washington, D.C., gave little power to its central government, which was a collateral reason for its failure.*
mamma	An organ of female mammals that contains milk-producing glands; a breast or udder; also, an instinctive infantine utterance.
	WORDS IN CONTEXT: *Many babies gain their first nourishment from **mamma**.*

After studying the words above, use them in the sentences below.

1. One of the most important things a bettor looks at is the horse's _____.
2. The labor union's marching song was "_____Forever."
3. They were my _____in trying to get the principal fired.
4. Today's feminists are the spiritual_____ of Susan B. Anthony.
5. In the United States,_____, a baby's utterance, is accented on the first syllable; in England, it is commonly stressed on the last syllable.

Test Yourself: Write the word that best fits the meaning given below.

1. list of ancestors _____
2. strongly bound together _____
3. loosely organized but united in purpose_____
4. product of earlier generations _____
5. offers milk _____

On a separate sheet of paper, write a sentence using each of these words.

DID YOU KNOW?
Charles Darwin waited 22 years after writing *On the Origin of Species* before he published it. Why? He was afraid of the backlash he would receive when it was published, so he wanted to gather more proof for his ideas. When he finally published the book, after hearing that other scientists with similar theories were preparing to publish their own, his book did indeed meet fierce resistance—as it still does today in some quarters.

coterie	A close circle of friends who share a common interest or background; a close-knit group distinguished from "outsiders." A **coterie** was originally an organization of peasants united to hold land from a lord.
	WORDS IN CONTEXT: *Alternative computing consists of enthusiastic **coteries** of users of nonstandard computer platforms or operating systems, such as Linux, Amiga, and Be. Even Macintosh users are sometimes thought to constitute a **coterie**.*
clan	A group of people with interests in common; clique, set.
	WORDS IN CONTEXT: *A **clan** was an early form of social group composed of several families claiming descent from a common ancestor, bearing the same family name, and following the same leader.*
domain	Land belonging to one person; estate; ownership; dominion; territory under one government or ruler.
	WORDS IN CONTEXT: *The landowner stood on a mountain on his property and surveyed his **domain**.*
patrimony	Property or a trait inherited from one's father or ancestors.
	WORDS IN CONTEXT: *The heir found that his **patrimony** included several large properties.*
once removed	This indicates a difference of one generation.
	WORDS IN CONTEXT: *This concept, often misunderstood, can be explained with this example: Your mother's first cousin is your first cousin, **once removed**. This is because your mother's first cousin is one generation younger than your grandparents, and you are two generations younger than your grandparents—a one generation difference.*

After studying the words above, use them in the sentences below.

1. All the many magazines, broadcast stations, publishing houses, and satellite programmers were part of his vast_____.
2. She wasted her _____and needed to borrow from friends.
3. Their Scottish_____ paraded in black and gold kilts.
4. The_____ of Oxford friends made countless movies together.
5. Sarah and Betty are first cousins; Betty has a daughter, Betsy, who is Sarah's first cousin_____.

Test Yourself: Write the word that best fits the meaning given below.

1. a group with common interests, today mostly socially _____
2. property ruled over _____
3. earned only by birth _____
4. congenial group _____
5. indicates a one generation difference_____

On a separate sheet of paper, write a sentence using each of these words.

DID YOU KNOW?
Did you ever hear the original adult version of "Pop Goes the Weasel," before someone turned it into a children's song? Here goes:
Up and down the City Road
In and out the Eagle.
That's the way the money goes,
Pop goes the weasel.

patronymic	Derived from the name of a father or ancestor; showing descent from a given person as by the addition of a prefix or suffix.
	WORDS IN CONTEXT: *The **patronymic** Stevenson indicates that he was Steven's son; the **patronymic** O'Brian, indicates that he was a descendent of Brian.*
godparent	A person who sponsors a child, as at baptism, and assumes responsibility for its faith; godmother or godfather.
	WORDS IN CONTEXT: *Mr. and Mrs. Stevenson agreed to be **godparents** of Michael O'Brian.*
extraction	In connection with kinship, extraction means origin, descent, source.
	WORDS IN CONTEXT: *He was of Eastern European **extraction**.*
phalanx	In discussing family, a phalanx is a group of individuals united for a common purpose; also, an ancient military formation of infantry in close and deep ranks with shields joined together and spears overlapping.
	WORDS IN CONTEXT: *The men marched together onto the stage in a **phalanx**, showing their unity.*
genitor	One who begets or creates; a natural father as distinguished from a foster or stepfather.
	WORDS IN CONTEXT: *The young man, who had lived with a loving foster father for years, became curious about his **genitor** and set out on a search for him.*

After studying the words above, use them in the sentences below.

1. Strictly speaking, no one can become a part of the Mafia unless he is of Sicilian_____.
2. To be a _____is an honor, but usually it brings little responsibility.
3. Most _____names have become so commonplace that no one thinks of their historic meaning.
4. He was ushered into the courtroom behind a_____ of lawyers.
5. The baby's _____was established by matching the DNA of man and baby.

Test Yourself: Write the word that best fits the meaning given below.

1. honored by child of family or friends _____
2. family background _____
3. connective family names_____
4. collection of supporters_____
5. natural father_____

On a separate sheet of paper, write a sentence using each of these words.

DID YOU KNOW?
The word *wedlock* does not imply the lock of marriage. *Wed* comes from Old English—a pledge—and *lac* means an action. Wedlock is what happens when you act on a pledge.

Sensitive Words

Sensitivity encompasses many areas of feeling and thought. Here we take a look at some words that express them.

DAY 1

empathy	sapid	nuance	felicitous	disquietude

DAY 2

aphasia	sensuality	sentimental	sensuous	huffish

DAY 3

thanatopsis	saturnine	ecstatic	sensibility	sensorium

DAY 4

sufferance	endurance	seraphic	empyrean	fervid

DAY 5

emotive	impressionable	susceptive	transported	sensate

DAY 6

percipient	anaphrodisiac	aesthete	delectation	perturbation

DAY 7

titillation	luxuriate	cathexis	gusto	esurient

empathy	The projection of one's own personality into the personality of another to understand him or her better; ability to share in another's emotions or feelings; personally responsive. **WORDS IN CONTEXT:** *Because she had grown up in Africa, she felt **empathy** for the young African boy.*
sapid	Agreeable to the mind; interesting; engaging; having a pleasing taste; savory. **WORDS IN CONTEXT:** *The docent made a **sapid** remark about the art in the museum.*
nuance	A slight or delicate variation in tone, color, meaning; a shade of difference. **WORDS IN CONTEXT:** *The lecturer's remarks were insightful and **nuanced**, so the experts in the audience did not question him.*
felicitous	Used or expressed in a way suitable to the occasion; aptly chosen; having the knack of expressing oneself in an appropriate and pleasing way. **WORDS IN CONTEXT:** *In translating the novel from the French, the translator made word choices that were apt and **felicitous**.*
disquietude	a state of worry or uneasiness; anxiety **WORDS IN CONTEXT:** *We were filled with **disquietude** as we sat in the hospital waiting for information about our brother who had been in an accident.*

After studying the words above, use them in the sentences below.

1. The candidate's language appeared to his audience to grow less _____ as the race heated up.
2. He surprised the students with profound and _____ comments about their work.
3. The preacher's secret was his ability to feel _____ for his congregation.
4. The _____ analysis at the end of the chapter made me like the work better.
5. We felt _____ as we stood among the crowd waiting for the election returns.

Test Yourself: Write the word that best fits the meaning given below.

1. intellectually attractive_____
2. identification with others_____
3. pleasing expressions_____
4. showing shades of difference_____
5. anxiety, uneasiness _____

On a separate sheet of paper, write a sentence using each of these words.

DID YOU KNOW?
Where does the expression *whipping boy* come from? Church historians say that whipping boys were actually identifiable people. Edward VI had a whipping boy who took his licks for him, as did Charles I. When Henry I of France left Protestantism and joined the Catholic Church in 1593, a bishop and a cardinal were sent to Rome to take the king's punishment. They knelt in St. Peter's singing and at each verse received a blow on their shoulders. Thus was King Henry absolved.

aphasia	A loss or disturbance of the ability to comprehend the meaning of words.
	WORDS IN CONTEXT: *After his third stroke, he developed* **aphasia** *and was no longer able to comprehend the books he had cherished for so long.*
sensuality	The state or quality of being sensual; fondness for or indulgence in sensual pleasures, which in some may lead to lasciviousness and lewdness.
	WORDS IN CONTEXT: *After hearing him read his poetry, she was aware of his* **sensuality**, *so she did her best not to arouse him.*
sentimental	Having or showing tender, gentle, or delicate feelings, as in aesthetic expression; having or showing such feelings in an excessive, superficial, or maudlin way, mawkish; influenced more by emotion than reason; acting from feeling rather than practical motives.
	WORDS IN CONTEXT: *Every greeting card she found was too* **sentimental** *for her taste, so she created her own.*
sensuous	Of, derived from, based on, affecting, appealing to, or perceived by the senses; readily susceptible through the senses; enjoying the pleasures of sensation.
	WORDS IN CONTEXT: *The fabrics in the shop—silks, satins, velvets, and soft wools—were* **sensuous** *to the touch.*
huffish	Peevish, sulky, or irritable.
	WORDS IN CONTEXT: *They saw that their father was in a* **huffish** *mood, so they waited to speak to him about their problem until after dinner.*

After studying the words above, use them in the sentences below.

1. She pretended to be aloof, but her innate _____ shone through.
2. Everything about him, from the fitted jeans he wore to the way he walked, was _____ to his women colleagues.
3. The film was so sappy and _____ as to be laughable.
4. She exhibited _____ when she could no longer write a letter or comprehend letters sent to her.
5. The woman came to the door at their knock, but by her _____ manner they could tell that she would buy no Girl Scout cookies from them this day.

Test Yourself: Write the word that best fits the meaning given below.

1. absorbing what the senses offer _____
2. touching, feeling, enjoying _____
3. hyped feelings _____
4. loss of the ability to read or write _____
5. irritable _____

On a separate sheet of paper, write a sentence using each of these words.

DID YOU KNOW?
Author Vladimir Nabokov experienced synesthesia. In his autobiography *Speak, Memory,* he said that as a boy he told his mother that the colors on his letter-and-number blocks were inaccurate. What he meant by that is unclear, unless it was that the colors called up the wrong sense impression for him. His mother understood, though; she had the condition herself, as does Vladimir's son, Dimitri.

thanatopsis	A view or musing about death.
	WORDS IN CONTEXT: *Thanatopsis is a word coined by William Cullen Bryant in his poem by that name. Thanatos means "death" in Greek, topsis means "view." Similar in meaning is the more frequently used word thanatology.*
saturnine	Sluggish, cold, and gloomy in temperament; born under or influenced by the planet Saturn.
	WORDS IN CONTEXT: *Saturn is the technical name for lead in Middle English; therefore, any reference to Saturn, as in **saturnine**, connotes lead: sluggish, cold, and dull, and even lead poisoning.*
ecstatic	Said of one who is overpowered by emotion, joy, grief, passion, extreme emotional exaltation; filled with intense delight that overpowers the senses and lifts one into a trancelike state.
	WORDS IN CONTEXT: *She was **ecstatic** to find that her father was still alive after his disappearance 10 days before.*
sensibility	The capacity for physical sensation; the power to respond to stimuli; the ability to feel; the capacity for being affected emotionally or intellectually, whether pleasantly or unpleasantly; receptiveness to impression; delicate, sensitive; awareness or responsiveness; liability to be offended.
	WORDS IN CONTEXT: *The writer found that some of the words in his book had offended the **sensibilities** of readers, but he had written the truth as he saw it.*
sensorium	The seat of sensation in the brain of human beings and other animals
	WORDS IN CONTEXT: *The **sensorium** is the center to which sense impressions are transmitted by the nerves.*

After studying the words above, use them in the sentences below.

1. Horror films adversely affected his delicate _____.
2. She was _____ about her promotion.
3. His _____ demeanor affected the entire room, making everyone in it feel gloomy.
4. Depressed more and more by the reversals, he created a private _____ in his mind.
5. At the concert in the art museum, she felt her _____ overloaded with a plethora of stimuli.

Test Yourself: Write the word that best fits the meaning given below.

1. contemplating the end _____
2. heavy weight _____
3. emotional exaltation _____
4. delicate responsiveness _____
5. the brain's center of sensation _____

On a separate sheet of paper, write a sentence using each of these words.

DID YOU KNOW?
The mimosa (*M. pudica*) is called the "sensitive plant" because it is believed by some to mimic the sensitivity of animals. Its leaves fold up at the lightest touch. Sir Walter Scott had this to say in *Marmion, Intro, canto* IV:
And one whose name I may not say,—.)
For not Mimosa's tender tree
Shrinks sooner from the touch than he.

sufferance	The power or capacity to endure pain or distress; tolerance. **WORDS IN CONTEXT:** *His powers of **sufferance** were great, but he felt he was beginning to reach their limit.*
endurance	The ability to withstand pain, distress, fatigue without flinching; holding up under stress. **WORDS IN CONTEXT:** *The climber's **endurance** was tested as she tackled Mount Everest.*
seraphic	Angelic, as one of the heavenly beings surrounding the throne of God, represented as having three pairs of wings (Isaiah. 6:2); the highest order of angels. **WORDS IN CONTEXT:** *The faces of the members of the choir during the oratorio appeared **seraphic**.*
empyrean	The highest heaven; among the ancients the sphere of pure light or fire; among Christian poets, the abode of God; the sky, the celestial vault, the firmament. **WORDS IN CONTEXT:** *Dante and others speak of the **empyrean** in their work.*
fervid	zealous, impassioned. **WORDS IN CONTEXT:** *He was a **fervid** book collector and had amassed tens of thousands of volumes.*

After studying the words above, use them in the sentences below.

1. She bore a calm and _____ look as she walked down the aisle.
2. The defensive line's _____ melted in the fourth quarter.
3. The actress had reached _____ status in the Hollywood pantheon.
4. He held his job only through the _____ of his father-in-law.
5. A _____ basketball fan, he would not miss a Duke game.

Test Yourself: Write the word that best fits the meaning given below.

1. heavenly place_____
2. never giving up _____
3. at the top _____
4. willing to give another chance_____
5. passionate _____

On a separate sheet of paper, write a sentence using each of these words.

DID YOU KNOW?
Speaking of empyrean, Milton wrote of it in *Paradise Lost* III, 56.
Now had the
   Almighty Father
   from above,
From the pure
   Empyrean where
   he sits
High thron'd above
   all height, bent
   down his eye.

emotive	Characterized by expressing or producing emotion.
	WORDS IN CONTEXT: *The teacher in the actor's workshop instructed the students in how to be **emotive**.*
impressionable	Easily affected by impressions: capable of being influenced intellectually, emotionally, and morally.
	WORDS IN CONTEXT: *The young parents understood that children are **impressionable**, so they were careful about the language, visuals, and ideas to which their kids were exposed.*
susceptive	Having a sensitive nature or feelings; susceptible; receptive.
	WORDS IN CONTEXT: *The child was **susceptive** to colds in the winter, so his mother paid special attention to the temperature in his room.*
transported	In speaking of sensitive words, transported refers to strong emotion, especially of delight or joy; rapturous, being carried away.
	WORDS IN CONTEXT: *She was **transported** by the music of Chopin that filled the room.*
sensate	Endowed with physical sensation
	WORDS IN CONTEXT: *All **sensate** creatures can feel pain, but can they feel joy?*

After studying the words above, use them in the sentences below.

1. _____ teenagers see a great many violent movies.
2. Byron's romantic poetry _____ the two readers.
3. She was _____even in her quiet hours.
4. Realizing that she was _____to hypnosis, she tried that as a way to stop smoking.
5. Being_____himself, he could not bear to see pain inflicted on any living creature.

Test Yourself: Write the word that best fits the meaning given below.

1. exhibiting feeling_____
2. accepting, physically or mentally_____
3. subject to outside influences _____
4. carried away _____
5. capable of physical sensation _____

On a separate sheet of paper, write a sentence using each of these words.

DID YOU KNOW?
The quotation on the previous page from John Milton is a "periodic sentence" in which the subject and verb are delayed until the end of it—or until just before the period. In this one, you must read 19 words before you get to "bent down his eye" —the subject and verb. Sometimes this is done to build interest and create anticipation in the reader. Sometimes it's used for poetic effect. Here, Milton does both.

percipient	Referring to one who perceives keenly and readily. **WORDS IN CONTEXT:** *The professor noticed one especially* ***percipient*** *student among a class of ordinary pupils.*
anaphrodisiac	Lessening of sexual desire caused by a substance, food, drink, drug, environment, or social order. **WORDS IN CONTEXT:** *The girls who had dated a particular college student joked in the dorm that they would take up a collection to buy him an* ***anaphrodisiac***. *The atmosphere at the monastery was decidedly* ***anaphrodisiac***.
aesthete	One highly sensitive to art and beauty; one who artificially cultivates artistic sensitivity or makes a cult of art and beauty; a word often used derogatorily to connote effeteness and decadence. **WORDS IN CONTEXT:** *At the end of the nineteenth century, a group of* ***aesthetes*** *was so influential that the period was declared the Age of Decadence.*
delectation	Delight, enjoyment, entertainment. **WORDS IN CONTEXT:** *The banquet was sumptuous, and the entire evening a* ***delectation***.
perturbation	The fact or condition of being unsettled, disordered, confused or agitated; also a disturbance in the regular or expected order of things **WORDS IN CONTEXT:** *At his father's death, he felt great* ***perturbation*** *along with his sadness.*

After studying the words above, use them in the sentences below.

1. With his foppish dress, he presented himself as a dandy and _____, a self-invention he enjoyed.
2. In the highly-charged sexual environment of Times Square, the market for _____ has not grown lately.
3. With his keen eye, he had become a _____ appreciator of art and architecture.
4. She was such a delightful woman, every moment spent with her seemed to him a _____.
5. The villagers experienced great _____ when the volcano erupted.

Test Yourself: Write the word that best fits the meaning given below.

1. quick study _____
2. pleasurable _____
3. sexual reducer _____
4. artistically prideful _____
5. a state of being disordered, agitated, or troubled _____

On a separate sheet of paper, write a sentence using each of these words.

DID YOU KNOW?
What is the background for the expression "Catch-22"? Joseph Heller used it to great effect in his 1961 novel of that name. It's that odd catch that prevents a U.S. Air Force pilot from requesting a leave on the basis of insanity. It seems that a person "would be crazy to fly more missions and sane if he didn't, but if he is sane, he had to fly them. If he flew them, he was crazy and didn't have to; but if he didn't, he was sane and had to." You figure it out—if you're crazy or sane enough. This novel became especially popular during the era of the Vietnam War.

titillation	A state of being excited or stimulated. **WORDS IN CONTEXT:** *Titillate derives from the Latin, "to tickle."*
luxuriate	To grow with great abundance; to expand or develop greatly; to live in great luxury, take great pleasure in life, and revel. **WORDS IN CONTEXT:** *The women decided to take the day off to luxuriate at a spa.*
cathexis	Concentration of psychic energy on a single person, place, thing or aspect of the self. **WORDS IN CONTEXT:** *The unbalanced man had such a cathexis on the film celebrity that he was arrested for stalking her.*
gusto	To enjoy, taste, love life; appreciate enthusiastically with zest, great vigor. and liveliness. **WORDS IN CONTEXT:** *The group of aging women decided to form a club, wear red hats, and live the rest of their lives with gusto.*
esurient	Hungry, greedy. **WORDS IN CONTEXT:** *An esurient former head of the New York Stock Exchange was questioned about the enormous amount of money he left with and the excessive pay of his cronies.*

After studying the words above, use them in the sentences below.

1. The advertising campaign called it a beer with _____.
2. She set aside other tasks so she could _____ in her grand new home.
3. The _____ of his life was his effort to free the unfairly convicted man.
4. Much fashion advertising attempts to _____ viewers.
5. Her_____personality motivated her ambition to succeed at any cost.

Test Yourself: Write the word that best fits the meaning given below.

1. obsessively focused _____
2. mentally geared up for sex _____
3. love of life _____
4. to enjoy oneself immensely_____
5. greedy and hungry _____

On a separate sheet of paper, write a sentence using each of these words.

DID YOU KNOW?
Who wrote *The Autobiography of Malcolm X*—the activist who became a Black Muslin, then broke with the group to form the Organization of Afro-American Unity? Better known for his book *Roots,* the author Alex Haley actually wrote Malcolm X's autobiography in the year of Malcolm's death, 1965.

Impressive Words

Many of the following words are unusual, and some are infrequently used, but they are all fun to know. Be the first one on your block to know them.

DAY 1

salmagundi   anthropophagous   faundious   gilravage   senescence

DAY 2

solipsism   apodyterium   oppugn   apopemptic   girandole

DAY 3

prognathous   supererogation   hirsute   ophiolatry   anandrious

DAY 4

hinny   nacre   omphalos   quidnunc   dactylograms

DAY 5

cognoscenti   machinations   imprecations   sororal   galactophagous

DAY 6

ulotrichous   peruke   exsuperate   quiddity   facinorous

DAY 7

exulcerate   ectomorphic   endomorphic   mesomorphic   aleatory

salmagundi	Any mixture or medley; literally, a dish of chopped meat, eggs, flavored onions, anchovies, vinegar, and oil.
	WORDS IN CONTEXT: *Salmagundi is the name of a literary magazine that contains short articles, essays, poetry, and bits and pieces of literary writing.*
anthropophagous	Man-eating, cannibalistic.
	WORDS IN CONTEXT: *The scholars studied the culture that was once **anthropophagous.**.*
faundious	Eloquent.
	WORDS IN CONTEXT: *His address to the members was lengthy and **faundious**.*
gilravage	To feast, make merry, or party in an excessive or riotous manner.
	WORDS IN CONTEXT: *The students were invited to **gilravage** around a classmate's swimming pool after the prom.*
senescence	The process or condition of growing old
	WORDS IN CONTEXT: *When the roof leaked, and rain came into their bedroom, the owners had to acknowledge the **senescence** of the estate they had inherited.*

After studying the words above, use them in the sentences below.

1. Archaeologists found the skulls of ancient people they suspected to be victims of an _____culture.
2. _____speech was what one expected of the drama teacher.
3. In the castle, a _____was in progress, with music, dancing, and feasting.
4. We didn't know exactly what was in the dish, but we called it _____.
5. Their grandfather liked to talk about_____and the wisdom he had gained in his later years.

Test Yourself: Write the word that best fits the meaning given below.

1. high-toned speech_____
2. big party _____
3. eat people _____
4. fish dish _____
5. growing older _____

On a separate sheet of paper, write a sentence using each of these words.

DID YOU KNOW?
Who said, "A little knowledge is a dangerous thing?" It was the English writer Alexander Pope, but he was, as most people claim to be, misquoted. What he actually said was, "A little learning is a dangerous thing."

solipsism	The theory that the self can be aware of nothing but its own experiences and states, or that nothing exists or is real but the self.
	WORDS IN CONTEXT: *The therapist thought that the patient's **solipsism** was damaging his relationships with other people.*
apodyterium	A dressing room, from the Greek originally, a room in which clothes were deposited by those preparing for a bath.
	WORDS IN CONTEXT: *He folded his clothes and placed them in the **apodyterium** before diving into the indoor swimming pool.*
oppugn	To oppose with argument; criticize adversely; call in question; controvert.
	WORDS IN CONTEXT: *The debaters had the material to **oppugn** their rivals' argument.*
apopemptic	A farewell or leave-taking; a valedictory.
	WORDS IN CONTEXT: *The retiring opera singer's concert was her **apopemptic** to the Metropolitan.*
girandole	A rotating display, as of fireworks; a branched candleholder, sometimes backed with a mirror; a piece of jewelry, such as an earring, having one large stone surrounded by several small drops.
	WORDS IN CONTEXT: *Although **girandole** means several disparate things, let us imagine here a mirror to which branched burning candles are affixed in holders.*

After studying the words above, use them in the sentences below.

1. The mansion had a white marble _____ near the Jacuzzi.
2. At commencement one graduate gave an _____ to his high school days.
3. The woman's _____ gave her a very narrow focus on the outside world.
4. Every argument I could come up with for going, my father found a way to _____.
5. Barbara and Tom watched the _____ of fireworks over the bay in Seattle.

Test Yourself: Write the word that best fits the meaning given below.

1. argue against _____
2. a fond farewell _____
3. dressing room _____
4. self-referenced _____
5. earrings with a central stone and several drops _____

On a separate sheet of paper, write a sentence using each of these words.

DID YOU KNOW?
From where did we get the expression "to get off scot free"? In Old English "scot" meant a payment or a portion of a payment. Getting off scot free meant that one didn't have to meet that obligation.

prognathous	Having the jaws projecting beyond the upper face.
	WORDS IN CONTEXT: *The thing that made him appear tough and pugnacious was his* **prognathous** *jaw, which stuck out as if asking to be punched.*
supererogation	The act of doing more than what is required or expected.
	WORDS IN CONTEXT: *He was required to read three outside books for his English class, but given his tendency for* **supererogation***, he, of course, read five.*
hirsute	Bristly, hairy, shaggy.
	WORDS IN CONTEXT: *Until he shaved his beard and moustache, his girlfriend would not kiss his* **hirsute** *face.*
ophiolatry	The worship of snakes.
	WORDS IN CONTEXT: *Back in the hills, the writer ran across a church in which* **ophiolatry** *was practiced, and he watched the parishioners handling snakes.*
anandrious	lacking virility, impotent
	WORDS IN CONTEXT: *The patient explained his concern, and his doctor diagnosed him as* **anandrious** *but told him the problem could be solved.*

After studying the words above, use them in the sentences below.

1. He was asked to paint the fence, but with his usual _____, he painted the barn too.
2. He was proud of his _____ jaw, because he thought it helped him get acting parts in the theater.
3. Dad overlooked the scruffy appearance of his _____ son, hoping the teenager would grow out of this phase.
4. People choose many things to worship, but one of the most curious cults is that of _____.
5. Although the impotent man was _____, he found a solution to his problem.

Test Yourself: Write the word that best fits the meaning given below.

1. jutting jaw _____
2. hairy _____
3. a passion for pythons _____
4. overachieving _____
5. without virility _____

On a separate sheet of paper, write a sentence using each of these words.

DID YOU KNOW? What does the word *pythonic* mean, and where did it come from? It means huge, gigantic, and gargantuan, and we get it from the mythological serpent that Apollo killed.

hinny	The offspring of a male horse and a female donkey.	
	WORDS IN CONTEXT: *Hinny comes from* hinnire *the Latin word for "whinny." (Maybe hinnies whinny because they are nearly always sterile.)*	
nacre	Mother-of-pearl—the hard, pearly internal layer of certain marine shells, such as the pearl oyster and abalone, used in making buttons and artwork.	
	WORDS IN CONTEXT: *The mother-of-pearl that forms the background of David Anthony's* Sea Forms *was **nacre** from the oysters found near his beach home.*	
omphalos	The navel; a central point; a rounded stone in Apollo's temple at Delphi regarded as the center of the world by the ancients.	
	WORDS IN CONTEXT: *Friends jocularly derided their meditative friend for contemplating his **omphalos** too much.*	
quidnunc	An inquisitive, gossipy person; busybody.	
	WORDS IN CONTEXT: *Some called the neighborhood busybody a yenta; others called her a **quidnunc**.*	
dactylograms	Fingerprints.	
	WORDS IN CONTEXT: *The detective found **dactylograms** on the safe that had been cracked and compared them to those in his files.*	

After studying the words above, use them in the sentences below.

1. The medallion on her necklace was made of creamy, lustrous_____.
2. He was such a silent, thoughtful man that he was sometimes accused of scrutinizing his_____.
3. Some called her a yenta; others called her nosy; I called her a_____.
4. Product of two four-legged animals with different pedigrees:_____.
5. At the police station, the officer ordered a set of the suspect's_____.

Test Yourself: Write the word that best fits the meaning given below.

1. into everyone's business _____
2. no one is born without one _____
3. grandma's favorite button_____
4. close relative of a mule_____
5. the swirly patterns on your fingertips _____

On a separate sheet of paper, write a sentence using each word.

DID YOU KNOW?
Where did we get the word *gigantic*? It was from the race of extremely enormous folks— giants—who warred against the Olympian gods of Greek mythology and lost.

cognoscenti	People with special knowledge in some field, especially the arts; experts; persons of superior taste; connoisseurs. The singular form of the word is **cognoscente** (pronounced "con-yoh-shen'-tee" or "cawg-noh-sen'-tee") **WORDS IN CONTEXT:** *Alice appealed to some friends among the* **cognoscenti** *to help her find a gallery to show her art, because she considered these people to be in the know.*
machinations	Artful or secret plots or schemes, especially with evil intent. **WORDS IN CONTEXT:** *George did not trust Phillip at all, for he had seen some of Phillip's business* **machinations** *firsthand when they had worked together.*
imprecations	Evocations or prayers for a curse to fall on some person or thing. **WORDS IN CONTEXT:** *The witches in the play* Macbeth *with their words, "Bubble, bubble, toil, and trouble," called down* **imprecations** *on the drama about to unfold.*
sororal	Of or characteristic of a sister; sisterly. **WORDS IN CONTEXT:** *Wendy, who had no natural sister, had a long-time* **sororal** *relationship with Tracy, her best friend.*
galactophagous	One who drinks milk; a milk-fed animal. **WORDS IN CONTEXT:** *People who are* **galactophagous** *are purportedly healthier than others, but fat-free is best.*

After studying the words above, use them in the sentences below.

1. Gregory wanted to join the board of the Metropolitan Opera, because he thought the group to be among the music_____.
2. Ellen, my cousin, greeted me in a _____way.
3. Charlotte was in a black mood and called down _____on the man who had dumped her.
4. The politician's _____in using attack ads and nasty rumors to hurt his rival's chances at the ballot box were sure to catch up with him in the end.
5. The _____ nonagenarian told the reporter that he ate an apple a day along with drinking a glass of milk, and to those habits he attributed his longevity.

Test Yourself: Write the word that best fits the meaning given below.

1. like a female sibling _____
2. curses _____
3. in-group with special knowledge_____
4. distasteful plots and schemes _____
5. a person who sports a milk mustache _____

On a separate sheet of paper, write a sentence using each of these words.

DID YOU KNOW?
Where did we get the word *gargantuan*? The comic writer Rabelais gave us the word in his outrageous novel *Gargantua and Pantagruel*.

ulotrichous	Having wooly, crisp, and tightly twisted hair.
	WORDS IN CONTEXT: *His genes had given him **ulotrichous** hair, which annoyed him, but many of his friends envied it.*
peruke	A periwig; a wig of the type worn by men in the seventeenth and eighteenth centuries, usually powdered and having the hair gathered together in the back with a ribbon.
	WORDS IN CONTEXT: *In the paintings, the founding fathers of the United States wore **perukes**.*
exsuperate	To rise above, overtop, surpass, overcome.
	WORDS IN CONTEXT: *Richard thought there was no task or difficulty that he could not, with determination, **exsuperate**.*
quiddity	The essential quality of a thing; essence; also, a trifling distinction or quibble.
	WORDS IN CONTEXT: *The **quiddity** of the forest—its dense trees, dark soil, and cool shadows—was what drew the hiker to it.*
facinorous	Extremely wicked. From the Latin word for "bad deed."
	WORDS IN CONTEXT: *A **facinorous** man kidnapped Ellen's elderly father and robbed him.*

After studying the words above, use them in the sentences below.

1. Dressed to perform in *1776*, Bob and Jerry looked smashing in their_____.
2. Carl let his _____hair grow until it resembled a small bush; Carla cut hers to a sculptured nap.
3. The climbers of Mr. Everest had many difficulties to_____, but finally one of them reached the top.
4. The _____of Margaret's thinking, teaching, and behavior was always deeply moral and ethical.
5. The_____ serial killer was finally apprehended.

Test Yourself: Use the word that best fits the meaning given below.

1. to keep on trucking _____
2. essential kernel _____
3. powdered and beribboned _____
4. thick and curly_____
5. consummately evil _____

On a separate sheet of paper, write a sentence using each of these words.

DID YOU KNOW?
What is the origin of the word colossal? Again our language goes back to antiquity. The Colossus of Rhodes, a huge bronze statue, straddled the harbor of Rhodes, a Greek island, where ships passed between its huge, gigantic, gargantuan legs. The Greek word to describe such immense statues was colossal.

exulcerate	To cause ulcers in; to fret, to irritate, to annoy; also, to break out in ulcers. **WORDS IN CONTEXT:** *The rowdy behavior and noise of the four small children was enough to **exulcerate** their mother.*
ectomorphic	A slender physical type of person, characterized by the predominance of structures developed from the ectodermal layer of the embryo—skin, nerves, brain, and sense organs. **WORDS IN CONTEXT:** *Emily found a job as a fashion model, having been born with an **ectomorphic** physique.*
endomorphic	The abdominal physical type of person, who carries his or her weight in the abdomen. **WORDS IN CONTEXT:** *Having been born with an **endomorphic** body type, James finds it necessary to exercise regularly and watch his diet carefully.*
mesomorphic	The muscular or athletic physical type of person, characterized by the predominance of structure developed from the mesodermal layer of the embryo—muscle, bone, and connective tissue. **WORDS IN CONTEXT:** *Carl, the tennis champion, has a **mesomorphic** body type.*
aleatory	Dependent upon chance, luck, or an uncertain outcome; in music, using or consisting of sound sequences played at random or arrived at by chance, as by throwing dice. The adjectival form is **aleatoric**. **WORDS IN CONTEXT:** *His **aleatoric** approach to life led him to be a gambler.*

After studying the words above, use them in the sentences below.

1. He had a tendency to _____ when he was under pressure at his firm.
2. Though his body was _____ rather than muscular, he was a fine runner.
3. No matter how carefully she watched her diet, Maria, with an _____ body type, had trouble losing the spare tire around her middle.
4. He was built to be an athlete, _____ in body type, disciplined, and determined.
5. He could read music, but he also practiced _____ by playing random notes.

Test Yourself: Write the word that best fits the meaning given below.

1. skinny _____
2. chubby _____
3. well-toned _____
4. prone to internal lesions _____
5. dependent upon chance _____

On a separate sheet of paper, write a sentence using each of these words.

DID YOU KNOW?
Where did those vandals who smashed your mailbox and turned over your garbage can come from? The name for those wicked people who willfully or maliciously deface or destroy property harkens back to the Vandals, a Germanic people who overran Gaul, Spain, and North Africa in the fourth and fifth centuries A.D. And in 455 A.D. they sacked Rome. Our word derived from the Latin, *vandalus*. The Germanic term was *Wandal*.

Wise Words

Wisdom is a valued characteristic, and the English language has many words to describe the various ways and means of being wise.

DAY 1

| lucubration | sagacious | erudite | trenchant | sententious |

DAY 2

| prescient | gravitas | pundit | noetic | Apollonian |

DAY 3

| serene | venerable | perspicacious | oracular | profundity |

DAY 4

| eudaemonia | autodidact | polymath | acuity | discriminating |

DAY 5

| reverenced | emeritus | judicious | argute | penetrating |

DAY 6

| wiseacre | acumen | mentor | sobriety | discerning |

DAY 7

| provident | prudent | sapient | gumption | astute |

lucubration	Laborious work, study, or writing, especially that done late at night; something produced by such study; learned or carefully elaborated work.
	WORDS IN CONTEXT: *A literary composition is sometimes humorously referred to as a **lucubration**, especially if the work suggests pedantry.*
sagacious	Referring to one who perceives acutely; one having or showing keen perception of discernment, sound judgment, and foresight.
	WORDS IN CONTEXT: *The man was selected for a judgeship because he was viewed as **sagacious**.*
erudite	Learned, scholarly; having or showing a wide knowledge gained from reading.
	WORDS IN CONTEXT: *The group of **erudite** scholars was appointed to edit the encyclopedia.*
trenchant	Keen, penetrating, incisive, effective, distinct, cutting, sharp.
	WORDS IN CONTEXT: *She made a **trenchant** remark about the opinion rendered by the Supreme Court.*
sententious	When said of people, being full of intelligence or wisdom and sometimes pomposity; when said of words—full of meaning.
	WORDS IN CONTEXT: *He wrote a long **sententious** essay filled with Latin quotations.*

After studying the words above, use them in the sentences below.

1. He chose the university for graduate school that he believed had the most _____ faculty.
2. His comments, however penetrating and _____, annoyed many listeners.
3. Knowing her to be _____ in real estate matters, I asked her for advice before buying.
4. Preparing legal briefs requires _____.
5. The lecturer's pointed and pompous interpretation of the poem was _____.

Test Yourself: Write the word that best fits the meaning below.

1. extremely knowledgeable _____
2. wise _____
3. difficult preparation _____
4. sharp and incisive _____
5. full of meaning _____

On a separate sheet of paper, write a sentence using each of these words.

DID YOU KNOW?
How did the word *woman* come to us? It's a compound of the Old English word *wif* (from which we get "wife"), which meant an adult human female and "man," which meant a human being or an adult male as it does today.

prescient	Describes one who has apparent knowledge of things before they happen or come into being; possessing foreknowledge.
	WORDS IN CONTEXT: *The senator's comments about the way the political situation would evolve turned out to be* ***prescient***.
gravitas	Weight, heaviness, graveness, solemnity, or sedateness of manner or character; earnestness.
	WORDS IN CONTEXT: *A person described as having* ***gravitas*** *is generally thought of as grave and serious, carrying the weight of experience.*
pundit	A person who has, or professes to have, great learning; actual or self-professed authority.
	WORDS IN CONTEXT: ***Pundit*** *actually means "a learned person" in Sanskrit, and in India a* ***pundit*** *is a Brahman who is learned in Sanskrit and Hindu philosophy, law, and religion—a bit more elevated in learning than in the United States, where almost anyone who has a public platform for espousing his or her views is often called a* ***pundit***.
noetic	Existing or originating in the intellect; given to or involving purely intellectual speculation.
	WORDS IN CONTEXT: *My ideas are strictly* ***noetic***, *but time will tell whether they will have any basis in fact.*
Apollonian	Of a theoretical or rational nature, clearly defined, well-ordered, harmonious, noble, serene, dignified. **Apollonian** originally referred to the traits of the Greek mythological figure, Apollo, god of the sun, medicine, music, prophecy, and poetry.
	WORDS IN CONTEXT: *His writing style, unlike his manner of dress, was quite* ***Apollonian.***

After studying the words above, use them in the sentences below.

1. As a philosopher, he could offer _____thoughts without challenge.
2. The vice president was supposed to bring _____to the ticket.
3. It was amusing how _____she seemed to be about how I would do in law school.
4. Anyone who had ever worked a day in a prosecutor's office apparently qualified as a _____on cable television.
5. The judge was of an _____ nature: noble, serene, rational, and dignified.

Test Yourself: Write the word that best fits the meaning below.

1. thoughtful style_____
2. mysterious foreknowledge _____
3. years of wisdom _____
4. commentator _____
5. traits originally associated with Apollo _____

On a separate sheet of paper, write a sentence using each of these words.

DID YOU KNOW? The word *wizard*—meaning sorcerer and male witch—is a compound of "wise"—learned and sensible—and "ard," a suffix that was usually a pejorative, as in drunkard and coward. It meant, then, "a so-called wise man."

serene	Clear, bright, unclouded, calm, peaceful, tranquil, quiet; not disturbed or troubled.
	WORDS IN CONTEXT: *Practicing her yoga daily appeared to make her **serene** and clear-headed.*
venerable	Worthy of respect or reverence by reason of age and dignity, character and position; impressive because of age or historic or religious associations.
	WORDS IN CONTEXT: *In the Anglican Church, **venerable** is a title given to an archdeacon; in the Roman Catholic Church, **Venerable** is a title given to persons who have attained the lowest of the three degrees of sanctity, the others being beatification and canonization.*
perspicacious	Ability to see through; refers to one who is clear in statement or expression; easily understood, lucid.
	WORDS IN CONTEXT: *Readers noted that the commentary of the committee chosen to study the document was **perspicacious**.*
oracular	Wise, prophetic, mysterious; having the nature of an oracle.
	WORDS IN CONTEXT: *In Greek myth, the oracle made pronouncements, told the future, and influenced behavior, such as in the case of Oedipus; from this is derived the word **oracular**.*
profundity	Great depth, especially depth of intellect, feeling, or meaning. **Profundity** comes from the Latin *pro* ("before") and *fundus* ("bottom"); ergo, great depth.
	WORDS IN CONTEXT: *Her comments on the panel were lacking in **profundity**.*

After studying the words above, use them in the sentences below.

1. The _____professor attracted an auditorium full of students for every lecture.
2. He was a _____teacher, the kind I cherished in an advanced mathematics class.
3. Her _____demeanor calmed everyone around her.
4. His speaking style was so_____ that everyone thought he was smart.
5. The listeners remarked upon the_____of the scientist who spoke to the group.

Test Yourself: Write the word that best fits the meaning below.

1. tranquil style _____
2. sees clearly and is lucid _____
3. years of wisdom _____
4. makes mysterious pronouncements _____
5. depth _____

On a separate sheet of paper, write a sentence using each of these words.

DID YOU KNOW?
How did the word *mesmerize* come to us? Franz Anton Mesmer was an eighteenth-century physician who believed that magnetic powers resided in his body. During one public presentation of his powers in Paris he caused people to sleep, dance, and go into convulsions. The magnetic power Mesmer thought he possessed was actually his ability to hypnotize people of which he was not aware. One of his pupils popularized the term, and mesmerism came to mean "hypnotic or irresistible attraction."

eudaemonia	A state of happiness achieved by a life of activity governed by reason.
	WORDS IN CONTEXT: *In the philosophy of Aristotle, **eudaemonia** (derived from the Greek words "good" and "demon") was the chief universal goal, which could be achieved by an active, rational life.*
autodidact	A person who is self-taught.
	WORDS IN CONTEXT: *One student in our class, an older gentleman, was an **autodidact** who wanted to complete his education with some professorial guidance.*
polymath	A person of great and diversified learning.
	WORDS IN CONTEXT: *The academic committee recommended hiring a **polymath** to lead interdisciplinary studies.*
acuity	Acuteness, keenness in thought and vision.
	WORDS IN CONTEXT: *The **acuity** of the leader of the book club was apparent to the other members.*
discriminating	Able to draw fine distinctions; perceptive; fastidiously selective.
	WORDS IN CONTEXT: *Margaret was a woman of such **discriminating** intellect that people of all ages came to her for advice when they were in doubt.*

After studying the words above, use them in the sentences below.

1. He fancied himself a_____, willing to offer an opinion on anything.
2. Her _____about science awed her classmates.
3. It was as if he had slipped into a state of_____.
4. Should we respect more a product of schools or an_____?
5. His_____mind made him an ideal choice for president of a university during times of unrest.

Test Yourself: Write the word that best fits the meaning below.

1. educating oneself _____
2. intellectual bliss _____
3. widely trained _____
4. sharp thinker _____
5. able to make fine distinctions_____

On a separate sheet of paper, write a sentence using each of these words.

DID YOU KNOW?
What was a "genius" originally? In Roman mythology this was a guiding spirit received at birth that followed a man from cradle to grave. Genius guided a man's fortunes, determined his character, and eased his death. Only men had Genius; women had Juno, their own attendant spirit. The sense of "natural talent and inclination" became attached to the word. Finally, "native intellectual power of a grand type" and "one who possesses such power" came to be associated with genius in the eighteenth century.

reverenced	One who evokes a deep feeling of respect, love, and awe, as for something sacred; venerated; revered.
	WORDS IN CONTEXT: *My grandfather was **reverenced** for his wisdom and kindness.*
emeritus	One who has served out one's time; retired from active service, usually for age, but retains one's rank or title, as in professor emeritus.
	WORDS IN CONTEXT: *Dr. Heilbrun was given the title Professor of English **Emeritus** for her long years of service and her acuity.*
judicious	Having, applying, or showing sound judgment; wise and careful.
	WORDS IN CONTEXT: *Meg and Peter made **judicious** decisions about how they would raise and educate their children.*
argute	Keen, sharp, subtle, and shrewd.
	WORDS IN CONTEXT: *The **argute** qualities of the young man prompted his college advisor to suggest entrepreneurial work.*
penetrating	insightful; able or seeming to be able to see into innermost parts; piercing, acutely perceptive
	WORDS IN CONTEXT: *The reporters gave us a **penetrating** look into the culture in the Sudan.*

After studying the words above, use them in the sentences below.

1. After serving as chairman of the board for 29 years, he became chairman _____ when he reached his 72nd birthday.
2. Rather than heading out in the storm, they settled on a _____ plan to work at the hotel that night and leave the next morning.
3. Her _____ nature made her a successful public relations consultant.
4. The Pope is a _____ figure to many people.
5. Jerry read aloud to me the _____ comments about the economy that the columnist had researched and interpreted.

Test Yourself: Write the word that best fits the meaning given below.

1. reward for valuable service _____
2. honored _____
3. carefully thought out _____
4. alert _____
5. piercing _____

On a separate sheet of paper, write a sentence using each of these words.

DID YOU KNOW?
The poem that concludes Lewis Carroll's *Through the Looking Glass* is an acrostic. Read down the first letters of each line of the poem, and you will find the name of the young girl Alice Pleasance Liddell, for whom Carroll wrote the book.

wiseacre	One who thinks himself wise or who wishes to be thought wise. Pronounced "whiz'-uh-ker," from the Dutch meaning "a wise sayer"), the word originally meant a soothsayer, a wise or learned person. **Wiseacre** has come to be associated with a foolish person who has an air of wisdom. The term is usually used pejoratively, as one would say "wise guy." **WORDS IN CONTEXT:** *The class clown thought himself smart and funny, but he was viewed as a **wiseacre** by his classmates.*
acumen	Keenness and quickness in understanding and dealing with a situation; shrewdness. **WORDS IN CONTEXT:** *The parents applauded their son's **acumen** in dealing with the college authorities and winning a grant to study abroad.*
mentor	A wise, loyal adviser; teacher or coach. **WORDS IN CONTEXT:** *In Greek myth, **Mentor** was the loyal friend and adviser of Odysseus and teacher of his son, Telemachus.*
sobriety	Temperance or moderation, especially in the use of alcohol; seriousness, sedateness. **WORDS IN CONTEXT:** *Her **sobriety** and gravitas made her a good candidate for the judgeship.*
discerning	Perceptive, keen. **WORDS IN CONTEXT:** *Our manager's **discerning** view of the political situation in the office eased the anxiety of everyone.*

After studying the words above, use them in the sentences below.

1. He displayed great _____ in the negotiation.
2. _____, not extremism, was needed under the circumstances.
3. The older woman served as a _____ for the ambitious young woman.
4. Her comments were so habitually facetious that her family called her a _____.
5. An extraordinarily_____teacher diagnosed the young man's reading difficulties.

Test Yourself: Write the word that best fits the meaning given below.

1. easily grasped _____
2. quick to grasp _____
3. trusted helper_____
4. careful state _____
5. clear-sighted _____

On a separate sheet of paper, write a sentence using each of these words.

DID YOU KNOW?
The word *malapropism*, meaning a word misused but close enough to the correct word to create a comic effect, came from a character, Mrs. Malaprop, who boldly misused words. This character is found in Richard Sheridan's *The Rivals.* "Malapropisms" literally means "things out of place."

provident	Providing for future needs or events; exercising or characterized by forethought; prudent or economical; thrifty.
	WORDS IN CONTEXT: *It appeared to the widow that the time was* **provident** *for investing her inheritance in the stock market.*
prudent	Capable of exercising sound judgment in practical matters, especially those in one's own interest; cautious and discreet in conduct; circumspect, not rash.
	WORDS IN CONTEXT: *After the accident, the victim searched for a* **prudent** *lawyer to argue her case.*
sapient	Full of knowledge, wise, sagacious, discerning.
	WORDS IN CONTEXT: *The words of our adviser were* **sapient,** *and we agreed to follow her recommendations.*
gumption	Courage and initiative; enterprise and boldness. The original meaning of **gumption** was "shrewdness in practical matters; common sense"—connotations the word still carries.
	WORDS IN CONTEXT: *It took a lot of* **gumption** *to outbid the other customers at the auction.*
astute	Keen in judgment, crafty.
	WORDS IN CONTEXT: *It took a particularly* **astute** *judge of human nature to succeed as director of Human Resources at Xeron Corporation.*

After studying the words above, use them in the sentences below.

1. He displayed _____ in standing up to the bully.
2. Sagacious and wise, she showed a discerning and _____ understanding of the issues.
3. Given the faltering economy, the trustees knew they must not only be prudent but also _____ in managing the endowment.
4. Considering the future, given the unsettled conditions, the leaders needed to be _____ in their approach to the use of the available military resources.
5. She was _____ in her analysis of the foundation's needs and hired people who could successfully fill the empty offices.

Test Yourself: Write the word that best fits the meaning given below.

1. well planned by forethought _____
2. skillfully pragmatic _____
3. knowledgeable _____
4. determination_____
5. shows good judgment _____

On a separate sheet of paper, write a sentence using each of these words.

DID YOU KNOW?
Which witty Irish-English playwright made Victoria Station in London famous in literature? That would be Oscar Wilde in *The Importance of Being Earnest.* **Here, Jack Worthing, who is sueing for the hand of the daughter of snobby Lady Bracknell, tells the lady that he was born in a handbag in the cloakroom in Victoria Station.**

Intemperate Words

Words, attitudes, acts, and conditions of intemperance—lack of moderation—cause hard feelings and sometimes damage those around them. Here are a few.

DAY 1

| flagrant | duplicitous | acrimonious | pernicious | flagitious |

DAY 2

| perverse | derisive | disparaging | reprehensive | eldritch |

DAY 3

| arbitrary | malignant | excoriating | barnumize | dipsomaniacal |

DAY 4

| venomous | impertinent | vexatious | obsessive | prejudicial |

DAY 5

| impudence | horrific | contumacious | odious | implacable |

DAY 6

| blistering | dyspeptic | invidious | histrionic | immoderate |

DAY 7

| turbulent | dissolute | callow | dour | barratry |

flagrant	Glaringly bad, notorious, outrageous.
	WORDS IN CONTEXT: *The act was a **flagrant** violation of the law.*
duplicitous	Deceitful; showing hypocritical cunning or deception; double-dealing.
	WORDS IN CONTEXT: *One of the brothers found that the other had been **duplicitous** in dividing the inheritance.*
acrimonious	Bitter and caustic in temper, manner, or speech.
	WORDS IN CONTEXT: *The argument among the board of directors was so **acrimonious** that the chairman adjourned the meeting for the day.*
pernicious	Something (a disease, remark, attitude) that does great injury by insidiously undermining or weakening.
	WORDS IN CONTEXT: ***Pernicious** anemia insidiously undermines one's health.*
flagitious	Guilty of, or addicted to, extremely brutal or cruel crimes; viscious; scandalous; heinous.
	WORDS IN CONTEXT: *The author wrote that the remorseless government persisted in its **flagitious** project.*

After studying the words above, use them in the sentences below.

1. Everyone knew how_____ the two-timing girl was with her boyfriends.
2. The harsh, _____statement spoiled their relationship.
3. He got two free throws because of the _____foul.
4. Whenever the tense family got together, the atmosphere was_____.
5 The man was sentenced to life in prison for his_____crimes.

Test Yourself: Write the word that best fits the meaning given below.

1. unnecessarily harsh_____
2. insidious_____
3. cunningly dishonest_____
4. glaring _____
5. viscious and shameful_____

On a separate sheet of paper, write a sentence using each of these words.

DID YOU KNOW?
A play by Irish playwright John Millington Synge that opened at the Abbey Theatre in Dublin in 1907 prompted 500 policemen to gather outside. *The Playboy of the Western World* generated a riot because people objected to new ideas presented by the play.

perverse	Deviating from what is considered right or good; improper; stubbornly contrary; persisting in error or fault.
	WORDS IN CONTEXT: *Mary found Jim's attitude about taking care of their elderly father **perverse** and selfish.*
derisive	Showing contempt or ridicule; provoking derision.
	WORDS IN CONTEXT: *The hecklers in the audience were **derisive** about the candidate's position.*
disparaging	Referring to a slighting remark or action; a lowering in esteem; discrediting, belittling, deprecating. In Middle English, *disparagen* meant to marry one of inferior rank, thus lowering the esteem of the person of higher position. From this word, we get **disparaging**, a discrediting or depreciating of a person's worth.
	WORDS IN CONTEXT: *While his hotly contested divorce was in progress, the professor's critiques of students' papers became more **disparaging** than previously.*
reprehensive	Referring to the act of finding fault with; criticizing, reproving, rebuking, or censuring.
	WORDS IN CONTEXT: *The judge's comments were **reprehensive** as he sentenced the criminal to prison.*
eldritch	Extremely weird, almost to the extent of being frightening.
	WORDS IN CONTEXT: *Her **eldritch** demeanor caused the children to think she was a witch.*

After studying the words above, use them in the sentences below.

1. The _____ man was disliked for his constant criticism and fault-finding of his neighbors.
2. His slighting and _____ remarks about her clothes belittled her.
3. The law professor's contempt for first-year students was revealed in his _____ manner.
4. The nasty way he treated people and things smaller than himself let us know that he was _____ from the time he was a child.
5. The appearance and manner of Caliban in Shakespeare's *The Tempest* is quite _____.

Test Yourself: Write the word that best fits the meaning given below.

1. ridiculing_____
2. abnormal behavior_____
3. cruelly critical_____
4. rebuking_____
5. very eerie_____

On a separate sheet of paper, write a sentence using each of these words.

DID YOU KNOW? What German dramatist who created groundbreaking literature by using music, song, masks, commentators, projectors, and grand movements is best known for his character Mack the Knife in *The Threepenny Opera*? **ANSWER:** Bertolt Brecht, an experimenter in drama, also wrote *Mother Courage, The Life of Galileo,* and *The Caucasian Chalk Circle.*

arbitrary	Based on one's preference or whim; capricious; not fixed by rules but left to one's judgment or choice.
	WORDS IN CONTEXT: *They thought their father's instructions about the use of the car were **arbitrary** and unfair.*
malignant	Having an evil influence, very harmful, dangerous, virulent; in health, likely to cause death.
	WORDS IN CONTEXT: *Jim's behavior had a **malignant** influence on the members of the group, so they decided not to include him in their discussions again.*
excoriating	Denouncing harshly; flaying, stripping the skin from, especially with words.
	WORDS IN CONTEXT: *The producer's remarks about the final editing of the film were **excoriating**, so the editors went back to work to revise it.*
barnumize	To advertise extravagantly with lavish, sometimes comical, display. The word derives from the circus showman P.T. Barnum, who specialized in overwrought advertising and puffery.
	WORDS IN CONTEXT: *The remake of the classic movie was **barnumized** so thoroughly that it became more profitable than the superior original on which it was based.*
dipsomaniacal	Having a morbid craving for alcohol; being persistently drunk.
	WORDS IN CONTEXT: *His **dipsomaniacal** nature landed him in jail more than once.*

After studying the words above, use them in the sentences below.

1. Cancer is often, but not always, a _____ disease.
2. The coach flayed the team with an _____ assessment of its performance.
3. To attract attention to their opposition to his views, the students decided to _____ the visit of the political candidate by dressing as chickens and flapping their arms around making clucking noises.
4. The judge's decision seemed _____ at best.
5. They took their _____ neighbor to the rehab clinic to dry out.

Test Yourself: Write the word that best fits the meaning given below.

1. criticizing viciously _____
2. presented in outlandish display to attract attention _____
3 capricious_____
4. venomous _____
5. habitually drunken _____

On a separate sheet of paper, write a sentence using each of these words.

DID YOU KNOW?
Tennessee Williams wrote a play that suggested that the central character was cannibalized? Well, that's one way of interpreting this mystifying play, *Suddenly Last Summer.*

venomous	Poisonous, full of venom; spiteful, malicious.
	WORDS IN CONTEXT: *Father warned us to stay out of the woods because* **venomous** *snakes had been found there.*
impertinent	Not showing proper respect or manners; insolent, saucy, impudent; also, not pertinent, irrelevant, having no connection with a given matter.
	WORDS IN CONTEXT: *My son made* **impertinent** *remarks to his sister, so I sent him to his room.*
vexatious	Annoying, troublesome, distressing.
	WORDS IN CONTEXT: *The* **vexatious** *fact that it rained every day during our short week in Florida put everyone out of sorts.*
obsessive	Referring to one who is haunted or troubled of mind to an abnormal degree; greatly preoccupied; possessed of an idea, desire, or emotion that cannot be got rid of by reasoning.
	WORDS IN CONTEXT: *After they moved across the country, the woman was* **obsessive** *about getting all the boxes unpacked and the house in order.*
prejudicial	Forming an adverse judgment or opinion beforehand or without examination of the facts; a preconceived preference or idea; bias; irrational suspicion or hatred of a particular group, race, or religion. **Predjudicial** comes from Latin meaning "to prejudge."
	WORDS IN CONTEXT: *On appeal, Microsoft claimed that the judges' not-so-casual comments to the press prior to the antitrust hearings had been highly* **prejudicial.**

After studying the words above, use them in the sentences below.

1. It is _____ that we have to go to so much trouble just to vote.
2. His cheeky, _____ manner toward the professor offended others in the class.
3. She maintained a cheerful style, yet everyone knew there was _____ spite underneath the surface.
4. The choreographer was _____ about getting the routine perfect.
5. The candidate was rejected for a Supreme Court appointment because he showed a _____ opinion about civil rights.

Test Yourself: Write the word that best fits the meaning given below.

1. cocky demeanor _____
2. annoying events _____
3. utterly focused _____
4. fiercely vicious _____
5. biased judgment _____

On a separate sheet of paper, write a sentence using each of these words.

DID YOU KNOW?
Virginia Woolf's name is in a drama she did not write. You can probably guess that it's Edward Albee's *Who's Afraid of Virginia Woolf?*—the name is a play on the children's story about the Big, Bad Wolf. And why should anyone be afraid of this brilliant, thoughtful writer? Well, some people may be wary of eccentric, independent, suicidal women.

impudence	Showing contempt; shamelessly bold or disrespectful; insolent.
	WORDS IN CONTEXT: *The school principal scolded the boy for his **impudence** in the classroom.*
horrific	Having the power to horrify or to induce fear.
	WORDS IN CONTEXT: *The ghost story was too humorous to be truly **horrific**.*
contumacious	Obstinately resisting authority; insubordinate, disobedient.
	WORDS IN CONTEXT: *The **contumacious** student had been warned over and over to improve his behavior and was finally suspended from school for a week.*
odious	Arousing or deserving hatred or loathing; disgusting, offensive.
	WORDS IN CONTEXT: *Her **odious** and arrogant attitude kept her from being voted into the club.*
implacable	Incapable of appeasement; inflexible; inexorable
	WORDS IN CONTEXT: *He found his manager to be extremely **implacable**, so eventually he quit.*

After studying the words above, use them in the sentences below.

1. His _____to everyone, including his parents, caused discord.
2. The referee's_____ wrong call cost them the game.
3. The Marines know how to handle _____recruits.
4. Their _____performance truly frightened the audience.
5. Since his political rival appeared to be_____, the candidate had to change his strategy and appeal to the voters' good sense.

Test Yourself: Write the word that best fits the meaning given below.

1. offensiveness _____
2. refusal to follow rules _____
3. terrifying_____
4. too cocky for one's own good _____
5. inflexible_____

On a separate sheet of paper, write a sentence using each of these words.

DID YOU KNOW? Christopher Isherwood wrote the novel *Goodbye to Berlin* (1935) on which the musical drama and film *Cabaret* were later based. The book, which deals with the rise of Nazism, was adapted for the stage by John Van Druten as *I Am a Camera* (1951); the story later became *Cabaret* (1966).

blistering	Severely beating, or lashing out with words harsh enough to cause a blister; also, the formation of a raised patch of skin caused by a burn or chafing. **WORDS IN CONTEXT:** *The police officer gave a **blistering** assessment of the work of one of the patrolmen who had acted rashly when confronting a suspect.*
dyspeptic	One who is gloomy and grouchy, especially as a result of suffering from impaired digestion; a bellyacher. **WORDS IN CONTEXT:** *The union boss was **dyspeptic**, so the members of the committee decided not to approach him that day.*
invidious	Exciting ill will, odium, envy; giving offense by discriminating unfairly. **WORDS IN CONTEXT:** *The mother accused the teacher of making **invidious** comparisons between her two sons.*
histrionic	Theatrical, dramatic, overacted or overacting, affected, over the top. **WORDS IN CONTEXT:** *The teenage girl's **histrionic** behavior about her curfew was ignored by her mother, who recalled how dramatic she had been in her own youth.*
immoderate	Extreme, excessive, exceeding a reasonable degree of propriety or necessity. **WORDS IN CONTEXT:** *Because she found herself to be eating an **immoderate** amount of food, she vowed to go on a diet.*

After studying the words above, use them in the sentences below.

1. After his _____ comments to the umpire, the manager was ejected.
2. He is so grumpy and _____ in the morning that we avoid him.
3. Most people agreed that the hyperactive female lead in the play was _____.
4. Her _____ casting of the play invited envy and ill will among the cast.
5. He found himself spending an _____ amount of time on his schoolwork, so he decided to take the weekend away from his studies.

Test Yourself: Write the word that best fits the meaning given below.

1. bellyacher _____
2. overly dramatic _____
3. unfair decision _____
4. scathing comment _____
5. excessive _____

On a separate sheet of paper, write a sentence using each of these words.

DID YOU KNOW?
A novel by Laurence Sterne (1767) contains several blank pages, uses a stream-of-consciousness style, and has virtually no plot. It's *Tristram Shandy,* still considered avant-garde today because of its experimental form. It initially purports to be the "autobiography" of Mr. Shandy (it begins with his birth), but it's basically about the escapades of his Uncle Toby and the opinions of Shandy's father.

turbulent	Full of commotion or wild disorder; marked by or causing turmoil; violently agitated, tumultuous. **WORDS IN CONTEXT:** *The air was* **turbulent**, *so the plane had to turn back to Chicago.*
dissolute	Loosened, lax, and unrestrained; dissipated, immoral, profligate, debauched. **WORDS IN CONTEXT:** *In the Bowery, the tourists noted several* **dissolute** *men drinking from bottles in brown paper bags.*
callow	Young and inexperienced; immature; fledgling. *Callow* derives from an Old English word meaning "bald" and "bare," indicating a young bird that is lacking the feathers needed for flying. **WORDS IN CONTEXT:** *The baby African grey parrots were utterly* **callow** *after hatching, but they grew rapidly to near adulthood.*
dour	Hard, stern, severe; obstinate; sullen; forbidding. **WORDS IN CONTEXT:** *The man who opened the door to the old house that the children had heard was haunted had a* **dour** *expression on his face.*
barratry	Stirring up quarrels or groundless lawsuits, a word that comes from Old French meaning "deception or cheating." **WORDS IN CONTEXT:** *Jimmy's* **barratry** *in contesting a legal will made his siblings hire lawyers needlessly to defend themselves.*

After studying the words above, use them in the sentences below.

1. He was a _____ boy, out of his league at the sophisticated prep school.
2. After fighting in the war, which had scarred his psyche, the ex-soldier became _____.
3. Dr. Drake was a _____ headmaster who intimidated the students.
4. The flood waters were _____, causing great damage to homes on the coast.
5. The judge threw the frivolous case out of court on grounds of _____.

Test Yourself: Write the word that best fits the meaning given below.

1. a mere fledgling _____
2. strict and stern _____
3. lax and dissipated _____
4. tumultuous _____
5. filing groundless lawsuits _____

On a separate sheet of paper, write a sentence using each of these words.

DID YOU KNOW?
Who was the Tolstoy character who killed herself by leaping under a train? This character was Anna Karenina in the eponymous novel. (Remember "eponymous"?) She was a passionate, daydreaming, Russian, married woman who took a lover. Her creator punished her for rebelling against the norms of society by having her fling herself under a train.

Abused Words

Many of the words in this week's assignment are abused—often by people who should know better. Learn to use them correctly once, and you will never have to think about them again.

DAY 1

amount/ number	myself	climactic/ climatic	anti/ ante	citizen/ resident

DAY 2

comprise/ compose	core/ corps	fewer/ less	comprehensive/ comprehensible	aggravate/ irritate

DAY 3

as/ like	emerge/ immerse	veracious/ voracious	clandestine/ covert	each other/ one another

DAY 4

yoke/ yolk	callous/ callus	forbear/ forebear	tenant/ tenet	gourmet/ gourmand

DAY 5

proscribe/ prescribe	ordinance/ ordnance	foreword/ forword	envelop/ envelope	broach/ brooch

DAY 6

recur/ reoccur	rout/ route	populous/ populace	poring over/ pouring over	debauched/ debouched

DAY 7

amend/ emend	biannual/ biennial	bazaar/ bizarre	prone/ supine	blond/ blonde

amount **number**	Things you can weigh. Things you can count. **WORDS IN CONTEXT:** *The **amount** of material we moved today was 25,000 pounds. The **number** of boxes we moved was 200.*
myself	Many people who should know better use **myself** when they mean *me*. For example, the honoree said, "I thank you for the banquet for my wife and myself." Think of it this way: If you left out "my wife," would you say "Thank you for the banquet for myself"? Sometimes people use **myself** incorrectly because they are not sure whether to say *I* or *me*, so they weasel around the question by saying **myself**: "The science project was done by Owen and myself." (Would you say "The science project was done by myself, if Owen were not involved"? Both sentences call for the word *me*, not **myself.** Generally, **myself** is correctly used as an intensifier. **WORDS IN CONTEXT:** *I **myself** could not go, so Walter went in my place. I take good care of **myself**. I bathed **myself** in the lake at camp. I have not seen the film **myself**, but my sister saw it. Use **myself** in a sentence only if you have already used I.*
climactic **climatic**	Refers to a climax. Refers to weather. **WORDS IN CONTEXT:** *The **climactic** point in the evening was a speech given by the Nobel Laureate in Literature. The **climatic** news—possible tornadoes in our area—was not encouraging.*
anti **ante**	This is a prefix meaning "against." This is a prefix meaning "before." **WORDS IN CONTEXT:** *He was accused of **anti**-Semitism, (Add a hyphen following **anti** when it precedes a capitalized word or a word that begins with the letter i, as in **anti**-intellectual.) An anteroom is an entryway, or the room before a lobby in a hotel. The antebellum years were the period before the Civil War. (Notice there is no hyphen after ante.)*
citizen **resident**	A person who holds political rights in a nation; one is a **citizen** of a nation only—not of a state, county, region, or city. A person who lives in an area. **WORDS IN CONTEXT:** *Robert is a British **citizen**, but he is a **resident** of the United States. Robbyn is a **resident** of Connecticut and a **citizen** of the United States.*

After studying the words above, use them in the sentences below.

1. I called him on the phone _____, so I know he was aware of the change.
2. The play came to a_____ conclusion when the woman walked out and slammed the door.
3. The _____room was crowded with visitors waiting for the inner doors to open.
4. We read the _____news in the paper and worried about an approaching tornado.
5. The _____death penalty group stated its objections to the governor.
6. The _____of chairs around the table was 14.
7. The _____ he paid for the table and chairs was more than he had anticipated.

Test Yourself: Write the word that best fits the meaning given below.

1. used to describe things you can count _____
2. someone who lives in an area_____
3. used in discussing something you can weigh_____
4. used when discussing weather_____
5. one who shares in political rights of a nation _____
6. used when discussing the climax of an event_____
7. belongs to a nation_____
8. used after I has already been used, but not used to mean me_____
9. resides in a particular area _____

On a separate sheet of paper, write a sentence using each of these words.

DID YOU KNOW?
A writer once set out to write a novel without employing the most frequently used letter in the alphabet—*e*. He did it in 50,000 words. Ernest Vincent Wright in 1939 wrote *Gadsby*. The only *e*'s that occur in the book are in his name.

comprise **compose**	To contain. *The whole **comprises** the parts.* To put together. *The whole is **composed** of parts.* **WORDS IN CONTEXT:** *The program **comprised** five panels. The program was **composed** of five panels.*
core **corps**	Center. A group of people. **WORDS IN CONTEXT:** *Walter, the leader, was the **core** of the group. The **corps** of Girl Scouts attended the same camp.*
fewer **less**	Refers to items that can be counted. Refers to general amounts. **WORDS IN CONTEXT:** *I took **fewer** courses this year than I did last year. At her college, she paid **less** for the semester than I did.*
comprehensive **comprehensible**	Complete. Understandable. **WORDS IN CONTEXT:** *We found the scope of the student's research **comprehensive**. Beyond being **comprehensive** in research, the study was also concise, clear, and **comprehensible**.*
aggravate **irritate**	To make an existing condition worse. To make the skin itch, either literally or metaphorically. **WORDS IN CONTEXT:** *The tennis player's shoe **aggravated** the blister on his heel. As I jogged, the cold wind **irritated** my cheeks, and when I came home, my wife's attitude **irritated** me.*

After studying the words above, use them in the sentences below.

1. _____people than he had invited came to the lecture.
2. He ate the apple and threw the _____into the waste can.
3. His analysis of the report was_____, and the committee applauded.
4. The weight of the new truck was _____than that of the last truck he drove.
5. Why he got the bill was_____, because he had neglected to pay the mortgage.
6. A _____of Boy Scouts marched in the Memorial Day parade in Centerport.
7. He _____his paper for the philosophy class by combining the ideas of three thinkers.
8. His paper _____ the thoughts of Aristotle, Hegel, and Nietzsche.
9. The sharp wind began to _____ her sunburn.
10. The insecct bites began to _____ his arms.

Test Yourself: Write the word that best fits the meaning below.

1. to contain _____
2. to put together _____
3. complete_____
4. understandable _____
5. you can count it_____
6. general amounts _____
7. a group, as of people_____
8. center, as of an apple_____
9. to make an existing condition worse_____
10. to make the skin itch _____

On a separate sheet of paper, write a sentence using each of these words.

DID YOU KNOW?
Who wrote an acclaimed novel in 1969 called *Naked Came the Stranger* that was published under the name Penelope Ashe? That would be some 20 people who wrote it as a lark, each writing a chapter independently. Its publication under the pseudonym of Penelope Ashe was a hoax.

as **like**	Use the conjunction **as** to introduce clauses. Use the preposition **like** to introduce prepositional phrases.
	WORDS IN CONTEXT: *He sings the aria **as if** his heart were breaking. She looks **like** a film star. **Like** Jesse, Cleve ate all of his vegetables. Tia is **like** me in loving to read. She learned to dance, just **as** she learned to swim: practice, practice, practice. He does not dance **like** Fred Astaire, but he is an able partner.* **TIP:** *Please do not use **like**, as in "**Like**, what did you make on the history test?" or "I'm **like** really tired of writing term papers." This locution sounds, **like**, illiterate.*
emerge **immerse**	To come into view. To plunge into.
	WORDS IN CONTEXT: *Just as I rounded the corner, a car **emerged** from the side road. He **immersed** himself in the lake and immediately felt better.*
veracious **voracious**	Truthful. Extremely hungry.
	WORDS IN CONTEXT: *The witness called the defendant a hard-working, loyal, and **veracious** man. The bear that attacked the campsite had a **voracious** appetite, assuming that the campers' accounts had been **veracious**.*
clandestine	Underhanded, furtive, crafty; from the Latin *clam* meaning "secretly, in private." **Clandestine** implies an attempt to conceal an action itself, instead of or in addition to the identity of the sponsor or doer of the action.
covert	Concealed, hidden, under cover. From the Latin "to cover," **covert** implies an attempt to hide or conceal the doer or sponsor of an action rather than to conceal the action itself.
	WORDS IN CONTEXT: *The **clandestine** group gathered information to help overthrow the opposition government. A **covert** action, the bombing of the bridge, was wrongly blamed on the opposition but had actually been carried out by the tyrannical government in power.*
each other **one another**	Involving two. Involving more than two.
	WORDS IN CONTEXT: *The couple looked lovingly at **each other** across the dinner table. The four little girls on the first row in the theater looked at **one another** and giggled.*

After studying the words above, use them in the sentences below.

1. John knew Phillip to be_____, so he never doubted him.
2. The government took _____action to free the hostages without making the captors aware of its responsibility.
3. Sandra _____her beach towel in the ocean, so it would be cool to lie upon.
4. _____her mother before her, she has prematurely white hair.
5. A _____group of government operatives undertook intelligence gathering about the enemy for many years without being detected.
6. I felt_____, so I ate my steak and my partner's steak, too.
7. He _____from the sauna and headed for the swimming pool.
8. He spoke spontaneously _____ the thoughts came into his mind.
9. Wendy and David grabbed_____'s hands and began to run.
10. In the circle, Wendy, David, Tim, and Jill grabbed _____'s hands and began to dance.

Test Yourself: Write the word that best fits the meaning given below.

1. use to introduce a clause _____
2. use to introduce a prepositional phrase _____
3. involving two _____
4. involving more than two _____
5. extremely hungry_____
6. truthful _____
7. describing an action whose perpetrator is concealed _____
8. describing an action that is kept secret_____
9. to plunge into_____
10. to come into view _____

On a separate sheet of paper, write a sentence using each of these words.

DID YOU KNOW?
A novel by an American writer contains a sentence of 823 words and takes up three pages. Yes, William Faulkner wrote that sentence in *The Sound and the Fury*.

yoke yolk	A binding device. The yellow of the egg. **WORDS IN CONTEXT:** *The two were* **yoked** *together by marriage and children. To make the meringue, she discarded the egg* **yolk***.*
callous callus	Emotionally hardened. Hardening of the skin. **WORDS IN CONTEXT:** *The senior citizens thought the tax collector had a* **callous** *attitude toward them. The tennis player was bothered by the* **callus** *on her foot.*
forbear forebear	To cease or refrain from. An ancestor. **WORDS IN CONTEXT:** *They asked him to* **forbear** *practicing his trumpet at night. I learned that Grover Cleveland was my* **forebear***.*
tenant tenet	A person who rents a house or an apartment. A doctrine. **WORDS IN CONTEXT:** *The landlord thought the woman an ideal* **tenant***, so he allowed her to stay longer than her lease called for. The* **tenets** *of their church proscribed alcoholic beverages, so they did not drink.*
gourmet gourmand	A connoisseur of food; one who knows a great deal about the preparation and service of fine food. One who eats a great deal; a consumer of large amounts of food. **WORDS IN CONTEXT:** *The chef at the new restaurant was nervous because he had heard that a* **gourmet** *society was in the dining room waiting to order. The man who came to dinner was a* **gourmand***, and the hostess was relieved when he finally left.*

After studying the words above, use them in the sentences below.

1. During his strenuous diet, he had to _____ carbohydrates of any kind.
2. The original _____ of our apartment wanted to return, so we had to find another place.
3. The couple grew _____ about the political situation after their son was called up.
4. We were told to make omelets with the whites of the egg, but it tasted weird without the _____.
5. The_____ of our club forbid meetings on weekends.
6. One of Tom's _____ was Thomas Jefferson, and he never let us forget it.
7. The _____ on my foot came from hiking 10 miles in poorly fitted shoes.
8. The _____binding the two oxen allowed them to pull heavy loads.
9. Although he was a gluttonous_____, his highly discriminating tastes were those of a true_____.

Test Yourself: Write the word that best fits the meaning given below.

1. a binding device _____
2. hardening of the skin _____
3. an ancestor _____
4. the yellow of the egg _____
5. a doctrine_____
6. a person who rents a house or an apartment _____
7. emotionally hardened _____
8. cease or restrain from_____
9. one who eats a lot_____
10. a connoisseur of food _____

On a separate sheet of paper, write a sentence using each of these words.

DID YOU KNOW?
A novel of the 1930s called *The Well of Loneliness* by Radclyff Hall was enormously controversial because of its subject matter. It was the first American novel to deal with lesbianism.

proscribe **prescribe**	To prohibit or condemn. To order something. **WORDS IN CONTEXT:** *The rules of the club **proscribed** admitting more than one new member a year. The doctor called to **prescribe** an antiviral medication for her patient.*
ordinance **ordnance**	A law. Weapons and ammunition. **WORDS IN CONTEXT:** *In the small town, there was an **ordinance** against shooting off fireworks within the city limits. The general demanded more **ordnance** to protect his troops.*
foreword **forward**	An introduction to a work. Onward. **WORDS IN CONTEXT:** *She asked the famous author to write a **foreword** for her book. At the signal, the band marched **forward**.*
envelop **envelope**	To surround or cover. Container for a letter. **WORDS IN CONTEXT:** *We felt the crowd **envelop** us as we walked into it. I looked for an **envelope** for the note I wrote to my brother.*
broach **brooch**	To make a hole in something; to begin a discussion. An ornament such as a decorated pin to attach to a blouse or dress. **WORDS IN CONTEXT:** *Whitney **broached** the subject of an allowance increase to her father, Craig, after she had made him his favorite dinner. Florrie wore the antique **brooch** her grandmother had left her.*

After studying the words above, use them in the sentences below.

1. The editor told the author that she needed a scientist to write the _____to her textbook.
2. In the courthouse records, we found an _____against tearing down the fence.
3. To _____ the medication, my physician had to call the pharmacy.
4. The rules of the contest _____contestants from being younger than 18.
5. They wrote a plan to move them _____professionally and financially in five years.
6. We took heavy rain capes to_____ us in our walk through the rain forest.
7. The soldiers stored the _____out of sight of the enemy.
8. The lady added a new _____ to the others already decorating her sequined blouse.
9. Whitney found a manila_____ in which to mail her college application.
10. He had the nerve to _____ the subject of his brother's alleged infidelities in the presence of the brother's wife.

Test Yourself: Write the word that best fits the meaning given below.

1. ammunition and weapons _____
2. an introduction to a work_____
3. a container for a letter _____
4. to open a conversation _____
5. an ornamental pin_____
6. move ahead_____
7. to surround or cover _____
8. a law _____
9. to order something _____
10. to condemn or prohibit_____

On a separate sheet of paper, write a sentence using each of these words.

DID YOU KNOW? According to science fiction writer Ray Bradbury, the temperature at which books will burn is Fahrenheit 451, also the name of the novel by Bradbury. It is a futuristic tale in which authorities demand that all books be burned. Filmmaker Michael Moore adapted the title for a political film.

recur **reoccur**	To happen again frequently. To happen again once. **WORDS IN CONTEXT:** *Tornadoes were a **recurring** event that spring in Kansas. We got new locks, hoping a burglary would not **reoccur**.*
rout **route**	A huge defeat leading to confusion or disorder. The way to a destination; a specific numbered road or highway. **WORDS IN CONTEXT:** *The team suffered a **rout**, and nobody could understand what happened. To get from Joplin, Missouri to Oklahoma City, people once took **Route** 66. When the interstate highway system was completed alternative **routes** were feasible.*
populous **populace**	Containing many people. The common people. **WORDS IN CONTEXT:** *It was a **populous** city on the waterfront. The **populace** was unhappy about the new taxes.*
poring over **pouring over**	Gazing steadily or earnestly; reading or studying carefully and attentively; meditating deeply, pondering. Sending forth a stream or flow of liquid. **WORDS IN CONTEXT:** *She sat in the library **poring over** the history book. He stood in the shower, the water **pouring over** his head.*
debauched **debouched**	Morally corrupted; dissipated; said of one who has over-indulged in sensual pleasures. (Pronounced "de-bo(t)cht'.") **Debauched** comes from an Old French word meaning "to separate or lead away from." Refers to one who has emerged or issued from a small area into an open area, as of a person or persons emerging from an auto, train, or buggy. (Pronounced "de-boosht'.") **Debouched** comes from the Latin words for "out of" and "a mouth or opening." **WORDS IN CONTEXT:** *In the movie, when the group returned from Las Vegas, they appeared **debauched**. The couple **debouched** from the taxi and walked toward the hotel.*

After studying the words above, use them in the sentences below.

1. In the election, the most _____ states have the most votes.
2. In the Friday night game, the Wildcats _____ the Indians and prompted a wild atmosphere in the stands.
3. He stood in the shower after the game with water _____ him.
4. I asked directions about the _____ we should take before driving to Texas.
5. At the rally, it seemed that the entire _____ of the city had turned out.
6. Anna was _____ her math book when the phone rang.
7. My headache kept _____ every Friday before physics class.
8. His mother told Jim that if his behavior of the day before ever _____ she would cut off his allowance.
9. A woman in a ball gown _____ from the limousine.
10. Returning from their all-night round of clubbing, the students looked _____.

Test Yourself: Write the word that best fits the meaning given below.

1. to happen again once _____
2. to happen again frequently _____
3. studying intently _____
4. a huge defeat _____
5. the way to a destination _____
6. the common people _____
7. containing many people _____
8. sending forth a stream of water _____
9. emerged or issued from a small space to a large one _____
10. corrupted, dissipated, sensually over-indulged _____

On a separate sheet of paper, write a sentence using each of these words.

DID YOU KNOW?
Abraham Lincoln took an author by the hand and greeted her with, "Is this the little woman who made this great war." According to historical reports, Lincoln so greeted Harriet Beecher Stowe, who some said incited the Civil War with her book, *Uncle Tom's Cabin*.

amend **emend**	To make a formal change. To correct. **WORDS IN CONTEXT:** *The city council voted to* **amend** *the charter. The editor* **emended** *the writer's statement.*
biannual **biennial**	Twice a year. Once every two years. **WORDS IN CONTEXT:** *We needed to meet every two years, so we set up* **biennial** *conferences. The periodical was issued only* **biannually**, *but its editor hoped to make it a quarterly.*
bazaar **bizarre**	A marketplace. Strange or odd. **WORDS IN CONTEXT:** *In Turkey, we went to a* **bazaar** *to shop. The costumes at the Halloween party were* **bizarre**.
prone **supine**	Lying on one's stomach. Lying on one's back. **WORDS IN CONTEXT:** *The children lay* **prone** *in the backyard, watching the ants. The adults lay* **supine** *in the backyard, watching the clouds.*
blonde **blond**	This is a noun to be used for a female. This is a noun to be used for a male. Used as an adjective, **blond** can describe either sex: Both the man and the woman have **blond** hair. **WORDS IN CONTEXT:** *The* **blonde** *in the photograph is Susan; the brunette is Tracy. The* **blond** *in the turtleneck is Bob; the brunet in the golf shirt is Jay. (Notice the male spelling* brunet *and the female spelling* brunette.*)*

After studying the words above, use them in the sentences below.

1. Carrie thought Jon's behavior was becoming_____, and she worried about him.
2. The_____ issue of the journal had come only once, so we expected the last one soon.
3. Jennifer lay _____on the bed, her nose buried in her pillow.
4. The church was having its annual_____, and we looked forward to the sales.
5. Once every two years, our group met for our _____get-together.
6. David lay _____under the tree, watching the squirrels run up and down the trunk.
7. The meeting was called to _____ the bylaws.
8. "I want to _____ the comment I made last night," Foster told the group.
9. The _____entered the hair salon to have her bleached hair retouched.
10. The red-haired boy beat the_____one in the male division of the races.
11. The _____ girl and _____ boy in the photograph are sister and brother—both have their mother's dark hair.

On a separate sheet of paper, write a sentence using each of these words.

DID YOU KNOW?
What was the first type-written book manuscript (1875) in America? Mark Twain's *The Adventures of Huckleberry Finn,* which was typed on a Remington. *Life on the Mississippi* was also typewritten that year. Twain did not announce those facts because he didn't want to give testimonials or explain how to operate a typewriter.

Words on Words

Some words about words and those who use them.

DAY 1

| hortatory | epicene | anachronism | abecedarian | alexia |

DAY 2

| adumbration | ambiguity | ampersand | analogous | concinnity |

DAY 3

| anaphora | riposte | anthology | orotund | antepenult |

DAY 4

| pleonasms | exundate | fugacious | mimetic | apocopated |

DAY 5

| fabulize | manqué | imputation | inexplicable | aphorisms |

DAY 6

| moniker | nefandous | nescience | opsimath | aperçu |

DAY 7

| opprobrium | arcane | ataraxia | funicular | comiconomenclaturist |

hortatory	Exhorting or encouraging a person or group. **WORDS IN CONTEXT:** *The commencement speaker gave a **hortatory** address to the graduates.*
epicene	Belonging to one sex but having characteristics of the other or of neither; effeminate, unmanly; also, a noun, as in Latin or Greek, having only one grammatical form to denote an individual of either sex. **WORDS IN CONTEXT:** *An **epicene** man was standing on the corner speaking to a woman who was clearly a woman.*
anachronism	An error in computing time or fixing dates; reference of an event to the wrong date or time period; anything done or existing out of date. **WORDS IN CONTEXT:** *In the movie, a Native American with his bow and arrow sported a smallpox vaccination scar on his upper arm—an **anachronism** that got past the film editors.*
abecedarian	Pertaining to the alphabet or one teaching or learning the rudiments of the abecedary—a primer. **WORDS IN CONTEXT:** *She was an **abecedarian** teacher in elementary school.*
alexia	"Word blindness," a disorder in which cerebral lesions cause loss of the ability to read. **WORDS IN CONTEXT:** *The physician told Cheryl that her inability to read was caused by a disorder called **alexia**.*

After studying the words above, use them in the sentences below.

1. The_____ in the novel, such as placing machine guns in the hands of British soldiers during the American Revolution, spoiled it for most readers.
2. The child began learning to read with a special _____study.
3. Notre Dame coach Knute Rockne was famous for his _____pregame speeches.
4. The parade of _____figures outside the bar caused some people to flee.
5. Eric had a hard time learning to read in the first grade, and his problem was finally identified as _____.

Test Yourself: Write the word that best fits the meaning given below.

1. enthusiastic language _____
2. out of historical context_____
3. basic learning of letters _____
4. indeterminate sexuality_____
5. inability to read caused by a brain disorder _____

On a separate sheet of paper, write a sentence using each of these words.

DID YOU KNOW? What is contradictory about the title of Ken Kesey's novel, *One Flew Over the Cuckoo's Nest?* Cuckoos do not build nests. They lay their eggs in other birds' nests. The title befits the novel about a perfectly sane man who commits himself to a mental institution, where the inmates often seem more sane than those who run it.

adumbration	An outline form; shading in a painting; a shadowy figure or a faint description.
	WORDS IN CONTEXT: *On a poster, the architect **adumbrated** the planned housing complex.*
ambiguity	Double or dubious meaning; equivocal expression; uncertainty.
	WORDS IN CONTEXT: *There was such **ambiguity** in the wording of the proposal that the committee refused to accept it.*
ampersand	The symbol &, which stands for the word *and*
	WORDS IN CONTEXT: *The sign said: "Joan **&** David's Bookstore."*
analogous	Similar in attributes, circumstances, relations, or use.
	WORDS IN CONTEXT: *The bristles or quills on other animals are **analogous** to hair on humans.*
concinnity	A skillful, harmonious arrangement of parts; elegance in literary style; from Latin, meaning "to place fitly together, arrange in good order."
	WORDS IN CONTEXT: *His letters from overseas were models of **concinnity**; unfortunately, the post office often mangled them en route.*

After studying the words above, use them in the sentences below.

1. The lawyers thought an _____ was not elegant enough in the name of their firm, so he opted to spell out the word.
2. The place that Meryl Streep holds in movies is _____ to the place that Ethel Merman once held in musical theater.
3. He larded his speech with _____ so that his opponents could not be sure about his plans.
4. The _____ she offered was all I could learn about him.
5. Suzanne's writing professor complimented her on the skillful _____ with which her papers were organized.

Test Yourself: Write the word that best fits the meaning given below.

1. abbreviation _____
2. confusion, deliberate or otherwise _____
3. similar to another _____
4. partial information _____
5. harmonious arrangement of parts _____

On a separate sheet of paper, write a sentence using each of these words.

DID YOU KNOW?
July 16 is called "Bloomsday" because it's the day Leopold Bloom set out to walk the streets of Dublin in James Joyce's *Ulysses.* On this date, Joyce devotees read the book aloud from start to finish at a New York theater called Symphony Space.

anaphora	The repetition of the same word or phrase in several successive clauses.
	WORDS IN CONTEXT: *The speaker used* **anaphora** *to sway the crowd: " I came to see; I came to understand; I came to help you plan."*
riposte	A sharp, swift response or retort; also, in fencing, a sharp, swift thrust made after parrying an opponent's lunge.
	WORDS IN CONTEXT: *His* **riposte** *to the obnoxious man at the bar made us laugh.*
anthology	A collection of works—prose, poetry, essays, reprints, or a combination of these—in one volume.
	WORDS IN CONTEXT: *The class read an* **anthology** *of the short stories of John Updike.*
orotund	Said of the voice: clear, strong, deep, resonant; said of a speaking or writing style: bombastic or pompous.
	WORDS IN CONTEXT: *His voice was pleasant, clearly audible, and* **orotund***.*
antepenult	The third syllable from the end of a word. (The second from the end is the **penult,** and the final syllable is the **ultimate**.)
	WORDS IN CONTEXT: *The antepenult of the word* antepenult *is the syllable "te."*

After studying the words above, use them in the sentences below.

1. His ability to make a _____ made him a successful debater.
2. The _____ of the century's best sports writing gave me many interesting evenings.
3. _____ is a classic trick of political orators.
4. He was an old-fashioned television anchor with an _____ voice.
5. The syllable "tith" is the _____ in the word antithesis.

Test Yourself: Write the word that best fits the meaning given below.

1. deep and resonant _____
2. a volume bringing together a subject in common _____
3. parry, then attack _____
4. stylistic repetition _____
5. third from the end _____

On a separate sheet of paper, write a sentence using each of these words.

DID YOU KNOW?
Where does the expression "let the cat out of the bag" come from? It's related to the expression "pig in a poke," if that helps. Once farmers brought pigs to market in a bag or "poke" to sell. Sometimes an unscrupulous farmer would put a cat in the bag, rather than a pig. If someone bought the bag without examining its contents first, that person bought "a pig in a poke." But if the bag was opened and the substitution discovered, the buyer had let the cat out of the bag.

pleonasms	The use of more words in a sentence than are necessary to express the meaning; redundancy of expression; superfluous words or phrases themselves.
	WORDS IN CONTEXT: *The overuse of too many superfluous, unnecessary, not needed, redundant words, phrases, and clauses in a sentence or a group of words with a subject and verb is called a **pleonasm**. The preceding sentence is an example of one.*
exundate	To overflow.
	WORDS IN CONTEXT: *The hurricane in Florida caused the river to **exundate** and flood our house.*
fugacious	Passing away quickly; fleeting, ephemeral; in botany, falling soon after blooming, as some flowers do.
	WORDS IN CONTEXT: *The summer shower was **fugacious**, ending as quickly as it began.*
mimetic	Having an aptitude for mimicry or imitation; characterized by mimicry.
	WORDS IN CONTEXT: *The actor we hired to perform at my sister's birthday party had strong **mimetic** skills and imitated the speech of everyone in the room to entertain us.*
apocopated	Cut off, especially the last letter or syllable of a word.
	WORDS IN CONTEXT: *In some parts of the South, where people commonly say, "runnin'" "jumpin'" and 'swimmin,'" standard English is **apocopated**.*

After studying the words above, use them in the sentences below.

1. The actor Robin Williams is noted for his _____ skills.
2. Their romance was as _____ as a spring snowfall.
3. The donors filled the basket with coins until it appeared to_____.
4. Editors were shaken when they had to deal with his copy filled as it always was with_____.
5. The girl_____her word when she said, "I want to go dancin'."

Test Yourself: Write the word that best fits the meaning given below.

1. too much to be contained_____
2. far, far, far more than necessary _____
3. dies so soon it's barely noticeable_____
4. entertaining copier _____
5. cut off_____

On a separate sheet of paper, write a sentence using each of these words.

DID YOU KNOW?

In his poem, "Under Ben Bulben," W. B. Yeats ends with these lines: "Cast a cold eye/ On life, on death/ Horseman pass by!" The last three words were borrowed by Larry McMurtry for the title of a novel, *Horseman Pass By*, which was later made into the film *Hud*.

fabulize	To invent fables; to concoct narratives of myth or legend that teach a lesson.
	WORDS IN CONTEXT: *Her mother, a storyteller, could* **fabulize** *any small event by elaborating on a kernel of fact.*
manqué	Would-be; potential but unrealized; that which falls short of the goal.
	WORDS IN CONTEXT: **Manqué** *is placed after the noun it modifies, as in scholar* **manqué**, *artist* **manqué**. *He presented himself as an artist, but he was actually an artist* **manqué**.
imputation	The act of charging, or the fact of being charged. with fault, crime, and so forth; accusation.
	WORDS IN CONTEXT: *The* **imputation** *of guilt for the death of his friend by drowning hung over him like a black cloud.*
inexplicable	Inexpressible, unexplainable; that which cannot be unfolded, untwisted, or disentangled; very complex.
	WORDS IN CONTEXT: *Her behavior on the trip during which she offended everyone she met was* **inexplicable** *to me. (The preferred pronunciation of the tongue-twister is "in-eks'-pli-ka-bul.")*
aphorisms	Concise statements of a principle in any science; principles or precepts expressed briefly and pithily; maxims.
	WORDS IN CONTEXT: *The "***Aphorisms** *of Hippocrates" were short, memorable statements of scientific principles.*

After studying the words above, use them in the sentences below.

1. The police officer's_____ was that the man had stolen the money.
2. The critic devastated his performance to the point of calling him an actor_____.
3. To the rest of us, it was _____that he would rebuild his house on the coast after the fourth hurricane took his last house away.
4. The Brothers Grimm could _____on the tiniest of ideas.
5. Our grandmother taught us lessons or principles about life in such colorful_____that we never forgot them.

Test Yourself: Write the word that best fits the meaning given below.

1. not nearly as good as he thinks he is _____
2. inventions of a storyteller _____
3. accusation _____
4. unexplainable _____
5. principles stated in short, memorable statements_____

On a separate sheet of paper, write a sentence using each of these words.

DID YOU KNOW?
From which book of the Bible did Hemingway borrowed the title of his 1926 novel *The Sun Also Rises*? This comes from Ecclesiastes 1:5, which refers to the futility of human struggle in the larger nature of things. The sun rises, the wind blows, and man's effort is as nothing.

moniker	A person's name or nickname, also spelled monicker. **WORDS IN CONTEXT:** *In light banter, John asked the boy, "What's your **moniker**?"*
nefandous	Not to be spoken of; utterly unmentionable; abominable. **WORDS IN CONTEXT:** *In his home, the subject of sex was **nefandous**.*
nescience	Absence of knowledge; ignorance. **WORDS IN CONTEXT:** *He was a likable person with a pleasing manner, but his **nescience** kept him from succeeding.*
opsimath	A late bloomer or one who learns late in life. **WORDS IN CONTEXT:** *He worked to support his orphaned brothers and sisters when he was young, so he entered college late in life as an **opsimath**.*
aperçu	A summary, synopsis, or outline. From the French. **WORDS IN CONTEXT:** *The author, Simon Singh, wrote a brilliant **aperçu** of the Big Bang theory.*

After studying the words above, use them in the sentences below.

1. His name was George Herman Ruth, and he also had another _____: Babe.
2. _____plays an important part in many negative criticisms of evolution.
3. After awhile, incest became a_____subject in our family.
4. He wrote his first opera at age 50, marking him as a classic_____.
5. The graduate student gave the class an _____of the works of Tolstoy.

Test Yourself: Write the word that best fits the meaning given below.

1. lack of learning _____
2. seeker of knowledge at a late age _____
3. unspeakable_____
4. that by which you are known _____
5. a summary or outline _____

On a separate sheet of paper, write a sentence using each of these words.

DID YOU KNOW?
Who used Shakespeare's words "brave new world" in the title of his work of satire aimed at utopians and advocates of a planned society? Shakespeare wrote them in *The Tempest*. Aldous Huxley borrowed them for his novel of that name.

opprobrium	The disgrace attached to conduct considered shameful; the imputation of this disgrace; infamy; reproach.
	WORDS IN CONTEXT: *Society viewed with **opprobrium** his abandoning his family.*
arcane	Hidden, secret; known only to a few insiders.
	WORDS IN CONTEXT: *The new employee was about to learn the **arcane** language and mysterious ways of the fashion world.*
ataraxia	Freedom from disturbances of mind or passion; stoical indifference.
	WORDS IN CONTEXT: *The Buddhist teachings she absorbed contributed to her serene **ataraxia**.*
funicular	A mountain railway on which counterbalanced cars on parallel sets of rails are pulled up and lowered by cables.
	WORDS IN CONTEXT: *The **funicular** carried us up to Sacre Cour church, but we walked down.*
comicono- menclaturist	A collector of funny names of real people.
	WORDS IN CONTEXT: *One name in a list collected by a serious **comiconomenclaturist** was a Dr. B.N. Paine, a physician in New York.*

After studying the words above, use them in the sentences below.

1. After his stressful week of work, he spent the weekend at a spa, sinking into a state of_____.
2. In some places, skiers ride to the top of the hill on a_____.
3 Almost every profession develops its _____words and customs.
4. When his lies were confirmed, the senator was heaped with_____ by his angry colleagues.
5. The _____ had these names in his file: Governor Ima Hogg, Mary Etta Roach, Rea Polster, and the podiatrist, Dr. Charles Footlick.

Test Yourself: Write the word that best fits the meaning given below.

1. up and down the mountain _____
2. mysteries known to a few _____
3. strong reproach_____
4. idyllic calm_____
5. serious collector of funny names _____

On a separate sheet of paper, write a sentence using each of these words.

DID YOU KNOW?
What does a cat have to do with the catgut used in many stringed instruments? Nothing at all. These strings are made from sheep gut. But the Latin for "guitar," *cithara* (hard c), was shortened to "kit," and the strings for instruments were referred to as "kit guts." Some misunderstanding—perhaps *catachresis* — along the line turned that into catguts.

Works Consulted

ART

Griffin, Benjamin, *In the World of Music and Art,* Barron's, New York, 1991.
Janson, Horst W., *History of Art,* 4th ed., Abrams, New York. 1991.

ARCHITECTURE

Fleming, John, et al., *Penguin Dictionary of Architecture,* 4th ed. Viking Penguin, New York, 1991.
Hunt, William D., Jr., *Encyclopedia of American Architects,* McGraw-Hill, New York, 1980.
Kostof, Spiro, *A History of Architecture: Settings and Rituals,* Oxford University Press, Boston, 1985.

MUSIC

Baker, Robert M., "A Brief History of the Blues," thebluehighway.com/history.html
Collier, James L., *The Making of Jazz: A Comprehensive History,* Dell, New York,1979.
Goulding, Phil G., *Ticket to the Opera,* Faucett Columbine, New York, 1996.
Hoffman, Miles, *NPR Classical Music Companion,* Houghton Mifflin, New York, 1997.
Kamien, Michael, *Music: An Appreciation,* 3th ed., McGraw-Hill, New York, 1984.
Kennedy, Michael, *The Oxford Dictionary of Music,* Oxford University Press, New York, 1985.
The New Grove Dictionary of Music and Musicians, 29 vols., Stanley Sadie, ed., Oxford University Press, New York, 2001.
Priestly, Brian, *Jazz on Record: A History,* Billboard Books, New York, 1991.
The Rolling Stone Encyclopedia of Rock and Roll, Jon Pareles and Patricia Romanowski, eds., Rolling Stone Press, New York, 1991.

DRAMA

Allardyce, Nicoll, *World Drama,* Harcourt, Brace & World, New York, undated.
Bentley, Eric, *The Life of the Drama,* Atheneum, New York, 1979.
The Crown Guide to the World's Great Plays, from Ancient Greece to Modern Times, Joseph T. Shipley, ed., Crown Publishers, NY, 1984.
Macgowan, Kenneth, and William Melnitz, *The Living Stage,* Prentice-Hall, Englewood Cliffs, NJ, 1955.
McGraw-Hill Encyclopedia of World Drama, 5 vols., McGraw-Hill, New York, 1972.
The Reader's Encyclopedia of World Drama, John Gassner and Edward Quinn, eds., Thomas Y. Crowell Co., New York, 1969.

PHILOSOPHY

Adler, Mortimer J., *Adler's Philosophical Dictionary, 125 Key Terms for the Philosopher's Lexicon,* Scribner Reference, New York, 1995.
Adler, Mortimer J., *The Four Dimensions of Philosophy,* McMillan Publishing Co., New York, 1993.
Copleston, Frederick C., *History of Philosophy, 9 vols.,* Doubleday, New York, 1985.
Durant, Will, *The Story of Philosophy,* Pocket Books, New York, 1983.

Eichhoefer, Gerald W., *Enduring Issues in Philosophy,* Greenhaven Press, San Diego, CA, 1995.
Masterpieces of World Philosophy, Frank N. Magill, ed., HarperCollins, New York, 1990.
The Stanford Encyclopedia of Philosophy, Stanford University Press, Palo Alto, CA, 1999.
Urmson, James O., *A Concise Encyclopedia of Western Philosophy and Philosophers,* 3d ed.,
    Unwin Hyman, Boston, 1990.

PSYCHOLOGY

Blake, Toni, *Enduring Issues in Psychology,* Greenhaven Press, San Diego, CA, 1995.
Hunt, Morton, *The Story of Psychology,* Doubleday, New York, 1993.
Nordby, Vernon J., and Calvin S. Hall, *A Guide to Psychologists and their Concepts,* Freeman
    and Company, San Francisco, CA, 1974.

FOREIGN WORDS

Carroll, David, *The Dictionary of Foreign Terms in the English Language,* Hawthorne Books,
    New York, 1973.
Dubois, Marguerite-Marie, *Larousse's English-French Dictionary,* Pocket Books, Simon and
    Schuster, New York, 1955.

LEGAL WORDS

Kling, Samuel G., *The Legal Encyclopedia and Dictionary,* Pocket Books, Simon and Schuster,
    New York, 1970.
Walker, David M., *The Oxford Companion to Law,* Clarendon Press, Oxford, 1980.

LITERATURE

Abrams, M. H., *A Glossary of Literary Terms,* 3d ed., Holt, Rinehart and Winston, New York,
    1971.
Baldick, Chris, *The Concise Oxford Dictionary of Literary Terms,* Oxford University Press,
    Boston, 1991.
Dictionary of Cultural Literacy, E. D. Hirsh, Jr., Joseph F. Kett, and James Trefil, eds., Houghton-
    Mifflin, Boston, 1988.
Encyclopedia of World Literature in the 20th Century, vols. I and II, Wolfgang Bernard
    Fleischmann, ed., Frederick Ungar Publishing Co., New York, 1967–1969.
Herduck, Donald E., *African Authors: A Companion to Black African Writing,* Black Orpheus
    Press, Harrow, UK, 1973.
Ousby, Ian, *The Cambridge Guide to Literature in English,* Cambridge University Press, Boston,
    1993.
The Oxford Anthology of English Literature, vols. I and II, Frank Kermode, John Hollander,
    Harold Bloom, Martin Price, J. B.Tripp, Lionel Trilling, gen. eds., Oxford University Press,
    New York, 1973–1979.
The Oxford Companion to English Literature, 5th ed., Margaret Drabble, ed., Oxford University
    Press, Boston, 1985.
Thomas, Owen, *Metaphor and Related Subjects,* Random House, New York, 1969.

POETRY

Ciardi, John, *How Does a Poem Mean?,* Houghton Mifflin Co., Boston, 1959.
Cleveland, Ceil, *In the World of Literature,* Barron's, New York, 1991.

Lederer, Richard, and Michael Gilleland, *Crazy English,* Pocket Books, New York, 1990.
Perrine, Laurence, *Sound and Sense,* Harcourt, Brace & World, New York, 1963.
Simpson, Louis, *An Introduction to Poetry,* St. Martin's Press, New York, 1986.
Zen Flesh, Zen Bones, Paul Reps, ed., Doubleday Anchor Books, Garden City, NY, 1961.

MYTHOLOGY

Bell, Robert E., *Women of Classical Mythology,* Oxford University Press, New York, 1991.
Boswell, Fred, and Jeanetta Boswell, *What Men or Gods Are These" A Genealogical Approach to Classical Mythology,* The Scarecrow Press, Metuchen, NJ, 1980.
Bush, Douglas, *Mythology and the Renaissance Tradition in English Poetry,* Pageant Book Co., New York, 1933.
———, *Mythology and the Romantic Tradition in English Poetry,* Pageant Book Co., New York, 1937.
Cotterell, Arthur, *The Encyclopedia of Mythology,* Anness Publishing, London, 1996.
Norton, Dan S., and Rushton Peters, *Classical Myths in English Literature,* Rinehart & Company, New York, 1952.
Rose, H. J., *Handbook of Greek Mythology,* E. P. Dutton & Co., New York, 1950.
Lorousse Greek and Roman Mythology, Joel Schmidt and Seth Berardete, eds., McGraw-Hill Book Co., New York, 1980.

BIBLE

Asimov, Isaac, *Asimov's Guide to the Bible, vol. I, "The Old Testament,"* Doubleday & Company, Garden City, NY, 1968.
———, *Asimov's Guide to the Bible, vol. II, "The New Testament,"* Doubleday & Company, Garden City, NY, 1969.
Blair, Edward P., *Abingdon Bible Handbook,* Abington Press, Nashville, TN, 1975.
Panati, Charles, *Sacred Origins of Profound Things,* Penguin Books, New York, 1996.
Sellier, Charles E., *Ancient Revelations of the Bible,* Bantam Doubleday, New York 1995.

WORDS

Ammer, Christine, *Have a Nice Day—No Problem,* Dutton, New York, 1992.
Bowler, Peter, *The Superior Person's Book of Words,* David R. Godine, Boston, 1985.
Bremner, John B., *Words on Words,* Columbia University Press, New York 1980.
Brooks, Brian S., and James L. Pinson, *The Concise Handbook for Media Writers and Editors,* St, Martin's Press, New York, 1989.
Buckley, William F., *The Right Words,* Harcourt Brace, New York, 1996.
Dickson, Paul, *Dickson's Word Treasury,* John Wiley & Sons, New York, 1992.
Elster, Charles Harrington, *There's a Word for It!* Scribners, New York, 1996.
Freeman, Morton S., *The Story Behind the Story,* ISI Press, Philadelphia, 1985.
Krieger, T. D., *The Portable Pundit,* Warner Books, New York, 2000.
McWhorter, John, *Doing Our Own Thing,* Gotham Books, New York, 2004.
Nunberg, Geoffrey, *The Way We Talk Now,* Houghton-Mifflin, Boston, 2001.
Onions, C. T., *Oxford English Dictionary of Etyomology,* Oxford University Press, New York, 1966.
Partridge, Eric, *Usage and Abusage,* British Book Center, London, 1965.
Rees, Nigel, *Dictionary of Catchphrases,* Cassell Publishers, London, 1995.
Safire, William, *Watching My Language,* Random House, New York, 1997.
———, *Spread the Word,* Times Books, New York, 1999.

Smith, Ken, *Junk English,* Blast Books, New York, 2001.

Winchester, Simon, *The Meaning of Everything, The Story of the Oxford English Dictionary,* Oxford University Press, New York, 2003.

Yogoda, Ben, "The Adjective—So Ludic, So Minatory, So Twee," *Chronicle of Higher Education,"* Feb. 20, 2004.

GENERAL

The American Heritage Dictionary of the English Language, William Morris, ed., Houghton-Mifflin Company, Boston, 1973.

Baker, Sheridan, *The Practical Stylist,* Thomas Y. Crowell, New York, 1973.

Berliner, Barbara, *The Book of Answers: The New York Public Library Telephone Reference Services's Most Unusual and Entertaining Questions,* A Fireside Book, Simon and Schuster, New York, 1990.

Born, Roscoe C., *The Suspended Sentence,* Charles Scribners, New York, 1986.

The Concise Columbia Encyclopedia, Columbia University Press, New York, 1983.

Evans, Ivor, *Brewer's Dictionary of Phrase and Fable,* Harper & Row, New York, 1989.

Jackson, R. W., *The Diabolical Dictionary of Modern English,* Delacorte Press, New York, 1986.

New World Dictionary of the American Language, 2d college edition, David B. Guralnik, ed., World Publishing Company, New York, 1976.

The New York Public Library Desk Reference, 2d ed., Paul Fargis, Sheree Bykofsky, eds., Prentice Hall, Englewood Cliffs, NJ,1989.

The Oxford Universal Dictionary, C. T. Onions, ed., Clarendon Press, Oxford, 1955.

Pearson, Will, Mangesh Hattikudur, Elizabeth Hunt, *Mental Floss Presents: Condensed Knowledge,* Harper Resource, HarperCollins, New York, 2004.

DID YOU KNOW?

Berliner, Barbara, *The Book of Answers,* The New York Public Library, Simon & Schuster, New York, 1992.

Cleveland, Ceil, *In the World of Literature,* Barron's, New York, 1991.

Evans, Ivor H., *Brewer's Dictionary of Phrase and Fable,* 14th ed., Harper & Row Publishers, New York, 1989.

Mordoch, John, and Myron Korach, *Common Phrases and Where They Come From,* The Lyons Press, Guileford, CT, 2001.

Pearson, Will, et al., *Hooked on Books Calendar, Mental Floss Magazine,* New York, 2004.

Why Do We Say It? Castle, Secaucus, NJ, 1985.

Word Mysteries and Histories: From Quiche to Humble Pie, Editors of American Heritage Dictionary, Houghton Mifflin, Boston, 1986.

ABOUT THE AUTHOR

Ceil Cleveland is an English professor who formerlly taught writing and literature at New York University and was chief editor for Columbia University periodicals. She has recently relocated to the Research Triangle of North Carolina.